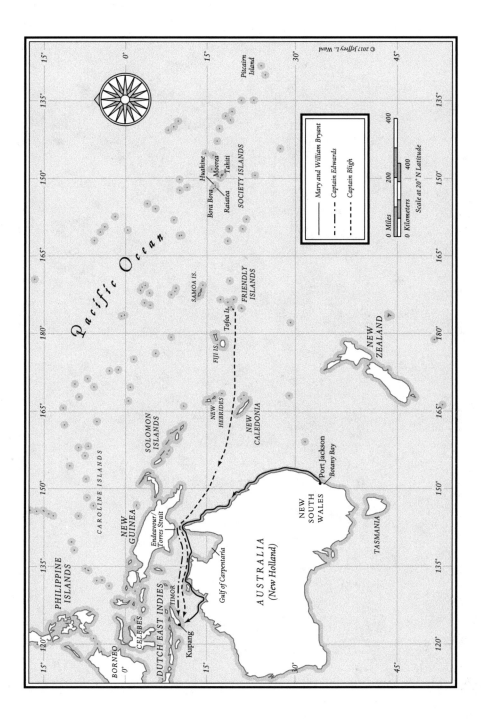

© 2017 Jeffrey L. Ward

PARADISE IN CHAINS

PARADISE IN CHAINS

The *Bounty* Mutiny and the Founding of Australia

DIANA PRESTON

B L O O M S B U R Y

NEW YORK · LONDON · OXFORD · NEW DELHI · SYDNEY

Bloomsbury USA
An imprint of Bloomsbury Publishing Plc

1385 Broadway	50 Bedford Square
New York	London
NY 10018	WC1B 3DP
USA	UK

www.bloomsbury.com

First published 2017
© Diana Preston, 2017

ISBN: HB: 978-1-63286-610-3
        ePub: 978-1-63286-612-7

Library of Congress Cataloging-in-Publication Data

Names: Preston, Diana, 1952– author.
Title: Paradise in chains : the Bounty Mutiny and the founding of Australia / Diana Preston.
Description: New York : Bloomsbury USA, an imprint of Bloomsbury Publishing Plc, 2017. |
Includes bibliographical references.
Identifiers: LCCN 2017002518 | ISBN 9781632866103 (hardcover) | ISBN 9781632866127 (ePub)
Subjects: LCSH: Bounty Mutiny, 1789. | Bligh, William, 1754–1817—Travel. | Prisoners—
Travel—History—18th century. | Prisoners—Australia—Botany Bay (N.S.W.)—History—
18th century. | Escapes—History—18th century. | Ocean travel—History—18th century. |
Survival at sea—History—18th century. | Islands of the Pacific—Description and travel. |
Australia—History—1788–1851. | Islands of the Pacific—History—18th century.
Classification: LCC DU20 .P74 2017 | DDC 996.18—dc23 LC record available at https://lccn
.loc.gov/2017002518

2   4   6   8   10   9   7   5   3   1

Typeset by Westchester Publishing Services
Printed and bound in the U.S.A. by Berryville Graphics Inc., Berryville, Virginia

CONTENTS

INTRODUCTION

*O*n July 2, 1792, the *London Chronicle* reported the arrival of one of King George III's warships at Portsmouth on England's south coast:

> News from Botany Bay from His Majesty's ship, the *Gorgon*. The infant colony is in greatest distress being in want of every necessity of life and by no means in that fertile state represented . . .
>
> The following were [among] passengers on the *Gorgon*. Captain W. Tench . . . Captain Edwards of the *Pandora*, upwards of a hundred men, women and children of the Marine Corps, ten mutineers from the *Bounty* and several convicts that made their escape from [Botany] Bay to Batavia in an open boat though the distance is not less than 1,000 leagues . . .

As well as informing its readers of the precarious state of the convict colony founded four years before, this short account also brought together three of the greatest and most dramatic stories of survival at sea. The mutineers were some of those from the *Bounty* who, after they had put William Bligh over the side with members of his loyal crew to make his celebrated 3,600-nautical-mile, forty-seven-day, open-boat journey to Kupang on Timor, had returned to Tahiti and remained there when Fletcher Christian and the hard core of the mutineers headed for Pitcairn Island.

Captain Edward Edwards, dispatched aboard the *Pandora* to hunt down the mutineers, had seized them on Tahiti and imprisoned them in harsh conditions in a dark roundhouse on deck that had become known, perhaps predictably, as "Pandora's Box." When the *Pandora* was wrecked on the Great Barrier Reef in August 1791, Edwards and the other survivors made a sixteen-day, 1,200-nautical-mile journey in four open boats to Kupang.

The convicts had "made their escape" from the penal colony in March 1791. They included—and some said were led by—a woman, Mary Bryant, née Broad. Their open-boat journey of 3,254 nautical miles from Port Jackson, modern-day Sydney, again to Kupang had taken sixty-nine days. Here, in bitter irony, Captain Edwards had arrested them and shipped them home

with the mutineers on the *Gorgon* to face trial. Captain Watkin Tench—
referred to by the *London Chronicle*—was an officer who, with many other
marines, was returning from service as one of the initial guards of the penal
colony established in 1788. By coincidence, they found themselves aboard the
Gorgon with the escaped convicts of whose fate they had until then been
ignorant.

The ideas behind the penal settlement and the *Bounty*'s breadfruit voyage
to Tahiti had a common origin: Britain's attempts to exploit its discoveries
made in the Pacific in the third quarter of the eighteenth century by Captain
James Cook and others. At one stage they had been planned as a single
venture—an idea only formally abandoned a week before the convict fleet's
departure. The two stories would become further intertwined when, in 1805,
Captain Bligh was appointed governor of the penal colony where in 1808 he
would again suffer a mutiny. A verse circulating in Sydney would ask:

> *Oh Tempora! Oh Mores! Is there*
> *No* Christian *in New South Wales to put*
> *A stop to the Tyranny of the Governor.*

Cook's first expedition, from August 1768 to July 1771—the many objec-
tives of which had included observing the transit of Venus—had owed
much to the enthusiasms of members of the Royal Society—then, as now,
Britain's foremost scientific institution. Leaders in the "Age of Enlightenment," they were eager to understand the mechanics and geography of the
universe, the earth's place in them, and the reasons underlying their own
existence. Cook's voyage was also one of discovery designed to reveal more
about the Pacific and the possible existence there of a great southern continent, and, in so doing, to assess the scope for extension of British trade, fore-
stalling French, Spanish, and Dutch rivals. He surveyed New Zealand and
made the first European landings there and on the east coast of Australia,
which he claimed for Great Britain and named New South Wales, after Wales
in his homeland.*

The impetus for British attempts to exploit these discoveries was the
American War of Independence and the subsequent loss of the American

---

*The name "Australia" was first used by Matthew Flinders in 1804 on a hand-drawn map.

colonies. Britain no longer had priority in its trade with its former colonies, compelling it to seek new markets. A particular problem was finding a source of sustaining cheap food for the slaves on the sugar plantations of the British West Indies, to which breadfruit from the Pacific, which the *Bounty* was sent to obtain, was believed to be the solution. The British government had also been accustomed to transport to the American colonies prisoners convicted of crimes not considered to merit death but too serious to allow them to return to Britain's streets. After exhausting other possibilities, the authorities turned to Botany Bay in New South Wales as a destination, which also offered opportunities for trade and use as a staging post for British merchantmen in the Pacific.

These decisions had a profound impact on the region's people. Earlier British encounters with them in the Pacific, and in Tahiti in particular, had already significantly contributed to the discussion of "the noble savage" and whether a society based on man's inherent moral qualities had advantages over those ruled by laws imposed by religious and social hierarchies. These debates, and descriptions of the undoubted beauty and charm of the Pacific islands, gave a not entirely accurate and highly romantic view of them as a Utopian paradise, later sustained by the Romantic poets and later still enhanced by Paul Gauguin's paintings.

The story of the four decades between the first arrival of the British in Tahiti in 1767 and the arrival of William Bligh in New South Wales as governor is as much one of outstanding characters—sometimes heroic, sometimes flawed, and sometimes somewhere in between—as of ideas and of clashes between cultures and societies. At least as much as Cook and Bligh, the naturalist Sir Joseph Banks stands out. He accompanied Cook on his first voyage, enjoying the amorous favors of Tahiti's beautiful women, and searched so hard for botanical specimens that Cook named Botany Bay after his and his associates' efforts there. For forty-two years he was president of the Royal Society and he was the key figure behind the eventual choice of Botany Bay as the destination to which British convicts should be trans- ported, behind Bligh's breadfruit expedition and—sixteen years after the *Bounty* mutiny—Bligh's appointment as governor of New South Wales.

Another key figure was Captain Arthur Phillip, the phlegmatic son of a poor German immigrant to Britain, who became a naval officer, spied for Britain against the French, and then served as the commander of the first convict fleet and, following its arrival in 1788, as the first governor of the penal colony. There he displayed remarkable even-handedness in his treatment of guards and prisoners and attempted, if not always successfully, to maintain good relations with the local Aboriginals.

James Boswell spans events first as a commentator on the early parts of the story, describing his conversations with Dr. Samuel Johnson on the virtues of "civilization" compared to life in a more "natural" state, in his attempts to join Cook's second voyage, and later as the champion of Mary Bryant and the other escaped prisoners.

Influence was exerted and positions and promotions obtained through many interlocking circles. As the achievements of Cook and Phillip—both from poor backgrounds—show, advancement was not always dependent on wealth and privilege, though these clearly helped. Those with influence promoted those with whom they had previously served and found able and congenial. Family links as well as those of education were valuable. Freemasonry, with its emphasis (despite its rituals) on rationalism as distinct from mystic explanations, was at one of its high points—Cook, Bligh, Banks, Boswell, and others were masons. Regional links mattered: Cornishmen were especially prominent in the *Bounty* and Botany Bay stories, while close associations between families in Cumberland and the Isle of Man influenced the aftermath of the *Bounty* mutiny.

People from the Pacific are also major figures. Purea, "queen" of one of Tahiti's clans, not only seduced Banks but immediately recognized the potential of Europeans to assist her in increasing her power. Tu, one of her successors as the dominant figure on Tahiti, brought such ambitions to fruition, profiting from his closeness to the new arrivals to secure muskets and in the end their active help in establishing his dynasty as paramount in Tahiti. Omai, a Tahitian, eventually visited Britain as did Bennelong, an Aboriginal, giving a human face to accounts of exotic new lands. Jenny, a Tahitian woman, provided one of the few independent accounts of Fletcher Christian's voyage to Pitcairn Island and his life and death there.

Yet in 1767, as a British naval ship nosed through the reefs toward a mist-wreathed island, no one aboard or ashore could possibly foresee how profoundly both the Pacific and western worlds would change in the years that followed.

I

"NO OTHER GODS BUT LOVE"

*F*orewarned by swift-paddled canoes from outlying islands of the approach of what they would recall as an "amazing phenomenon," the tawny-skinned occupants of a hundred outrigger canoes peered into a bank of thick morning fog. Slowly the outline of "a floating island" propelled by divine power and inhabited by gods appeared, filling them with "wonder and fear": HMS *Dolphin*, a 24-gun, 113-foot-long, 508-ton British frigate under the command of thirty-nine-year-old Cornishman Samuel Wallis.

As Wallis strained his own eyes, a sweep of jagged green peaks emerged through the drifting mist. At the sound of breaking surf ahead he gave orders to begin depth sounding. He, like all his hundred-fifty-strong crew, was exhausted after months of scouring the South Pacific for the fabled continent "Terra Australis Incognita." Ship's master George Robertson described how the glimpse of land "filled us with the greatest hopes imaginable . . . We now supposed we saw the long wished for Southern Continent, which has been often talked of but never before seen by Europeans." In fact, that morning of June 19, 1767, they had just become the first Europeans to reach Tahiti, the largest of an island archipelago in the South Pacific.*

When the fog cleared further the sailors lining the rails saw the high-prowed, thirty-foot-long Tahitian canoes festooned with red feathers racing toward the *Dolphin* through the surf, the islanders' curiosity and wonder seeming to more than match their own.

A Tahitian stood up in one of the leading canoes and hurled a plantain branch into the sea—unknown to Wallis's men, a priest making a gesture of welcome. Then as the canoes drew closer, "one fine brisk young man"

---

*Tahiti lies at S17°40', W149°25'.

leapt from one, seized hold of the *Dolphin*'s rigging, and scrambled aboard. Others quickly followed. Eager for fresh food, the sailors imitated the gruntings of pigs, the flapping and clucking of chickens, and the crowing of cocks. When the Tahitians failed to understand their antics the crew brought out the few turkeys, sheep, and goats they had aboard. The islanders had never seen such creatures. When a goat butted one of them from behind they all dived overboard in fear, one pausing to snatch from a midshipman's head "a gold-laced hat."

Slowly Wallis's men coaxed them back, offering beads and nails. Aboard once more, the Tahitians explored the ship, seizing anything they liked the look of; in Tahitian culture a successful thief was considered to have won the protection of Hiro, a powerful god. With those still in canoes also clamoring vociferously for goods and beginning "to be a little surly," Wallis feared the situation might get out of control and ordered his gunners to fire a warning shot from the *Dolphin*'s cannon. The islanders, who were ignorant of gunpowder, cannon, and muskets, fled back to the shore.

With lookouts posted at the mast tops to watch for surf breaking on reefs and changes of color in the bright water indicating shallows, Wallis began navigating Tahiti's southwestern coast, searching for a safe harbor. He quickly saw enough of the 120-mile-long curving shoreline to realize it was an island and not the much-sought-after great southern continent Terra Australis Incognita (the "Unknown South Land").* However, he and his crew were already struck by the "most beautiful appearance possible to imagine" of Tahiti, its "fine pasture land," rivers, waterfalls, neat settlements with thatched houses "like long farmers' barns," and lush palm groves.

Watching from the shore, some of the Tahitians recalled a recent prophesy by one of their priests following the chopping down of a sacred tree during an intra-island conflict that newcomers of an unknown kind would arrive and that "this land will be taken by them. The old order will be destroyed and sacred birds of the land and the sea will . . . come and lament over what the lopped tree has to teach. [The newcomers] are coming upon a canoe without an outrigger."

The islanders grew so suspicious that when a shore party commanded by the *Dolphin*'s Virginia-born master's mate John Gore tried to land from

---

*The mythical Terra Australis Incognita had been believed to exist since antiquity and thought to be a great and probably fertile landmass balancing, as on a pair of scales, the lands of the northern hemisphere. It appeared as such on early maps.

the ship's cutter, they attacked with slingshots. Though Wallis, following his Admiralty orders to invite local inhabitants "to trade and show them every kind of civility and regard," had given strict instructions that the local people were not to be harmed, Gore fired his musket loaded with buckshot at a Tahitian warrior before ordering the cutter back to the *Dolphin*.

On June 22, the winter solstice in Tahiti when—of course unknown to Wallis—custom forbade canoes to put to sea, Wallis ordered the ship's boats to be lowered to take further soundings, and sailors and scarlet-jacketed marines to go ashore to search for supplies and water. The marines fired more shots at islanders they thought were threatening them in what was only the beginning of a series of further confrontations over the next forty-eight hours. The Tahitians, after unsuccessfully trying to put back on his feet one of their fellows hit by a musket ball, began to believe that the scarlet-coated marines squinting down the barrels of their muskets might be blowing into their weapons and named the muskets *pupuhi roa*—"breath which kills at a distance." Red was the color of their war god, Oro, who used thunder and lightning to enforce his power. Thus the red-clad marines, with the flash and bang of their weapons, seemed all too likely to be Oro's minions bent on avenging the islanders' disrespect to their gods.

Nevertheless, early on June 24 the *Dolphin*'s crew, by now seeking a safe anchorage in Matavai Bay and having grounded the *Dolphin* once already to the amusement of the islanders, saw several large war canoes approaching fast. As well as men each carried young women who, standing on high platforms, performed "a great many droll wanton tricks." These included exposing their genitals while their companions shouted and chanted. Wallis's crew, deprived of female company for months, interpreted the "so well proportioned" women's gestures as sexual enticement and rushed to the ship's rails but, in fact, Tahitians believed that by exposing themselves toward the *Dolphin* the women were opening a portal for their ancestral gods, allowing them to channel their power against the newcomers. As the war canoes drew nearer, some of their occupants furiously whirled slingshots over their heads to discharge stones at the *Dolphin* and its now sexually aroused crew.

Fearing his ship was again in danger, Wallis first ordered muskets to be fired and then, when the attackers persisted, the firing of cannon loaded with grapeshot and cannonballs. A cannonball split one great war canoe in half. Others were soon splintered and sinking and many aboard them were injured or dying, staining the translucent turquoise water red with blood. Among the wounded, hit in the shoulder by a musket ball, was a young man named Omai, originally from the neighboring island of Raiatea, who would become well known to later European visitors. Ship's master George Robertson wrote of how terrible those on shore must have felt "to see their nearest and dearest of friends dead and torn to pieces in such a manner as I am certain they never beheld before. To attempt to say what these poor ignorant creatures thought of us, would be taking more upon me than I am able to perform." After this admission of the understandable mutual incomprehension that was so often to prevail between islanders and Europeans, he added "some of my messmates thought they would now look upon us as demi Gods, come to punish them for some of their past transgressions."

Wallis now decided to claim Tahiti by right of conquest and went ashore with an armed party to hold a ceremony for the purpose. As the scarlet-coated marines began to drill, the islanders—now seemingly convinced that these new arrivals were indeed demigods—slowly approached waving plantain branches and making signs of submission. Members of the Tahitian aristocracy followed, including one white-bearded old chief crawling on hands and knees in abasement. Others offered gifts of pigs. Gradually more amicable relations were established, helped by the Tahitian women, encouraged by their menfolk, offering their favors to the sailors. George Robertson wrote, "All the sailors swore that they never saw handsomer made women in their lives and declared they would all to a man live on two thirds allowance rather than lose so fine an opportunity of getting a girl apiece . . . We passed this night very merry supposing all hostilities were now over and to our great joy it so happened."

Wallis and his men were successful in bartering for fresh food and water, offering the islanders in return knives, hatchets, and iron nails. The only iron the islanders had seen before was from a ship wrecked without survivors on a reef off a distant outer island. Such was the islanders' passion for anything iron that Wallis's men were soon extracting nails surreptitiously from the Dolphin's hull to reward sexual favors. So great was their commander's concern that their depredations would irrevocably weaken his ship, they risked flogging if caught.

When they arrived, many of the sailors had been sick with scurvy, their gums black and bleeding, their teeth loose, their nails cracked, their urine green, their joints aching and stiff, and purple oozing ulcers covering their limbs. Others, including Wallis and several of his officers, had serious stomach disorders. Now with fresh food and the warmth of the island all began to recover. One of the island's noblewomen, named Purea, befriended Wallis, ordering him to be given food and carried by her servants to her home, a large thatched dwelling one hundred and twenty feet long and supported on fourteen carved pillars. In its shade she put four young women to gently massaging his limbs and those of other suffering officers. When in the process the ship's surgeon removed his wig, the surprise of the Tahitians was immense.

Later Purea would dine aboard the *Dolphin*—unlike Tahitian women of lower status, custom permitted her to eat with men. During her visit Robertson described her as "a strong well-made woman about five foot ten inches high . . . very cheerful and merry all the time she was on board." On a later visit she asked Robertson to strip so that she could examine his body and, when he did, was surprised by his pale skin and "my breast being full of hair." She probed and felt the muscles of his thighs and arms as if testing his strength. "This seemed to please her greatly and she eyed me all round and began to be very merry and cheerful and, if I am not mistaken by Her Majesty's behaviour afterwards, this is the way the ladies here try the men before they admit them to be their lovers."

After five weeks, Wallis prepared to sail home. Despite the initial violent deaths, relations between his crew and the islanders had become so close that many on both sides were in tears. Aboard the departing *Dolphin* were many ceremonial gifts, including a plaited string of her hair Purea had presented to Wallis as a symbol binding him to her and a string of pearls she had given him for the British queen. As Purea watched the final preparations for leaving, Robertson recalled, "This great friendly woman took no manner of notice of what she got from us but shaked hands with all that she could come near. She wept and cried, in my opinion with as much tenderness and affection as any wife or mother could do, at the parting with their husband or children." Despite her grief she took care to stash away safely a red pennant from the *Dolphin* given to her by Wallis. She intended to have it sewn on to a sacred banner made of bark and banyan and flown with great ceremony on her clan's *marae*—a sacred meeting and worship place consisting of a raised stone platform—as a symbol of the earthly power she hoped to obtain through Wallis for herself and her clan when he returned, as he promised he would.

When the *Dolphin* reached England in May 1768, Wallis learned that Philip Carteret, commanding HMS *Swallow*, which had originally been part of his own expedition but had become separated from the *Dolphin*, had also returned having discovered, among other places, Pitcairn Island (some 1,200 nautical miles southeast of Tahiti), which he named after one of his midshipmen. Wallis quickly submitted to the Admiralty his meticulous charts and in his report eulogized the beauty of Britain's lush, fertile new possession and suggested further exploration of the region. Yet the accounts of Tahiti's beautiful and sexually available women published in the newspapers and in pamphlets—despite the Admiralty's attempts to keep Britain's discovery secret—most caught the public imagination. In one a sailor described how "the [Tahitian] men brought down their women and recommended them to us with great eagerness which made me imagine they want a breed of Englishmen amongst them."

Interest in Tahiti grew further as the reports of a French expedition filtered through to Britain. While Wallis had been homeward-bound, Louis-Antoine de Bougainville—navigator, diplomat, and mathematician—had also reached Tahiti. In tribute to Tahiti's "celestial women" he named the island New Cythera after the island near where the goddess Venus (Aphrodite) reputedly sprang from the sea, and he in turn claimed it for France.

His two ships, the *Boudeuse* and the *Etoile*, arrived early in April 1768. The Tahitians had quickly realized both the futility of opposing the occupants of "floating islands" with force and that the attractions of their beautiful women were one of the best ways to please and placate them and secure the iron goods they wanted. De Bougainville wrote that as his ships approached the shore the number of canoes shooting through the surf and thronging around the vessels made navigation difficult. The canoes' noisy occupants were

crying out "taio" which means friend and gave a thousand signs of friendship; they all asked nails and earrings of us. The canoes were full of women who for agreeable features are not inferior to most European women and who in point of beauty of the body . . . vie with them all. Most of these fair females were naked . . . The men . . . pressed us to choose a woman and to come on shore with her; and their gestures which were by no means ambiguous denoted how we should form an acquaintance with her. It was very difficult amidst such a sight to keep at work four hundred young French sailors who had seen no women for six months. In spite of all our precautions, a young girl got on board and stood on the quarterdeck near a hatchway open to give air to those heaving the capstan below it. The girl carelessly dropped a cloth which covered her and appeared to the eyes of all beholders such as Venus showed herself to the Phrygian shepherd having indeed the celestial form of that goddess . . . The capstan was never heaved with more alacrity than then.

De Bougainville's cook, who had slipped ashore against his orders, returned "more dead than alive." As soon as his feet touched the beach, the Tahitians seized and undressed him so that "he thought he was utterly lost, not knowing where the [actions] of those who were tumultuously examining every part of his body" would end. However, they soon returned his clothes and his possessions and beckoned a girl to him, "desiring him to content those desires which had brought him ashore. All their persuasive arguments had no effect; they were obliged to bring the poor cook on board who told me that I might reprimand him as much as I pleased but that I could never frighten him so much as he had just now been frightened on shore."

Even though he described the *Etoile* as a "hellish den where hatred, insubordination, bad faith, brigandage, cruelty and all kinds of disorders reign," the botanist Philibert Commerson had less reason to feel a lack of female companionship than any other man aboard de Bougainville's ships. He had smuggled on to the *Etoile* his mistress and housekeeper disguised as his valet, Jean Baret. By dint of restraining her breasts and pushing cloth down the front of her breeches she had not been detected during the long voyage to Tahiti. However, some of the islanders quickly grew suspicious and surprising her on the beach collecting shells with Commerson stripped her, as they had done the cook, and revealed her sex much to their amusement. Recovering from her ordeal, "Jean Baret" would continue the voyage, becoming the first woman known to have circumnavigated the globe.

Despite his mistress's attractions, Commerson was smitten with Tahiti and its people during the French vessels' stay of only thirteen days. He painted a beguiling, sensuous picture and compared the island to Thomas Moore's Utopia. The Tahitians were free

of any vice and prejudice, without any requirements and dissensions . . . Born under the most beautiful of skies, fed on the fruits of a land that is fertile and requires no cultivation, ruled by the heads of families rather than by kings, they know no other Gods but love. Every day is dedicated to it. The entire island is its temple, every woman its altar, every man its priest. And what sort of women? you will ask. The rivals of Georgians in beauty, and the sisters of the utterly naked Graces. There neither shame nor modesty exercise their tyranny . . . the

action of creating a fellow human being is a religious one . . . Strangers are all
welcome to share in these delightful mysteries . . . so that the happy Utopian
continually enjoys both his own feelings of pleasure and the spectacle of those
of others.

Even though the Tahitians were as skillful "as the pickpockets of Paris" he
questioned whether they were thieves at all. "Is the right of ownership a
natural one? No, it is purely a convention," he wrote, and continued that
Tahitians were simply following the laws of nature, citing philosopher Jean-
Jacques Rousseau's views in support of his own.

Accounts such as those of Commerson and de Bougainville, who himself
referred to Tahiti as "the true Utopia," ascribed to the Tahitian islands many
of the virtues of natural law based on man's innate and unconscious sense
of morality, compared to laws dictated by religious leaders or secular rulers
for their own benefit, a distinction then being debated animatedly in Europe
by Denis Diderot, Rousseau, and others. To some, Tahiti represented a lost
golden age and the Tahitian people epitomized "the noble savage"—a term
first coined in 1672 by the English poet and playwright John Dryden in these
lines from his play *The Conquest of Granada*:

I am free as nature first made man,
Ere the base laws of servitude began,
When wild in the woods the noble savage ran.

Rousseau suggested *Robinson Crusoe* as the first book a child should
read because its hero Crusoe discarded western self-consciousness in favor
of survival on his deserted island. Diderot wrote *A Supplement to de Bougainville* in which fictional characters including a South Sea islander debated.
The work criticized European society and questioned institutions such as
marriage and the family which Diderot thought designed to safeguard and
retain property through man's control of woman's fertility rather than for
the happiness of society. He also queried the benefits of European intrusion
into the islanders' lives, suggesting that if European ideas and religion were
introduced the islanders would soon become "almost as unhappy as they [the
Europeans] are."

Not everyone agreed with such radical views. Many continued to support
the thesis propounded by the English philosopher Thomas Hobbes in his
1651 book *Leviathan* that if man had remained in the savage state without

institutions, law and government there would be no industry, no navigation, no trade, "no knowledge of the face of the earth . . . no arts, no letters, no society and which is worst of all, continual fear and danger of violent death, and the life of man solitary, poor, nasty, brutish and short."

Debate, whether at the philosophical level about the relative virtues of Tahitian and European society, or on the more popular one about the island's life of ease and titillating sexual freedom, drew added attention to the Pacific. Its sixty-four million square miles covering a third of the earth's surface and containing 45 percent of the planet's total surface waters still remained to Europeans a region of almost unimaginable vastness and mystery. In 1513 Spaniard Vasco Núñez de Balboa tramped over the Isthmus of Panama and, standing on a peak in Darien, was the first European to sight the ocean that he named the Mar del Sur, the "southern sea." Seven years later Ferdinand Magellan, a Portuguese captaining a Spanish fleet, became the first European to sail across what he named the Mar Pacifico, the "peaceful sea," for its favorable winds.

Like many of the voyagers who ventured after him, Magellan's fleet of five vessels was riven by dissent and mutiny. Even before he had sailed through the straits that now bear his name from the Atlantic into the Pacific, he had put down a full-fledged insurrection, killing two of his captains and marooning a third. He spared most of the other mutineers since he needed them to work his ships. One of those mutineers—the Basque pilot Juan Elcano, commanding the only remaining ship of his fleet—completed the first circumnavigation of the world after Magellan had been killed in a skirmish with the local people in the Philippines.

For two hundred years, Spain dominated the Pacific, dispatching lumbering annual treasure galleons from its possessions in the Philippines across to its settlements in Mexico. Even in Wallis's time, Spain still claimed the Pacific, citing the treaties of Tordesillas, brokered by the Pope in 1494, and of Zaragoza in 1529 that had divided the "new world" between Spain and Portugal.

Britain had first ventured into the Pacific in 1578. In what became the second circumnavigation of the world in a single vessel, Elizabethan adventurer Francis Drake rounded the Horn in the *Golden Hind* to attack Spanish possessions in the Pacific. Like Magellan, he too suffered mutiny in the Atlantic. The leader was Thomas Doughty, one of his captains, who resented the authority of Drake—a simple mariner—over himself, "a gentleman," and attempted to usurp Drake's position. Drake tried Doughty on a charge of seeking to overthrow the voyage, found him guilty, and sentenced him to death. He allowed Doughty the gentleman's privilege of being beheaded rather than hanged. Afterward he mustered his company and addressed them: "Here is such controversy between the mariners and the gentlemen, and such stomaching between the gentlemen and the mariners, it doth make me mad to hear it. But, my masters, I must have it left. For I must have the gentleman to haul and draw with the mariner, and the mariner with the gentleman. Come, let us show ourselves all to be of one company and let us not give occasion to the enemy to rejoice at our decay and overthrow."

Drake went on to wreak havoc among the Spanish possessions in the Pacific and when he returned home in 1580 his booty was rumored to amount to half a million pounds and even to have funded the fleet in which he and others defeated the Spanish Armada in 1588. Vestiges of the distinction between gentlemen born to command and mariners would persist into the times of Cook and Bligh in the tensions between officers, such as lieutenants and captains holding the king's commission, and warrant officers. The latter included the sailing master (often simply known as "the master" and responsible for the ship's navigation), the bosun or boatswain (responsible for the rigging, sails, and all the ship's gear), the gunner (responsible for the guns and powder), and the carpenter (responsible for the maintenance of the hull, masts, and spars), all possessed of essential skills but usually of a lower social status.

A century later, English buccaneer and naturalist William Dampier became the next Briton to circumnavigate the world. In the intervening hundred years Abel Tasman had on two expeditions between 1642 and 1644 sailed without landing along parts of the north Australian coast, which he named New Holland. He did land on the southern island now named Tasmania after him, but which he named Van Diemen's Land. He also became the first European to sight New Zealand. However, after a deadly attack by Maoris on a boat that he had tried to send ashore he veered away, again without landing, believing New Zealand to be a single island.

Dampier initially started his voyaging as a buccaneer, crossing the Pacific from Mexico to Guam in 1686 in the *Cygnet*. There he saw breadfruit and, a meticulous recorder of the natural world, gave the first description in English of these trees "which I did never hear of anywhere else." They were "as big and high as our largest apple trees" with glossy dark green leaves and fruits "as big as a penny loaf." He also explored the process that metamorphosed the fruits into bread:

> When the fruit is ripe, it is yellow and soft: and the taste is sweet and pleasant. The natives of this island use it for bread: they gather it when full grown, while it is green and hard; then they bake it in an oven, which scorcheth the rind and makes it black: but they scrape off the outside black crust, and there remains a tender thin crust, and the inside is soft, tender and white, like the crumb of a penny loaf. There is neither seed nor stone in the inside, but all is of a pure substance like bread.

After a series of adventures, the *Cygnet's* exhausted, fractious crew, including Dampier, landed on January 4, 1688, on the northwestern coast of New Holland (Australia) in what is now known as King Sound to repair and careen their vessel. They became the first Britons to step ashore, while Dampier was the first to give the world detailed impressions of the new land. He thought it an unforgiving landscape in which none of the few trees "bore fruit or berries." The men briefly encountered some Aboriginal people carrying lances and pieces of wood "shaped like a cutlass"—probably boomerangs.

After breaking from the buccaneers, Dampier reached Britain again in autumn 1691. With the benefit of his copious notes, he wrote a book entitled *A New Voyage Around the World* followed by *A Discourse of Trade Wind, Breezes, Storms, Seasons of the Year, Tides and Currents of the Torrid Areas throughout the World*. The latter included the first global wind maps incorporating the Pacific as well as the other oceans. The *New Voyage* itself described much new flora and fauna and introduced to the English language words such as avocado, barbecue, breadfruit, cashew, and chopsticks.

The *New Voyage*, which Cook, Banks, and Bligh would carry on their expeditions, also contained the first published description of the Aboriginal people of New Holland, characterizing them as "the miserablest people in the world." Apart from their human shape, the Aboriginals differed "little from brutes." They were "tall, strait-bodied, and thin, with small long limbs." They had "great heads, round foreheads, and great brows." Their eyelids were "always half-closed, to keep the flies out of their eyes; they being so troublesome here, that no fanning will keep them from coming to one's face."

He described them as "long visaged and of a very unpleasing aspect, having no one graceful feature in their faces" with their "great bottle noses, pretty full lips and wide mouths." Their hair was "black, short and curled like that of a negroe." Their speech was gutteral, rising from "deep in the throat."

Yet the unpublished draft of Dampier's book presented a different, more objective picture with no comments about "brutes" or "unpleasing aspects." The people were "of good stature but very thin and lean," which he attributed to "want of food." Their hair was "matted-up like a negroe's" but this was "for want of combs." It would be long if combed out. Perhaps when Dampier's journals were being readied for publication he was encouraged to "sensationalize" his physical descriptions of a people inhabiting a land so remote and unknown, or perhaps an editor did so for him.

Dampier shows compassion, even admiration, for a people whose existence seemed hard. He looked on their landscape through European eyes. Not realizing that it was rich in "bush tucker" if, like the Aboriginals, you knew where to seek it, he wrote that "the earth affords them no food at all . . . neither herb, root, pulse nor any sort of grain for them to eat . . . nor any sort of bird or beast that they can catch, having no instruments wherewithal to do so." He believed they depended for their food on the sea but that apart from dugong and turtle the sea did not appear "very plentifully stored with fish."

Following the bestselling success of his books, Dampier was taken up by society and in particular by the Royal Society, Britain's first and still premier scientific institution, founded in 1660. As a result, in a highly unusual move in 1698, the Admiralty, acting in conjunction with the Royal Society, commissioned Dampier into the navy to return to New Holland to undertake discoveries "for the good of the nation" and to bring back natural history specimens.

For what was to be the English government's first expedition officially to combine exploration and science Dampier was allotted a 292-ton, fifth-rate warship named the *Roebuck* already not in the best condition. He set out in early 1699 and was soon quarreling with his second in command, Lieutenant Fisher, who suspected Dampier intended to seize the *Roebuck* and return to piracy. At Tenerife, according to one crewman, "upon a very frivolous occasion" Fisher "gave the captain very reproachful words and bade him kiss his arse and said he did not care a turd for him." He apologized but the truce was short-lived. By the time the *Roebuck* reached Salvador de Bahia in Brazil the two had come to blows and Fisher was in irons. When Dampier asked Fisher to moderate "his scurrilous language" and false abuse of him, he yelled that "the captain might kiss his arse for while in confinement he would speak as he pleased." Abuse and bad language either by a commander, as in the case of Bligh, or against him as here, were frequently cited as a major grievance in court-martials about disputes on British naval ships in the eighteenth century. Dampier meanwhile challenged the rest of his crew. Were they planning to mutiny? Of course, they answered "no." Dampier nevertheless slept "with small arms upon the quarterdeck" with those officers he trusted, "it scarce being safe for me to lie in my cabin, by reason of the discontents among my men."

After putting Fisher ashore in Bahia, Dampier continued his voyage.

He had intended to round Cape Horn and approach New Holland from the east but the season and weather prevented him. Had it not, he might have discovered the east coast of Australia long before Cook. Instead, traveling around the Cape of Good Hope he once more reached its western coast, where he assiduously recorded what he saw and collected numerous botanical specimens, many now preserved in Oxford University.

On the way back to Britain, the leaking *Roebuck* foundered off Ascension Island. Dampier saved all his crew and many of his specimens. On his return he faced a court-martial for his treatment of Fisher. The court believed Fisher's charge of ill-usage but not Dampier's countercharge of "mutinous behaviour" and fined Dampier his entire salary for the voyage. His book on the expedition, *A Voyage to New Holland*, contained much new information about the lands he had visited. However, neither it nor his oral reports encouraged further British expeditions to New Holland, considered a barren land, or to the Pacific.

The next British venture into the region was in 1740 when the Admiralty dispatched a squadron of seven ships commanded by Commodore George Anson to attack the Pacific coast of Spanish South America. In the interim the lure and romantic mystery of the South Seas had led foolish British investors to pile their money into the stock of the chimerical South Sea Company, leading to the financial crisis known as the "South Sea Bubble," which in 1720 almost brought down the British economy.

Although Anson enjoyed some initial successes against the Spaniards, scurvy quickly became rife, killing some 1,300 crewmen compared to four who died in action. The vessels of Anson's fleet lost contact with each other. Eventually he reached home in his own ship the *Centurion*, having circumnavigated the globe and captured the annual Manila galleon that took treasure from the Philippines to the Mexican coast for transhipment to Europe.

The crews of Anson's other ships were much less fortunate, in particular that of HMS *Wager*, which lost a mast in a storm and was wrecked on rocks just off the Chilean coast. Most of the crew got ashore but, once there, morale and discipline began to disintegrate even more quickly than the wreck of the *Wager*. The ship's commander, Lieutenant David Cheap, had with him only two commissioned officers but several warrant officers, including the sailing master, the gunner John Bulkeley, and a number of midshipmen, among them John Byron (the Romantic poet's grandfather) and Henry Cozens. Soon quarrels broke out, with ordinary sailors arguing that since their pay had stopped with the loss of their ship so had the authority of their officers. Copious amounts of alcohol seem to have been recovered from the wreck. Three weeks after the *Wager* hit the rocks, Cheap accused Cozens of being drunk and, after an argument, struck him. A few days later Cozens, again drunk, complained to the purser about the allocation of rations. The purser believed he was acting mutinously and cried out. Cheap rushed up and shot Cozens, wounding him in the head, and thereafter refused him any medical care from the surgeon. Cozens, who was popular, died in agony some days later, leading to a breakdown of relations between Cheap and most of his men.

Nevertheless, the crew continued strengthening the *Wager's* longboat and two other small boats rescued from the wreck with a view to sailing to civilization. Bulkeley proposed to lead the boats back through the Magellan Strait to Portuguese Brazil. Cheap would have none of it although he had no plan of his own. A few weeks later most of his crew colluded in Cheap's arrest and imprisonment. Subsequently they abandoned him and his few loyalists and set out south in the boats for Brazil. After navigating the Strait of Magellan during a hazardous voyage of two thousand miles, they reached the Rio Grande in Portuguese territory. During the voyage the *Wager's* purser had died. Bulkeley commented, "He died a skeleton for want of food. This gentleman probably was the first purser belonging to His Majesty's service that ever perished with hunger." Pursers were notorious for profiteering from food supplies and keeping the best for themselves. Allegations of profiteering would feature large in the claims of the mutineers against Bligh, who acted as the *Bounty's* purser as well as its commander.

Cheap and three others, including John Byron, eventually reached Britain after traveling up the coast of Chile to Santiago. After their return and that of Bulkeley's party, there was an expectation that Bulkeley would be court-martialed for mutiny. However, the Admiralty preferred not to act either on this or on charges that Cheap had killed Cozens without due cause, showing a leniency it would later display toward actions of others in distant oceans such as some of the *Bounty* mutineers. Shortly afterward, Parliament passed a new act that clarified that the crews of wrecked naval vessels remained subject to naval discipline.

John Byron's naval career thrived. In 1764, the Admiralty entrusted him with the command of a voyage of exploration to the South Pacific with the aim of locating Terra Australis Incognita. He was given HMS *Dolphin* and completed the first circumnavigation of the world in less than two years (July 1764 to May 1766) but made few discoveries. Byron missed the chance of being the first European to land on Tahiti, sailing just north of it and acknowledging on his return to Britain that he might well have passed close to a significant body of land: "We saw vast flocks of birds which we observed towards evening always flew away to the southward. This is a convincing proof to me that there is land that way and, had not the winds failed me in the higher latitudes I make no doubt but I should have fell in with it and in all probability made the discovery of the southern continent."

Encouraged, in 1767 the Admiralty dispatched Samuel Wallis to make a further search for the continent in the *Dolphin*, which thus became the first ship to circumnavigate the world twice.

II

"THE TRUEST PICTURE OF ARCADIA"

*B*efore the *Dolphin* and Wallis returned on May 20, 1768, the Royal Society and the Admiralty had already been planning for some time an expedition to the Pacific to observe the transit of Venus across the face of the sun, due in June 1769. They believed that these observations, together with those of the transit made elsewhere, would be important in calculating the distance between the earth and the sun and other planets. They had, however, decided no specific location for their Pacific observation. Wallis's report of his discovery of Tahiti with its "safe, spacious and commodious harbour" changed all that. Tahiti seemed an ideal, not to say heaven-sent, location for their celestial observations.

Despite their vagueness about where in the Pacific to make their sightings, the joint preparations of the Admiralty and Royal Society were so advanced by the time of Wallis's return that they had already purchased a three-year-old Whitby-built collier "at a cost of 2840 pounds, 10 shillings and 11 pence, a . . . bark of the burthen of 368 tons," which they renamed HMS *Endeavour*. The Admiralty had also appointed James Cook, newly promoted from the warrant officer rank of master to the commissioned rank of lieutenant, to command her, and the Royal Society was preparing to nominate Joseph Banks as the head of the scientific staff.

James Cook had risen through the ranks of the Royal Navy by merit at a time when background and patronage were more often key to promotion. The forty-year-old Yorkshire-born son of a Scottish farm worker had at the age of sixteen been apprenticed to a grocer in the port of Staithes near Whitby on the northeast coast of England. Eighteen months later, inspired to go to sea, he persuaded his master to apprentice him instead to a Quaker ship owner. He served aboard several Whitby colliers, rising to the position of master before, with war with France imminent, in 1755 he joined the Royal Navy as an ordinary able seaman. Soon, the tall (over six-foot), dark-eyed, and handsome Cook had passed the necessary exam to be warranted a sailing master, licensed to navigate and handle a king's ship. During the wars with France in Canada, he earned praise for his accurate charting—sometimes under fire—of the St. Lawrence River, which helped General James Wolfe take his troops up the river to storm the Heights of Abraham, capture Quebec, and end the prospect of North America becoming a French possession.

After the war, the Admiralty appointed Cook Surveyor of Newfoundland, where he again impressed with his new charts and a successful observation of an eclipse of the sun—for which he received the praise of the Royal Society. His skills in surveying and astronomy made him an obvious choice to command the expedition to the South Seas. He clearly helped select the *Endeavour*, knowing the good handling and sea-holding capabilities of such Whitby coal vessels.

Joseph Banks was from an altogether more privileged background. He was born in February 1743 in London, the son of parents who owned considerable estates in Lincolnshire and Yorkshire. His father died when he was young, leaving Banks extremely wealthy. His annual income was six thousand pounds, compared to Cook's naval pay for the expedition of ninety pounds a year, an ordinary sailor's of twelve pounds, a farm laborer's around fourteen pounds, the botanist in charge of the Chelsea Physic Garden's fifty pounds, the first director of the British Museum's two hundred pounds, and Dr. Johnson the lexicographer's income of three hundred pounds—which kept Johnson and his household in some comfort. Banks studied at Harrow, Eton, and Oxford University's Christ Church College, where he became deeply interested in botany and an admirer of the Swedish pastor and pioneering botanist Carl Linnaeus, who had introduced a new way of classifying animals and plants which, he boasted, was so straightforward that even a woman could understand it.

When appointed to the Pacific expedition to which he contributed ten thousand pounds of his capital—a sum equivalent to more than a million pounds today—Banks was pleased: "the South Sea at least has never been visited by any man of science." He took with him on the *Endeavour* Dr. Daniel Solander, a renowned Swedish pupil of Linnaeus; two artists; a clerk; a man to look after his numerous scientific instruments; two valets; and two black servants. (They were servants, not slaves. Slavery had never been authorized by statute in Great Britain and four years after the *Endeavour* sailed, Lord Mansfield, in a historic court judgment, would find it illegal under common law, describing it as "so odious that nothing can be suffered to support it" and freeing a slave who had reached Britain whose master had tried to reclaim him.) Unfortunately, both black servants would perish early in the voyage in the snows of Tierra del Fuego during a disastrous shore expedition.

In addition to Banks's team, an astronomer and his assistant and Cook and his eighty-strong crew made up the ninety-three men crammed into the *Endeavour*, which was just over one hundred feet long and just under thirty feet wide. As a merchant vessel it would have carried a crew of around two dozen. Among Cook's men were twelve marines whose task was to assist Cook to protect his ship against external threats and any internal dissent. The *Endeavour*'s third lieutenant was the American John Gore, now thirty-eight, who had already circumnavigated the world twice with Byron and then Wallis. Twenty-five-year-old Charles Clerke, a notorious practical joker who had circled the globe with Byron, was the master's mate. The increased numbers meant Cook had to share the captain's cabin, known as the great cabin—around fifteen feet by twenty feet—with Banks and Solander, their instruments, their extensive library including Dampier's volumes on the South Seas, and, in due course, their growing store of specimens.

Final preparations to sail were made during the next few weeks, including the stowing of 7,800 pounds of sauerkraut to combat scurvy, 185 pounds of Devonshire cheese, four tons of beer, 608 gallons of rum, barrels of gunpowder for the guns, and much more. There were also four pigs, seventeen sheep, and two dozen chickens to accommodate in pens on deck until required for food, as well as two favorite greyhounds of Banks to find space for. Cook now received his final orders from the Admiralty. After he had completed his observation of the transit of Venus he was "in pursuance of His Majesty's pleasure hereby required and directed to proceed to the southward in order to make discovery of the [southern] continent." He should also explore the true nature of the island of New Zealand reported by Tasman more than 120 years previously.

The *Endeavour* left Britain in August 1768. Eight months later, Banks's journal entry for April 13, 1769, announced their arrival in Tahiti: "This morn early came to anchor in Port Royal [Matavai Bay] . . . Before the anchor was down we were surrounded by a large number of canoes who traded very

quietly and civilly for beads chiefly, in exchange for which they gave coconuts, breadfruit, both roasted and raw, some small fish and apples." After
landing, Banks walked across the island with Cook and Gore who, as a
previous visitor, had learned some words of the Tahitian language. Banks
was entranced by "breadfruit trees loaded with a profusion of fruit and giving
the most grateful shade I have ever experienced, under [which] were the habitations of the people, most of them without walls; in short the scene . . . was
the truest picture of an arcadia."

Their intended destination was Purea's dwelling but Gore became puzzled
to find "almost everything was altered for the worst" since his visit with
Wallis. He scarcely recognized any of the somewhat apprehensive-looking
local people trailing behind them. Purea's *marae* had disappeared. So, too, had
her great thatched palace. Only a few carved pillars remained standing. Gradually, Cook discovered that after Wallis's departure there had been fighting
on the island and the faction led by Purea and her husband had been defeated
and displaced. The apprehension on the faces of the new inhabitants of the
area arose from their concern about Wallis's known closeness to Purea and
their fear he might have returned to avenge her and dispossess them.

These people, under their chief, whom Banks named Hercules "for the
large size of his body," therefore sought to appease Cook and his men with
gifts such as perfumed bark cloth and food. However, the success of their
efforts at appeasement was rather spoiled when Solander and the ship's
surgeon had their pockets picked, losing a pair of opera glasses and a snuffbox,
respectively.

Cook soon identified a site for the observatory at the northeastern tip of
Matavai Bay at what became known as Point Venus and began construction.
Improving relations between Britons and Tahitians were again disrupted
when the marines guarding Point Venus shot dead a Tahitian who, after
distracting one of their comrades, had stolen his musket. Two other Tahitians
were wounded in the marines' random firing. The islanders seemed to accept
the shooting philosophically as a suitable punishment for failing to succeed
in the theft. Banks, however, said: "If we quarrelled with those Indians we
should not agree with angels!" One of the artists, Sydney Parkinson, a
Quaker, was distressed that the marines had fired with "the greatest glee
imaginable as if they had been shooting at wild ducks," regretting "what a
pity that such brutality should be exercised by civilised people upon
unarmed ignorant Indians."

Relations between the islanders and the British began to improve once more, following the same pattern of friendship interspersed with violence that would continue to typify relations between the British and most Pacific islanders. One day Banks saw a new party approaching his tent. It was led by Purea. "Our attention," he wrote, "was now entirely diverted . . . to the examination of a personage we had heard so much spoken of in Europe. She appeared to be about forty, tall and very lusty, her skin white and her eyes full of meaning. She might have been handsome when young," he continued, before adding ungallantly, "but now few or no traces of it were left." She was as delighted to see the British and in particular those who had served on the *Dolphin* as they were to see her.

Banks, who had a reputation as a man about town, even a rake, in Britain and was reputedly engaged to be married, soon formed a close relationship with one of Purea's attendants whom he described as a "fine Grecian girl . . . my flame" while, he claimed, holding off Purea's own attentions. His friendship with both women led to an incident among the most popularly celebrated and exaggerated after the *Endeavour* returned to Britain. One evening Banks, having "stripped myself" of clothes, including his breeches as well as a fine white jacket and silver-frogged waistcoat, was sleeping in one of Purea's large canoes, probably with her servant, his "flame," and not with her. Purea was however close by when he awoke to find that his garments had been purloined. An embarrassed Banks had to return to the ship partly clad in Tahitian cloth, although he eventually recovered his clothes.

The incident did not dissuade him from continuing such amours, even reputedly coming close to a duel with the ship's doctor over one woman. To Banks in Tahiti love was "the chief occupation, the favourite nay almost the sole luxury of the inhabitants; both the bodies and souls of the woman are modelled into the utmost perfection for that soft science. Idleness, the father of love, reigns here in almost unmolested ease." He enjoyed dancing with the Tahitian women, describing how "I was . . . prepared by stripping off my European clothes and putting me on a small strip of cloth around my waist, the only garment I was allowed to have, but I had no pretensions to be ashamed of my nakedness for neither of the women were a bit more covered than myself."

Well aware of the siren reputation of Tahitian women, Cook took a relaxed attitude to his men's sexual relations with them so long as these hampered neither the observations of the transit nor his ship's operations.

Nearly all of his officers and men took mistresses. Sydney Parkinson wrote, "most of our ship's company procured temporary wives . . . with whom they occasionally cohabited; an indulgence which even many reputed virtuous Europeans allow themselves in uncivilised parts of the world, with impunity; as if a change of place altered the moral turpitude of fornication . . . [and thus] suppose that the obligation to chastity is local and restricted only to particular parts of the globe." However, Parkinson was perhaps writing a little hypocritically for home consumption since, when Banks took a woman into a tent to enjoy her favors, "the first thing he saw was shyboots Parkinson in bed with the girl's sister."

Cook himself, who had married seven years previously, would always remain celibate. Misinterpreting his restraint for impotence, the Tahitian women described him as "old and good for nothing." Cook worried about the spread of the venereal disease, with which he decided the men of de Bougainville's "French" expedition must have infected the locals. The Tahitians called it "the British disease." Indeed, it was widespread in British sailors, among whom the expression "one night of Venus, six months of mercury" (the supposed cure for venereal disease) was common for good reason.

Cook did, however, do his best to understand the local customs, often eating with the island's leaders. Once he was offered the meat of a vegetable-fed dog and although most of his men would not touch it, he, Banks, and Solander did. Cook recalled "it was the opinion of everyone who tasted of it that they never ate sweeter meat." Banks observed and described for the first time in English what we now call surfing or bodyboarding. The Tahitians swam out beyond the surf, taking with them parts of a broken old canoe. "Their chief amusement" was to climb onto the wood "and opposing the blunt end to the breaking wave were hurried in with incredible swiftness. Sometimes they were carried almost ashore but generally the wave broke over them before they were half way," whereupon they dived beneath the wave and swam out to repeat the operation.

Banks also noticed that when the Tahitian women wished to express grief they would lacerate their cheeks "with great force six or seven times" with shark's teeth until "a profusion of blood" flowed. Although he did not like the smell of the monoi oil with which then, as now, Tahitians of both sexes anointed themselves, he admired the islanders' cleanliness: "These people are free from all smells of mortality and [the smell of] their oil . . . must be preferred to the odiferous perfume of toes and armpits so frequent in Europe."

All noticed how many local people were heavily tattooed, particularly on the legs and buttocks. The word itself is Tahitian, brought into English by Banks: "I shall now mention their method of painting their bodies or 'tattow' as it is called in their language. This they do by inlaying the colour of black under their skins . . . The colour they use is lamp black . . . Their instruments for pricking this under the skin are made of bone or shell, flat, the lower part . . . cut into sharp teeth . . . I saw this operation performed . . . on the buttocks of a girl about fourteen years of age." Several of the *Endeavour*'s crew returned to England with tattoos of their own.

No visitor, however, understood fully the complexities of Tahitian society, including the many religious taboos, and therefore Europeans unwittingly caused needless offense by straying onto the great stone *maraes* or harming sacred trees. In particular they did not then comprehend the role of the *arioi*, a powerful society of well-born young Tahitians of both sexes who enjoyed free love but who, if they wished to remain in the society, were required to kill any child produced as a result of their lovemaking.

The observation of the transit of Venus on June 3, 1769, went well. Afterward, Cook conducted a tour of the island before deciding to depart for New Zealand and the search for the southern continent. Despite Cook's abilities as a leader, the lure of Tahiti was such that as that time approached, he faced desertions and even incipient mutiny. As the Point Venus encampment was being dismantled two marines deserted. Cook, for the first but not the last time in his voyages, had some of the local leaders held hostage to ensure their people delivered the miscreants back to the ship, a stratagem that on this occasion worked. Cook had the deserters imprisoned and, when the *Endeavour* returned to sea, given twenty-four lashes. He had had other sailors flogged during the voyage to Tahiti and while on the island for theft, but he did not impose the death penalty for any crime on either his men or on Tahitians who had stolen from him, writing: "That thieves are hanged in England, I thought no reason why they should be shot in Tahiti."

After Banks had planted watermelons, lemons, limes, and oranges, the crew of the *Endeavour* made their final farewells. Purea, as she had when Wallis left, wept copiously. Aboard the *Endeavour* as it sailed were two Tahitians—Tupaia, Banks's *taio* or sworn friend who, as well as being a Tahitian priest, was a skilled navigator and now understood enough English to interpret; and his servant. Cook had opposed their boarding but as Banks wrote, "the captain refuses to take him on his own account . . . I have therefore resolved to take him. Thank heaven I have a sufficiency and I do not know why I may not keep him as a curiosity, as well as some of my neighbours do lions and tigers at a larger expense than he will probably ever put me to."

Tupaia was to prove highly useful as a navigator and translator when, leaving Tahiti after a stay of three months, Cook sailed on through the South Pacific islands. The expedition reached and then thoroughly explored and charted the coasts of New Zealand, finding that it was two main islands and not the one Tasman had thought. Thereafter, Cook turned the *Endeavour* west in search of the still undiscovered lost continent. On April 19, 1770, the lookout spotted land. Banks wrote, "At 10 [the next day] it was pretty plainly to be observed; . . . sloping hills covered in part with trees or bushes but interspersed with large tracts of sand." The hills had "the appearance of the highest fertility."

The *Endeavour* navigated along the coast, anchoring on April 28 in what Cook called a "capacious, safe and commodious bay" where they would remain for nine days. Cook commanded the first landing party but told his wife's young cousin Isaac Smith, a member of his crew, "Isaac, you shall land first." Cook wrote, "The great quantity of new plants etc Mr. Banks and Dr. Solander collected in this place occasioned my giving it the name of 'Botany Bay.'" The *Endeavour*'s men also encountered the local Aboriginal people, who seemed to wish for little to do with them. Banks found they differed greatly from the description by Dampier, "in general . . . a faithful relator." Their hair was sometimes "lank as a European's, in others a little crisped" but not "at all resembling the wool of negroes." The people were "naked as ever our general father was before his fall."

Continuing up the coast, they sighted almost immediately what "appeared to be safe anchorage" where they did not stop, but which Cook named Port Jackson, today's Sydney. Sailing on, the *Endeavour* struck the Great Barrier Reef off what Cook named "'Cape Tribulation' because here all our troubles begun," holing the vessel. Cook beached his ship near what is now Cook-town and began repairs. Here they encountered many other Aboriginal people. Cook described them as "a dark chocolate [colour] . . . their hair was black, lank, cropped short and neither woolly nor frizzled . . . Some parts of their bodies had been painted with red and one of them had his upper lip and breast painted with streaks of white . . . Their features were far from being disagreeable, the voices were soft and tunable." Some had bones through their noses. Despite their lack of possessions, Cook thought them "far happier than we Europeans . . . They live in a Tranquillity which is not disturbed by the Inequality of Condition." They were, Banks wrote, "content with little, nay almost nothing. Far enough removed from the anxieties attending upon riches or even the possession of what we Europeans call common necessaries," they drew no distinction between rich and poor, having no understanding of luxuries such as "strong liquors, tobacco, spices, tea etc." Among them "Providence seems to act the part of a leveller."

Banks also observed and described the kangaroo: "Quadrupeds we saw but few . . . The largest was called by the natives 'kangooroo.' It is different from any European and indeed any animal I have heard or read of [with] the singular property of running or rather hopping upon only its hinder legs, carrying its fore bent close to its breast . . . it hops so fast . . . it easily beat my greyhound who though he was fairly started at several killed only one."

After seven weeks, with the *Endeavour* repaired, Cook sailed on. On August 22, 1770, he landed on what is now known as Possession Island and "once more raised English colours and in the name of His Majesty King George III took possession of the whole eastern coast [of New Holland] . . . by the name of New South Wales." The *Endeavour* reached Batavia (modern Jakarta) in the Dutch East Indies in October 1770. Cook had lost none of his men to scurvy on his long voyage but while in Batavia dysentery and malaria struck, killing several including the ship's surgeon and Tupaia and his servant. Shortly after leaving the pestilential port many others, among them the artist Sydney Parkinson, died. Thirty-four succumbed in total—more than a third of the *Endeavour*'s complement.

The *Endeavour* reached England in July 1771, having covered thirty thousand miles as Cook and his men explored and charted more than five thousand miles of new coastline. On his return Cook's account and that of Banks, together with the latter's drawings, artifacts, and specimens (which included 3,600 species of plants—1,400 new to Europe's botanists and a substantial addition to the total of 6,000 previously recognized), excited great interest and enthusiasm about the Pacific. The public's attention centered not on New Zealand and New South Wales but once more on the stories of the Tahitians' sexual freedom and their lack of inhibitions, making love openly and promiscuously. Some like John Wesley, the Evangelical founder of Methodism, were shocked by the notion of "men and women coupling together in the face of the sun and in the sight of scores of people," a practice he thought contradicted the doctrine of man's shame after his fall in the Garden of Eden.

Many others perceived a commendable lack of hypocrisy or guilt in Tahiti's women compared with the mores of British society where, even in what was a relatively permissive age, respectability enforced certain conventions and deceptions. Georgiana, Duchess of Devonshire, the leading political hostess of her day and a friend of Banks, conducted a well-known affair with Charles Grey and lived in a ménage à trois with her husband and his mistress. Yet when she became pregnant by Grey, her husband forced her to terminate the affair. She was dispatched to the continent to give birth and the child was adopted.

James Boswell, friend of Banks, biographer of Dr. Samuel Johnson, and admirer of Rousseau, was an inveterate and self-confessed womanizer. As well as taking many other mistresses, after he had visited Rousseau he had an affair with his hero's long-term mistress. Boswell also consorted with whores on bridges and on London's street corners when drunk. In the morning he woke up not only with a hangover and on occasion venereal disease but also with an overwhelming sense of guilt and self-loathing perhaps traceable back to his Calvinist Scottish upbringing.

Moral pressures were stronger at all levels of society on women and perhaps strongest among the middle classes where, as Diderot suggested, concerns about paternity and property were acute. Among working people, if an unmarried young woman became pregnant all would be well if she quickly married the father (if single).* If the young woman did not marry, there followed disgrace, dismissal from her job (if, as many servants were, she was impregnated by her master), expulsion from her family, and quite often a descent into crime and prostitution.

The British press, then as now, published "kiss-and-tell" stories. One anonymous sailor from the *Endeavour* was quoted as saying of Tahiti: "The women are extremely lascivious . . . They are not very decent in their amours having little regard to either place or person. A virgin is to be purchased here with the unanimous consent of the parents for three nails and a knife. I own I was the buyer of such commodities." Even the official account of the voyage, compiled by Dr. John Hawksworth from the journals of Cook, Banks, and others, succumbed to a combination of outrage and lascivious wonder, describing how Tahitian young women danced with "motions and gestures beyond imagination wanton . . . a scale of dissolute sensuality wholly unknown to every other nation . . . and which no imagination could possibly conceive."

---

*Academic studies show some 40 percent of first baptisms to couples of this period occurred fewer than eight and a half months after their marriage.

Almost immediately on his return to Britain Banks ended his engagement to wealthy heiress Harriet Blosset, who was said to have received a substantial settlement of five thousand pounds from him for breach of promise. Society gossips quickly associated this story with those circulating of Banks's exploits on Tahiti. Cartoons and verses satirized his behavior. One cartoon showed Banks's breeches being surreptitiously stolen while, oblivious, he was deep "in flagrante delicto" with "the Tahitian queen"—Purea. Banks's breaking of his engagement and his previous reputation as a rake were not the only reasons for such ribaldry. So too, surprisingly, was his passion for botany. Versifiers worried Banks's "sensitive plant" might wilt if not handled appropriately. In a satirical "Epistle from Mr Banks, Voyager, Monster-hunter and Amoroso to Oberea [Purea] Queen of Tahiti," a lovesick Banks writes:

> I own the plants thy love has given to me,—
> But what a plant did I produce to thee!

Such double entendres reflected Linnaeus's explicit statement that his system for classifying plants was based on their male and female reproductive organs: "The calyx is the bedchamber . . . the filaments the spermatic vessels, the anthers the testes, the pollen the sperm, the stigma the vulva, the style the vagina." The *Encyclopaedia Britannica* was appalled: "A man would not naturally expect to meet with disgusting strokes of obscenity in a system of botany."

Not everyone was impressed by the eulogies of Banks and others of the *Endeavour's* crew about the ease of life on Tahiti as this exchange between Boswell, the friend of Banks and Rousseau, and Dr. Johnson—no believer in the "noble savage"—shows:

BOSWELL: "I am well assured that the people of Tahiti who have the bread tree, the fruit of which serves them for bread, laughed heartily when they were informed of the tedious process necessary with us to have bread—ploughing, sowing, harrowing, reaping, threshing, grinding, baking."

JOHNSON: "Why sir, all ignorant savages will laugh when they are told of the advantages of civilised life. Were you to tell men who live without houses, how we pile brick upon brick, and rafter upon rafter, and that after a house is raised to a certain height, a man tumbles off a scaffold, and breaks his neck, they would laugh heartily at our folly in building; but it does not follow that men are better without houses. No, sir" (holding up a slice of a good loaf), "this is better than the bread tree."

Although a libertine and a member of the notorious Hellfire Club, the First Lord of the Admiralty, the Earl of Sandwich, was a hardworking man who enacted many naval reforms and is usually credited as the founder of the Royal Marine Corps.* He prided himself on his efficiency, demanding brief memoranda and promising to deal speedily with one-page documents whereas anyone who made him turn over a page "must wait my leisure." The undoubted success of Cook's and Bank's expedition led to an immediate decision by Sandwich for a second voyage to make further discoveries in the South Seas. Two ships, both again Whitby-built colliers, were purchased and renamed, respectively, HMS *Resolution* and HMS *Adventure*.

Banks, sometimes not a modest man—"how immense has been the improvement of botany since I attached myself to the study," he once boasted—assumed he would now be in effective command, with Cook in a subordinate role. Indeed the Earl of Sandwich, his friend, encouraged him to think so, ordering the *Resolution* to be modified, against Cook's advice, to meet Banks's request for an extra deck to give more space for himself and his scientists. However, when the modified vessel was on sea trials she proved top-heavy and in danger of capsizing. Charles Clerke, who was to be Cook's second lieutenant, wrote: "By God, I'll go to sea in a grog tub if required, or in the *Resolution* as soon as you please, but must say I think her by far the most unsafe ship I ever saw or heard of." Sandwich promptly ordered the modifications to be removed. Thereupon a piqued Banks, according to an onlooking midshipman, "swore and stamp'd upon the wharf, like a mad man." He subsequently declined to go.

Cook, promoted to Master and Commander, was confirmed in command. The *Resolution* and the *Adventure* sailed in June 1772, taking with them twelve of the men who had sailed on the *Endeavour*, including Isaac Smith, Cook's

---

*The sandwich is certainly named after him for requesting meat between two slices of bread to avoid breaking off from what he was doing, but opinion is divided whether he first asked for one because he did not want to break off from gambling or so that he could continue working at his Admiralty desk.

wife's cousin, and Charles Clerke. Among the newcomers were George Vancouver, then a fifteen-year-old midshipman, and twenty-one-year-old James Burney, the brother of the novelist Fanny Burney. As botanists, Cook took at short notice after the loss of Banks a German church minister named Johann Forster and his son George. While resupplying in Madeira, Cook was surprised when a young man who called himself Burnett presented himself at the gangplank claiming to be a botanist and an associate of Banks. Unlike in the case of Commerson's mistress, "Burnett" was soon discovered not to be a man at all but one of Banks's mistresses, whom he'd intended to smuggle aboard and whom he had been unable—or perhaps had forgotten—to inform that he would not, after all, be sailing.

After a voyage in high southern latitudes where his ships became the first to cross the Antarctic Circle, Cook in the *Resolution* returned to New Zealand where he was reunited with the *Adventure*, which he had lost touch with in fog. Cook later headed for the fertile, friendly Tahitian islands to resupply before returning south where, having again lost contact with the *Adventure*, the *Resolution* reached 71 degrees 10 minutes south, a farthest south record that stood for nearly fifty years. After a further visit to Tahiti he descended south yet again. En route he came upon an uninhabited surf-fringed island some one thousand nautical miles northeast of Botany Bay which he named Norfolk Island. Cook was immediately struck by the suitability of the great spruce pines he found there for naval masts.

Proceeding far south again, he mapped, claimed, and named the island of South Georgia after his king. Then, convinced there was no more land to be found in the southern ocean at these latitudes, he headed home. He wrote in his journal, "I flatter myself that the intention of the voyage has in every respect been fully answered, the southern hemisphere sufficiently explored and a final end put to the searching after a southern continent, which has at times engrossed the attention of some of the maritime powers for near two centuries past and the geographers of all ages."

He would also report on an important secondary object of his voyage: the testing of the accuracy of the marine chronometer developed by John Harrison and thus its utility for measuring longitude. On his first voyage Cook had used the lunar distance method, which required a sextant to measure the angular differences of stars from the moon. On this second voyage he carried with him a copy of Harrison's H4 chronometer made by Larcum Kendall, known as K1, and some other chronometers. Only K1 proved sufficiently accurate for use in calculating longitude, as observations made at Point Venus, whose location had been precisely determined during the transit of Venus, demonstrated. On his return Cook informed the Admiralty, "Mr. Kendall's watch has exceeded the expectations of its most zealous advocates."

While in Tahiti Cook had discovered that civil strife had again altered the balance of power and he and his men had to get to know new leaders. Purea still visited but was a much-diminished figure. Nevertheless, nearly all the crew retained a very favorable impression of the islands and their people. One newcomer called Tahiti "the Paradise of those Seas." Naturalist Johann Forster likened it to Virgil's depiction of the Elysian Fields with the people delighting in "the grassy groves of the happy ones . . . and the homes of the blessed." Forster also shrewdly identified the temptation to desert for men whose prospects in their own homeland were poor:

> If we fairly consider the different situations of a common sailor on board the *Resolution* and of a Tahitian on his island, we cannot blame the former if he attempt to rid himself of the numberless discomforts of a voyage around the world, and prefer an easy life, free from cares . . . the most favourable prospects of future success in England which he might form in idea, could never be so flattering to his senses as the lowly hope of living like the meanest Tahitian . . . he must earn his subsistence in England by the sweat of his brow while this oldest curse on mankind is scarcely felt at Tahiti.

Forster's son George, however, questioned the effect of their visit on the islanders: "If the knowledge of a few individuals can only be acquired at such a price as the happiness of nations, it were better for the discoverers, and the discovered, that the South Sea had still remained unknown to Europe and its restless inhabitants." Cook too worried about the Tahitians: "To our shame as civilised Christians, we debauch their morals already too prone to vice, and we introduce among them wants and perhaps disease which they never before knew, and which serve only to disturb the happy tranquillity which they and their forefathers enjoyed. If anyone denied the truth of this assertion let him tell me what the natives of the whole extent of America have gained by the commerce they have had with Europeans."

When Cook arrived back in Britain aboard the *Resolution* at the end of July 1775 after a voyage of just over three years, he found that the *Adventure* had preceded him by a year. Omai, the young islander wounded in the encounter with Wallis on Tahiti and taken aboard the *Adventure* in Huahine, an island northwest of Tahiti, had become the first Polynesian to visit Britain and had been taken up by British society. Joseph Banks assumed a proprietorial interest in the young man, buying him the best clothes, teaching him English and English manners and taking him to meetings of the Royal Society as well as to stay for some time with the Earl of Sandwich at his home. There he was rumored to have had a number of affairs with women entranced by the exotic, not to say erotic, lure of the South Seas. Censorious evangelicals suggested that Banks and Sandwich, instead of bringing Omai into the light of Christianity, had merely taught him "to make refinements on sin in his own country."

Omai had proved a quick learner, even if he reputedly greeted King George III on first meeting him with "How do King Tosh." Banks took him to the state opening of the British parliament where King George deprecated "the daring spirit of resistance" in the New England colonies. Omai attended race meetings and many other social events as well as inspecting the British fleet with Banks and the Earl of Sandwich. He even learned to skate during the extremely cold winter of 1776 when the Thames froze over and he became proficient in backgammon and chess. At Banks's instigation Sir Joshua Reynolds painted him. When Fanny Burney met him with her brother James, who had returned on the *Adventure* as second lieutenant, she wrote, "He rose and made a very fine bow . . . As he had been to Court, he was very fine. He had on a suit of Manchester velvet, lined with white sateen . . . lace ruffles and a very handsome sword which the King had given to him. He is tall and very well made, much darker than I expected to see him but had a pleasing countenance. Indeed he seems to shame education for his manners are so extremely graceful and he is so polite, attentive and easy that you would have thought he came from some foreign Court."

According to James Boswell even Dr. Johnson was impressed when he met him: "He was struck by the elegance of his behaviour, and accounted for it thus, 'Sir, he had passed his time . . . only in the best company so that all that he had acquired of our manners was genteel. As a proof of this, sir, Lord Mulgrave and he dined one day at Streatham. They sat with their backs to the light fronting me, so that I could not see distinctly; and there was so little of the savage in Omai, that I was afraid to speak to either, lest I should mistake one for the other."

Omai's time in Britain was soon to draw to a close. After Cook's report of his successes, which led to his promotion to post-captain, Lord Sandwich and the Admiralty were soon planning another Pacific expedition, this time to search for the Northwest Passage through the Arctic from the west, long sought by many countries. However, the authorities wished to keep their real objective a secret and the return of Omai with many gifts to his homeland seemed to provide the perfect cover.

III

"WHAT COULD YOU LEARN, SIR? WHAT CAN SAVAGES TELL, BUT WHAT THEY THEMSELVES HAVE SEEN?"

$\mathcal{T}$he Admiralty originally intended to appoint Charles Clerke to lead their new expedition but were delighted when Cook, at dinner with Lord Sandwich one evening, stood and volunteered to command it. Despite his disappointment, Clerke agreed to serve as Cook's second-in-command and captain of the *Discovery* which was to accompany a refitted *Resolution* on this voyage. Soon afterward Clerke was arrested for debt, one of the forty thousand Britons to whom this happened annually, often for small sums. Imprisoned in the King's Bench debtors' prison in London, he caught one of the diseases rampant in the country's prisons—a severe chest infection he would later discover was consumption (tuberculosis). It took Lord Sandwich's intervention to secure his release just in time to join the *Discovery* before she sailed. Virginian John Gore was appointed first lieutenant of the *Resolution*, with James King as the *Resolution*'s second lieutenant. James Burney became the *Discovery*'s first lieutenant and David Nelson, an employee of Joseph Banks, was appointed the expedition's botanist.

Twenty-one-year-old William Bligh was appointed the *Resolution*'s master. Like many other sailors at this time, including Samuel Wallis, he was from a Cornish family. Born on September 9, 1754, he was the only child of a customs official and his wife, both of whom had been previously married. His mother, who had a grown-up daughter from another marriage, was forty-one at his birth. Destined for the sea at an early age, he was entered at seven years old on the muster roll of HMS *Monmouth* as a captain's servant. However, he probably did not serve aboard. Persuading a captain to add to his roll a young boy was common and mutually beneficial. The boy would gain theoretical sea time toward that required to become a commissioned officer. The captain would have a nonexistent mouth for which he could claim the cost of food from the Admiralty.

William Bligh's first sea experience probably came as an able seaman and then midshipman in 1770, a few months after his mother had died and two after his father had remarried again. He did not make particularly fast progress toward a commission. His last appointment before the *Resolution* was to the *Ranger*, a small naval vessel based in the Isle of Man and tasked with preventing the smuggling for which the islanders—like the people of Bligh's home county of Cornwall—were notorious, most inhabitants sympathizing more with the perpetrators than with the revenue officials. Around this period he took and passed the examinations to be warranted a ship's master—a noncommissioned rank that could be the dead end for a naval career. Bligh, however, signaled his continued ambition by passing his lieutenant's examination before sailing on the *Resolution* and was probably hoping that his experience with Cook would secure that rank for him. Cook wrote that in general he was looking for able men who "could be usefully employed in constructing charts, in taking views of the coasts and headlands near which we should pass, and in drawing plans of the bays and harbours in which we should anchor." How Bligh came to be selected for the post of the *Resolution*'s master is not recorded. However, he must have had some reputation in that regard.

As she awaited the final orders for departure in Plymouth Sound, the *Resolution* was surrounded by sixty-two troop transports carrying Hessian mercenaries to fight against the rebellious American colonists. A commentator reflected on "the singular and affecting circumstance that at the very instant of our departure upon a voyage the object of which was to benefit Europe by making fresh discoveries in North America there should be the unhappy necessity of employing others of His Majesty's ships, and of conveying numerous bodies of land forces to secure the obedience of those parts of that continent which had been discovered and settled by our countrymen in the last century."

On July 12, 1776, eight days after the thirteen rebel American colonies signed the Declaration of Independence, the *Resolution* finally sailed. Standing together on the deck as the vessel headed out to sea, Cook and Bligh would have made an oddly assorted pair. The forty-seven-year-old Cook at over six feet would have towered above the twenty-one-year-old Bligh, who was scarcely more than five feet tall. Cook's dark features would have been weathered and sea-beaten, while Bligh was always noted for his blue eyes and pale skin, "of an ivory or marble whiteness" beneath his dark hair. Bligh quickly grew to look up mentally as well as physically to Cook, who would become the role model for many of his own command practices. Bligh noted how Cook insisted on pain of flogging that his men consume sauerkraut, wort of malt, and orange and lemon juice to avoid scurvy, how Cook also insisted on them dancing on deck to provide exercise as a further guard against disease, and how Cook demanded from his crew cleanliness of both their persons and their quarters. He would also remember how Cook preferred a three-watch system for the running of his ship under which crews were split into thirds to work the ship in shifts in contrast to the two-watch system that was standard on most naval ships.

One man not on board was James Boswell, whose in-person pleas to accompany Cook on the voyage to learn about people in a pure state of nature Cook had turned down, by now wary of supernumeraries who might turn out to be prima donnas. Samuel Johnson had been equally discouraging: "What could you learn, sir? What can savages tell, but what they themselves have seen? Of the past, or the invisible, they can tell nothing. The inhabitants of Tahiti and New Zealand are not in a state of pure nature, for it is plain they broke off from some other people. Had they grown out of the ground, you might have judged of a state of pure nature."

After touching on Tasmania and revisiting New Zealand—landing where some of the *Adventure*'s men had been killed and eaten by Maoris on the previous voyage—the ships reached the Friendly Islands, Tonga, in 1777. There, by now stripped of illusions about how the local people would behave and increasingly exasperated by thefts and no doubt increasingly exhausted after long years at sea, Cook resorted more quickly than previously to flogging both islanders and crewmen and to hostage-taking to secure the return of stolen goods.

In August 1777, the *Resolution* and *Discovery* anchored in Matavai Bay in Tahiti, where Cook went ashore with Omai. To his surprise Cook received a lukewarm welcome but quickly discovered the reason. Two Spanish ships had visited the island, depositing for a time two Catholic missionaries. The Spaniards had told the Tahitians they ruled the world and that they had defeated the British and in fact killed Cook himself. Cook's presence in the flesh, with the help of a fireworks display and a large quantity of sacred red feathers obtained in the Friendly Islands, soon mended relations. Cook, Omai, and the ships' officers were now greeted formally by Tu, a young man in his late twenties who had established himself as the island's supreme chief.

Purea, the Britons discovered to their dismay, had died. Even taller than Cook, Tu welcomed the British regally but was entirely unimpressed by Omai's boasting about Britain and his friendship with "King Tosh" as well as his displays of his finery and other gifts.

While on Tahiti, Cook visited a *marae* where a human sacrifice was being made to increase Tu's martial power or *manna* in an anticipated battle with the people of the neighboring island of Moorea. The human sacrifice had seemingly already been made when Cook arrived but he witnessed the eye being removed and ceremoniously placed on a leaf and inserted in Tu's mouth to give him the strength of Oro, the god of war. Among the most venerated objects was the sacred Tahitian banner onto which the *Dolphin's* pennant presented to Purea by Wallis had been sewn. Shortly afterward some of the Tahitian chiefs were offended by Cook's refusal to join them in an attack on Moorea and outraged by Omai telling them that if they sacrificed a man in England they would be hanged for murder.

Nevertheless the crews continued to enjoy the pleasures of Tahiti. One first-time visitor recalled: "The overflowing plenty, the ease in which men live and the softness and delightfulness of the clime, the women are extremely handsome." Another enthused, "In these Elysian fields immortality alone is wanting . . . We had not a vacant hour . . . we wanted no coffee houses to kill time nor Ranelaghs or Vauxhalls." (These were London's pleasure gardens, illuminated by thousands of lanterns by night, and centers of entertainment of all sorts from concerts and fancy-dress balls to firework displays and fire-eating.) He witnessed a dance whose performance "bespoke an excess of joy and licentiousness. Most were young women who put themselves into several lascivious postures, sometimes they put their garments aside and exposed with seemingly very little sense of shame those parts which most nations have thought it modest to conceal." In fact, he was mistaken about the purpose of the dance. It was again not eroticism but designed to arouse Oro.

After presenting to Tu a picture of himself painted by his ship's artist, John Webber, and guided by Omai in his canoe, Cook and his ships sailed through the reefs across to Moorea, which he had not previously charted. There the friendly relations the expedition first established deteriorated quickly after two goats belonging to the vessels and put ashore to graze were stolen, leading an irate Cook to overreact by ordering the destruction of many of the islanders' canoes. Some of his crew deplored his "cruel ravages" but Omai took a leading part in the mayhem. According to a German crewman he "executed the greater part of this destruction and behaved much worse than the Europeans."

Sailing on to the island of Huahine, where Omai had joined the *Adventure*, Cook put him ashore and established him on a small farm where his men helped build paddocks for the horses, cows, and goats that King George III had given him—and that were all unknown in the islands until the arrival of the Europeans.* As the time for departure grew closer a young marine deserted, only to be captured by Cook and Bligh when sleeping garlanded with flowers between two women in a canoe, brought back to the ship, and flogged. Shortly afterward two other crewmen—a midshipman deeply in love with a Tahitian woman and one of the gunner's mates—also deserted. After they were recaptured with some difficulty, Cook assembled his crews and told them all deserters would be sure to be captured, dead or alive.

Leaving a weeping Omai and the islands behind for what would be the last time, Cook again mused that the islanders could never go back to their previous halcyon existence: "My real opinion [is] that it would have been far better for these poor people never to have known our superiority in the accommodation and arts that make life comfortable . . . indeed they cannot be restored to that happy mediocrity in which they lived before we discovered them . . . for by the time that the iron tools of which they are possessed are worn out they will have almost lost the knowledge of their own. A stone hatchet is, at present, as rare a thing amongst them, as an iron one was eight years ago."

Voyaging on, Cook and his men became the first Europeans to reach the Hawaiian Islands, which he named the Sandwich Islands after the First Lord of the Admiralty. There they found the women just as generous with their favors as the Tahitians and the whole population equally keen on purloining articles from the ships and their crews.

Beginning their search for the Northwest Passage, Cook's ships sighted the northwest coast of America, in what is now Oregon, in March 1778. Working his ships farther north, Cook passed the wild shores of a large island (later to be named after his midshipman George Vancouver, who would make further surveys in the area), and landed in the island's Nootka Sound,

---

*The islanders coined the name "man-carrying pig" for the horse.

which he charted. Pushing onward, the crews traded furs with the Inuit and passed through the volcanic Aleutian Island chain before crossing the Arctic Circle. Not long afterward Cook "perceived a brightness in the northern horizon like that reflected from the ice, commonly called the blink." Soon, at 70 degrees 44 minutes north, they met a barrier of ice and had to turn back, returning eventually to the Sandwich Islands. There, as they anchored in January 1779 in a bay on the island of Hawaii called Kealakekua, an area which they had not previously visited, they were warmly welcomed by Hawaiians, who believed them to be gods.

Leaving after two and a half weeks, the two ships quickly ran into a fierce storm that split the *Resolution*'s foremast. Cook, now fifty years old, returned to Kealakekua Bay, where the Hawaiians were surprised to see those they had considered divine returning with a damaged ship. As a consequence they were much less welcoming as sailors and marines brought ashore the damaged foremast to be repaired—a process that would take some days.

Thefts from the ships became ever more frequent and blatant. Mutual distrust spilled over into confrontations, in one of which midshipman Vancouver and the *Discovery*'s master were hurt and some of their equipment stolen. Already determined to stop the Hawaiians imagining "they have gained advantage over us," Cook woke the next morning, February 14, 1779, to find that the *Discovery*'s cutter had been stolen during the night from where it had been moored half under water to preserve it against warping.

By now thoroughly angry, he ordered four boats—two from each ship— to blockade the bay, allowing no canoes to escape while he landed to retrieve the cutter either by direct action or by taking the leading chief of the island hostage to secure its return. Bligh was put in charge of the *Resolution*'s cutter. Soon spotting canoes attempting to leave the bay, he set off in hot pursuit and, closing in on them, gave the order to his marines to fire—which they did, together with those in one of the other boats, wounding some of the canoeists, including a priest, and forcing the canoes back to shore.

Cook meanwhile had landed some distance away, accompanied by Lieutenant Molesworth Phillips of the marines and nine of his men, to secure the island's chief. Lieutenant John Williamson, the *Resolution*'s Third Lieutenant—a close friend of Bligh's, and a fellow freemason, but according to his men a bully and "a very bad man and great tyrant"—hovered just offshore in the *Resolution*'s launch together with its pinnace. Cook was bringing the chief back towards the beach when a hubbub broke out among the nearly two thousand Hawaiians now thronging the shore. Some officers later thought its cause was the news of the attack on the canoes by Bligh and the others and the wounding of the priest.

Whatever the cause, the Hawaiian warriors began to crowd around Cook and shortly attacked him with clubs and stones. Cook and the marines fired once but then the marines, abandoning any attempt to reload, dropped their muskets and ran back toward the sea, pursued by the Hawaiians. Lieutenant Phillips, wounded in the shoulder in his attempts to defend Cook, swam across to the pinnace, which had remained close in, before jumping back into the sea to drag aboard by his hair one of his marines who was floundering in the water. Lieutenant Williamson in the launch, to the manifest disgust of some of his crew, rather than going to the defense of Cook—who could not swim—immediately headed the launch back toward the *Resolution* despite Cook's gesturing him to come closer to the shore. Cook tried to protect himself but was soon felled, and clubbed and stabbed to death among the rocks on the shoreline, together with four marines.

In the aftermath of Cook's death, Bligh was among the advocates of taking a bloody revenge on the Hawaiians, but Charles Clerke, now in command in Cook's place, refused to take any such drastic actions. Subsequently he ordered Bligh to take a party ashore again to bring back to the ship Lieutenant King; William Bayly, one of the expedition's astronomers; and some marines and sailors, who had been working on the *Resolution's* damaged foremast and making celestial observations in another part of the bay, which had remained peaceful. Skeptical about the need to leave, King told Bligh to stand on the defensive while he returned to the *Resolution* to confirm the orders to abandon the camp. After he departed, Bligh, in what King would claim was direct defiance of his explicit orders and despite protests from Bayly, opened fire on nearby villagers, killing some. Eventually King returned to the encampment and the Britons quickly withdrew to the safety of the ships, taking with them the half-repaired foremast.

Cook's death led to a series of promotions and changes of responsibility, though not for Bligh. Lieutenant Gore became commander of the *Resolution*. One of Bligh's subordinates—a master's mate—was promoted over his head to be a lieutenant as another had been earlier in the voyage. The *Resolution* and *Discovery* continued their expedition, making a full survey of the Sandwich Islands and exploring some of the coast of Siberia including the Kamchatka Peninsula, where Clerke died from the tuberculosis he had contracted in the debtors' prison. His death sparked another round of promotions. Bligh again failed to benefit despite his claim that after Cook's death "C. Clerke being very ill in a decline he could not attend the deck—publicly gave me the power solely of conducting the ships and moving as I thought proper." Another of Bligh's master's mates was, however, made a junior lieutenant.

John Gore now took command of the expedition and brought the two ships back to Britain in October 1780. Upon their return there were further promotions, among them for King, Phillips, and Williamson. Yet again William Bligh was not included. Perhaps the events surrounding Cook's death had something to do with it. Bligh's own journal for the voyage no longer exists, believed lost on the *Bounty*, but he later annotated King's version of what happened at the encampment and elsewhere, calling it "a pretty old woman's story" and claiming that "whenever any dangerous situation should be taking place King was always being ill."

Bligh also blamed Lieutenant Phillips and his marines for Cook's death rather than his friend Lieutenant Williamson, despite many other accounts praising Phillips, in particular for his rescue of the marine from drowning, and damning Williamson for cowardice. Captain Clerke had apparently been collecting reports on Williamson's behavior as material for a possible court-martial but, according to Phillips, when Clerke died Williamson broke open the captain's desk and stole the relevant papers. According to a midshipman, Williamson formed "a mason's lodge" on the *Resolution* by "bribing [the sailors] with brandy and got them to promise as brothers they would say nothing of his cowardice when they came back to England."*

Although exactly what happened in Kealakekua Bay that day will never be entirely clear, one certainty is that sailing master William Bligh was one of the very few of the expedition's officers who did not profit from Cook's last voyage, failing in his expectation to be rewarded for his endeavors by promotion to lieutenant. To add insult to injury, Bligh found that many of the charts of the voyage—for which he rightly claimed to have been responsible—were being presented to the Admiralty as the work of another of his master's mates, Henry Roberts, newly promoted to lieutenant.

---

*Nearly two decades later Williamson was court-martialed for disobedience to orders and cowardice at the battle of Camperdown, at which Bligh himself served honorably. Called as a witness, Bligh did not condemn his old colleague; but on the overwhelming evidence of others Williamson was convicted of disobedience and dismissed from further service.

His indignation reached a new high when the third volume of the official account of the voyage, prepared by King and dealing with the period after Cook's death, appeared in 1784. In it, Roberts was credited in print for what Bligh considered his charts. Bligh later wrote on a copy of the volume: "None of the maps and charts in this publication are from the original drawings of Lieutenant Henry Roberts. He did no more than copy the original ones from Captain Cook who besides myself was the only person that surveyed and laid the coast down in the *Resolution*. Every plan and chart from Captain Cook's death are exact copies of my works."

In the nearly four years between the *Resolution*'s return and the publication of that volume much had happened in William Bligh's life and career. His father, who had been widowed and remarried yet again for a fourth time, had died three months after the return of Bligh, his only son. Bligh was employed as master on a succession of naval ships in the wars against European powers who were supporting the American rebels, eventually achieving his long-delayed and ardently desired promotion to a junior lieutenancy.

Soon after his return on the *Resolution* and immediately after his father's death, he had revisited the Isle of Man during a period of leave. There he met—or much more likely renewed the acquaintance from his previous visits on the *Ranger* of—Elizabeth Betham, the twenty-seven-year-old daughter of the head of the Isle of Man's customs service. Within a few weeks, and only four months after the *Resolution* had docked, the couple were married. A little over nine months later, Betsy, as she was known to the family, gave birth to a daughter, with a second daughter to follow not long after.

The signing of the Treaty of Paris in 1783 ended the wars and confirmed the independence of the thirteen colonies. The peace led to a speedy rundown of the British navy. Many officers, including Bligh, were placed on half-pay, in his case around thirty-five pounds a year. This was far from a sufficient sum to keep a wife and family in a genteel way and Bligh was now a family man.

Fortunately, Elizabeth Bligh's relations were well placed to help, having influential connections both familial and friendly. A distant relation in the navy had had a hand in Bligh's belatedly receiving a commission. Now Elizabeth's maternal uncle Duncan Campbell was best placed to help. He was a wealthy merchant owning vessels trading with the West Indies as well as the prison hulks anchored in the Thames and holding the prisoners who, until the rebellion of the American colonies, would have been transported by him to those very lands for a considerable profit. Campbell arranged for Bligh to secure the Admiralty's permission to command one of his merchant vessels plying the West Indian trade and gave him a magnificent salary of five hundred pounds per annum.

When the account of Cook's last voyage was published in 1784, Campbell intervened with the Admiralty, urging Bligh's claim that many of the charts credited to Roberts were his, and successfully gained Bligh a share of the royalties. The bulk went to Captain Cook's widow, whereas Roberts got nothing.

IV

"THERE ARE VERY FEW INHABITANTS"

$\mathcal{T}$he independence gained by the thirteen colonies had changed much for Britain and necessitated a rethink of her strategy toward the rest of the world. Despite some face-saving naval victories toward the war's end, in particular at the Battle of the Saints against the French in the West Indies, Britain had suffered a loss of prestige in the eyes of other European powers. More tangibly, she had lost the guarantee of the profitable trade—both import and export—with the colonies. The potential loss of this trade pushed the authorities to look east to Asia for a market for the increasing amount of manufactured goods the developing pace of the Industrial Revolution (in which Britain was the world leader) was producing. The government also feared the perception of a renewed British vulnerability might tempt other powers, in particular the Netherlands, France, and Spain, to interfere politically and militarily with Britain's new aspirations.

Even more practically, the British government had lost the destination to which they transported their convicted felons, the number of whom was increasing with the discharge at the war's end of so many soldiers and sailors lacking both settled roots and employment. The punishment of transportation had evolved from the middle of the seventeenth century. By the time of the American Revolution, the practice was for the government to appoint a contractor to whom they paid five pounds for each felon transported to the North American colonies. There the contractor profited further by selling, normally to plantation owners, the indentured labor of the convicts, usually for seven or fourteen years—the main periods for which convicts were sentenced to be transported overseas—for sums ranging from ten to twenty-five pounds for males and a little less for women. Rewards for the recovery of missing indentured convicts often featured in the colonial newspapers among those for runaway slaves.

In 1772, forty-six-year-old Duncan Campbell had been appointed to the profitable position of the government's sole contractor for transportation to the colonies, having been a junior partner of the previous contractor for fourteen years. During the American Revolution the transport of convicts dwindled to a halt. (Estimates of the total numbers of prisoners transported to the American colonies in the eighteenth century vary widely from perhaps the most likely figure of forty thousand to fifty thousand to a more improbable one hundred thousand.) A shrewd, not to say calculating, businessman, Campbell now discussed with government what to do with felons who would previously have been transported. The authorities agreed to Campbell's self-serving proposal that they should be sentenced to hard labor and housed by him in de-masted ships—hulks—anchored in the Thames, whence they would be sent ashore daily in chains to undertake hard labor such as stone breaking or digging gravel or sand from the riverbanks.*

In July 1776, Campbell was formally appointed overseer of convicts on the Thames, with an incentive to keep costs low to maximize his profits from the twenty-eight pounds per annum the government paid him for each prisoner. The hulks—soon known as "Campbell's academies for crime"—became notorious. After visiting them John Howard, Britain's first penal reformer, condemned them as breeding grounds for disease as poorly clothed, poorly fed inmates were crammed together in the holds of old vessels floating in pools of rubbish and ordure. The shore-side portholes were closed to prevent noxious smells from the insanitary conditions troubling shore dwellers, thus depriving prisoners of light. There was insufficient headroom between decks for even those of middle height to stand upright beneath the beams. Where hammocks were provided, the weight of the iron fetters often prevented convicts from climbing into them. Nearly a quarter of inmates died from disease within a year.

When Howard and the utilitarian philosopher and prison reformer Jeremy Bentham inspected the hospital on one of the vessels, Campbell prudently "declined going down" with them into the hold and "soon called us out."†

---

*Among the first people sent to the hulks was Peter Le Maitre, sentenced to five years for stealing medals from the Ashmolean Museum in Oxford where he was a don at the university.

†Bentham developed his own concept of a "panopticon" prison—a vast circular prison where each cell was visible from the center. To his great frustration it was never built in his lifetime. However, the now disused Presidio Modelo penitentiary built in Cuba in the 1920s closely follows his concept.

In response to successive adverse reports, Campbell undertook small incremental improvements in conditions, presumably reducing his profits a little each time. However, conditions remained harsh and discipline fierce, with miscreants flogged. Prisoners sometimes rioted and there were many escape attempts. In September 1776, Campbell's overseers put down two mass escapes, killing three prisoners and badly wounding more than twenty-five.

An observer described the prisoners working ashore with "fetters on each leg, with a chain between, that ties variously, some round their middle, others upright to the throat. Some are chained two and two; and others whose crimes have been enormous, with heavy fetters. Six or seven [guards] are continually walking about with them with drawn cutlasses, to prevent their escape and likewise to prevent idleness . . . so far from being permitted to speak to anyone, [the convicts] hardly dare speak to each other." Some commentators decried freeborn Britons being turned into slaves. Campbell soon had walls built around the prisoners' work areas to prevent escapes but also to keep out prying eyes.

By the end of the American War of Independence, Campbell had three hulks on the Thames and there were two others—one in Plymouth harbor and one in Portsmouth. However, continuing complaints about the hulks from both reformers and locals worried about the spread of disease and dangerous escapees, and from magistrates and other local worthies about the increasing number of felons and consequent overcrowding of the prisons on shore, led the authorities to consider options for the renewed transport of felons overseas. Among destinations investigated were Canada, the Falkland Islands, and West Africa, where a few men were actually sent, but swiftly died. In 1784, an attempt was made to transport some convicts aboard a ship named the *Mercury* to Georgia, without the approval of the American state's authorities. It ended when, still off the English coast, the convicts mutinied, seized the ship, imprisoned the crew, and succeeded in reaching the port of Torbay in Devon, where many escaped. Another proposal briefly mooted was to trade convicted prisoners for white Christians captured by Barbary pirates and enslaved in North Africa.

Eventually a proposal to establish a penal colony in New South Wales—which had not been visited by any British ship, nor by any foreign one, since Cook had claimed it for Britain in 1770—began to gain traction. The first to suggest the possibility of a convict settlement there was Joseph Banks to a parliamentary committee in 1779 while Cook's third expedition was still in progress. Despite the amusement at his amorous exploits on Tahiti and his walking away from Cook's second voyage, Banks had become a pillar of the establishment and a friend and adviser to King George III, a man of a similar age to his own. In 1774 he had secured the king's agreement to turning the king's garden at Kew—originally conceived as a pleasure garden like that at Vauxhall—into a botanical garden. Through the gardens he introduced species such as magnolias, hydrangeas, fuchsias, peonies, monkey-puzzle trees, and cranberries (one of North America's only three indigenous fruits) to Britain. He thus established Kew as a major repository for plants he then bred—if necessary in hothouse conditions—and dispersed throughout Britain's overseas possessions wherever he thought they could be of benefit. The poet Samuel Taylor Coleridge found Banks and his garden an excellent source of cannabis and Indian hemp—two of the drugs with which he liked to experiment.

Another breeding project on which Banks himself was beginning to work was the improvement of Britain's sheep flock. As the Industrial Revolution gathered pace, cotton started to supplant wool in several applications. In some, such as summer wear and underwear, it was because of its inherent properties, in others partly because British wool was too coarse to spin effectively by machine. Banks, who had a personal interest in the topic as a Lincolnshire land and sheep owner, set about a breeding program to improve the fleece of British flocks so that a fine wool thread could be produced. Central to it was the import of Spanish merino sheep, which had fine fleeces. Since the Spaniards knew they held a considerable commercial advantage they refused to supply Banks; but he obtained specimens clandestinely through Portugal. Soon he had established a breeding flock for the king at Kew.

At the end of 1778, Banks was elected President of the Royal Society (a post he held until 1820). In 1779 he told the parliamentary committee that New South Wales, and Botany Bay in particular, might be a suitable destination for convicts. The earth was sufficiently fertile to sustain a European settlement, with plenty of fish and good water; the climate was good, "similar to that about Toulouse in the South of France"; and the local people few and, "though armed with lances," timorous—they "constantly retired from our people when they made the least resistance." Provided the expedition was well supplied with equipment and seeds for grain and vegetables, Banks suggested the settlement would become self-sufficient within a year. Despite Banks's considerable enthusiasm and eloquence, the committee did not then take up his suggestion.

In 1783 James Matra, a slightly mysterious figure who had sailed as a midshipman on the *Endeavour* where he had become friends with Banks, and who was a loyalist displaced from the newly independent American colonies, approached Banks with ideas on New South Wales. Subsequently he put forward his own proposals that a colony be established there for displaced American loyalists like himself. Such a colony would be good for trade and would also have strategic benefits, giving Britain a secure entry into the Pacific. In response to queries from the authorities he also agreed that it would make a fine settlement for convicts. "Let it be here remarked," Matra wrote, "that [the convicts] cannot fly from the country, that they have no temptation to theft, and that they must work or starve." So good was the climate and soil that in twenty or thirty years the goods they produced might "cause a revolution in the whole system of European commerce and secure to England a monopoly of some part of it and a very large share in the whole."

Sir George Young, a future admiral and well experienced in the navigation of the Indian Ocean, agreed emphatically with Matra and produced a proposal along similar lines. He also included the suggestion that the area could be used to grow "that very remarkable plant" the fibrous New Zealand flax—sometimes known as New Zealand hemp—which he concluded, on the basis of the specimens brought back by Banks and Cook, to be a suitable raw material for making sail canvas and ropes and hawsers, all much in demand for the navy. He emphasized that a settlement would also be a good and secure staging post for the China trade in tea and silks. Again the government did not respond but set about exploring other options to little avail.

In 1785, the British government established a committee under Lord Beauchamp to hear evidence about where might prove a suitable location for a penal colony. Matra gave evidence and Young submitted a paper, but most attention was paid to the testimony of Banks. Reiterating many of the arguments he had put forward six years earlier, he said he had "no doubt that the soil of many parts of the eastern coast of New South Wales . . . is sufficiently fertile to support a considerable number of Europeans." The timber looked suitable for "house building and ship building," and women could be imported from Pacific islands to make up any discrepancy in the numbers of male and female convicts. There were "very few inhabitants" and such as there were wandered from place to place "like the Arabs," abandoning their dwellings "which are framed with less art or rather less industry than any habitations of human beings probably that the world can show." "From the fertility of the soil, the timid disposition of the inhabitants, and the climate being so analogous to that of Europe," the area was in his view preferable above all others. Duncan Campbell was also called to the committee to give some estimates of the costs of transportation to Botany Bay, which he suggested would be some thirty to forty pounds per prisoner, depending on the numbers to be transported and the size of ships used and including an element of profit for the chosen contractor.

The Beauchamp committee, however, in its report instead recommended a site on the southwest coast of Africa for the colony and the government sent out a vessel to reconnoiter that area, but on his return the captain's report was unfavorable. Therefore, in the summer of 1786 the British government under Prime Minister William Pitt (the Younger), his Secretary for Home Affairs Lord Sydney, and Sydney's Under Secretary Evan Nepean, a Cornishman and former naval purser, were still searching for a site for the penal colony while pleas from the authorities responsible for the overflowing prisons to make a decision were becoming overwhelming. Botany Bay now seemed the only viable option and Nepean reworked Campbell's calculations, suggesting that the cost of transporting 750 convicts, three regiments of marines to guard them, and maintaining the colony for three years would be about thirty-two pounds per convict per year, perhaps 15 percent more than keeping a prisoner on a hulk—"too trivial to be a consideration with Government."

Probably helped by Banks, Nepean produced a plan "for effectually disposing of convicts, and rendering their transportation reciprocally beneficial both to themselves and to the State, by the establishment of a colony in New South Wales . . . (from whence it is hardly possible for persons to return without permission) . . . [and] providing a remedy for the evils likely to result from the late alarming and numerous increase of felons in this country, and more particularly in the metropolis." The plan gave the detailed requirements for the establishment of a colony for some seven hundred to eight hundred convicts, with a governor, judges, and surgeons, as well as marines to protect the colony and guard the prisoners. It reiterated Banks's proposals that "a further number of women from the Friendly Islands [Tonga], New Caledonia etc . . . may be procured without difficulty" to rectify any imbalance between the sexes and thus avoid "disorders"—such as fighting among the men over the women—or "gross irregularities"—a euphemism for homosexuality. The document also laid out other advantages of a settlement in New South Wales, including the growing of tropical products such as spices and cotton, thus lessening Britain's dependence on its European rivals' colonies for them. The proposal described the area as a potential source for naval supplies not only of New Zealand flax—Catherine the Great's Russia was threatening to exploit its near monopoly of hemp— but also of pine for masts and other ships' timber. To the latter end, the colonization of Norfolk Island would become a subordinate aim of the venture.

By the end of August 1786, the government had announced its decision to send a fleet to transport convicts to Botany Bay. Public reaction was mixed. One Birmingham newspaper editorialized that "besides providing a place for our convicts from which all escape will be impracticable, the settlement may be otherwise highly beneficial to our Asiatic commerce." The *Morning Chronicle* conceded that since the convicts might in the end prove useful to Britain, there would be no harm in some expenditure to establish the colony. On the other hand, the *Daily Universal Register* suggested the colony would become "a nest of pirates" and, if not, the colonists would quickly claim independence as the Americans had done. Other papers predicted that Dutch or Spanish forces would soon arrive to overwhelm the settlers.

Preparations went swiftly ahead that autumn. The selection of a commander for the transportation fleet, who would become the governor of the colony on arrival, was a particular priority. Like that of Captain Cook, the authorities' choice was not of a well-connected insider but of a man from a humble background, Arthur Phillip. He had already demonstrated the qualities required for the job: good maritime experience, a level head, proven ability to act independently far from superiors, initiative tempered with discretion, as well as the ability to control subordinates without conflict.

Phillip was born in London on October 11, 1738, the son of an immigrant teacher of "the languages" from Frankfurt in Germany who probably later went to sea before dying when Arthur was still a child. The family lived in some penury before at thirteen the young Phillip was sent to a Greenwich school for the sons of dead or disabled seamen. After serving briefly on a whaler, Phillip joined the navy at the age of seventeen in 1755. By November 1770 he was a fourth lieutenant, his relatively slow advancement at least in part due to a period out of the navy after his marriage at the age of twenty-four to a rich widow seventeen years his senior. The marriage, which was childless, did not last and the couple separated in 1769, with his wife keeping her property and income. Why they separated is unknown, as is whether the self-contained Phillip married for money, whether he had little need for marital or female companionship, or whether he just became bored with life ashore and wished to return to sea.

At the Admiralty's suggestion, Phillip joined the navy of Portugal—Britain's ally—where he served with "great zeal and honour" in South America as a ship's captain in conflicts between Spain and Portugal. At the end of his secondment he re-joined the British navy. A report from the Portuguese viceroy in Rio de Janeiro gives a rare insight into Phillip's character at this period: "As regards his disposition, he is somewhat self-distrustful; but, as he is an officer of education and principle, he gives way to reason and does not, before doing so, fall into those exaggerated and unbearable excesses of temper which the majority of his fellow countrymen do . . . an officer of great truth and very brave; and is no flatterer, saying what he thinks, but without temper or want of respect."

During his renewed service in the British navy as a first lieutenant, Phillip became a firm friend of Evan Nepean, then a naval purser and like himself from a relatively humble background, being the son of a shipwright. In 1784, after Nepean's move to the home office and with tension rising with France, Nepean arranged with the Admiralty for Phillip to go to France with a generous allowance of one hundred fifty pounds to spy on the French naval and coastal defenses in and around Toulon on the Mediterranean coast. Well suited temperamentally to such a task, possessing the requisite knowledge of French and of the sea, Phillip continued in this role until in September 1786 he was appointed to command the first convict fleet at a salary of one thousand pounds per annum, plus his naval pay.

While Phillip was making preparations for the fleet's departure—no doubt often consulting Banks—Banks himself was promoting another South Seas scheme that he considered could form part of the convict fleet's task: the transport of breadfruit plants from Tahiti to the West Indies to provide food for the slaves there.

Just as William Dampier had praised the qualities of the breadfruit after his own Pacific voyage, Banks had written after his time on the *Endeavour*: "In the article of food these happy people [the Tahitians] may almost be said to be exempt from the curse of our forefather; scarcely can it be said that they earn their bread with the sweat of their brow when their chiefest substance, breadfruit, is procured with no more trouble than that of climbing a tree and bringing it down." The official published account of the *Endeavour* voyage built on his words: "If a man plants ten [breadfruit trees] in his lifetime, which he may do in about an hour, he will completely fulfil his duty to his own and future generations as the native of our less temperate climate can do by ploughing in the cold winter, and reaping in the summer's heat, as often as these return." Breadfruit thus began to symbolize a Pacific Garden of Eden, a kind of manna from heaven as freely available as the islands' beautiful women, only waiting to be plucked from the tree.

Once Banks was back in Britain, the breadfruit became prominent among the plants he was soon proposing be reared at Kew and then dispatched to other British possessions where their cultivation might prove commercially beneficial. His colleague and friend Dr. Solander advocated it as "universally esteemed as palatable and nourishing as bread itself and one of the most useful vegetables in the world."

When the war with the thirteen colonies cut Britain's West Indian plantations off from a supply of food, leading to starvation among some of the slaves, pressure to import breadfruit to the Caribbean began to build on Banks and the British government. In spring 1775, the West Indies Committee, consisting of British West Indian merchants and plantation owners, discussed the introduction of the breadfruit (and also the mangosteen). Shortly afterward, they posted a one-hundred-pound reward to "the captain of an East India ship or any other person" bringing to Britain "the true breadfruit tree in a thriving vegetation." The following year the Royal Society of Arts offered its gold medal to anyone who brought back "six plants in a growing state."

However, the very circumstances—the war with the colonies—that heightened West Indian interest in the breadfruit meant that the Admiralty had other priorities and could spare no resources to bring breadfruit plants from the Pacific. After the war ended and with relations with the now independent colonies uncertain, the plantation owners sent one of their number, Hinton East, to London to lobby once more for a breadfruit voyage.

Preeminent among those to whom East talked was Joseph Banks. Although immersed in the discussion about the convict colony, Banks needed no convincing and began to work up a scheme whereby the two ventures could be combined. After depositing the convicts in Botany Bay, one of the convict transports could be refitted there and travel on to New Zealand to pick up New Zealand flax plants and then on to Tahiti for breadfruit plants. He secured the approval of his friend King George and put the proposal to Prime Minister Pitt and his government, who in February 1787 agreed to his plan that the breadfruit voyage be combined with the transportation of convicts to New South Wales. Their decision was made all the easier by information that Britain's arch-rival France was planning a voyage for breadfruit.

However, as Banks worked through the plan, the reality of difficulties such as availability of good wood and skilled shipwrights and carpenters likely to be faced in Botany Bay in refitting a ship for a breadfruit voyage bore down on him. By the end of March 1787, he was convinced that a separate voyage for breadfruit was "more likely to be successful" and put forward detailed plans to that effect for a voyage from Britain to Tahiti and then direct to the West Indies. The government swiftly agreed and on May 5, 1787—a week before the departure of the convict fleet—Lord Sydney gave authority to the Admiralty to proceed. Banks, at the King's suggestion, was asked to make the arrangements.

Not everyone, however, was pleased. The antislavery movement was gaining pace. The Society for Effecting the Abolition of the Slave Trade was formed that year, 1787. Its Quaker members, banned as dissenters from being MPs, found a parliamentary champion in MP William Wilberforce, a correspondent of Banks, who began to press their case assiduously. Abolitionists saw the transhipment of the breadfruit not as the bringing of manna but as a perversion of enlightened science aiding the exploitation of human beings, just as they would oppose transportation as a kind of virtual slavery.

No detailed record exists of William Bligh's selection for what would be his first Royal Navy command. Bligh was in the West Indies commanding Duncan Campbell's ship *Britannia* when the breadfruit voyage was approved. However, the influence of Campbell is clear. Already well known to Banks, with his twin West Indies and convict interests Campbell would have been involved with him in both decisions and subsequent arrangements and thus in an excellent position to lobby for Bligh. The only surviving records of Campbell's involvement are a letter he wrote on May 2, 1787, in which he said, "I wish Bligh home soon, as thereby he may stand a chance of employment in his own line," and a later one in which he wrote, "Bligh is now fitting out a small ship in the King's service which I helped to procure him the command of . . . to bring the breadfruit plant."

The thirty-two-year-old Bligh was indeed well qualified for the appointment by virtue of his previous voyage to Tahiti and his knowledge of West Indian waters. His lack of speedy advancement and recent naval appointments meant that the position would be likely to be attractive to him.

Bligh did not dock in the Thames from the West Indies until August 5. There he learned of his appointment and wrote the first of what would be many fulsome letters to Banks: "I have heard the flattering news of your great goodness to me, intending to honour me with the command of the vessel you propose to go to the South Seas, for which, after offering you my most grateful thanks, I can only assure you I shall endeavour, and I hope succeed, in deserving such a trust."

V

"VILLAINS AND WHORES"

The eleven ships that made up the "First Fleet," as it became known, were the 612-ton, 24-gun man-of-war HMS *Sirius* as Arthur Phillip's flagship; the sturdy 170-ton armed sloop HMS *Supply*; three store ships—the *Borrowdale*, *Fishburn*, and *Golden Grove*; and six relatively new three-masted merchant ships that had been chartered by the authorities to carry the convicts. The largest of the convict ships—the 452-ton *Alexander*, which would carry more than two hundred convicts—was only 114 feet long and 31 feet broad. The others were the *Scarborough*, which would also carry more than two hundred prisoners, and the smaller *Charlotte*, *Lady Penrhyn*, *Friendship*, and *Prince of Wales* (the latter a late addition as the number of convicts selected for transportation grew), which would each transport about one hundred.

Carpenters in the Deptford dockyards labored to refit the transport ships to turn cargo holds into living quarters.* Here the prisoners would sleep on broad shelves running along either side of the hull on which four convicts would share a space only seven feet long and six feet wide. Headroom between decks was only four feet five inches, so that during their waking hours all but the shortest would have to stoop. An officer noted that the carpenters were also ordered to construct "very strong and thick bulkheads filled with nails" to run "across from side to side in between the decks abaft the mainmast with loopholes to fire between the decks in case of irregularities. The hatches are well secured down by cross bars, bolts and locks and are likewise nailed down from deck to deck with oak stanchions. There is also a barricade of plank about three feet high, armed with pointed prongs

---

*No below-main-deck plans of the first fleet's transport ships appear to have survived.

of iron on the upper deck . . . to prevent any connection between the marines and ship's company with the convicts."

On January 6, 1787, the process of loading the convicts began. At Woolwich, transportees from Campbell's prison hulks, Newgate Prison, and elsewhere—many with heavy irons on their legs—were rowed across the River Thames to the *Alexander* and the *Lady Penrhyn*, which was to carry only women. Many were ragged, louse-infested, and skeletally thin. An appalled Arthur Phillip complained to his friend Evan Nepean: "The situation in which the magistrates sent the women on board the Lady Penrhyn, stamps them with infamy—tho' almost naked, and so very filthy that nothing but clothing them could have prevented them from perishing, and which could not be done in time to prevent a fever, which is still on board that ship, and where there are many venereal complaints that must spread in spite of every precaution I may take hereafter and will be fatal to themselves." Phillip had already insisted to Home Secretary Lord Sydney, Nepean's political master, that he would accept no responsibility for deaths that might result from poor rations, paltry medical supplies, and overcrowding of his fleet. Now he told Nepean, "Let me repeat my desire that orders immediately may be given to increase the convict allowance of bread. Sixteen pounds of bread for forty-two days is very little." Some weeks earlier he had also complained that "no kind of surgeons' instruments" had been put aboard any of the ships, making it "very difficult to prevent the most fatal sickness amongst men so closely confined."

The prisoners' poor state had more to do with the wretched conditions they had endured on Campbell's prison hulks and in the jails than any profiteering by the contractor selected to provision the First Fleet. Just as Phillip had feared, "jail fever"—typhus—indeed spread, killing eleven male prisoners aboard the *Alexander*. The remainder were hastily taken ashore while sailors cleansed the vessel with the traditional naval remedies of creosote and quicklime. Despite these precautions, five more prisoners died after they were reloaded. By April 11, Phillip had further cause for concern: "By some mistake 109 women and children are put on board the Lady Penrhyn, tho' that ship was only intended to carry 102, and with propriety should not have more than two-thirds of that number."

The Admiralty Navy Board remained deaf to Phillip's complaints, just as they did to his requests for clothing for the female prisoners and more food for all. The board assured him blandly that since "the confinement on shipboard will not admit of much exercise, this allowance will be found more advantageous to the health of the convicts than full allowance." The diet the authorities proposed for the prisoners consisted largely of hard ship's biscuit (often referred to by sailors as "bread"), pottage made of dried peas, and salt beef.

The prisoners expected to survive on these rations were the product of Britain's chaotic and somewhat contradictory eighteenth-century penal system. The number of crimes punishable by death rose steadily through the century from about fifty in 1688 to 170 in 1765 and some two hundred by the century's end. Many of the new capital crimes were in fact the product of subdivision of old ones, and most of the rest were designed as deterrents to protect the rights to personal property, so heavily defended and jealously cherished in Britain and so lightly regarded in the South Seas.

However, the number of executions did not rise in proportion to the increasing number of capital crimes as might have been expected. On the contrary they began to decline so that by 1800 the number of crimes theoretically punishable by death began to overtake the number of people—two hundred or so—executed each year in England and Wales, which then had a combined population of around eight million. The only exception to this reduction in the number of hangings was a spike in the period 1783–86 after the return of more than 160,000 footloose soldiers from the American wars and before the introduction of transportation to New South Wales.

The ways in which criminals escaped execution for capital crimes were several and varied. For some offenses long on the statute book the accused could plead "benefit of clergy" under which, as a vestige of ecclesiastical privilege, they would avoid the death penalty provided they could recite a passage of scripture—usually the Fifty-First Psalm, nicknamed the "neck verse" because it could save one's neck. In other cases recommendations for mercy made by judges or juries were often accepted. In London, for example, only about one third of those sentenced to death were executed.

Often, the fate of the accused depended on the mood or temperament of the judges and juries. While the law stipulated maximum sentences, the severity of those imposed by judges varied widely and without much obvious logic. Either of their own volition or at a sympathetic judge's direction, juries that had the task of valuing stolen property would often estimate it just below the level at which a death sentence would apply. Sometimes juries would convict only on lesser charges, for example of petty larceny, which did not carry the death sentence, rather than grand larceny, which did. Sometimes, they might ignore evidence and acquit if sympathetic to the accused's plight, for example if the accused had been starving or had a dependent family to support. The reintroduction of transportation provided a welcome alternative sentence to the judges, juries, and those exercising the royal prerogative of mercy, removing the feeling that they were returning to the streets felons who might commit further crimes. Britain's justice system was, however, by no means "soft." Penal reformer John Howard pointed out that Amsterdam—a city with a population about one third of Georgian London's—had only had five executions in total in an eight-year period, whereas the annual rate in London was twenty to twenty-five.

At least half of those to be transported came from the stews and "hell houses" of London, even though Britain's capital made up only some 10 percent of the population. Many of these Londoners spoke "the flash or kiddy language" of the underworld—an "unnatural jargon" one officer called it—that sometimes needed a translator to interpret during their trials. Many may well have committed their crimes or been apprehended when under the influence of alcohol. In 1750 one in four houses in some parts of London was a drinking house or pub. In Westminster it was one in eight. Half of the wheat sold in London's markets was destined to be turned into gin and other alcohol. Londoners at this time are estimated to have drunk around 11.2 million gallons of alcohol each year.

Though some attempts were made to select on grounds of age, and the average age of those transported was around twenty-seven, the oldest was an eighty-two-year-old rag-and-bone woman named Dorothy Handland, convicted of perjury, while the youngest was nine-year-old chimneysweep John Hudson, who had been dispatched by his master through the skylight of a chemist's house in London's Smithfield to thieve for him.

No one aboard the First Fleet was a convicted murderer, since murder was not an offense punishable by transportation. The great majority were being transported for crimes against property: theft, breaking and entering, or stealing livestock. John Nicolls, a young and clearly ambitious assistant to a London hair merchant and perfumer, had been convicted at the Old Bailey of stealing nearly fifteen pounds, together with a large assortment of combs, razors, hair switches, powders, powder puffs, and pomades, and a looking glass sufficient to set himself up in business. Esther Abrahams, a young unmarried Jewish dressmaker from London's East End, who had recently given birth to a daughter, Rosanna, in Newgate Prison, had stolen twenty-four yards of black silk lace, presumably to use in her trade. John Martin, one of ten black men transported on the First Fleet, had purloined a veritable wardrobe of clothes—coats, breeches, waistcoats, and a woman's petticoat and gown—from a house. A sympathetic jury valued his booty at thirty-nine shillings—just below the forty shillings that would have made it a capital crime.

London prostitutes Charlotte Springmore and Mary Harrison had thrown acid on another woman's clothing for encroaching on their "turf"—the Black Swan gin shop near Petticoat Lane. Their defense that "there are so many sly whores now it is impossible for a public whore to get her living" had not impressed the judge, who had decided to rid the country of such "abandoned characters." Many were being transported for far less. Seventy-year-old Elizabeth Beckford had taken a few pounds of Gloucester cheese from her mistress's larder. Thomas Chaddick, a black man from the West Indies, had taken twelve cucumbers from a kitchen garden to stifle his hunger; while fifteen-year-old John Wisehammer had snatched a packet of snuff from the shop of a Gloucester apothecary.

Several forgers, swindlers, or receivers of stolen goods were among those being transported. William Parr, described in court records as a "noted swindler," had been sentenced at Liverpool in 1785 for cheating a shopkeeper. An Old Bailey jury had convicted Londoner William Hogg of "deception and forgery" for stamping wares with a fake hallmark and lion in order to pass them off as products of the Worshipful Company of Goldsmiths—an offense considered so serious that he received fourteen years.

Only 14 percent of the prisoners had been convicted of robbery with violence, and many of those had originally been condemned to death before having their sentences commuted. The latter included a unique band of female highway robbers: twenty-one-year-old Mary Broad, the daughter of fisherman William Broad and his wife, Grace, from Fowey, a port on the southern Cornish coast, and her two accomplices, Catherine Prior and Mary Haydon, both born in Devon. They had been arrested the previous year for attacking a female traveler on the main road out of Plymouth. Local magistrates had sent the women to Exeter to be tried at the Lenten Assizes, where they had appeared before high-court judges on circuit, Sir Beaumont Hotham and Sir James Eyre, charged with "feloniously assaulting Agnes Lakeman, spinster, on the King's Highway, putting her in corporeal fear and danger of her life on this said highway and violently taking from her person and against her will one silk bonnet (value 12d) and other goods to the value of £11.11s." One other female transportee, Mary Pile, was described as a "female highwayman" but only because she dressed as a man; her conviction was for stealing from a fellow lodger in an inn where the two were sharing a bed. Mary Broad and her confederates were also almost unique in that they had no male accomplices.*

Later court records described Mary Broad as dark-haired, gray-eyed, and five feet four inches in height—tall for a woman of that time. She gave no place of birth or residence, simply describing herself as a "forest dweller," and the brief record of the trial gives no clues about what had driven her from her home in Fowey to live rough. Fowey had once been a prosperous port, exporting tin, wool, and fish to continental Europe, and so economically and strategically important that in the Middle Ages two blockhouses had been built to protect it against French raiders. In 1415, one hundred archers had sailed from Fowey to fight for Henry V at Agincourt.

However, by Mary Broad's time, Fowey was in decline. Cornwall had been hard hit by a succession of natural disasters. Bad summers and resultant poor harvests had pushed up the price of corn. The winter of 1785–86 had been unusually harsh. Worst of all, the shoals of fish, especially pilchards, on which many depended for food and for trading—salted pilchards were exported from Fowey as far as Naples and Bilbao—had failed to arrive off the coast. A decade later, local people still recalled these times when "the fish were so scarce that the families of the fishermen lived solely on limpets which at other times they could not be prevailed upon to eat." At the same time, Cornwall, already one of the poorest counties, was suffering from the policies of the government in far-off London, which imposed a tax on salt imported from France—essential for the curing of fish and the extraction of its oil. It was also allowing landowners to fence off areas of what had been common land, depriving many of a place to graze their livestock.

Perhaps the prospect of starvation had forced Mary Broad to leave Fowey and turn to highway robbery or perhaps she did so to help her family to survive. Certainly the harsh economic conditions were driving many to crime. A 1785 issue of the *Sherborn Mercury* warned its probably already nervous readers that "highway robberies threaten the traveller, whether by night or day—the lurking footpad lies, like a dangerous adder on our roads and streets . . . making night hideous."

The jury lost little time in finding Mary Broad and her companions guilty, upon which one of the judges, a black cap atop his curled wig, had informed

---

*Mary Haydon was sometimes known as Mary Shepherd and Catherine Prior as Catherine Fryer.

them they would first be returned to jail and then taken "to a place of execution and there hanged by the neck until you are dead." However, once the Assizes were over, as was customary, Hotham and Eyre reviewed the list of condemned to decide which men and women to recommend to Home Secretary Lord Sydney as worthy to receive "the Royal mercy." Four nerve-shredding days after their trial the three women learned that instead of being executed they were to be "transported beyond the seas . . . as soon as conveniently may be" for seven years.

Loaded onto an open cart in shackles and exposed to the elements and the jeers of passersby, they had been taken the forty-five miles across Dartmoor back to Plymouth, where they were put aboard the prison hulk *Dunkirk* to await their transportation. When, on a chill gray day in January 1787, the three were rowed across to the anchored convict transport *Charlotte*, which had now arrived in Plymouth, Mary Broad and Catherine Prior were pregnant. Probably during their ten months on the *Dunkirk*, like some other female prisoners who were young and pretty enough, they had found themselves a "protector" among the marines guarding them.

The *Charlotte*'s quota of prisoners was eighty-four men and twenty-four women. Among the men transferred from the *Dunkirk* to the *Charlotte* were three whose fortunes would become entwined with Mary's. William Bryant, a Cornish fisherman, had been charged at the Launceston Assizes of March 1784 with "feloniously and knowingly receiving contraband cargo and using the name of Timothy Cary." The jury had acquitted him of smuggling contraband—indeed few West Country juries then had much appetite to convict for an offense so rife and from which so many benefited. Smuggled brandy, wine, and tobacco —the most profitable contrabands—were to be found in the homes of even the most respectable members of the local communities. A judge in the Cornish town of Bodmin reputedly wryly told a man just acquitted of smuggling: "You will leave this Court with no stain upon your character except that you have been acquitted by a Bodmin jury." However, in Bryant's case the jury were less forgiving of his using a false identity—considered as "forgery"—and the judge sentenced him to seven years' transportation for that crime.*

The second man, James Martin—a sallow-skinned, black-haired Irishman in his late twenties, originally from Antrim—had worked as an estate laborer

---

*In 1824 the mayor of Mary Broad's birthplace Fowey was accused of smuggling.

at Powderham Castle in Devon, belonging to the powerful Courtenay family. At the same Exeter assizes as Mary Broad, the jury convicted him of stealing iron bolts with a total value of four shillings for which Hotham and Eyre sentenced him to death, a sentence commuted like Mary's to transportation for seven years. The third man, James "Banbury Jack" Cox, had been convicted at Exeter two years earlier for stealing five shillings' worth of lace and sentenced to transportation for life.

The senior officer of marines responsible for guarding the convicts aboard the *Charlotte*—Watkin Tench—already knew Mary Broad and the three men well because he had served on the *Dunkirk*. Tench understood from personal experience what it was to be a prisoner. He did not come from a military or naval background. His father, a dancing master and proprietor of a "most respectable boarding school in Chester," had ensured that his son received a good education. Tench could, for example, recite John Milton's *Paradise Lost* from memory. Tench had studied briefly in Paris, becoming fluent in French and exploring the libertarian ideas of philosophers like Rousseau, Diderot, and Voltaire. After joining the marines at eighteen, he fought in the American war, only to be captured when, in 1778, a French squadron forced his ship HMS *Mermaid* aground in Delaware Bay. Tench spent three months as a prisoner of war in Maryland before a prisoner exchange enabled him to return home. In 1782, he was promoted to Captain-Lieutenant by Major General Collins, whose son David—a fellow marine officer appointed the new colony's Judge-Advocate—was sailing with Captain Phillip on the *Sirius*.

With the American war over, Tench—by then in his late twenties and serving with the marine detachment guarding the prisoners aboard the *Dunkirk*—was among those who answered the Admiralty's call for volunteers to sail to Botany Bay "to enforce due subordination and obedience" among the convicts and "for the defence of the settlement against incursions of the natives," signing up for a three-year tour of duty. Before sailing he also agreed with Debrett's publishers in London that he would record his impressions of the new colony for publication.

Perhaps because of his own experiences, Tench was one of the few marines to express sympathy for the convicts, describing how "an opportunity was taken, immediately on their being embarked, to convince them, in the most pointed terms, that any attempt on their side either to contest the command or to force their escape, should be punished with instant death; orders to this effect were given to the sentinels in their presence; happily, however . . . so desperate a measure" was unnecessary, "the behaviour of the convicts being in general humble, submissive and regular; indeed I should feel myself wanting in justice . . . were I not to bear this public testimony of the sobriety and decency of their conduct."*

Also aboard the *Charlotte* was thirty-one-year-old John White, the new colony's chief surgeon. Sharing Phillip's concern about the prisoners' dismal conditions, he wrote to Evan Nepean urging "the necessity of having fresh provisions served to the whole of the convicts while in port" and warning that otherwise many would succumb during the voyage to "a scorbutic taint"—scurvy. White's passion had some effect; fresh meat and vegetables eventually arrived. His advocacy also helped the marines, worried that having "voluntarily entered on a dangerous expedition" in the new colony they would be expected to survive without rum, something they regarded as "indispensably requisite for the preservation of our lives" and "without which . . . we cannot expect to survive the hardships" of "change of climate" and "extreme fatigue." More sympathetic to their concerns than the convicts' plight, the authorities responded generously, sending on board a three-year supply of wine and tobacco as well as rum.

Lieutenant of marines Ralph Clark, the Edinburgh-born son of a "gentleman's gentleman" posted to the convict transport *Friendship*, did not share Tench's and White's humanitarian outlook, frequently deriding the convicts as "villains" and "whores" in his journal. His principal concern as the fleet prepared to sail was parting from his young wife, Betsey Alicia, whose miniature he was carrying with him, and their two-year-old son. He had asked to be allowed to take his family with him and a sympathetic Phillip had argued his case to the authorities. They had turned the request down, which Clark thought "a great hardship," particularly since the expedition's only chaplain, the Reverend Richard Johnson, was bringing his new young wife with him. A chaplain had only been appointed because William Wilberforce had pressed his friend Prime Minister William Pitt to send one and the thirty-one-year-old Johnson, an Evangelical Methodist from Yorkshire, had been selected. A bachelor when appointed, he sought a suitable wife to aid him in his ministry and, just one month after accepting the chaplaincy and five months before sailing, married Mary Burton.

Another lieutenant of marines, William Dawes, posted to the *Sirius*, was a gifted amateur astronomer recommended by the Astronomer Royal. The

---

*Some have suggested that the empathetic Tench might have fathered Mary Broad's child but there is no evidence to substantiate this.

Board of Longitude had equipped him with instruments, including three telescopes and a ten-inch sextant, and asked him to observe a comet expected to streak across the heavens during the voyage. Dawes's routine duties included witnessing the daily winding of the handsome Kendall chronometer, K1. Cook had taken K1 on his second and third voyages, praising it as his trusty friend; Bligh as his sailing master had used it on the third voyage; and now the Board of Longitude had allocated it to Phillip. With its white enamel dial and finely polished steel hands, it was essential to the fleet's accurate navigation.

Forty-nine-year-old Captain John Hunter, Phillip's second-in-command on the *Sirius*—and his replacement as governor if he became incapacitated or ill—would also witness the winding of K1. Hunter, born in the port of Leith just outside Edinburgh, had at one time considered ordination in the Church of Scotland but chose instead to join the navy. He passed his lieutenant's exams at twenty-three but despite an obvious aptitude for navigation and chart-making, and though serving with distinction in several campaigns, remained without an actual lieutenant's commission for twenty years. However, once he secured it, further promotion came quickly. Philip Gidley King, Hunter's junior by some twenty years though commissioned two years earlier, was also aboard the *Sirius*. A Cornish draper's son, King had served twice under Phillip who, appreciating his abilities, had been quick to appoint him second lieutenant aboard his flagship and clearly regarded him as his protégé.

Perhaps strangely, not a single member of the crew of Cook's *Endeavour* when it visited New South Wales joined those manning the convict fleet, although some—like William Peckover and Isaac Smith, cousin of Cook's wife, Elizabeth, and the first to land in Botany Bay—remained in naval service, Smith with the rank of post-captain. Once at sea Phillip would have to rely on Cook's charts and other written accounts, supplemented by recollections of any conversations he had had with Banks, Matra, and others.

By the middle of March 1787, to Phillip's satisfaction the fleet was assembling off Portsmouth in the lee of the Isle of Wight. He had been requesting this move for some time since here the transports would be sufficiently far from land to allow the prisoners sometimes to be loosed from their fetters—heavy ankle shackles attached to long chains so that prisoners could be linked together in groups of four or sometimes six, and sometimes wrist irons as well—and allowed up on deck for fresh air. However, the careful measures taken to keep the prisoners—especially the nearly two hundred women—segregated were already breaking down. During a random roll call on April 19, five women on the *Lady Penrhyn* were discovered in the crew quarters—an offense for which three crewmen were flogged and the women put in irons.

While he awaited the final convicts and the last supplies the Admiralty was prepared to give him, Phillip faced another problem. Though the naval crews of the *Sirius* and the *Supply* had received two months' pay in advance, the crews of some of the convict transports and the store ships—merchant seamen not subject to naval discipline—had received nothing for seven months and were refusing to obey orders. King thought that "the seamen had a little reason on their side." Captain Phillip hastily arranged for them to be paid and also agreed to their request to be allowed a final night ashore before the fleet sailed. Some never returned.

In the early hours of May 13, 1787, the First Fleet finally sailed, still without the extra supplies of food and clothing Phillip had requested. Led by the *Sirius*, the eleven ships headed out into the English Channel. Aboard were more than 1,400 people. Just over half of them were convicts, of whom nearly two hundred were women. The remainder included, as well as the ships' companies, 250 marines with around fifty members of their families. With the fleet was HMS *Hyaena*, a 24-gun frigate that was to serve as escort for the first three hundred miles in case any of the convicts should attempt anything similar to the 1784 mutiny on the *Mercury* convict transport, especially since some of those same mutineers were aboard Phillip's fleet. Propelled by a freshening wind, the ships bucked and rolled. Aboard the *Lady Penrhyn*—an especially bad sailer—many of the women were soon retching in the cramped darkness.

Confined belowdecks, none of the prisoners had the comfort of a last look at his or her fast-receding homeland, which—even if they served out their sentences—they were unlikely to see again. No provision had been made to transport time-served prisoners back to Britain. Before sailing, Tench—given the "tiresome and disagreeable" task of censor—had read the final letters to their loved ones of those convicts who could write or could persuade someone to do so on their behalf. He knew how many felt oppressed by "the impracticality of returning home, the dread of a sickly passage, and the fearful prospect of a distant and barbarous country." Yet once the moment of departure had come he thought they seemed not mutinous but resigned, even relieved, though some could not suppress "the pang of being severed, perhaps forever, from their native land . . . in general, marks of distress were more perceptible among the men than the women."

Newspapers reported the convicts' departure. Just as accounts of Tahiti had done, the venture intrigued the public, inspiring humorous ballads, a new country dance, and even an opera, which one reviewer thought "partly moral and partly comic." The *Gentleman's Magazine* erroneously assured its readers that everything had been done "to render everything as permanently comfortable to the unhappy convicts as the nature of the case will admit . . . Even trifles have been thought of. One instance as a proof, they now have comfortable beds." Another paper reported equally incorrectly that "each transport ship . . . has two guns loaded with grapeshot pointed down the hatchway where the convicts are to be and which will be fired on them should riot or mutiny happen." Some thought the convicts' lot far too easy. One London commentator predicted that "to be rewarded with the settlement in so fertile a country cannot fail of inducing every idle person to commit some depredation that may amount to a crime sufficient to send him there at the expense of the public."

VI

"THE FINEST HARBOUR IN THE WORLD"

$\mathcal{T}$oward evening on May 20, with the fleet two hundred miles west of the Scilly Isles, HMS *Hyaena* turned for home after "the usual salute of three cheers." Since so far from land there was little risk of the prisoners trying to escape, Phillip signaled those masters "who had convicts on board to release from their irons such as might by their behaviour have merited that indulgence," though "on the least appearance among them of irregularity" they were to be confined again "with additional security." Lieutenant Watkin Tench on the *Charlotte* thought this a "humane order," though others, among them Lieutenant Ralph Clark aboard the *Friendship*, considered it rash "for so great a number to be out of irons at once." Indeed, that day a prisoner on the *Scarborough* claimed to have evidence "of a design formed among the convicts on board . . . to mutiny and take possession of the ship." He identified two ringleaders and, though the men vigorously protested their innocence, Phillip sentenced them to two dozen lashes and to be transferred in irons to another ship.

Concerned to keep the prisoners healthy, Phillip ordered them to be allowed on deck twice a day and encouraged to wash both themselves and their clothes. They emerged blinking into the daylight from their fetid, almost pitch-black quarters, without portholes and where no candles or lanterns were allowed for risk of fire. The only light came from the hatches when they were open and the only ventilation from sails erected on deck by the open hatches and angled to catch and channel the breezes belowdecks. During rough weather the hatches had to be battened down and prisoners survived as best they could in the stinking fumes rising from the bilges and the claustrophobic darkness.

The fleet made good progress to Tenerife in the Canary Islands, where Phillip planned to take on further supplies. As the ships approached, thick fog obscuring the peak of volcanic Mount Teide cleared to reveal an island that from a distance looked to Lieutenant King "no more than a heap of rocks," though he had heard it was "fruitful and plentiful." The ships anchored half a mile off the town of Santa Cruz and next morning Phillip dispatched King to the governor to apologize that his flagship the *Sirius* had not fired a salute on arrival "on account of our being so much lumbered with casks etc on the gundeck."

Over the next week, Phillip ensured that all—convicts and non-convicts alike—were well fed, including a pound of fresh beef a day. Using the powers granted to him to submit certified bills for payment by the British Treasury, he also purchased rice, pumpkins, onions, figs, mulberries, limes, wine, and water for the voyage ahead. In dispatches to London he reported that eight convicts had died while eighty-one prisoners and marines had suffered illness, including ten convicts who had venereal disease. He also wrote that "in general the convicts have behaved well . . . They are quiet and contented, tho' there are amongst them some complete villains." One such "villain"— twenty-four-year-old John Power, convicted at the Old Bailey for stealing timber—"had the address, one night, to secrete himself on the deck [of the *Alexander*], when the rest were turned below; and after remaining quiet for some hours, let himself down over the bow of the ship, and floated to a boat that lay astern, into which he got, and cutting her adrift, suffered himself to be carried away by the current, until at a sufficient distance to be out of hearing when he rowed off." A search party eventually found him hiding among some rocks after failing to persuade the captain of a Dutch East Indiaman to take him on board. Phillip ordered him to be returned to his ship and kept "heavily ironed."

On June 10, 1787, with the ships well stocked with provisions and their water casks full, the fleet sailed, following a course that would enable them to profit from prevailing currents and the pattern of the trade winds that would push them first across to Rio de Janeiro and then back across the South Atlantic down to Cape Town. As the voyage continued, the fresh food Phillip had purchased—especially the antiscorbutic limes— had its effect and the convicts' health steadily improved. However, as Tench noted, the weather was becoming "intolerably hot" and, approaching the Equator, heavy tropical rains began to fall. Surgeon White would not allow the convicts on deck when it rained "as they had neither linen nor clothing sufficient to make themselves dry and comfortable after getting wet."

To cleanse the increasingly fetid air belowdecks, the ships' crews resorted to such "preventives" as "frequent explosions of gunpowder, lighting fires . . . and a liberal use of that admirable antiseptic, oil of tar." Phillip also ordered water in the ships' bilges—where filth of every description from dead rats to rotting feces collected—to be pumped out daily "to keep them sweet and wholesome," but the crew of the *Alexander* neglected this task. Surgeon-General John White—called to the ship to discover why sickness had broken out—found prisoners overcome by a poisonous cloud that "had by some means or other risen to so great a height that the panels of the cabin, and the buttons on the clothes of the officers, were turned nearly black by the noxious effluvia. When the hatches were taken off, the stench was so powerful that it was scarcely possible to stand over them."

The "enervating effects of the atmospheric heat" took their toll particularly on the female prisoners. White was called to treat women who, "perfectly overcome by it, frequently fainted away; and these faintings generally terminated in fits." Yet "so predominant was the warmth of their constitutions, or the depravity of their hearts, that the hatches over the place where they were confined could not be suffered to [be open] during the night, without a promiscuous intercourse immediately taking place between them and the seaman and marines" who could buy a woman with only a pannikin of rum. On the *Friendship*, though it was explicitly forbidden to consort with female prisoners, four sailors broke through a bulkhead into the women's accommodation and persuaded four to accompany them to their own quarters. When they were discovered the men were flogged and the women put in irons—far too lenient a punishment in Lieutenant Clark's view: "If I had been the commander, I should have flogged the four whores also."

Conditions must have seemed desperate to the six-months-pregnant Mary Broad aboard the *Charlotte*. The daily ration of water, by now fetid, was only three pints—a quantity, in Surgeon White's view, "scarcely sufficient to supply that waste of animal spirits the body must necessarily undergo, in the torrid zone, from a constant and violent perspiration, and a diet consisting of salt provisions." In the debilitating conditions, some women became unruly. Aboard the *Friendship* Elizabeth Barber—convicted for violent theft with a knife—wrote a letter of complaint to Phillip about the shortage of drinking water. A few days later, as Clark alleged, "very much in liquor," she abused the *Friendship*'s doctor, Mr. Arundell, "in a most terrible manner and said that he wanted to **** her and called him all the names she could think of." When the ship's captain ordered her to be put in irons, she began abusing him "in a much worse manner than she had done the doctor . . . in all the course of my days I never heard such expressions from the mouth of a human being." The captain ordered her to be gagged but before this could be done she shouted that "she should see us all thrown over board before we got to Botany Bay . . . I wish to God she was out of the ship . . . I would rather have a hundred men than to have a single woman." Soon afterward she got into a fight with three other women. The captain "ordered the sergeant not to part them but to let them fight it out."

Meanwhile Barber's fellow prisoner on the *Friendship*, pickpocket Elizabeth Dudgeon, one of the four "whores" recently found in the crew's quarter, was flogged with a rope for, as Clark put it, "being impertinent" to the *Friendship's* captain. "The corporal did not play with her, but laid it home, which I was very glad to see . . . then ordered her to be tied to the pump. She has been long fishing for it, which she has at last got until her heart's content."

On August 5, as the fleet sailed into Rio de Janeiro, a boat well loaded with oranges, plantains, and bread came alongside and its occupants—three Portuguese and their six slaves—began a brisk trade with those leaning eagerly over the side. During these transactions, Surgeon White wrote, "we discovered that one Thomas Barrett, a convict, had, with great ingenuity and address, passed some quarter-dollars which he, assisted by two others, had coined out of old buckles, buttons belonging to the marines, and pewter spoons during their passage from Tenerife. The impression, milling, character, in a word, the whole was so inimitably executed that had their metal been a little better, the fraud, I am convinced, would have passed undetected." White was astonished that men kept under constant surveillance without access to any open flame had managed it: "Hardly ten minutes ever elapsed, without an officer of some degree or other going down among them. The adroitness, therefore, with which they must have managed, in order to complete a business that required so complicated a process gave me a high opinion of their ingenuity, cunning, caution, and address." The twenty-nine-year-old Barrett, being transported for stealing household goods, was in fact an accomplished engraver. Though he was relatively lightly punished, a marine later caught trying to pass off one of Barrett's fake coins in Rio received two hundred lashes.

While Lieutenant Dawes immediately set up a temporary observatory on an offshore island to check that the K1 chronometer was still keeping accurate time, Phillip again took on supplies, including rum, wine, and starchy cassava as a substitute for ship's biscuit, together with numerous plants and seeds, from coffee and cocoa to bananas, guavas, tamarinds, and prickly pears, for planting in Botany Bay. He also purchased ten thousand musket balls since, through an oversight, his fleet had only been supplied with enough ammunition for immediate use. Phillip had written from Tenerife to Lord Sydney asking that a ship be dispatched at once with "musket balls . . . paper for musket cartridges . . . and armourer's tools to keep small arms in repair." He had also again asked for clothes for the female prisoners, without which "we shall be much distressed." To clothe the many prisoners who were "nearly naked" Phillip specified that the sacks of "Russia"—a strong brown cloth woven from jute—in which the cassava had come on board "be used hereafter in clothing the convicts."

On September 4, the fleet left Rio, soon to be driven by strong westerlies across the ocean toward Cape Town. In the early hours of September 8, aboard the *Charlotte* Mary Broad "was delivered of a fine girl," as Surgeon White recorded. She was soon having to nurse her baby in squally weather so rough that some of the ships "rolled prodigiously" and a male prisoner, William Brown, "bringing some clothing from the bowsprit end, where he had hung them to dry," fell overboard from the *Charlotte* and drowned before a boat could reach him.

On October 6, according to Advocate-General David Collins, "four seamen of the *Alexander* transport were sent on board the *Sirius*, under a charge of having entered into a conspiracy to release some of the prisoners while the ship should be at the Cape of Good Hope, and of having provided those people with instruments for breaking into the fore-hold of the ship (which had been done and some provisions stolen)." Phillip ordered the four sailors to be confined on board the *Sirius* and sent four of the *Sirius*'s men to replace them.

A week later, the fleet anchored safely in Table Bay and next morning Phillip ordered a thirteen-gun salute to honor the governor. Since the Dutch colony at Cape Town was the last place the fleet could take on provisions, Phillip started negotiating at once. However, on asking the governor for supplies of flour and corn he learned that "the Cape had been very lately visited by that worst of scourges—a famine, which had been most severely felt by every family in the town, his own not excepted." As a result, Phillip took longer than he had hoped to negotiate for supplies, and prices were exorbitant. Nevertheless, he purchased five hundred animals, including a bull, a bull calf, seven cows, one stallion, three mares, and three colts together with rams, ewes, goats, and pigs, so that each ship became "like another Noah's Ark." Phillip made room for the cattle aboard the *Sirius* by having eight guns dismounted. He also purchased what fresh fruit and vegetables he could find and—as he had in Rio—acquired "the rarest and best of every species both in plant and seed" from fig trees and bamboo to sugarcane, quinces, oak, and myrtle for planting in the new colony. To strengthen the prisoners for the final but most difficult part of their voyage across the Indian and Pacific Oceans he ordered that while in port they be given daily "one pound and an half of soft bread . . . a pound of fresh beef, or mutton, and three quarters of a pound for each child, together with a liberal allowance of vegetables."

Meanwhile, in St. Phillip's church, at Mary Broad's request, the Reverend Richard Johnson christened her daughter Charlotte after the transport on which she had been born. Phillip's officers admired Cape Town's strong fortifications, handsome houses, churches, and "most excellent" gardens but Collins saw "with horror" evidence of the severe punishments meted out by the Dutch authorities to offenders: a row of gallows along the shore from which decomposing corpses swung in the breeze, flesh-smeared wheels on which people were executed by having their bodies smashed with iron rods, "a spiked pole for impalement," and posts to which the severed hands of thieves were nailed. Asking the source of the smoke rising from the hinterland they were told this came from fires lit by slaves who had fled their Dutch masters' cruelty.

On November 12, as in a rising wind the fleet prepared to sail for Botany Bay, Tench described how "a ship under American colours, entered the road, bound from Boston . . . The master, who appeared to be a man of some information, on being told the destination of our fleet, gave it as his opinion, that if a reception could be secured, emigrations would take place to New South Wales, not only from the old continent, but the new one, where the spirit of adventure and thirst for novelty were excessive." Yet Tench himself reflected that the fleet was about to leave far behind "every scene of civilization and humanized manners, to explore a remote and barbarous land." He was not alone in recognizing the uncertainties ahead. Collins wrote, "All communication with families and friends now cut off, we were leaving the world behind us . . . [for] the residence of savages."

With strong contrary winds, the waters of the Indian Ocean soon grew rougher. Sailors battened down the hatches on the convicts below while the wind blew chickens in their coops off the open decks into the sea. A queasy Clark complained that he had never known a ship roll as much as the

Friendship. A week after leaving Cape Town, Phillip found that instead of making progress, the fleet's distance from Botany Bay "had increased nearly an hundred leagues [three hundred nautical miles]." He decided to transfer from his flagship *Sirius* to the smaller, faster HMS *Supply* and sail ahead of the rest of the fleet to Botany Bay to identify a suitable place for the new settlement and begin clearing land. To assist him, Phillip took with him "several sawyers, carpenters, blacksmiths and other mechanics."

The rest of the fleet followed in two divisions. A chill, ghostly white fog descended, succeeded as Christmas approached by snow, hail, and tumultuous seas. Surgeon Arthur Bowes Smyth aboard the *Lady Penrhyn* described how "just as we had dined a most tremendous sea broke in at the weather scuttle of the great cabin and ran with a great stream all across the cabin, and as the door of my cabin was not to be quite close shut the water half filled it . . . No sleep all this night."

Among the prisoners, much of the talk was about what would happen when the fleet reached Botany Bay—a matter of especial concern to the women as rumors spread that regardless of their wishes they were to be shared out among the men. Phillip had earlier announced that he expected any who had formed "irregular liaisons" to marry on disembarking. By "irregular liaisons" he meant relationships between the prisoners—not those between women convicts and crewmen, of which there had been plenty. The "promiscuous intercourse" that had earlier shocked surgeon John White had continued: By the time the fleet had reached Rio two women on the *Friendship* were pregnant by sailors.

Reverend Johnson, who had brought with him four thousand books including Bibles, copies of the Book of Common Prayer, and such improving works as *Exhortations to Chastity*, announced that he would begin taking the names of couples in order to put up the marriage banns. Mary Broad and William Bryant were among the few who submitted their names. Though Tench later wrote "the two sexes had been kept most rigorously apart," male and female convicts had had the opportunity to meet while allowed up on deck for fresh air and exercise. Mary Broad and William Bryant had both been on the prison hulk *Dunkirk* and came from Cornish fishing communities. Their decision to marry was no doubt more pragmatic than romantic. It was obvious that the new colony would need skilled fishermen and they may have hoped for special treatment. Also, as Clark noted, Phillip's encouragement to the convicts to marry suggested that those who did wed might well enjoy special privileges—more privacy, better accommodation.

Whatever the case, the balance of advantage was on Mary's side. By marrying Bryant she gained a protector for herself and her daughter and it says something for the strength of her personality that he agreed to it. Young, strong, and with a "trade," he could have taken his pick among the women but instead chose to take responsibility not only for Mary but Charlotte, probably another man's child.*

In late December, Phillip and the *Supply* rounded the southeastern cape of Van Diemen's Land† and turned northward on the final leg of the journey up the coast of New South Wales toward Botany Bay, six hundred miles away. On January 5, as albatrosses wheeled high above, the leading ships of the main fleet followed. However, as the remaining ships led by the *Sirius* rounded the cape and headed north, they ran into "a perfect hurricane." Surgeon Bowes Smyth had never seen "a sea in such a rage, it was all over as white as snow." Violent winds sent the main yard of the *Prince of Wales* crashing down onto the deck and ripped the topsails from the *Golden Grove* before they could be furled. Beneath the battened-down hatches of the *Lady Penrhyn*, frightened women fell to their knees to pray for survival. From the *Sirius*, surgeon John White watched as "a very troublesome high sea" tossed the ships about beneath lowering skies. At about two P.M. came "one of the most sudden gusts of wind I ever remember to have known. In an instant it split our main sail; and but for the activity shewn by the sailors, in letting fly the sheets and lowering the top-sails, the masts must have gone over the side." Nearly every ship sustained some damage but fortunately the storm was short-lived. As the seas calmed and the *Charlotte* continued on her way northward, Tench rejoiced that his long confinement "on a service so peculiarly disgusting and troublesome"—the shipment of fellow human beings—was nearly over.

On the afternoon of January 18, HMS *Supply* rounded the southern arm of Botany Bay, Point Solander—named for Banks's Swedish botanist Daniel Solander—and anchored in its shallow waters, the first European vessel to do so since Cook's expedition eighteen years before. Phillip and his officers went ashore to search for fresh water but found none. Returning to their boat, they noticed a group of Aboriginal people gathered on another beach and Phillip ordered his men to row over to them. Though the locals shouted

---

*Some have suggested William Bryant could have been Charlotte's father, rather than a marine, but there is no evidence.

†Van Diemen's Land was not called Tasmania until 1856.

"in a menacing tone" and brandished their spears, an unarmed Phillip climbed from the boat and walked slowly toward them, proffering beads and mirrors. An Aboriginal stepped forward and gestured to Phillip to lay the gifts on the beach, then darted nervously forward to take them. He and his companions inspected them and, after Phillip and his men gestured that they were looking for water, showed them where to find it.

The *Alexander, Scarborough,* and *Friendship* arrived the next day and on the morning of January 20, the *Sirius* led in the remaining vessels. During the fleet's eight-month, 13,000-nautical-mile journey only forty-eight people had died—forty prisoners, five of their children, a marine, a marine's wife, and a marine's child. Reflecting what must have been universal relief, Surgeon White wrote that "to see all the ships safe in their destined port, without ever having, by any accident, been one hour separated, and all the people in as good health as could be expected or hoped for, after so long a voyage, was a sight truly pleasing." Surgeon Arthur Bowes Smyth thought it "pretty extraordinary how very healthy the convicts on board this ship in particular and the fleet in general have been during so long a passage and where there was a necessity of stowing them so thick together." Tench agreed, especially since "the people thus sent out were not a ship's company starting with every advantage of health and good living, which a state of freedom produces; but the major part a miserable set of convicts, emaciated from confinement, and in want of clothes, and almost every convenience to render so long a passage tolerable." More lyrically he wrote, "Ithaca itself was scarcely more longed for by Ulysses, than Botany Bay by the adventurers who had traversed so many thousand miles to take possession of it."

Those crowding the decks—who did not include the convicts, who were confined below—scanned the shore where dark naked figures sometimes emerged from the scrubby hinterland to stand in groups on the beach, watching. The landscape was not quite what the onlookers had anticipated from Cook's and Banks's description of a verdant, well-wooded, well-watered place ideal for settlement. Instead, it looked arid and unforgiving with only papery-trunked dusty eucalyptuses and stunted, scrubby bushes.

In line with his own instructions to "open an intercourse with the natives" and treat them with "amity and kindness," Phillip ordered that no violence be done to the local people and that everyone was to act in a friendly way toward them. However, when lieutenants King and Dawes went ashore, the Aboriginals "halloo'd and made signs for us to return to our boats . . . and one of them threw a lance wide of us to show how far they could do execution." King ordered a marine to fire a blank musket shot over the man's head and he fled. In subsequent days it became increasingly obvious that the Aboriginals indeed "desired us to be gone." Yet what no one appreciated was the Aboriginals' sense of violation as they watched the new arrivals tramping and hunting over their ancestral land and fishing in their water. Seeing sailors hauling in a fine catch, they began grabbing the fish "as if they had a right to them, or that they were their own." Surgeon White noted that they carried weapons "some of which were pointed and barbed with the bones of fish, fastened on with some kind of adhesive gum." The following day they belabored another fishing party with the shafts of their spears.

The new arrivals found the best way of placating them, according to King, was to offer clothes—greatcoats but especially hats, "their admiration of which they expressed by very loud shouts, whenever one of us pulled our hats off." He also described the Aboriginals' puzzlement over their visitors' sex: "They took us for women, not having our beards grown." He ordered one of his marines "to undeceive them" by dropping his trousers to reveal his genitals at which "a great shout of admiration" arose. The Aboriginals then pointed to "a great number of women and girls . . . all *in puris natura-bilis* [stark naked]—pas même la feuille de figeur [not so much as a fig leaf]" and "made signs for us to go to them and made us understand their persons were at our service." King declined and instead tied his handkerchief on one of the women "where Eve did the fig leaf," at which "the natives then set up another very great shout."

Everything he had observed confirmed Phillip's initial view that Botany Bay was no place to found a colony. Though its northern shores had "very good grass and some small timber trees," he saw no sign of the fine meadows described by Cook and Banks. Most of the hinterland looked unpromising for cultivation. He did not yet appreciate that this was in part due to differences in season: Cook had landed in late April, when rain would have regenerated the parched landscape. Furthermore, the bay itself was not only shallow but "very open, and greatly exposed to the fury of the South East winds, which, when they blow, cause a heavy and dangerous swell."

Phillip knew he had quickly to find a better spot, not least to preserve the health of the prisoners still locked below for most of the time in great heat. On January 22, he set out with a small party in three longboats to explore two inlets a few miles to the north that Cook had named Port Jackson and Broken Bay. Meanwhile, in case all else failed he ordered ground to be cleared just inside Point Solander for an encampment. To Phillip's relief, as his boats passed through the mile and a quarter gap between the sandstone heads, he saw opening before him the broad, sparkling sweep of Port Jackson extending some fifteen miles inland—"the finest harbour in the world," he later enthused to Lord Sydney, the first of many to do so—where "a thousand sail of the line may ride in the most perfect security." After sailing westward and surveying several coves he fixed on one, five miles from the Heads, where even close to the shore the water was deep enough for the largest ships to anchor and a large stream flowed down to the beach. He named it Sydney Cove in honor of the Home Secretary. To the Aboriginal inhabitants it was Warrane.

While Phillip went north, Tench explored Botany Bay and its hinterland. His encounters with the indigenous people intrigued him. Though he and his colleagues made them "various presents . . . our toys seemed not to be regarded as very valuable." Once again, the Aboriginals seemed more interested "of what sex we were." When Tench's party finally convinced them they were indeed male "they burst into the most immoderate fits of laughter, talking to each other at the same time with such rapidity and vociferation as I had never before heard. After nearly an hour's conversation by signs and gestures, they repeated several times the word *whurra*, which signifies begone, and walked away from us to the head of the bay." From this and other good-humored encounters, Tench wrote, "we began to entertain strong hopes of bringing about a connection with them. Our first object was to win their affections, and our next to convince them of the superiority we possessed: for without the latter, the former we knew would be of little importance."

Returning from his reconnaissance, Phillip ordered the fleet to prepare to sail to its new anchorage the next day. However as dawn rose the following morning, a breathless marine burst into Tench's cabin while he was still dressing to tell him a strange ship had been sighted. Tench "flew upon deck . . . when the cry of 'another sail' struck on my astonished ear." Not one but "two ships of considerable size" were beating across Botany Bay toward them. He wondered whether they were "Dutchmen sent to dispossess us" or perhaps store ships from England with the supplies Phillip had so urgently requested. According to Tench, "this mystery was at length unravelled and the cause of the alarm pronounced to be two French ships which, it was now recollected, were on a voyage of discovery in the southern hemisphere." Phillip decided "to postpone our removal to Port Jackson until a complete confirmation of our conjectures could be procured."

Pushed back by strong winds, the "strange ships" were unable to anchor but the next morning were seen to be back "in their former situation." Phillip sent a lieutenant across to them "to offer assistance and point out the necessary marks for entering the harbour." He returned with the news that the vessels were indeed French—*La Boussole* and *L'Astrolabe* on a voyage of exploration commanded by Comte Jean-François de la Pérouse. So far their journey had taken them around the Horn to Chile, the Sandwich Islands, Alaska, Siberia, and the coast of Korea before they had headed to the South Pacific. According to Tench, their "astonishment" at seeing the British ships "had not equalled that we had experienced for it appeared that . . . they had touched at Kamchatka" and there "learnt that our expedition was in contemplation."

Phillip found La Pérouse's arrival at this precise moment suspicious and he decided to sail forthwith for Port Jackson aboard the *Supply*, together with an advance party of officers, marines, and skilled manual workers selected from among the seamen of the *Sirius* and the convicts. Hunter was to follow in due course with the rest of the fleet. However, under the watching eyes of the French, the departure of the remaining vessels was chaotic. The *Charlotte* nearly grounded, then rammed the *Friendship*, which in turn hit the *Prince of Wales*. For the prisoners belowdecks, wholly reliant on their guards for information about what was happening, the waiting had already seemed interminable. Now, bracing themselves in the humid semi-darkness against the only too familiar rolling and pitching, they must have wondered how much longer it would be to journey's end.

The speedy *Supply* arrived on the evening of January 25 and anchored in the mouth of Sydney Cove. The next day, while awaiting the rest of the fleet, Phillip set the workmen to clearing ground that Collins described as "at the head of the cove, near the run of fresh water, which stole silently along through a very thick wood, the stillness of which had then, for the first time since the creation, been interrupted by the rude sound of the labourer's axe, and the downfall of its ancient inhabitants; a stillness and tranquillity . . . from that day were to give place to the voice of labour . . . and the busy hum of its new possessors."

By evening, though the other ships had still not arrived, Phillip ordered the *Supply*'s company to gather at the spot where they had first landed where, again according to Collins, "a flagstaff had been purposely erected and an Union Jack displayed." The marines fired volleys from their muskets "between which the governor and the officers . . . drank the healths of his Majesty and the Royal Family, and success to the new colony." With this brief and simple ceremony, Phillip took possession of Britain's newest colony.*

The day, which Collins recalled as "uncommonly fine," concluded with "the safe arrival of the *Sirius* and the convoy from Botany Bay—thus terminating the voyage with the same good fortune that had from its commencement been so conspicuously [our] friend and companion." Their arrival, though, had not been unobserved. Robert Brown, captain of the supply ship *Fishburn*, described how "natives on the shore hollered *Walla Walla Wha* or something to that effect and brandished their spears as if vexed at the approach."

---

*The site where Phillip and his men saluted the flag is in modern-day Loftus Street in Sydney, near the Customs House. January 26 is celebrated as Australia Day.

THE FLOATING GREENHOUSE

*W*ithin a week of Lord Sydney announcing the breadfruit expedition to the South Seas in May 1787, and four days before the convict fleet put to sea, the Admiralty issued orders to purchase a suitable vessel of no more than 250 tons. With Bligh not yet appointed to command, Joseph Banks inspected the ships on the Admiralty shortlist, accompanied by David Nelson, remembered by a shipmate on Cook's last voyage as "one of the quietest fellows in nature" and selected by Banks as the new expedition's botanist at a salary of fifty pounds a year. The Admiralty's list was indeed short—just two merchant vessels. Among three others that Admiralty officials had already rejected was Duncan Campbell's *Lynx*, which Bligh had commanded in 1785.

Convinced that even a ship of under two hundred tons would be "fully sufficient," Banks chose the smaller of the two offered by the navy—the three-masted, 215-ton coastal trader *Bethia*. After the Admiralty had beaten down the owner's asking price from £2600 to £1950, they dispatched the ninety-one-foot long, twenty-four-foot-four-inch-wide vessel, only three and a half years old and with a "pretty figure-head of a woman in a riding-habit," as Bligh would describe it, to the naval dockyards at Deptford for refitting. Work on her hull and rigging and the cost of equipping her would bring the final total to £6,406—three times the sum originally planned.

When the navy acquired a ship, their custom was to rename her. For the *Bethia*, Banks chose the name *Bounty* in fulsome recognition of the king's patronage of the expedition. Listed as His Majesty's Armed Vessel *Bounty*, she was to carry four four-pound cannon and ten half-pound swivel guns and have a complement of forty five men, though—as Bligh would point out to Banks—one of those was fictitious, "his pay going to the support of [sailors'] widows." Probably unknown to Bligh, Banks himself had initially wanted a crew of "no more than 30 souls" to leave plenty of space for the breadfruit plants.

On August 16, 1787, two days after the *Bounty* was confirmed as ready for sea, the thirty-two-year-old Bligh's appointment to command her was formally announced. However, over the coming weeks Bligh's satisfaction would be tempered by the Admiralty's refusal to promote him to captain. The Admiralty view was that the *Bounty* was too small to merit a captain in command. It justifiably pointed out that Cook had commanded the far larger *Endeavour* on his first voyage as a first lieutenant. In fact, Bligh would be the *Bounty*'s only commissioned officer. Also, because of lack of space, Bligh would sail without any marines to protect against external threat and also to reinforce the commander's authority and suppress unrest among the crew. Cook had never sailed with fewer than twelve marines.

Large ships did not necessarily enhance an expedition's chances of success. Byron and Wallis's HMS *Dolphin*, a 508-ton frigate, had required such a big crew—some 150 sailed with Wallis—that there had been insufficient space to store provisions for a long voyage. Furthermore, so many mouths could make it difficult to find enough food when landing in remote places. However, colliers of the type commanded by Cook—from *Resolution* at 462 tons, to *Endeavour* at 368 tons, *Adventure* at 336 tons, and *Discovery* at 299 tons—had proved large enough to carry sufficient supplies for a long voyage and marines but compact enough to be sailed by more modest crews. The *Endeavour*'s crew had numbered around eighty. By comparison, the cramped *Bounty* must have seemed to Bligh a disappointing choice even if, rather than undertaking a long voyage of exploration, he was sailing only to known destinations. Though Bligh would speak with affection of "my little ship," his father-in-law, Richard Betham, doubtless echoed his misgivings when he wrote: "Government, I think, have gone too frugally to work; both the ship and the complement of men are too small, in my opinion, for such a voyage."

The Admiralty held out the prospect of promotion to Bligh if, like Cook, his voyage was successful, but in the meantime he would have to maintain what he called his "poor little family"—he now had three daughters, of whom the youngest was epileptic, and his wife was pregnant again—on a lieutenant's pay of seventy pounds a year, compared to the five hundred pounds he had received in Campbell's employ as "a rum and sugar captain" and the ninety pounds paid to Cook for his first voyage. Bligh clearly hoped to eke out his pay by what extra he could make by acting as ship's purser since, as was common on smaller naval vessels, none was included in the *Bounty's* establishment. Criticism of pursers' self-serving parsimony was almost universal among naval ships' crews. Cook, too, had been his own purser and had not been exempt from complaints from his men.

The "dark and mysterious nature of pursery" certainly offered scope for profiteering, not to say corruption. The ship's purser was responsible for managing and dispensing all the provisions issued by the navy's Victualling Board at the start of a voyage. Though he did not purchase these stores himself, the purser was debited with their value on his account. To satisfy the Board that he had managed them efficiently, he was required to supply countersigned and detailed accounts of exactly how much had been consumed by each man and of any damage or wastage. At the end of a voyage he would be credited for any victuals he returned unused, hence the frequent accusations from crews that the purser stinted their rations for his own benefit. In addition, the purser's duties included the purchase at his own cost of "necessaries" such as coal, candles, hammocks, bedding, and lamp oil—on all of which he had a monopoly and for which he charged the crew against their future wages at prices he alone determined.

By custom the purser also acted as the crew's sole tobacco supplier and banker. Furthermore, during a voyage he was allowed to operate uniquely as a private contractor, trading with local people—on one occasion Cook purchased large numbers of turtles and chickens—and selling his purchases on to the crew, who often complained of unfair profiteering. Bligh clearly told others he expected to profit in this way. His father-in-law wrote to him that: "I'm most solicitous about the success of the voyage on your account, that it may not only be the means of your promotion, but attended with such emoluments as may enable you to live comfortably after the toils of the sea are past."

Although Banks had agreed to Bligh's appointment, when he met him for the first time aboard the *Bounty* at Deptford he wondered whether he had been right. He thought Bligh "very deserving" but was startled, as he wrote to Sir George Young, that Bligh seemed to know "little or nothing of the object of his voyage," adding that "unless you do interest the Captain himself or instruct him and inspire him with the spirit of the undertaking it is to very little purpose the vessel would sail." Banks had himself at once begun "inspiring" Bligh, telling Young that after "I had above an hour's discourse with him, he entered into the plan with spirit, was delighted with the idea of rendering such service to his country and mankind but declared if it had not been for my visit he never should have known anything of it." Whether Bligh really knew as little as Banks believed is debatable, but he convinced Banks he wanted to study botany. "He is become my pupil by accident. I will make him a botanist by choice," Banks wrote.

Bligh oversaw the final fitting out and equipping of his ship with energy and dispatch. Aware from sailing with Cook of the battering his ship would receive, he ordered the carpenters to shorten further the *Bounty*'s masts, which had already been cut down, and reduced the amount of iron ballast to be carried to aid the ship's stability from forty-five to nineteen tons, believing "too much dead weight in their bottoms" had brought many a ship to grief in high winds. He also had the hull sheathed in copper to protect the timbers against the tropical teredo shipworm. Examining the ship's boats, he rejected the eighteen-foot cutter supplied as inadequate, asking instead for one twenty feet long, and argued successfully that the twenty-foot launch should be replaced by one twenty-three feet long—the standard naval size. The *Bounty* would also carry a sixteen-foot "jolly boat."

With only one lower deck and an eleven-foot-deep hold beneath the main deck, living space on the *Bounty* was very limited. Most of the crew would sleep on the lower deck, including Bligh. As commanding officer, he would normally have expected to occupy the "great cabin" at the stern. However, carpenters had already adapted it to accommodate the breadfruit seedlings in accordance with Banks's exacting demands:

> The difficulty of carrying plants by sea is very great. A small sprinkling of salt water or of the salt dew which fills the air even in a moderate gale will inevitably destroy them if it is not immediately washed off with fresh water. It is necessary therefore that the [great] cabin be appropriated to the sole purpose of making a kind of greenhouse, and the key of it given to the custody of the gardener; and that in case of cold weather in going round the Cape a stove be provided by which it may be kept in a temperature equal to that of the intertropical countries.

As a result, as Bligh described, the great cabin was "extended as far forward as the after hatchway. It had two large skylights, and on each side three scuttles for air, and was fitted with a false floor cut full of holes to contain the garden-pots in which the plants were to be brought home. The deck was

covered with lead, and at the foremost corners of the cabin were fixed pipes
to carry off the water that drained from the plants into tubs placed below to
save it for future use."

Banks also specified that "no dogs, cats, monkeys, parrots, goats, or
indeed any animals whatever, must be allowed on board, except hogs and
fowls for the company's use; and they must be carefully confined to their
coops. Every precaution must be taken to prevent or destroy the rats . . . A
boat with green boughs should be laid alongside with a gangway of green
boughs laid from the hold to her, and a drum kept going below in the vessel
for one or more nights; and as poison will constantly be used to destroy them
and cockroaches, the crew must not complain if some of them who may die
in the ceiling make an unpleasant smell."

All this meant that the breadfruit, tended by the botanist David Nelson,
assisted by gardener William Brown, would have far better accommodation
than the forty-five men crammed aboard a ship that, as a merchant vessel,
had had a complement of only fifteen. Since as on the convict ships there
were no portholes, the crew's only source of light and fresh air belowdecks
would be the hatches by the ladderways. Bligh himself would occupy a poky
six- by seven-foot cabin amidships on the starboard side of the lower deck
near the rear ladderway and opposite the master's cabin where the keys
to the nearby arms chest were kept. He had his personal privy projecting
over the stern. His "dining room" would be a narrow space partitioned by
canvas walls from the sleeping quarters of the midshipmen and other officers. Amidships, the headroom was a mere five feet seven inches.

Thirty-three crewmen would eat and sleep in a space thirty-six by twenty-
two feet in the forecastle toward the bow, in odiferous proximity to pens
that would—in contravention of Banks's instructions—be filled with sheep
and goats as well as the pigs he had allowed and with headroom of barely
above six feet. Accommodation for the boatswain, carpenter, surgeon, clerk,
botanist, and gunner would be some tiny cubicles on "platforms"—
"cockpits"—newly fitted fore and aft in the hold beneath the lower deck.
With headroom of only five feet and accessed by ladder along dark narrow
companionways, they were extremely claustrophobic.

Bligh set about selecting his officers and crew and in many cases chose
either men who had sailed with Cook and/or himself or—in this age of
patronage—men with whom he or his wife's family, the Bethams, had
connections. Fletcher Christian, whom Bligh appointed as master's mate—a
senior petty officer—fitted both categories. At twenty-three, ten years Bligh's

junior and nearly nine inches taller, the dark, athletic Christian—strong enough to jump from one barrel straight into another—was the seventh of ten children born to lawyer Charles Christian. The Christians proudly traced their descent from King Edward I of England, while Fletcher's mother, Ann, came from a long-established Cumberland family, the Fletchers, for whom he was named. Though Charles and Ann Christian's home was rambling Moorland Close—described as "a quadrangular pile of buildings in the style of a medieval manor house, half castle and half farmstead" near Cockermouth in Cumberland (now Cumbria), which Ann had inherited—the Christians originated in the Isle of Man where from the Middle Ages a family member had often held the office of deemster, or judge.

When Fletcher was three years old his father died, leaving his mother to bring up her large family—six of her children survived into adulthood—in increasingly straitened circumstances. For a while Fletcher attended the Free Grammar School in Cockermouth where the poet William Wordsworth—six years younger and whose family, distantly related to the Christians, lived in a handsome house opposite the school—was also a pupil. Fletcher Christian next attended St. Bees School, founded in 1583 by the Archbishop of Canterbury. The school motto was *ingredere ut proficias*—"enter so that you may progress"—which Fletcher Christian clearly did. Edward, one of his three older brothers, himself a Cambridge University–educated lawyer, recalled how "allowed by all who knew him to possess extraordinary abilities . . . an excellent scholar," he had remained at school "longer than young men generally do who enter the navy," suggesting he might once have hoped for a career as a doctor or lawyer.

However, while Fletcher was at St. Bees, Ann Christian was declared bankrupt, largely through the financial folly of Fletcher's two oldest brothers, John and Edward. Other family members helped discharge some immediate debts but Moorland Close had to be sold. Ann Christian moved to the Isle of Man, where she was beyond the legal reach of debtors from the mainland and where she set up house for her younger children in Douglas, the island's chief port and town. She lived frugally on a small annuity but, as a member of the extensive and influential Christian family, was readily admitted to Isle of Man society. In 1780, William Bligh, recently returned from his voyage with Cook and shortly to marry Elizabeth Betham, was also in Douglas, where he stayed with Fletcher Christian's first cousin and her husband, Captain John Taubman, and may have first met Fletcher himself.

Bereft of financial support, Fletcher Christian probably consciously chose a career in the navy, where appointments and promotion were by examination and merit—even if tempered by influence and patronage—rather than the army, where officers' commissions and each subsequent promotion were purchased at some considerable expense. In 1783, aged eighteen, he signed on as a midshipman aboard HMS *Eurydice*, a twenty-four-gun sixth-rater on which he served for just over two years. He did well, winning temporary promotion to acting lieutenant while the *Eurydice* was in Madras in southern India. The *Eurydice*'s surgeon later told the third of Fletcher Christian's older brothers, Charles, by then a surgeon on the East Indiaman *Middlesex*, that the young man had "ruled in a superior pleasant manner." On his return, Fletcher Christian assured his family "it was very easy to make one's self beloved and respected on board a ship; one had only to be always ready to obey one's superior officers, and to be kind to the common men, unless there was occasion for severity, and if you are severe when there is a just occasion they will not like you the worse for it."

However, with Britain newly at peace Fletcher Christian's naval career, like that of so many others, stalled. Losing his temporary promotion to lieutenant, he found himself paid off. Like Bligh he now looked to the merchant fleet. John Taubman, the husband of Fletcher's cousin with whom Bligh had stayed on the Isle of Man, urged the young man to try to sail under "so experienced a navigator." Bligh, at that time commanding Duncan Campbell's *Britannia*, turned Christian down, explaining that he already had enough officers; merchant vessels like the *Britannia* were far more sparsely crewed than naval ships and had fewer officers.

Christian, however, offered to serve as an able seaman until a suitable vacancy arose, assuring Bligh that "wages were no object, he only wished to learn his profession, and if Captain Bligh would permit him to mess with the gentlemen, he would readily enter the ship as a fore-mast man, until there was a vacancy among the officers." He added: "We midshipmen are gentlemen, we never pull at a rope; I should even be glad to go one voyage in that situation, for there may be occasions, when officers may be called upon to do the duties of a common man." Bligh was won over. Fifteen months after returning from India, Christian, by now twenty-one, was back at sea aboard the *Britannia* under his new mentor.

The two men got on so well that Christian sailed with Bligh on a second voyage, initially as a gunner until Bligh promoted him to second mate. Christian clearly believed he had the measure of the man whom he described as "very passionate"—a term his contemporaries frequently used of Bligh—but also very kind to him. A shipmate observed that Christian "seemed to pride himself in knowing how to humour him." Conversely another—first mate Edward Lamb—thought Bligh foolishly overindulgent to his young protégé, constantly inviting him to dine and quite "blind to his faults"—a fact of which Lamb would, somewhat tactlessly, remind Bligh in later years. It was therefore unsurprising that Bligh himself recommended Fletcher Christian to the Admiralty for the position of master's mate aboard the *Bounty*—an act, Christian's brother Edward wrote, that his friends considered the cause of "a very great obligation."

In his previous naval career Fletcher Christian had, of course, been a midshipman and, though holding no commission, considered a "young gentleman" and a commissioned officer in waiting, as reflected by his temporary promotion to lieutenant. As the *Bounty*'s master's mate he would be a petty officer, a prospective warrant officer. However, the *Bounty*'s formal complement provided for only two midshipmen. To those positions Bligh, almost certainly at Banks's prompting, appointed fifteen-year-old John Hallett, son of a wealthy London architect acquainted with Banks, and twenty-year-old Thomas Hayward, recommended by William Wales, the secretary to the Board of Longitude of which Banks was a member and who had been the astronomer on Cook's second voyage.

Also aboard would be several other "young gentlemen," aspiring midshipmen who because there were no formal vacancies were entered in the ship's muster as able seamen. Edward Young—five foot eight, stocky, and minus several front teeth—was, according to the muster roll, from the West Indian island of St. Kitts and descriptions suggest he may have been of mixed race. He was said to be a nephew of Sir George Young, who had supported the proposal for a settlement in New South Wales. Indeed, it was probably through his connection with Banks that Sir George sought an opportunity for his young relation.

Twenty-one-year-old George Stewart—dark-eyed, narrow-chested, and altogether much slighter than Young—came from a family from the Orkney Islands off the north coast of Scotland that claimed descent from King Robert II of Scotland. Bligh had met him in 1780 when the *Resolution* called in Orkney on her return from the Pacific. Fifteen-year-old, fair-haired Peter Heywood from the Isle of Man was also well connected. Distantly related to Fletcher Christian, he was a descendant of Peter "Powderplot" Heywood, who had arrested Guy Fawkes and hence thwarted the infamous plot of November 5,

1605, to blow up King James I of England and Parliament. Heywood had entered the Royal Navy as a midshipman the previous year and Richard Betham had commended him warmly to Bligh as "a favourite of mine . . . and indeed everybody." He also noted that Heywood's father had recently lost his position as agent to the Duke of Athol, plunging the large Heywood family—Peter had ten brothers and sisters—into "a great deal of distress." (In fact, Heywood's father had mismanaged the duke's money and misappropriated several thousand pounds for his own use, both good grounds for dismissal, if not more, in an age when convicts were transported for stealing far, far less.) Before boarding the *Bounty*, young Heywood stayed with Bligh's wife, Betsy, in their tall, narrow house in Lambeth.*

The last "young gentleman," Robert Tinkler, was only twelve years old and Bligh would commonly refer to him as "the boy." Tinkler's thirty-five-year-old brother-in-law, John Fryer, from Norfolk would be the *Bounty*'s master. Recently married, Fryer had doubtless sought a place for Tinkler to please his new wife's family. He himself had never sailed the Pacific but Bligh thought him sufficiently capable to be responsible for navigating the ship— the very role he himself had fulfilled as Cook's sailing master. Fryer would be one of Bligh's warrant officers, appointed by warrant from the Navy Board, which conferred a number of privileges including, unlike midshipmen and petty officers, exemption from flogging.

The other warrant officers were forty-two-year-old gunner William Peckover, in charge of the *Bounty*'s cannon and powder and a veteran of all three of Cook's voyages, who spoke fluent Tahitian and preferred to visit Tahiti yet again rather than return to Botany Bay; thirty-eight-year-old ship's carpenter William Purcell, a combative man sailing for the first time on a naval as opposed to a merchant vessel, and thus unused to naval discipline; and bosun William Cole.

The ship's surgeon—the obese, inactive, and alcoholic Thomas Huggan— was also a warrant officer. He would be assisted by the younger and far more capable Thomas Denman Ledward, appointed as surgeon's mate by Banks just before the *Bounty* sailed, after an alarmed Bligh pointed out Huggan's likely uselessness on the voyage ahead: "My surgeon, I believe, may be a very capable man, but his indolence and corpulency render him rather unfit for the voyage."

---

*Bligh's house still stands opposite the former Bethlem Hospital for the Insane—"Bedlam"— now Britain's Imperial War Museum.

Below the warrant officers were the petty officers, the group to which Fletcher Christian formally belonged. The *Bounty*'s armorer was thirty-six-year-old, prematurely graying Joseph Coleman who, like Peckover, had sailed with Cook. The two quartermasters, whose duties included watch-keeping by the helmsman, were Liverpudlian John Norton, who had sailed with Bligh on Duncan Campbell's ships, and Peter Linkletter, from the Orkneys. Bosun's mate was twenty-seven-year-old James Morrison, a slender, sallow, well-educated man from Stornoway on the Isle of Lewis who had served in the navy as a midshipman and whose arm bore the scar of a musket ball wound from a naval engagement. He had recently passed the examination to be appointed a master gunner in the Royal Navy, satisfying his inquisitors not only that he knew "how to adjust a shot to a cannon and a due proportion of powder" and was "capable of taking or judging of heights and distances, especially at sea" but also that his "sobriety and obedience to command" could be relied upon. With the gunner's position on the *Bounty* already filled by Peckover, Morrison had had to content himself with a more junior post. Among his tasks would be to administer any floggings Bligh might order during the voyage. Charles Churchill, his hand disfigured by scars from "a severe scald," was Bligh's master-at-arms, responsible for small-arms drill. Nova Scotian Lawrence Lebogue, in his mid-forties, who had sailed with Bligh in the West Indies, was the *Bounty*'s sailmaker.

Among Bligh's complement of twenty-three able seamen was a stocky, badly pockmarked man with an ax scar on his foot who, though his real name was John Adams, had signed on under the alias of Alexander Smith, probably to conceal some past misdemeanor. He later said that he had been born in Hackney in East London "of poor but honest parents" and that his father had drowned in the Thames leaving "me and three more poor orphans." Able seaman William Muspratt, the cook's assistant, came from the village of Bray on the River Thames twenty-nine miles above London—a hub for the inland barge trade. A few months earlier his father had hanged himself from an apple tree; the inquest's verdict on the cause of death was "lunacy." Fifteen-year-old able seaman Thomas Ellison was yet another who had served under Bligh on Campbell's ships and was highly regarded by Campbell himself. To provide lively music for his crew to dance to both for distraction and for exercise to prevent disease—as Cook had believed in—Bligh took on a thin, pale, half-blind Irish fiddler from Kilkenny, Michael Byrne. To be his clerk Bligh chose the conscientious Edinburgh-born John Samuel and, as his personal servant and cook, John Smith.

While the *Bounty* was being finally readied for departure at Deptford, eight crewmen bolted. These included sailors transferred from other ships but also two men who had been taken by naval "press-gangs." (To meet the navy's recruitment needs, the Crown claimed the right to seize "seamen, seafaring men and persons whose occupations or callings are to work in vessels and boats upon rivers.") Hastily found replacements included able seamen William McKoy, a Scot, Matthew Quintal, and Isaac Martin, an American. Like the rest of the crew, all were volunteers, very rare for a naval vessel at this period. Samuel Johnson had archly observed that a sailor's life was like "being in a jail with the chance of being drowned" and that "a man in a jail has more room, better food, and commonly better company." Indeed, the realities of life in the navy included the certainty of bad food and low pay and the likelihood of flogging. Yet the lure of adventure and of fabled Tahiti as well as the constraints, lack of prospects, and often almost equally deprived conditions to be found ashore drew crewmen to the *Bounty*.

As the final preparations were being made Fletcher Christian spent an evening with his brother Charles, newly returned to England as the ship's surgeon aboard the *Middlesex*, who had a dramatic and disturbing tale to relate. Two weeks earlier as the *Middlesex*, a merchant vessel, had been nearing England, a seaman—after being goaded by "insults severe to my feelings," threatened with being flogged to death for supposedly insulting a passenger, and confined for a period in irons without being allowed "to do the necessary calls of nature in another place"—had menaced the captain, John Rogers, with a loaded pistol. When Rogers had ordered the man again to be put in irons, the first and second officers had attempted to intervene on his behalf, upon which Rogers had dismissed them from their posts for assisting in a "mutinous conspiracy" and ordered them to be locked in their cabins. In his log, Rogers claimed that Charles Christian had been party to the mutiny.

When the ship anchored in the Thames, members of the *Middlesex*'s crew wrote at once to the East India Company's directors, defending the conduct of the ship's company and blaming events on Rogers's brutal and irrational behavior. Charles Christian admitted intervening on behalf of the seaman but argued that he had done so from "a sudden ebullition of passion springing from human sympathy at seeing cruel usage exercised towards one who deserved far different treatment . . . an ingenious, unoffending, insulted, oppressed, worthy young man" whom he had considered it his human duty to defend against "the capricious orders of tyranny."

At the time the two Christian brothers met, the drama had not yet fully played out. The East India Company's directors later decided both sides were to blame. They censured Captain Rogers for not having informed them of his dispute with his officers and suspended the "mutineers" from their service—the seaman in perpetuity, the first officer for three years, and the second officer and Charles Christian for two years. Later, when the seaman and the two officers brought a civil law suit against Captain Rogers, Christian appeared as "the principal, the sole witness" and so impressed the judge with his "impartial and steady" testimony that he awarded the plaintiffs huge damages of three thousand pounds—a sum equivalent to perhaps three hundred thousand pounds today.

Charles's tale might have discouraged his younger brother about to embark on his own far voyage. Yet that night it seems that Fletcher's spirits were high. He was, as Charles recalled, full of "professional ambition and of hope," baring his muscular arm, and when Charles professed amazement at "its brawniness," boasting that he had acquired the muscles "by hard labour . . . I delight to set the men an example. I not only can do every part of a common sailor's duty, but am upon a par with a principal part of the officers."

With the *Bounty* ready to sail, in October the Admiralty instructed Bligh to sail to Spithead in the Solent at the entrance to Portsmouth harbor where he would receive his final orders. So contrary were the winds that he needed almost three weeks—until November 4—to bring the square-rigged vessel safely to anchor off Spithead, where just a few months earlier Phillip had received his orders for the convict fleet to sail. Bligh waited with growing impatience for his orders, which finally arrived on November 24. He was to make for Cape Horn and thence to the "Society Islands . . . in the southern ocean . . . where, according to the accounts given by the late Captain Cook . . . the breadfruit tree is to be found in the most luxuriant state." He was to take on board as many seedlings as he could in exchange for what the Navy Board called "such articles of merchandise and trinkets as it is supposed will be wanted to satisfy the natives." His £125 worth of trade goods included 2,800 steel blades, one thousand wooden-handled knives, some thousands of iron nails, forty-eight saws, and a collection of hatchets, rasps, files, and other implements so valued in the South Seas, together with looking-glasses, eighty pounds of red, white, and blue beads, more than two hundred stained-glass earrings, and half a dozen shirts.

From the Society Islands he was to sail on through the Endeavour Strait (in the southern part of the Torres Strait separating the northern tip of New Holland—Australia—from New Guinea), either to Prince of Wales Island in the Sunda Strait (between Java and Sumatra) or to the northern shores of Java itself, and there purchase other exotic trees—"mangosteen, duriens, jacks, nancas, lansas and other fine fruit trees of that quarter, as well as the rice plant," which he would buy not with gewgaws but with ducats and Spanish dollars specifically provided for the purpose. Then he was to round the Cape of Good Hope and make for the West Indies, where he was to leave half his plants in St. Vincent "for the benefit of the Windward Islands" and the other half in Jamaica, while retaining some plants "for his majesty's garden at Kew."

Bligh knew that the three weeks lost in waiting for these orders had already prejudiced his chances of reaching and rounding Cape Horn—the shorter route to Tahiti—before the deteriorating weather of the coming southern winter made that route impossible. On December 10 he wrote to Duncan Campbell:

> If there is any punishment that ought to be inflicted on a set of men for neglect, I am sure it ought on the Admiralty for my three weeks' detention at this place during a fine fair wind which carried all outward bound ships clear of the Channel but me, who wanted it most. This has made my task a very arduous one indeed for to get round Cape Horn at the time I shall be there. I know not how to promise myself any success and yet I must do it if the ship will stand it at all or I suppose my character will be at stake.

He also returned to his grievance at not being promoted to captain: "They took me from a state of affluence from your employ with an income of five hundred a year to that of lieutenant's pay four shillings per day."

In a further letter to Campbell, Bligh showed his continuing determination to be recompensed for every expenditure, writing, "I have found that Captain Cook and Clerke had a great many coals allowed them by government, and as I am at upwards of £42 expense for what is on board, I have solicited Mr. Nepean . . . to assist me in getting an allowance for the same as they are for the use of the plants and forge. I shall be very much obliged to you, Sir, if in the course of conversation you can back my solicitation with Mr. Nepean."

Refusing to let perceived injustices drop, he continued to bemoan to Banks that not only were other officers at his level being promoted but that it "would make a material difference to Mrs. Bligh and her children in case of any accident to me." Several days later he wrote again and yet more bitterly to Banks that the Admiralty's refusal to promote him was "a violation of all justice with respect to me," still disregarding the fact that Cook had made his first, more extensive, voyage into the unknown at no more elevated rank than his own. Underlying Bligh's resentment may have been a dispiriting recognition that the delay in sending him his final orders and the refusal to promote him probably had a common root—that the Admiralty did not consider the breadfruit voyage important. Certainly First Lord of the Admiralty Lord Howe did not share his predecessor Lord Sandwich's interest in voyages of science and exploration. More importantly, the Admiralty had more pressing things to worry about than a botanical expedition: a possible war with the Dutch. On September 29 Duncan Campbell had written to a friend that "everything here wears the appearance of war being at hand" and then complained, "seaman's wages and every naval store have of course risen to war prices."

As contrary winds continued to frustrate his departure, after obtaining Banks's approval Bligh asked the Admiralty for discretion to go via the Cape of Good Hope if the Horn route should prove impossible. On December 18 they gave it. Finally, on December 23, 1787—ten weeks after being ordered to sail to Spithead and at its third attempt—the *Bounty* finally battled out into the English Channel in winds so strong that one sailor fell from the yardarm on which he was perched trying to furl a sail, only saving himself "by catching hold of the main-top-mast-stay in his fall." In the days that followed, pounding seas "stove in our stern, and filled the cabin"—where the breadfruit would be stored—with water, damaging a large amount of ship's biscuit stored there. On deck, the winds and waves ripped seven barrels of beer free from their lashings into the sea. More seriously, the ship's boats were nearly lost overboard and only saved, Bligh wrote, with "great difficulty and risk."

It was not a promising start to the venture that Bligh, consciously following in the wake of the great Cook, hoped would profit both his country and himself. Too wrapped up in his own plans to consider the purpose of the convict expedition or perhaps considering it irrelevant, he thought: "The object of all the former voyages to the South Seas . . . has been the advancement of science, and the increase of knowledge. This voyage may be reckoned the first, the intention of which has been to derive benefit from those distant discoveries."

VIII

"THEY MUST BE WATCHED LIKE CHILDREN"

*O*n December 29, the gales died away, the weather brightened, and driven by northerly winds the *Bounty* at last made good progress. Like the convict fleet, her first port of call was Tenerife and, on January 5, the island's volcanic tip emerged through the haze. The next day, with his ship securely anchored, Bligh—ever a stickler for form and formality—chose Christian as his emissary to the governor "to acquaint him I had put in to obtain refreshments, and to repair the damages we had sustained in bad weather." He also instructed Christian to inform the Spanish governor that he "would salute, provided an equal number of guns were to be returned." The governor replied that while he was happy to supply whatever provisions Bligh needed he only returned an equal-gun salute to people "equal in rank to himself." Bligh called his response "extraordinary" and made no salute.

While Nelson the botanist roamed the hills in search of "plants and natural curiosities," Bligh bargained for provisions. Wine was of excellent quality and recalling a tactful suggestion of Lord Howe, Bligh purchased "two hogsheads of the best quality . . . equal to Madeira" for Banks and also 880 gallons of a cheaper wine "for the ship's use." However, he discovered it was the wrong season to buy fresh fruit and vegetables: "Indian corn, potatoes, pumpkins and onions, were all very scarce, and double the price . . . [they had been] in summer"—the time when the First Fleet had visited. The only fruit Bligh could find were "a few dried figs and some bad oranges." Fresh beef was also scarce and of such "miserable" quality that, bosun's mate James Morrison related, it was "for the most part thrown overboard as soon as it was served out by the people [the crew], who were not yet sufficiently come to their stomachs to eat what they supposed to be either an ass or mule."

These provisioning problems were a blow both to Bligh and to his crew, whose diet, unless it could be supplemented, would be not only dull but downright unpalatable. The staple was ship's biscuit made of wheat or pea flour, bulked out, some sailors claimed, with bone dust. Baked in batches in the royal dockyard kitchens, each biscuit was thick, brown, five inches across, and stamped in the middle. Alum was sometimes added to make the biscuit paler and hence more attractive, along with jalap—a Mexican root with a laxative effect—since alum was constipating. If stowed for any length of time, ship's biscuit tasted bitter and musty. It also became so infested with weevils and maggots that ships' cooks sometimes re-baked it. Some sailors chose to eat the biscuit either in the dark or with their eyes closed.

Meat was either salted beef or pork, packed in four-pound hunks into barrels but with so much gristle and bone that a piece weighing one pound was said to contain only twelve edible ounces, perhaps even less. Naval rules required that the oldest meat be eaten first but it was sometimes so hard and dry that sailors used it instead of ivory or bone to carve scrimshaw. Once a week, instead of meat a ration of raisins, currants, and flour might be doled out to each mess so the men could make puddings. A relatively recent addition to the naval diet, and one favored by Cook, was "portable" soup—also called "pocket soup" or "veal glue"—a meat broth boiled down into a thick paste that could be reconstituted. Breakfast was usually "burgoo": oatmeal porridge so lumpy and gelatinous that some preferred to boil ship's biscuit in water to make a stiff paste to which they added sugar when they could get it. They nicknamed it "Scotch coffee."

Unsurprisingly, given such fare and the tough physical conditions, alcohol was all-important and generously distributed in the navy. Sailors could expect a gallon of beer a day and, when that ran out, a pint of wine. In addition, twice a day sailors received a pint of grog: three parts water to one of rum, with a squeeze of lemon juice to ward off scurvy. The withholding of grog was often used as a punishment.

On January 10, the *Bounty* left Tenerife, the entire company according to Bligh "in good health and spirits." From the start of the voyage he had imposed a health regime as rigorous as Cook's, ordering the crew regularly to cleanse the ship with vinegar, air their bedding, and wash their clothes. Every Sunday, he inspected the personal cleanliness of each crew member, later writing: "Seamen will seldom attend to themselves in any particular and simply to give directions that they are to keep themselves clean and dry as circumstances will allow, is of little avail, they must be watched like children."

Also emulating Cook, Bligh divided the crew into three watches so that members of the watch would only be on duty for four hours out of twelve instead of—under the navy's usual two-watch system—six hours in every twelve. The benefits, in Bligh's view, were beyond dispute: "unbroken rest not only contributes much towards the health of a ship's company, but enables them more readily to exert themselves in cases of sudden emergency." The new arrangement of course required three men to take charge of the watches. Bligh chose Fryer and Peckover and also Christian, who on January 11 took command of the third watch.

Bligh now officially "made the ship's company acquainted with the intent of the voyage," explaining that he hoped to proceed to Tahiti without stopping by way of Cape Horn. "As the season was so far spent" that route might prove impossible but "at all events, he was determined to try." To ensure their provisions lasted, he was reducing the daily ration of ship's biscuit by one third—a decision, Morrison later wrote, that was "cheerfully" received.

However, a few days later, also according to Morrison, the first of a series of disagreements over food occurred. When Bligh ordered some casks of cheeses to be opened to air the contents, two cheeses were missing. Bligh insisted they had been stolen, at which the ship's cooper, Henry Hillbrant— responsible for making and repairing the ship's barrels—said that before the *Bounty* had left England John Samuel, who acted both as Bligh's clerk and his steward, had ordered that the cask be opened and the two cheeses sent to Bligh's lodgings. An apparently furious Bligh would not listen and "ordered the allowance of cheese to be stopped from officers and men till the deficiency should be made good and told the cooper he would give him a damned good flogging if he said any more about it."

Bligh's act sparked a simmering resentment. On the next meatless day, when cheese would normally have been served, the crew were given only butter, which they rejected because accepting it, Morrison wrote, "would be tacitly acknowledging the supposed theft." Meanwhile, seaman John Williams not only confirmed everything that Hillbrant had claimed, but added that he had been ordered to take ashore not just the cheeses but "a cask of vinegar and some other things." Whatever the truth, some of the crew at least thought Bligh was already practicing "the dark and mysterious art of pursery" and cheating them of their due.

With the air growing ever heavier and more humid as the ship neared the Equator, which they crossed on February 7 with some ceremony— though Bligh forbade the "brutal and inhuman" ducking of initiates from the yardarm—there was further trouble over food. This time the cause was the pumpkins Bligh had purchased in Tenerife, which were starting to spoil in the heat. According to Morrison, "they were issued to the ship's company in lieu of bread. The people, desiring to know at what rate the exchange was to be," asked Bligh's clerk, John Samuel, who informed them "they were to have one pound of pumpkin in lieu of two pounds of bread." When they refused, "on Mr. Bligh's being informed of it, he came up in a violent passion and called all hands, telling Mr. Samuel to call the first man of every mess and let him see who would dare to refuse it or anything else that he should order to be served, saying, 'You damned infernal scoundrels. I'll make you eat grass . . . before I have done with you.'" The result, Morrison continued, was that "everyone took the pumpkin . . . including the officers, who, though it was in their eyes an imposition, said nothing against it."

The supply of pumpkins eventually ran out and there, Morrison later wrote, "the grievance would have ended" if the men had not begun to notice that their ration of beef and pork appeared "very light" and asked Fryer to look into it "and procure them redress." When Fryer duly approached Bligh, his reaction was again explosive. Assembling all hands, he told them "everything relative to the provisions was transacted by his orders—and it was therefore needless to make any complaint, for they would get no redress—as he was the fittest judge of what was right or wrong." Furthermore, "he would flog the first man severely who should dare attempt to make any complaint in the future and dismissed them with severe threats." The seamen shrugged it off, "seeing that no redress could be had before the end of the voyage." However, the officers—Morrison named no names—"made frequent murmurings among themselves about the smallness of their allowance." When a cask was broached, Morrison later alleged, they saw with regret "all the biggest and best pieces culled out for Mr. Bligh's table."

Off the coast of Brazil, Bligh took advantage of a passing British whaler bound for Cape Town to send on board letters to Duncan Campbell, the Heywood family, and Joseph Banks. Maintaining the confident, cheerful, even airy tone he customarily used when reporting his progress, he made no mention of such bickerings. To Campbell he wrote of his men's "content and cheerfulness, dancing always from four until eight at night"; to the Heywoods of Peter's good progress; while he assured Banks that "we are now fit to go round half a score of worlds, both men and officers tractable and well disposed and cheerfulness and content in the countenance of everyone . . . I have no cause to inflict punishments for I have no offenders."

Bligh's efforts to safeguard his men's health continued unstinting. On February 18, with the *Bounty* in a region "between the NE and SE trade winds" (S21°) where "the calms, and rains, if of long continuance, are very liable to produce sickness," he ordered his men to use the ship's pumps to flush the bilges until the water ran out clear, to light fires between decks to dry out the ship, and to dry and air their clothes and bedding.

On Sunday, March 2, 1788, Bligh again publicly demonstrated his faith in Fletcher Christian when after divine service, he announced he was appointing him as acting lieutenant. For John Fryer, as the ship's master and the senior warrant officer, the promotion of his mate over his head must have been galling, just as Bligh must have resented the promotion of others over him on Cook's last voyage. Certainly, Fryer's general disgruntlement emerges from around this time. On March 10, he quarreled with seaman Matthew Quintal and reported him to Bligh for "insolence and mutinous behaviour." This left Bligh no option but to punish Quintal and he duly ordered Morrison to give him twenty-four lashes—the first flogging of the voyage. Quintal was stripped to the waist and bound hand and foot to an upright grating to receive his punishment. In his log Bligh wrote, "Until this afternoon I had hopes I could have performed the voyage without punishment to anyone"—not the impression his ragings about their demands for better food had given his crew.

As the air grew colder and danker, so that "the people might not suffer by their own negligence," Bligh ordered his crew to put aside their "light tropical clothing" in favor of clothes "more suited to a cold climate," of which he had laid in good stocks before leaving England. The crew's monotonous— and in their view meager—diet was occasionally enlivened by delicacies such as porpoise which, Bligh wrote, "was so well liked, that no part of it was wasted." By March 20, with whales spouting and the great seabirds of the southern ocean arcing high above, the *Bounty* neared the eastern shores of mountainous, snow-capped Tierra del Fuego. Bligh had never sailed around the Horn but thoroughly appreciated its hazards. For the moment, though, conditions looked promising. He wrote in his log that so far the region "has not shown itself with all the horrors mentioned by former navigators" but also that wintry weather could set in at any time so that "I have no right to lose a moment of time."

Aware that the "most difficult and grand part of our passage" lay ahead, Bligh ordered hot breakfasts—boiled wheat and barley mixed with sugar and butter—though Morrison complained that "the quantity was so small that

it was no uncommon thing for four men in a mess to draw lots for the breakfast and to divide their bread by the well-known method of 'who shall have
this?' "* On March 23 a sheep died and was served out to the crew in lieu of
pork and pease but, Morrison recorded, it being "nothing but skin and bones"
the men threw most of it overboard and instead ate "some dry shark supplied
in place, for a Sunday's dinner."

By late March, with the *Bounty* nearing the eastern approach to the
Magellan Strait, the gales Bligh had feared began battering the ship with such
force that instead of trying to sail into the strait Bligh pushed around east of
Staten Island and soon, as he later told Banks, "entered the Southern Ocean."
However, hopes of rounding Cape Horn proved short-lived. Early April
brought a violent gale that, Bligh wrote, "exceeded what I had ever met with
before . . . the sea, from the frequent shifting of the wind, running in contrary
directions broke exceeding high." The crew battled against "a storm of wind
and the snow fells so heavy that it was scarce possible to haul the sails up
and furl them from the weight and stiffness." Bligh ordered that a fire be kept
burning night and day and that the crewmen on watch dry their colleagues'
wet clothes.

As great waves crashed ceaselessly over her, the *Bounty* held steady against
the ferocious headwinds but needed to be constantly pumped. By April 12,
seawater was leaking through the planking of the main deck so badly that
Bligh turned over the great cabin "to those people who had wet berths, to
hang their hammocks in." Despite their efforts, everyone was dismayed
to realize at the end of every day "that we were losing ground; for notwithstanding our utmost exertions, and keeping on the most advantageous
tacks . . . the greater part of the time, we were doing little better than drifting
before the wind." The ship was rocking so violently that "the cook fell and
broke one of his ribs," while Surgeon Huggan fell down a ladderway and
dislocated his shoulder—whether alcohol had any part in his accident is not
recorded. The drenching seawater and bitter cold meant that a number of
crewmen—and Peckover the gunner at over forty in particular—were
suffering badly from rheumatism. Adding malt to the hot breakfasts did little
to help.

---

*To ensure food was distributed fairly, one man—his back to the rest—would divide it into
portions, each time calling out "who shall have this?" at which his colleagues would shout out
a name or draw lots.

With the full moon approaching, Bligh hoped the weather would change in their favor but "the event did not at all answer our expectations." At least the crew were able to supplement their diet. Bligh described how they "caught a good many birds" and, finding the taste too fishy, "tried an experiment upon them, which succeeded admirably. By keeping them cooped up, and cramming them with ground corn, they improved wonderfully in a short time . . . The pintada birds became as fine as ducks, and the albatrosses were as fat, and not inferior in taste to fine geese." The discovery was especially welcome since of all the livestock on board only the hogs had survived—"the sheep and poultry not being hardy enough to stand the severity of the weather."

On April 20, the wind died away, bringing a few hours' welcome calm, and Bligh ordered the slaughtering and serving of a hog. Toward noon, however, violent squalls from the west heralded yet more storms of snow and hail and Bligh accepted the inevitable: "I saw how hopeless, and even unjustifiable it was, to persist any longer in attempting a passage this way to the Society Islands. We had been thirty days in this tempestuous ocean. At one time we had advanced so far to the westward as to have a fair prospect of making our passage round; but from that period hard gales of westerly wind had continued without intermission, a few hours excepted which, to borrow an expression in Lord Anson's voyage, were 'like the elements drawing breath to return upon us with redoubled violence.'"

Bligh was worried about his "exceedingly jaded" crew. Eight were on the sick list, leaving only ten men "on whom the hard duty of furling and reefing principally fell" and who, "much harassed and fatigued," might soon sicken. He also knew that "I had not a moment to spare to make my passage to the Cape of Good Hope and refit so as to secure my getting to Tahiti in time." "To the great joy of every person on board," Bligh ordered his crew to bear away east for the Cape of Good Hope.

The *Bounty* was leaking so badly that, Bligh wrote, "we [were] obliged to pump every hour in our passage from Cape Horn." Yet as the weather improved, the hatches could again be opened and the work of drying and airing the ship could begin. On May 24, just six months after the departure of the First Fleet from Cape Town, the *Bounty* anchored safely twenty-five miles away in False Bay. Bligh was still consumed with regret that "had I been a fortnight sooner there, I could have made my passage round Cape [Horn] into the South Sea with the greatest ease."

His immediate priority was to make his ship watertight and seaworthy. Assisted by two Dutch caulkers, the carpenter Purcell began re-caulking the

Bounty's leaking seams. Lebogue, the sailmaker, oversaw the repair of the damaged sails and the rigging was thoroughly overhauled. Bligh himself checked the stores and provisions, finding to his dismay that much had been damaged, particularly the ship's biscuit. He was also anxious that his chronometer K2—a simplified, cheaper version of K1, which he had used on his voyage with Cook and which had gone with Phillip to New South Wales—was no longer functioning accurately. Taking it ashore to test it himself, he found it was slow by three and a half minutes and losing three seconds daily.

With the governor's help, Bligh arranged for fresh food to be brought from Cape Town but, like Arthur Phillip six months earlier, he was aghast at the prices "which were much dearer than when I was here in 1780"—the result of the recent famine. Five live sheep "cost four Spanish dollars each, and were so small that it answered better to purchase the mutton, for the ship's daily use, at four pence per pound." For reasons that are unclear but perhaps because goods were so costly in Cape Town, Bligh lent Fletcher Christian money—on the surface a gesture of trust and friendship, though Bligh sent the bill to Duncan Campbell with a request that one of Christian's brothers be asked to repay the loan with interest. According to Alexander Smith (John Adams), over the months to come Bligh would "frequently remind" his protégé of his generosity "when any difference arose. Christian, excessively annoyed at the share of blame which repeatedly fell to him in common with the rest of the officers, could ill endure the additional taunt of private obligations."

As with Arthur Phillip and his officers a few months earlier, the condition of the slaves in Cape Town shocked Bligh, who wrote of his distress at seeing "some of them carrying weighty burdens naked or what is worse in such rags that one would imagine could not fail to reproach the owners of a want of decency and compassion in not relieving such a degree of wretchedness of which they were the cause, and had every call on their humanity to remove."

Two days before leaving, Bligh wrote in customary self-congratulatory vein to Banks: "I am now ready for sea with my little ship once more in most excellent order and every man on board in very good health." His letter suggests that he had contemplated calling in at the new convict colony but then dismissed the idea: "I might wood and water at Botany Bay with little loss of time and it may be imagined I will do so, but I cannot think of putting it in the power of chance to prevent my accomplishing the object of the voyage. I shall therefore pass our friends there," but he assured his patron that "should any unforeseen accident drive me there I have a great many seeds and some fruit plants which I shall leave with them."

On July 1, the *Bounty* departed South Africa and, as had the convict fleet, soon encountered high winds "with much thunder, lightning and rain," which lasted a week. So violent were the seas that, Bligh noted, "the man at the steerage was thrown over the wheel and much bruised." However, by mid-August, despite yet more snow and hail, the *Bounty* was approaching Van Diemen's Land from the west and in the early hours of August 21 anchored safely in the deep clear water of Adventure Bay on its southern shores.* Bligh at once set out in a boat to search for places that he remembered as good sources of wood and water. Landing at the bay's western edge where the surf was not so fierce, he found a gully filled with rainwater. Looking around him he saw how stumps of trees felled by Cook's expedition had in the intervening years sprouted great shoots twenty-five feet high and fourteen inches thick.

Bligh quickly organized shore parties under Christian to fill water casks and fell timber. The pounding surf made the work of loading full casks into boats and rowing them back to the ship hazardous and cumbersome. The sawn wood had to be lashed into rafts and floated out. On August 23, while inspecting the work of the shore parties, Bligh criticized his carpenter, Purcell, for cutting planks that were, in his view, too long to be easily stowed, whereupon Purcell—unused to naval discipline and strongly inclined to resent aspersions on his competence—accused Bligh of only having come ashore "to find fault." To Bligh this was "most insolent and reprehensible" behavior and he ordered Purcell back to the *Bounty*, "there to assist in the general duty of the ship." Only the fact that, as he wrote, he "could not bear the loss of an able working and healthy man" prevented him from having Purcell locked up until he could be court-martialed. As Bligh—and no doubt Purcell—well knew, his options for dealing with the carpenter were limited. As a warrant officer, Purcell was exempt from flogging. With the *Bounty* expedition still at an early stage and his carpenter's skills essential to its success, to confine Purcell in his cabin until the ship's return to England where he could be court-martialed would have been foolish.

---

*Tobias Furneaux, Cook's second-in-command on his second voyage, had named the bay after his ship *Adventure* in 1773. Bligh, Nelson, Peckover, and Coleman, of course, knew it from their visit with Cook eleven years previously, in 1777.

Unchastened, Purcell continued to be obdurate, refusing Fryer's orders to help hoist water out of the hold. Bligh eventually subdued him by ordering that "no one should give him meat or drink until he worked." However, his challenge to Bligh's authority and the revelation of the limited sanctions available to Bligh gave others cause to reflect. Morrison later wrote that in Adventure Bay "were sown seeds of eternal discord between Lieut. Bligh and the Carpenter; and it will be no more than true to say, with all the officers in general." Bligh, Morrison alleged, "found fault with the inattention of the rest to their duty, which produced continual disputes."

Bligh set his men to fishing and they caught enough fish and spider-crabs to feed everyone though mussels plucked from the rocks made some sick—the result, Bligh thought, of "eating too many." Bligh himself continued his exploration of the bay, watching whales spouting and shooting gannets for food. With Nelson's help he also chose what he hoped would be a suitable spot to plant an extensive kitchen garden for any ships that passed that way in the future: "three fine young apple-trees, nine vines, six plantain-trees, a number of orange and lemon-seed, cherry-stones, plum, peach and apricot-stones, pumpkins, also two sorts of Indian corn, and apple and pear kernels."

On the night of September 1 came the first encounter with the Aboriginal people. Through the darkness Bligh's men spied the orange light of fires on low land near a promontory. The next morning, through their telescopes, they made out distant figures. Bligh hoped they would come closer and when they showed no interest in doing so determined to go after them, setting out in a boat. The surf was running too high for him to land so, ordering the dropping of a grapnel, he waited. An hour later he saw Nelson, who had gone ashore some time previously to botanize, emerge from woodland onto the shore. The botanist shouted that he had encountered some of the local people. "Soon after," Bligh wrote, "we heard their voices like the cackling of geese, and twenty persons came out of the wood, twelve of whom went round to some rocks, where the boat could get nearer to the shore than we then were. Those who remained behind were women." All were entirely naked and Bligh thought he recognized one man from his visit in 1777. Eager for a better view, Bligh ordered his crewmen to row closer so that he could "throw to the shore, tied up in paper, the presents . . . intended for them," holding up the items—beads and nails—before wrapping them. Though the people "ran very nimbly over the rocks" and caught the gifts "with great dexterity," they did not begin to open them until Bligh "made an appearance of leaving." Encouraged, Bligh ordered his men to row back toward them but at once they put the gifts down again. Bligh tried "throwing a few more beads and nails on shore, and made signs for them to go to the ship." Sitting on their heels, knees tucked into their armpits, they gestured him to land but with the thunderous surf still making this impossible, Bligh reluctantly departed. Curiosity roused, he continued to hope that the Aboriginal people "would have paid us a visit" but they kept their distance and all Bligh and most of his men saw were more fires in the night.

On September 5, the *Bounty* left Adventure Bay, dipping southeastward. Two weeks later, south of New Zealand, she passed some rocky islets covered with "white spots like patches of snow," which Bligh named the *"Bounty Isles."* Heading east they saw penguins and seals flipping through the water and smelled the acrid fishy stench of whales blowing. By trailing baited hooks the crew caught albatrosses—one with a wingspan of nearly eight feet—to fatten for the table as they had off Cape Horn.

On October 6, Bligh and his men gazed at a sea covered with phosphorescent plankton giving off "light like the blaze of a candle." That day, Surgeon Huggan informed Bligh that seaman James Valentine, who had taken ill in Adventure Bay, was dying. Having considered Valentine "one of the most robust people on board," Bligh was both astonished and angry, unequivocally blaming Huggan for negligence by allowing the arm from which he had bled the man to become badly infected.

On October 9, the day Valentine died, Bligh faced the most serious challenge to his authority so far when the boatswain and carpenter presented their expense books for the months of August and September for his approval and signature, which he duly gave. As was standard naval practice to prevent corruption, the books were next passed to another officer—in this case, Fryer—for countersignature. Fryer, however, stubbornly refused to sign unless Bligh gave him a signed note affirming "he had done nothing amiss during his time on board." Bligh's response was to summon the entire crew and then order the articles of war with its long list of offenses and punishments to be read out to them, at which, Bligh wrote in his log, "this troublesome man saw his error and before the whole ship's company signed the books." Bligh noted that he forgave Fryer but, according to Morrison, the master was anything but contrite, saying as he took the pen, "I sign in obedience to your orders but this may be cancelled hereafter."

Fryer may have believed that Bligh would doctor the books for his own benefit: The penalty for countersigning false accounts was cashiering from the navy. Alternatively, his short-lived rebellion may have been sparked by what he perceived as Bligh's slighting treatment of himself or he may have been upset by Bligh's blaming of Surgeon Huggan for the death of Valentine that same day. Whatever the case, Bligh was now on bad terms with three of his five warrant officers—Fryer, Purcell, and Huggan. Though the master and surgeon were formally Bligh's mess mates, Morrison states both now refused to eat with him, "each taking his part of the stock and retiring to live in their own cabins" and only speaking to their commander "with much apparent reserve." Of Fletcher Christian's relations with Bligh at this stage, all eye-witness accounts, including Bligh's, are silent, but in his growing isolation it seems more than likely that the captain relied increasingly on his protégé.

Over following days, Huggan angered Bligh further by diagnosing several crewmen with scurvy, which Bligh interpreted as an overt attack on his health regime. On October 19, gardener William Brown refused to join in that night's compulsory dancing session, excusing himself to the surgeon because of "some rheumatic complaints"—a condition, Bligh wrote in his log, that "the doctor insists . . . is scurvy." Bligh examined Brown himself and declared he could find no symptoms of the disease, but he ordered Huggan personally to dose Brown with essence of malt, much favored by Cook as a defense against scurvy.* As it was a Sunday, Bligh conducted his usual weekly inspection of the crew's health and cleanliness, afterward recording, 'I think I never saw a more healthy set of men . . . in my life." Purcell again proved stubborn. When Bligh ordered every man to drink "half a pint of beverage made of the elixir of vitriol"—another supposed defense against scurvy but in fact ineffective—the carpenter flatly refused, by his own later account saying, "I am well enough, and therefore I do not choose, nor won't take such stuff as this. I do not know what it is."

On October 25, having circled northward to catch the southeasterly trade winds, the Bounty approached the small hilly island of Maitea, only one hundred miles from Tahiti to which Bligh thought he and his crew would be the first European visitors since Cook's last expedition over a decade earlier. In fact, the convict transport Lady Penrhyn had called in three months earlier, after depositing her cargo of female prisoners at Port Jackson, which she had finally left in May.

*In fact, malt lacks any vitamin C.

The ship had been bound for China to collect a cargo of tea but with her sailors displaying the classic signs of scurvy, her captain had decided he must find somewhere with plentiful fresh food and on July 10 had anchored in Matavia Bay to a rapturous reception from islanders waving white bark cloth and plantain stems and—when the captain ordered the Union Jack to be run up—shouting *"Pahi no Tute!,"* "Cook's ship!" Before long they were climbing aboard. Young women danced on the deck with motions that the ship's surgeon thought "would in England be thought the height of indecency, and indeed they seem calculated to excite venereal desires to a great degree . . ." Many joined the sailors in their hammocks. The *Lady Penrhyn* spent two weeks before departing from the islanders, of whom the surgeon wrote, "There cannot be a more affectionate people."

Unaware of the *Lady Penrhyn's* visit, of course, and anxious to avoid any "ill-founded suppositions" that his men had brought venereal disease to Tahiti, Bligh ordered Huggan to examine every crewman for signs of it. Given his contempt for Huggan, it seems surprising that Bligh placed any confidence in his judgment and that he did not instead turn to his competent assistant, Ledward. However, several days earlier, after the surgeon's drunken behavior had reached new heights, Bligh had ordered his stinking cabin to be searched and cleaned out—a task "not only troublesome but offensive in the highest degree"—and his stock of liquor to be confiscated; and he now believed Huggan "perfectly cured in 48 hours." Huggan declared every man "perfectly free from any venereal complaint."

Bligh next posted on the mizzen-mast a list of "rules . . . for the better establishing a trade for supplies of provisions, and good intercourse with the natives of the South Seas." No one was "to intimate that Captain Cook was killed by Indians, or that he is dead" or to reveal that the purpose of the voyage was to obtain breadfruit trees until Bligh himself had broached it with the chiefs. Everyone was "to study to gain the goodwill and esteem of the natives; to treat them with all kindness; and not to take from them by violent means anything that they have stolen," while no one was ever to open fire "but in defence of his life."

Knowing the Tahitians' reputation for light fingers, the cost-conscious Bligh warned that if any man lost "arms or implements of any kind" in his care he would charge their value against the man's wages rather than the cost being borne by the ship and hence by himself as purser. Embezzling or selling "any part of the king's stores" was strictly prohibited. Bligh would appoint "a proper person or persons" to regulate trade and barter with the islanders and no one—officers included—was to trade "for any kind of provisions or curiosities" except through his officially appointed provider. By this means "a regular market will be carried on, and all disputes, which otherwise may happen with the natives will be avoided." It would also, Bligh knew, help him control the shipboard price of commodities.

The next day, October 26, 1788, as they sailed along Tahiti's eastern shores in the soft dawn light," Bligh identified the low, flat peninsula of Point Venus in Matavai Bay, just twelve nautical miles away. As the *Bounty* rounded the point and sailed into the lagoon through a break in the reef, "a great number of canoes came off to us. Their first enquiries were, if we were Tyos [*taios*], which signified friends and whether we came from 'Pretanee' (their pronunciation of Britain) or from Lima." Learning that the new arrivals were indeed from "Pretanee," chaos ensued as excited, flower-bedecked men and women "crowded on board in vast numbers, notwithstanding our endeavours to prevent it, as we were working the ship in . . . in less than ten minutes the deck was so full that I could scarce find my own people," Bligh wrote. In the midst of this confusion and prevented by contrary winds from sailing further in, Bligh anchored a mile offshore.

The *Bounty*'s long voyage "in direct and contrary courses" of 27,086 nautical miles—an average of more than one hundred miles a day—was over. Paradise awaited.

IX

"HERE NATURE IS REVERSED"

*O*ver the ten months during which Bligh had been voyaging to Tahiti, life in the new penal colony in New South Wales had been less than Paradise for both the convicts and their guards. Concerned by the presence of La Pérouse's vessels, one of Governor Arthur Phillip's first actions had been to set about fulfilling his orders to claim Norfolk Island—1,100 nautical miles (some two thousand kilometers) northeast—to "prevent it being occupied by the subjects of any other European power." Even before landing the bulk of the convicts, he ordered Lieutenant Philip Gidley King to take *Supply* with six months' provisions, farm animals, seeds to plant, and a small number of convicts, mostly volunteers, to establish a colony there. Among King's priorities would be to cultivate and harvest the island's wild flax, which Cook had enthusiastically described.

On January 27, 1788, the day after the raising of the Union Jack and while the *Bounty* was heading for the Equator, the male convicts were landed and set to felling timber and clearing tangled scrub—essential since, Judge-Advocate David Collins noted, trees clustered so thickly along the shore that "every man stepped from the boat literally into a wood." Soon "the spot which had so lately been the abode of silence and tranquillity . . . changed to that of noise, clamour and confusion" as the prisoners labored, guarded by marines sweating uncomfortably in their hot, tight red uniforms, all in turn watched by silent, naked figures peering cautiously from the bush.

The Aboriginal people inhabiting the region being so visibly appropriated belonged to some thirty clan groups including the Gweagal—two of whom had tried to prevent Cook and his men from landing in Botany Bay and been fired on many years before.* Other major groups were the Gadigal, whose lands stretched from the south head along the south side of Port Jackson, Gameyegal, Wangal, and Wallumedegal. The British would later call them collectively the "Eora people," from the word meaning "person" used by the indigenous people to describe themselves. They would call the British "the Berewalgal"—"people from a great distance off."

The Aboriginal people must have found astonishing the sight of a bull, cows, and horses—the first such creatures they had ever seen—being brought ashore. Lieutenant Tench indeed thought that any spectator of whatever background would have found the sights "highly picturesque and amusing. In one place, a party cutting down the woods; a second, setting up a black-smith's forge; a third, dragging along a load of stones or provisions; here an officer pitching his marquee, with a detachment of troops parading on one side of him, a cook's fire blazing up on the other."

The small rivulet flowing into Sydney Cove—one of the reasons Phillip had chosen to site the colony there—soon became its central axis. (It would later become known as Tank Stream when three tanks were dug in its sand-stone banks to store fresh water for the colony.) Phillip chose gently sloping land on the cove's eastern side for his own residence—in these early days a giant portable tented dwelling that had cost £125—and those of his guards and staff. A small number of the more trustworthy convicts would camp nearby. The marines' encampment was to be along the stream's western bank, near that of the male convicts, with the women's tents some distance away. Pondering where to position the astronomical instruments entrusted to him by the Board of Longitude, Lieutenant Dawes selected the cove's west-ernmost point, which he named Point Maskelyne after the astronomer royal. The indigenous people knew the spot as Tarra. Surgeon-General John White set up his hospital tents nearby, identifying an adjacent spot to grow vegetables for his patients. Like many officers, Lieutenant Clark did not enjoy his first night ashore under canvas, complaining of the "hard, cold ground" and "spiders, ants and every vermin that you can think of . . . crawling over me. I was glad when the morning came." On rising he consoled himself by shooting a parrot—"the most beautifulest birds that I ever saw."

To allow the male convicts to move and work freely, they were not kept in irons. Taking advantage of this, on February 5 a small group escaped into

---

*During Cook's visit, the Tahitian Tupaia had sketched three Gweagal men fishing from canoes—one of the earliest visual depictions of the indigenous population to reach Europe.

the bush and, finding an Aboriginal track, followed it seven miles south to Botany Bay. Encountering a shore party from the French ships, they pleaded with the Frenchmen to take them aboard either as political fugitives or as sailors. To La Pérouse, unwilling to antagonize the British, the convicts were merely "trouble and embarrassment." He gave them a day's food and told them to be gone, leaving them no option but to return to Sydney Cove, proof that this new land was in effect its own prison and that Phillip had little need to construct jails. Though Phillip had them flogged, they were fortunate La Pérouse turned them away. His ships were later lost in the New Hebrides (Vanuatu)—named by Cook in 1774—with no survivors.

The nearly two hundred women prisoners, who had been allowed on deck since the transports anchored, learned that they would land on February 6, becoming the first European women to set foot on the continent. Phillip, who had long been concerned about their scarecrow-raggedness, ordered new "slops"—dresses of coarse material—that he had been keeping back to be distributed to them. Not all were grateful. One woman, "upon being given her slops, and at the same time being told of the very indifferent character that she bore and how little she merited the slops, throwed 'em down on deck and would not have anything," Surgeon Bowes Smyth noted. Many, though, took great trouble over their appearance. Coming ashore after so many months of deprivation and hardship seemed a festive occasion, especially since the cove must have looked reassuringly green and hospitable, rather than the terrifying wilderness of their imaginings during the voyage. Soon after dawn, the first women began clambering down into the boats. Bowes Smyth thought them "dressed in general very clean and tidy" and that "some few amongst them might even be said to be well dressed."

Phillip had not anticipated what might happen as women arrived in the midst of so many sex-starved men. The trigger for what became mass rape was a sudden storm that broke just after six P.M. Bowes Smyth described how the last women "had not been landed more than an hour before they had all got their tents pitched or anything in order to receive them but there came on the most violent storm of thunder, lightning and rain that ever I saw." The lightning killed six sheep, two lambs, and one pig sheltering beneath a tree.

As the women ran for cover, the male convicts charged at them, dragging them down—young and old—onto the slippery ground to rape them. Seamen from the *Lady Penrhyn*, who had petitioned their captain for extra supplies of rum so they could "make merry upon the women quitting the ships," joined in, as did other sailors and some of the marines. Bowes Smyth wrote shudderingly: "It is beyond my abilities to give a just description of the scene of debauchery and riot that ensued during the night." As lightning flashed and thunder rolled around them, "some [were] swearing, others quarrelling, others singing, not in the least regarding the tempest, though so violent that the thunder shook the ship. [It] exceeded anything I ever before had a conception of, sailors almost all drunk . . . the heat almost suffocating." Only the few fortunate enough to have found "protectors"—Mary Broad with William Bryant, East London dressmaker Esther Abrahams and her Lieutenant of Marines George Johnston, fourteen-year-old Elizabeth Hayward, the youngest female prisoner, who had been taken in as their servant by the Reverend Johnson and his wife—were safe from being raped.

Though he must have been aware what was happening, Phillip did not attempt to intervene and the orgy lasted until dawn. At midday, however, "with music playing and colours flying," he summoned all the convicts to a specially cleared parade ground near the head of the cove. Dressed in his post-captain's frock coat of blue wool, white lapels edged in gold lace, sword by his side and medals gleaming on his chest, his senior officers by his side and two red boxes containing his commissions and letters patent from King George—still sealed—on a table before him, he ordered the mud-spattered prisoners, including the bruised and bloodied women, to squat down on the ground before him. Marines in red coats with white facings, black cocked hats, their muskets on their shoulders, formed a perimeter around them.

In a ceremony doubtless intended to awe, Judge-Advocate David Collins opened the two boxes, unsealed the documents inside, and read them out. Phillip was to be governor and captain-general of New South Wales, an area declared as extending from "Cape York [the extremity of the coast to the northward] in the latitude of 20 degrees 37 minutes South, to the South Cape [the southern extremity of the coast] in the latitude of 43 degrees 39 minutes South; and inland to the westward as far as 135 degrees of East longitude, comprehending all the islands adjacent in the Pacific Ocean, within the latitudes of the above-mentioned capes"—in other words "such parts . . . as were navigated by Captain Cook."

Phillip himself was empowered "to act entirely from his own judgement." He could appoint officials, pardon or punish offenders, and set up civil, admiralty, and criminal courts. Clark wrote, "I never heard of any one single person having so great a power vested in him as the Governor has by his commission." Indeed, within four days, Phillip would use his powers to establish a court of criminal judicature presided over by Judge-Advocate David Collins with six officers. Provided at least five of the seven members were in favor, the court could impose the death penalty. However, the officers would soon learn that Phillip had no powers in one area of major concern to themselves: He had no authority to grant them land, although he could assign one hundred acres to noncommissioned officers and fifty acres to privates after they had completed their service. All the governor could do for his officers was lend them land on which to graze animals or cultivate gardens.

After Collins had finished and marines had discharged three musket volleys between verses of the national anthem, Phillip addressed the convicts. Probably alluding to the previous night's rapes, he told them he was convinced "that there were a number of good men among them, who unfortunately, from falling into bad company, from the influence of bad women, and in the rash moment of intoxication, had been led to violate the laws of their country, by committing crimes which in the serious moments of reflection, they thought of with horror and shame." While he was prepared to "freely forgive and forget" what had happened, in future "the law should take its course." "Indiscriminate and illegal [sexual] intercourse" would not be tolerated and he commended matrimony. Marines would shoot any man attempting to enter the women's tents at night. Neither would he tolerate indolence: "Those who would not work, should not eat." Henceforth all would be subject to rigid discipline and anyone, convict and non-convict alike, found stealing livestock or food would be tried and, if found guilty, executed. At the end, Phillip and his officers withdrew to what should have been a pleasant meal of cold mutton only to find the meat full of maggots. "Nothing will keep 24 hours in this country," Clark grumbled.

Three days later, on Sunday, February 10, the Reverend Johnson christened the first European child born ashore in Sydney Cove and thus the first in New Holland—Elizabeth, daughter of marine Samuel Bacon and his wife Jane—together with the sons of two female prisoners born on board ship. He also conducted the first Christian marriages in New Holland. Mary Broad and William Bryant were last of the five convict couples to exchange vows. She marked a cross in the register, while he was able to sign his name. Looking on, liberal-minded Lieutenant Tench approved the official policy of encouraging matrimony since trying to keep the sexes apart would be "impracticable and . . . perhaps wrong." Ralph Clark was more cynical: "Several of the convicts were married yesterday," some of whom had "left wives and families at home."

Phillip's prohibitions on men visiting the women's camp soon proved ineffective. "Good God, what a scene of whoredom is going on there in the women's camp. No sooner has one man gone in with a woman but another goes in with her. I hope the Almighty will keep me free from them as he has hitherto done but I need not be afraid as I promised you, my tender Betsey . . . I will never have anything to do [with any woman] whatever except yourself, my dear wife," Clark wrote. He described how patrols caught "three seamen and a boy . . . in the women's camp and they were drummed out . . . the major sent for one of the women's petticoats and put it on the boy . . . I hope this will be a warning to them from coming into the whore camp—I would call it by the name of Sodom for there is more sin committed in it than in any other part of the world."

The first flogging in the colony was over a woman. Marine Private Bramwell was sentenced to "200 lashes on his bare back" for assaulting convict Elizabeth Needham, his clandestine lover on the voyage out from England. She had since begun a relationship with another man she intended to marry and, when Bramwell asked her to go into the woods with him for sex, refused—upon which he struck her. To the convicts, Bramwell's punishment was a tangible sign that Phillip intended all to be equal before the law; but it angered the marines who believed Phillip favored the convicts over them, so that "marines and sailors are punished with the utmost severity for the most trivial offences whilst the convicts are pardoned (or at least punished in a very slight manner) for crimes of the blackest dye." In fact, despite the marines' perceptions, among the first cases to come before Collins's criminal court was that of convict Sam Barsby, charged with striking a drum major, for which he received 150 lashes. Women too were flogged. On February 15 a female convict was lashed at the cart's tail for stealing from another woman.

Another early cause of tension with the marines was Phillip's rations policy, which was not to discriminate and for convicts to receive the same as officers and men—a weekly allowance of seven pounds of salt beef or four of pork, three pints of dried peas, seven pounds of flour, six ounces of butter, and half a pound of rice or an extra pound of flour for males. Women, however, would only receive two thirds that amount. "Could I possibly have imagined that I was to be served with, for instance, no more butter than any of the convicts," complained the marines' commanding officer, Major Robert Ross.

Phillip had meant it when he had stated that any theft of food would be a hanging offense. On February 27, Thomas Barrett, who had so ingeniously counterfeited quarter-dollars from buttons, spoons, and belt buckles while the transports had been in Brazil, was one of four men convicted of stealing butter, peas, and pork from the general store. Barrett was sentenced to hang that day, two of his confederates the following day, while the fourth man was to receive three hundred lashes. A large tree between the male and female camps was chosen as a gibbet. Clark, recovering from having a tooth so painfully extracted that "I thought that half of my head would have come off," described how "when the provost martial put a handkerchief about [Barrett's] head he turned as white as a sheet. Soon after the ladder was pulled from under him and he launched into the next world without a groan." Clark failed to mention that at the last moment, while the ashen and trembling Barrett waited, the convict who had volunteered for the role of hangman refused to go through with it until Major Ross threatened to shoot him. Afterward, Barrett's fellow convicts cut down his body and buried it beneath a tree. He was the first man executed in the new colony.

The next day, with rain still falling as if "heaven and earth was coming together" and after "the whole of the convicts sent a petition to the Governor begging that they might be forgiven," Phillip reprieved the three remaining culprits, whose punishment, instead, was banishment for a period to a small island in the harbor known as Pinchgut to live on bread and water.

The following day, two black convicts, Daniel Gordon and John Williams, were tried and convicted of stealing eighteen bottles of wine from the tent of a commissary clerk. Again, as Surgeon White described, Phillip showed mercy: "Williams being an ignorant black youth, the court recommended him to the governor as a proper object of mercy and he was accordingly pardoned. Gordon . . . had his sentence of death, while at the gallows, changed to banishment." The next day, Phillip pardoned another convict, about to be hanged for stealing flour, on condition that he would accept "the duty of the common executioner," which "reluctantly" he did. However, Phillip warned that thenceforth there would be no further reprieves for such crimes.

The indigenous people meanwhile kept their distance. Almost immediately on landing Phillip had dispatched a party under his second-in-command

Captain John Hunter to survey the harbor. During his explorations, Hunter encountered groups of Aboriginal people out fishing and watched them light fires in their canoes to cook their catch. They seemed friendly and the men accepted gifts, though they kept their women at a distance. Some allowed the sailors to examine their twelve-foot-long sharpened wooden spears, which they could hurl seventy yards. Their bodies were daubed white with, Hunter thought, "some degree of taste." In fact, Aboriginal people around Port Jackson commonly decorated themselves by smearing their bodies with red and white clay, fixing fish and animal bones in their hair, and making incisions in their skin called *gongara*.

A few days later, two elderly Aboriginal men carrying long spears approached Phillip's canvas house on the eastern side of the cove. Genuinely curious, as well as concerned to establish amicable relations, Phillip went to meet them. As a token of friendship and esteem he "bound some red bunting about their heads with some yellow tinfoil" and presented one with a hatchet. To Phillip's disappointment, the men refused to advance any farther, while one ostentatiously honed his spear point with an oyster shell. However, a young black boy off one of the ships who had come to look at them in turn excited their interest. Lieutenant Tench thought "they mistook him for one of themselves." They unfastened his shirt to examine his chest and, touching his hair, gestured that they would like some; so Surgeon Bowes Smyth cut off a lock. Tench was struck by this meeting between "the old and new lords of the soil" with "the old lords" not yet realizing that they had been dispossessed.

The "new lords" had been slower in establishing themselves than Phillip had anticipated. A particular problem was the lack of a plan for using the prisoners' labor to the settlement's best advantage. The convicts, Phillip wrote in his first reports home, were "naturally indolent, having none to attend them but overseers drawn from amongst themselves and who fear to exert any authority." He asked his officers to exhort the prisoners to work and remind them that slacking would be punished, but, as he told Lord Sydney on more than one occasion, the officers "decline[d] the least interference with the convicts," asserting that "they did not suppose that they were sent out to do more than garrison duty."

Compounding the problem, the prisoners were largely unskilled. Three months after arriving, Phillip complained to Lord Sydney that, since only twelve convicts were carpenters, "as many as can be procured from the ships have been hired to work on the hospital and storehouses." Also, their tools were inadequate. Though the First Fleet had been supplied with seven hundred axes, seven hundred hatchets, seven hundred spades, and seven hundred shovels, thanks to the contractors' penny-pinching profiteering they were of such poor quality that they blunted, buckled, and broke on the rock-hard ground.

Sydney Cove's verdant appearance—suggestive at first of rich English parkland bursting with useful timber—proved deceptive. Gum trees were so knotty the men struggled to cut them down. Eucalyptuses "from the size of a man's arm to 28-feet in circumference" were "either so very crooked, so rent or so rotten in the heart that we could scarcely get one sound or serviceable in a dozen." Surgeon White, anxious to see his hospital built, thought the timber "very unfit for the purpose of building . . . the worst wood that any country or climate ever produced." At least the tall, straight trunks of the succulent-looking giant cabbage-tree palms clustering along the stream in Sydney Cove made good supports for huts, but finding suitable materials to make walls was difficult. Interlaced saplings packed with mud—the centuries-old "wattle and daub" technique—proved too flimsy, collapsing in the heavy rains and blustering winds of those first weeks that caused Clark to write with horror of "terrible" nights of thunder and lightning and of dark "revengeful" skies.*

Phillip found a solution by asking convict James Bloodworth, a builder in his former life, to look for suitable clay and he discovered good deposits of red clay suitable for shaping and baking into bricks. At last, they could erect solid buildings, especially secure store-houses because provisions piled up in tents were far too vulnerable to theft. However, a new problem presented itself: The colony had no lime to make mortar. The only remedy was to grind up oyster and cockle shells "for burning into lime"—a slow process to which the women convicts were put, producing only limited mortar of very poor quality.

Female prisoners were allotted other building tasks, such as whittling wooden pegs to hold tiles in place and going into the bush to cut vegetation for thatching. Others became servants to officers—sometimes forming liaisons with them—or laundresses, going down to the creeks to wash the convicts' clothes. Sexual attacks on women continued. In March, two convicts were flogged for lying in wait for women as they went to wash after work.

---

*Since golden mimosa saplings were used, the mimosa became known as "wattle," the name it still bears in Australia—where it is now the national flower.

An underlying factor behind the men's behavior, as Phillip appreciated, was "the very small proportion of females" which "makes the sending out of an additional number absolutely necessary." However, he humanely dismissed the idea mooted by Joseph Banks and others in the early stages of the transportation project of sending "for women from the islands" since "in our present situation" this "would answer no other purpose than that of bringing them to pine away in misery." For some of the convict women themselves, the primitive conditions, hardships, and uncertainties were too much. Four fled into the bush, only to be shot at by marines who quickly recaptured three of them. The fourth vanished without a trace.

In early March, Phillip led a ten-day expedition to explore an inlet north of Port Jackson that Cook had named Broken Bay. Here he came across several groups of Aboriginal people, noticing that unlike those around the settlement, the women and children "had the little finger of the left hand taken off at the second joint, the stump of which was as well covered as if the operation had been performed by a surgeon." He and his companions also came across corpses laid out as if for ritual open air burial and heard Aboriginal people using the high, shrill call "Coo-ee" to communicate with each other in the bush.

Returning to Sydney Cove, Phillip found that HMS *Supply* was back from Norfolk Island having deposited King and his small band of colonists but bearing the surprising news that no flax whatever had been found on the island, though tall and magnificent pine trees suitable for masts indeed grew in profusion. Also, on the return voyage the *Supply* had discovered a crescent-shaped volcanic island that its commander, Lieutenant Henry Ball, had named Lord Howe Island after the First Lord of the Admiralty. The island was inhabited by large numbers of turtles—a possible valuable food source for the colony. Phillip at once dispatched the *Supply* to collect some but too late—the turtles had vanished.

By March 25—two months after the new arrivals had come ashore—all stores from the transports *Charlotte*, *Scarborough*, and *Lady Penrhyn* had been landed and the three ships, now chartered by the East India Company, were preparing to sail for Canton in China to fill their holds with tea. Phillip's officials took stock of the colony's supplies and the result was so worrying that Phillip cut the beef and pork rations. Unappetizing though the food was— the meat was tough, the butter rancid, and the flour and rice heaved with weevils—both convicts and guards regarded the reduction with dismay. As Tench described, "fresh provisions were becoming scarcer than in a blockaded town. The little live stock, which with so heavy an expense and through so many difficulties, we had brought on shore, prudence forbade us to use; and fish, which on our arrival, and for a short time after had been tolerable plenty, were become so scarce, as to be rarely seen at the tables of the first among us. Had it not been for a stray kangaroo, which fortune now and then threw in our way, we should have been utter strangers to the taste of fresh food. Thus situated, the scurvy began its usual ravages." As well as kangaroo—to Clark "the most extraordinary animal that I ever saw" and in White's view definitely "considered as a dainty"—broths made from stewed parakeets and crows were also eagerly consumed. Captain James Campbell of the marines, who had decided that the scheme of "forcing a settlement in such a country as this" while "romantic" was thoroughly misguided, wrote: "I am a perfect stranger to what our government intends saying of it, but I am myself fully convinced that the nation would save money by feeding their convicts at home upon venison and claret, clothing them in purple and gold, rather than provide for them here the worst fare that can be thought of."

Despite the land's fertile appearance, many of the newly planted crops withered or rotted. Nor did the colony's livestock prosper. Unable to withstand the heat, humidity, and inadequate diet, sheep sickened and died. In the increasingly pinched circumstances, fish provided a vital food source, though many prisoners were unused to eating fish in general and certainly not the rainbow-colored exotica in the harbor that were, Tench wrote, "unknown in Europe" but "extremely delicious and many highly beautiful." Since, according to Judge-Advocate Collins, William Bryant had "been bred from his youth to the business of a fisherman in the western part of England," Phillip had given him "the direction and management" of the colony's fishing boats, including selecting men to help him handle them and to haul the heavy drag nets with their weighted bottoms and top edges buoyed by floats known as seines. As a reward, Bryant could keep a proportion of the fish he caught and live with his new wife, Mary, and her daughter, Charlotte, in their own hut on the east side of the cove, well away from the main convict camps—a remarkably privileged position. Collins thought Bryant "wanted for nothing that was necessary, or that was suitable to a person of his description and situation."

Since Mary had grown up in Fowey—described by a contemporary as "a colony of fishermen" with air thick with "the effluvia" of pilchards —and was herself a fisherman's daughter, she too probably had useful skills. In Fowey women and children made seines and ropes and stood on the rocks "to watch the course of the fish," earning themselves the name of "'huers' from their setting up a hue to the fishermen." Mary probably also helped her father fish. If so, she would have known how to handle a boat in difficult conditions. A visitor to Fowey who rowed out to watch the fishermen at work wrote that "the waves drove with such strength through the mouth of the river that no small exertion was required to reach the distant fisher boats which were generally stationed in ten fathoms water and clear of all breakers."

Tench himself sometimes assisted at the nets, doing "many nights of public service from 4 P.M. to 8 A.M. hauling the seine in every part of the harbour of Port Jackson, and after a circuit of many miles and twenty or thirty hauls, seldom more than a hundred pounds of fish were taken, only seldom was there a glut." The problem was not only lack of fish—the new arrivals had not yet learned how numbers fluctuated with the seasons— but "the scarcity of boats." Phillip would have liked to build more but the carpenters were still busy constructing huts.

On May 1 the *Charlotte*, *Lady Penrhyn*, and *Scarborough* sailed for China. Several men tried to stow away and at least two—not convicts but sailors off the *Sirius* and the *Supply*—succeeded. Yet far from leaving deprivation behind, by the time the *Lady Penrhyn* reached the Kermadec Islands, northeast of New Zealand, some of her crew were too weak to stand and many had "swelled gums, the flesh exceeding black and hard, a contraction of the sinews, with a total debility"—the unmistakable signs of scurvy, which caused her to call in at Tahiti not long before the *Bounty*'s arrival there.

In June, Edward Corbett, the convict in charge of the settlement's cattle, vanished into the bush to avoid being tried for theft, leaving four cows and two bulls untended. They wandered off and were not seen again for several years, by which time they had become wild. Corbett himself returned nineteen days later to the settlement after attempting unsuccessfully to live among the Aboriginal people, who, though not hostile, had simply ignored him. He was tried, sentenced to death, and hanged the next day, together with twenty-year-old gentleman thief Sam Payton, who had taken advantage of celebrations to mark George III's birthday—when every marine was given an extra pint of porter and every convict half a pint of spirits—to loot the officers' tents. Surgeon White thought it curious how "in the agonizing moments of the separation of the soul from the body" the two men "seemed to embrace each other."

Not long after, in mid-July, the merchantmen *Alexander*, *Friendship*, *Borrowdale*, and *Prince of Wales* sailed for England, to be followed by the two remaining transports the *Golden Grove* and the *Fishburn*, leaving the colony with only two ships, the naval vessels *Sirius* and *Supply*. The departure of so many men for the "civilised" world was impossible to behold "without emotion," Tench wrote, "since on their speedy arrival in England perhaps hinged our fate; by hastening our supplies to us." Tench was one of the few to find any beauty in Sydney Cove—the shimmering expanse of the harbor, the densely wooded inlets from which bright-colored cockatoos and budgerigars rose in clouds, the highly scented shrubs "most of them entirely new to a European" and the tangled tawny infinity of the bush. Most of his comrades were desperate to leave and said so in the letters they sent home. Major Ross complained that "in the whole world there is not a worse country" and conjured a place the antithesis of Tahiti: "so very barren and forbidding . . . here nature is reversed; and if not so, she is nearly worn out, for almost all the seeds we have put into the ground has rotted" so that all but two who came out with him were "now most earnestly wishing to get away."

Ross also criticized Phillip, resenting what he perceived as Phillip's refusal to consult and unwillingness to delegate. He wrote to Undersecretary Evan Nepean that "what little we want, even to a single nail, we must not send to the Commissary for it, but must apply to His Excellency." Captain James Campbell, one of the irascible Ross's few friends, complained in similar vein that "this man [Phillip] will be everything himself—Never that I have heard of [does he] communicate any part of his plan for establishing a colony or carrying on his work to anyone—much less, consult them."

Phillip's own dispatches to London reveal his anxieties about the colony's future. To Lord Sydney, he expressed his hope that few convicts would be sent out that year or next unless they brought with them at least two years' provisions. He also cautioned against sending convicts on one ship and provisions on another since if the supply ship was lost it would be "fatal." To Nepean he wrote that "if fifty farmers were sent out with their families, they would do more in one year in rendering this colony independent of the mother country, as to provisions, than a thousand convicts." He pointed out that, since the captains of the transports had departed with the paperwork they had been given on first taking the convicts aboard, he himself lacked information about when their sentences would expire: "Some of them, by their own account, have little more than a year to remain and, I am told, will apply for permission to return to England, or to go to India, in such ships as may be willing to receive them." Since any time-expired convicts choosing to remain would require support for at least two years, the settlement would greatly benefit if "the most abandoned and useless were permitted to go to China, in any ship that may stop here."

As the last merchantman sailed out through the harbor's Heads, Phillip could only hope that the British government would respond quickly to his requests for further supplies, indeed that they might already be on their way. The colony lacked the most basic equipment. Surgeon John White's hospital, although now brick-built, had already blown down once because the mortar used to build it was so weak and was without any "blankets and sheets . . . although they are essential and absolutely necessary." Both "troops and convicts" were suffering from the effects of a salty diet and badly in need of "sugar, sago, oatmeal, barley, rice, currants, different spices, vinegar and portable soup, tamarinds, raisins and more saucepans," White also complained. At the same time, growing numbers of marines and prisoners alike were succumbing not only to scurvy but to cholera, flu, and infestations of parasites. Venereal disease—that scourge in Tahiti—was gaining "such a footing in this settlement, that I now doubt if it will ever be done away," Phillip wrote. Nevertheless, he tried. Collins described how the governor ordered "any man or woman having and concealing this disorder should receive corporal punishment, and be put upon a short allowance of provisions for six months." The Aboriginal people of course had no defenses against this and the other diseases spreading through the new arrivals and the Europeans began to find their corpses everywhere, along the beach and deep in the bush.

Though relatively peaceful at first, relations between the Aboriginal people and the Berewalgal, the British, began to deteriorate. In Tahiti, the Europeans regarded the islanders as thieves. In Port Jackson, as with so much else, it was the reverse. The indigenous people were startled by the newcomers' casual appropriation of their traditional hunting and fishing grounds and tried to stop them, sometimes challenging fishing parties and taking away their catch. Theft of their belongings also bewildered and angered them since, as David Collins noted, they were "accustomed to leave [them] under the rocks or loose and scattered upon the beaches." The Aboriginals were well used to bartering, using networks extending across vast distances to obtain raw materials and objects not available locally, but not to having their possessions stolen.

Before the transports had sailed, their crews, eager for souvenirs that would find a good market back home, had been especially guilty, stealing four-pronged fishing spears tipped with bone, teeth, or stingray spurs; fishing nets; fishing hooks made of wood or shells; and boomerangs. Despite Phillip's express prohibitions, the thieving continued, prompting the Aboriginals, in turn, to make off with stray shovels, spades, and pickaxes. Some also threw stones at convict work parties sent to dig red clay for Bloodworth's bricks on what had become known as Brickfield Hill.

On May 21, Aboriginals had attacked two young convicts, William Ayres and Peter Burn, both recovering from scurvy, who had gone into the bush to gather the small pointed leaves of the smilax glyciphylla—"a creeping kind of vine" whose leaves were used to make "sweet tea" that tasted pleasantly "like the liquorice root." Toward nightfall Ayres limped into the camp, a spear protruding from his back that Surgeon White found very hard to extract since it was "barbed and stuck so very fast that it would admit of no motion." By "dilating the wound to a considerable length and depth" he finally succeeded, finding that the spear "had penetrated the flesh nearly three inches." Ayres recovered. Of Burn, who had run into the undergrowth when Ayres was attacked, nothing could be found except his clothes, which were "torn, bloody and pierced with spears." A convict later came across his burned head in a bay near Sydney Cove.

Suspecting the attack was revenge for abuses inflicted on the Aboriginals, Phillip wisely and humanely forbade reprisals. In particular, he had heard rumors that Aboriginal women had been raped by some convicts. Though these women did not excite quite the same passions among the Europeans as had the women of Tahiti, a young surgeon of the *Sirius* thought: "There is in some of them a proportion, a softness, a roundness and plumpness in their limbs and bodies . . . that would excite tender and amorous sensations even in the frigid breast of a philosopher." Tench agreed with Phillip that "the unprovoked outrages committed upon them by unprincipled individuals among us caused the evils we had experienced."

However, a week later, one convict William Oakey, who had been cutting rushes for thatch, was found "most dreadfully mangled and butchered" among some mangrove swamps. Oakey was "transfixed through the breast with one of their spears." Two further spears were "sticking in him to a depth which must have proved mortal. His skull was divided . . . so much that his brains easily found a passage through. His eyes were out, but these might have been picked away by birds." The body of Samuel Davis, who had been working with him, was found virtually unmarked. White concluded he had hidden in the mangroves when the attack came only to die of "fear united with the cold and wet."

Again, some of the more enlightened questioned whether the Aboriginals had had cause to murder the men. Captain John Hunter noted that the two convicts had taken hatchets and bill-hooks with them, writing, "They might have been rash enough to use violence with some of the natives." Surgeon White too was "strongly inclined" to believe the Aboriginals must have been "provoked and injured by the convicts," while Lieutenant William Bradley thought the attack was retribution for the recent killing of an Aboriginal man in a canoe—perhaps the first death of an Aboriginal at the hands of the newcomers—writing, "I have no doubt but that this native having been murdered occasioned their seeking revenge."

This time, however, Governor Phillip decided he needed to discover whether the attackers—if he could locate them—had genuine grievances and, if they did not, "inflict a memorable and exemplary punishment." Taking Surgeon White, together with a small party of marines and two armed convicts who knew the bush to act as guides, he followed an Aboriginal track from where the men had died to the northwestern arm of Botany Bay. Here he found some three hundred people—men, women, and children—their canoes drawn up on the shore. Though the men had clubs, spears, and throwing sticks, they allowed Phillip—himself unarmed—to approach and present gifts of fish hooks, beads, and a mirror. As he did so, White wrote, the women danced and—as others had written of the Tahitian women—"threw themselves into some not very decent attitudes." A man showed Phillip what was clearly an ax wound to his shoulder while another gestured that one of the rush-gatherers had murdered an Aboriginal by cutting his stomach.

Deeply disturbed by what he had learned, Phillip returned to Sydney Cove and issued orders that only armed groups of six or more would thenceforth be allowed into the hinterland. However, he blamed the convicts, not the Aboriginal people, writing of the latter, "I think better of them from having been more with them." In his eyes, the Aboriginals had the same basic rights as anyone else but his attitude toward them—especially his continued refusal to permit reprisals—angered many. A female convict wrote that "the savages still continue to do us all the injury they can which makes the soldiers' duty very hard, and much dissatisfaction among the officers."

However, by October, Phillip's chief preoccupation was to secure further food supplies for the ten-month-old colony. The government farm he had established was not prospering. The convicts had on his orders sown wheat and corn, but most seeds had failed to germinate, leaving a crop so small it barely provided seed for the next season's planting. Watkin Tench, doubtless capturing the anxiety of many, thought "the dread of want in a country destitute of natural resource is ever peculiarly terrible." With provisions running low, Phillip cut the weekly flour ration by one pound. He also decided to send the *Sirius* to Cape Town to fetch grain and whatever flour and other provisions she could carry. To increase her speed and cargo capacity, he had her guns brought ashore, together with all her ammunition. On October 2, 1788, the *Sirius* departed just as the *Bounty* was about to arrive in the fabled paradise of pleasure and plenty—Tahiti.

KNIGHTS OF TAHITI

On October 26, 1788, with the *Bounty* safely moored in Matavai Bay, yet more Tahitians—men, women and children—clambered aboard with gifts of hogs and coconuts, though not, Bligh observed, breadfruit, which seemed worryingly scarce. The islanders asked eagerly for news of "Captain Cook, Sir Joseph Banks, and many of their former friends" and in particular whether it was true, as sailors from a ship that had called in three months earlier had told them, that Cook was dead. The ship was of course the *Lady Penrhyn*. David Nelson, fluent in Tahitian, assured them not only that this was incorrect and Cook was alive and well in "Pretanee" but that Bligh was his son, which Bligh thought "seemed to please them very much."

Bligh enquired after Omai, the young man who had so fascinated London society. On his final voyage Cook had left him in comfort on the nearby island of Huahine. Omai, the islanders told him, had died of a disease sent by the gods. Later Bligh learned that Omai had fought in a great battle against the combined armies of two neighboring islands, using the muskets he had been given by the British to assure victory, but after peace was concluded had died of natural causes.

That first night, worried about theft, Bligh insisted that the male Tahitians return ashore but allowed any women who wished to remain. Many did—the status of having a lover from "Pretanee" still outweighing the pockmarked skin, bad teeth, and poor physiques of many of the *Bounty*'s sailors as they had the dubious attractions of the *Lady Penrhyn*'s scurvy-ridden crew. Some delighted men found themselves with two women apiece.

Early next morning, before more islanders arrived as he knew they would, Bligh prudently worked the ship closer into the bay to anchor just a quarter of a mile off Point Venus. As the news of the *Bounty*'s presence spread, chiefs began appearing to be greeted courteously by Bligh in Tahitian. On his earlier visit with Cook he had learned a little of the language and on the voyage out Nelson had taught him more. Before long emissaries arrived from the man Bligh most wished to see—Tu, paramount chief of the Matavai region—who presented pigs and plantain trees as tokens of his friendship, and assured Bligh the chief was on his way. While he waited, Bligh went ashore, crunching over the black lava sand to revisit familiar haunts, including the spot where on Cook's third visit his shore party had pitched their tents. Returning to the *Bounty*, he found that the thieving had already begun. His men had caught a Tahitian trying to make off with a tin pot. A chief who had been escorting Bligh flew into such a violent rage that, Bligh wrote, it was only "with some difficulty that the thief escaped with his life." The chief told Bligh that if he ever caught another thief he should "order him to be tied up and punished with a severe flogging."

A further messenger from Tu arrived bearing the portrait of Captain Cook, painted by John Webber, Cook's artist on his last expedition, which Cook had presented to Tu with a request that it be shown to any visiting English ship "as a token of friendship." Since then it had become something of an icon before which the islanders made offerings to *"Toote Errie no Otaheiti,"* "Cook, high chief of Tahiti." The frame had been damaged and, the messenger told Bligh, Tu wished it repaired.

The next day Tu himself arrived. As a gesture of courtesy Bligh sent a boat under Fletcher Christian's command to bring him on board. The thirty-seven-year-old chief, "not less than six foot 4 inches in height and proportionately stout"—in fact over 280 pounds—arrived with his almost equally large twenty-four-year-old wife Iddeeah, a former champion wrestler, and a retinue of attendants. After Tu had bent to join noses—"the customary manner of saluting" between friends—with the much shorter Bligh, the chief informed him that he was now known formally as Tynah, since the name "Tu" had devolved to his eldest son, who, in line with Tahitian tradition, had on his birth become titular paramount chief. The child was only six and his father was continuing to rule but as regent on his son's behalf.*

Determined to establish good relations as soon as possible, Bligh presented Tu with a selection of the iron goods so sought after in Tahiti—"hatchets, small adzes, files, gimlets, saws" as well as looking glasses and the red

---

*To avoid confusion this book still refers to the father as Tu.

feathers—in this case flamingo wings from Cape Town—highly prized in Tahiti as offerings to Oro, god of war and fertility. To Iddeeah, Bligh gave earrings, necklaces, and beads until this "animated and intelligent" woman made clear that such gifts were well enough but she too had "a desire also for iron." Tu and Iddeeah asked to inspect the entire ship, including the dark, cramped cabin on the lower deck where Bligh slept. The consequence, as he had anticipated, was that "they took a fancy to so many things, that they got from me nearly as much more as I had before given them." When his royal visitors asked him to fire the ship's cannon, he also obliged and later entertained them to dinner. Tu ate first and because of his great rank was fed by an attendant, amazing Bligh by his consumption. "Indeed," Bligh wrote, there was "little reason to complain of want of appetite in any of my guests." As well as his dinner, during the time he spent with Bligh that day Tu also "ate four times of roast pork."

Bligh had already sent Nelson and Brown ashore to look for breadfruit trees and been encouraged by their reports that they were plentiful. However, he waited for the right moment to introduce breadfruit into the conversation with Tu and during that first meeting said nothing. Next day when he paid a courtesy visit to the chief—suffering in heat that to a man in naval uniform complete with hat "was scarce bearable"—he still said nothing, focusing instead on "the great numbers of children . . . and little ones," whom he delighted with presents of beads. The opportunity for which he was patiently waiting came several days later when he suggested to Tu and Iddeeah that he should visit Oparre, half an hour by boat to the west of Matavai Bay, to pay his respects to Tu's eldest son—the new paramount chief—who lived there. His real motive was "to see if Nelson would be able to procure [breadfruit] plants there."

During the short voyage, Tu told Bligh what had happened on the island since Cook's last visit—how "63 moons" after Cook's departure, warriors from a neighboring island had allied with men from another part of Tahiti to attack Tu and his people in Oparre. Many had been killed, forcing Tu and his family to flee into the mountains "leaving all their property to the mercy of the victorious party, who destroyed almost everything which they found not convenient to take away with them." The attackers had killed and eaten some of the cattle Cook had presented to Tu and driven the others away. As Tu related his grievances—harping in particular on the damage done to Cook's livestock—Bligh realized that he hoped "I would take vengeance on the people who had deprived him of them." He also realized how glad Tu was that the *Bounty* had come to Matavai Bay. The ship's arrival gave him both prestige and protection. He begged Bligh not to think of leaving Matavai, promising "you shall be supplied plentifully with everything you want. All here are your friends, and friends of King George: if you go to the other islands, you will have everything stolen from you."

Bligh saw his chance. Pointing out the "valuable presents" King George had sent, he asked, "Will not you, Tu, send something to King George in return?" "I will send him any thing I have," Tu replied, and began listing "the different articles in his power, among which he mentioned the bread-fruit." Just as Bligh had hoped and planned, he had achieved his objective but in a manner that "had every appearance of being undesigned and accidental." Bligh replied thoughtfully that breadfruit trees might indeed be what the king would like and, "much delighted to find it so easily in his power to send anything that would be well-received by King George," Tu promised a goodly supply.

Nelson had convinced Bligh that the seedlings would fare best if first reared in pots ashore. The next day Bligh moved the *Bounty* even closer to Point Venus, where in 1777 Cook had set up camp. To the Tahitians this was "holy ground" and they courteously invited Bligh to establish his shore camp on the exact spot. He at once sent a landing party to erect "a lodgement for the plants" and, with Tu's agreement, declared an exclusion zone "within which the natives were not to enter without leave." All the while, Bligh was still congratulating himself that "instead of appearing to receive a favour" he had convinced Tu and Iddeeah that "I was doing them a kindness in carrying the plants, as a present from them to the *Earee Rahie no Britanee* [Britain's supreme ruler]."

The *Bounty*'s mainsail and mizzenmast were brought ashore to be used in the construction of thatched shelters to protect the plants from sun, wind, and rain and his men turned some of the smaller sails into tents. By early November, the gathering of breadfruit seedlings was well under way, with Nelson and Brown finding willing helpers among the islanders who, Bligh noted with satisfaction, well understood how to care for the plants. To one side of the encampment, Nelson also laid out a garden where he planted a fig tree, pineapple plants, melons, and rose seeds brought from Cape Town. The nursery itself was guarded by a shore party commanded by Christian, assisted by young Heywood and four armed seamen working in rotation. Christian, Heywood, and the two gardeners were living permanently ashore as was Peckover, on his fifth visit to Tahiti. As a fluent Tahitian speaker with a good understanding of local customs, Peckover had been nominated by Bligh to oversee all trading with the locals.

Relations between the islanders and the *Bounty* men were good. Tahitians began bringing their broken iron tools—acquired from previous European visitors—to be mended by Coleman the armorer at his forge. The sailors' health rapidly improved as ailments—scurvy-related or not—disappeared with ample quantities of fresh fruit, meat, and coconut milk. The ship's cooks were soon overseeing the salting of hogs ready for the return voyage. With "each man allowed two pounds of the bones and such parts as were not fit for salting per day," as Morrison wrote, it was a time of plenty for all after the deprivations of the long voyage.

The Tahitian women continued to be everything the sailors had hoped and anticipated. Bligh did not object to the women living aboard and permitted his ordinary seamen ashore two at a time with no restrictions other than those he had laid down about respecting the islanders and not trading on their own account. Like Cook, he does not seem to have taken a lover, even though Tu hinted that because of his association with Cook and friendship with himself, Bligh could enjoy Iddeeah's sexual favors if he wished. Bligh also learned to his amazement from Tu's brother that Iddeeah slept not only with her husband but also with his servant—the man who fed him morsels of food at mealtimes. Some like James Morrison and George Stewart soon found a favorite woman and settled into something close to domesticity. Fletcher Christian formed a liaison with a strikingly beautiful chief's daughter, Mauatua, whom his fellow crewmen would nickname "Mainmast" for her height, but whom he called Isabella. During their stay on the island both he and Heywood were among those who had to pay the surgeon for treating their "venereals."

As well as their women, most of the crew soon acquired a special male friend or *taio*. Many—Christian and Heywood included—followed the Tahitian fashion of having themselves painfully tattooed, often on torsos, arms, and buttocks. Heywood chose the three-legged symbol of the Isle of Man for his right leg, while Morrison had the Order of the Garter tattooed around his left, complete with its motto *Honi soit qui mal y pense*—"Shame on him who evil thinks." Together with Christian, Stewart, and Martin, he also had tattooed on his left breast the star of Saint George—perhaps emulating the secret society, the Knights of Tahiti, formed by some of Cook's sailors on his second voyage.

As one languid day faded into the next, mindful of Banks's strictures that the health of the breadfruit was paramount, Bligh kept a close eye on the burgeoning nursery, logging with satisfaction the growing number of flourishing seedlings and praising the "very diligent and attentive" Nelson. At the same time, he was reacquainting himself with a place that with its clear, shimmering, turquoise lagoons, luscious vegetation, and attractive, welcoming inhabitants seemed to him truly "the Paradise of the World . . . if happiness could result from situation and convenience, here it is to be found in the highest perfection. I have seen many parts of the world, but Tahiti is capable of being preferable to them all."

Escorted almost constantly by Tu, he observed and documented the lives of the islanders, from their elaborate burial rites, during which an eye would be scooped from the corpse, to how women gave birth—Iddeeah personally demonstrated how Tahitian women squatted between the supporting arms of a male attendant, who stroked the woman's straining belly—to the Tahitian calendar. He began work on a Tahitian dictionary and even noted recipes for baking the delicious puddings of plantain and of breadfruit that the chiefs often sent as gifts.

Though Bligh saw much to enchant him, he was also sometimes shocked. Invited by Tu to one of the islanders' great celebratory feasts—a *heiva*—in the shade of a grove of breadfruit trees, he sat wrapped in a length of white bark cloth next to the similarly draped portrait of Cook as the festivities began. The men started "jumping and throwing their legs and arms into violent and odd motions, which the women kept time with, and as they were conveniently clothed for the purpose, their persons were generally exposed to full view, frequently standing on one leg and keeping the other up, giving themselves the most lascivious and wanton motions." The performers were some distance away but to Bligh's discomfort "were directed to come nearer, and they accordingly advanced with their clothes up, and went through the same wanton gestures."

On another occasion, four men started distorting their penises before him, one "with both hands seizing the extremity of the scrotum he pulled it out with such force the penis went in totally out of sight and the scrotum became shockingly distended (as far as the knees)." It was a demonstration of the generative powers of the penis, an incarnation of the source of life, but too much for Bligh who, to "much laughter amongst the spectators," asked the performers to stop. From his previous visit, Bligh knew about the islanders' uninhibited sexual exuberance and had some understanding that it was linked to their religious and cultural beliefs. Even so, he deplored their "numerous sensual and beastly acts of gratification," including sodomy and oral sex, complaining that "even the mouths of women are not exempt from the pollution, and many other ways they have of gratifying their beastly inclinations."

The aspect of Tahitian life that most disturbed Bligh was the society of the *ariori*, which he had first encountered with Cook and to which many young aristocratic young Tahitians—male and female—belonged. Though he knew the *arioi* were highly respected and the male members were formidable warriors, their custom of strangling their newborn young because they were not allowed to have children and remain within the *arioi* perplexed him. Tu told Bligh that, while a young *arioi* himself, "his first-born child was killed as soon as it came into the world." Bligh also learned that Tu's sister and her husband had "had eight children, every one of which was destroyed as soon as born." Yet, Bligh noted, this couple had adopted as their heir a nephew "of whom they are excessively fond."

A puzzled Bligh sought some rational explanation for the *ariois'* casual infanticide. Since the Tahitians were clearly not "devoid of natural affection," killing their infants was not, he decided, "an act of choice in the parents" but perhaps the result of "some barbarous superstition." He wondered whether it might be linked to the island's relatively dense population, suggesting that in a place that until recently "probably had not an idea of the existence of other lands," it was "not unnatural that an increasing population should occasion apprehensions of universal distress."

Celibacy was an obvious solution but he had another, more novel one, which, "however fanciful . . . seems to merit some attention," he wrote:

> While we see among these islands so great a waste of the human species, that numbers are born only to die; and, at the same time, a large continent so near to them as New Holland, in which there is so great a waste of land uncultivated, and almost destitute of inhabitants; it naturally occurs, how greatly the two countries might be made to benefit each other: and gives occasion to regret that the islanders are not instructed in the means of emigrating to New Holland, which seems as if designed by nature to serve as an asylum for the superflux of inhabitants in the islands. Such a plan of emigration, if rendered practicable to them, might not only be the means of abolishing the horrid custom of destroying children, as it would remove the plea of necessity, but might lead to other

important purposes. A great continent would be converted from a desert to a populous country; a number of our fellow-creatures would be saved: the inhabitants of the islands would become more civilised; and it is not improbable, but that our colonies in New Holland would derive so much benefit as to more than repay any trouble or expense, that might be incurred in endeavouring to promote so humane a plan.

Why not, Bligh asked, bring "a people without land to a land without people?"

Much of Bligh's time was taken up with entertaining Tu, his family, and other chiefs on whose continued goodwill the expedition's success depended. Tu and Iddeeah frequently slept aboard the *Bounty* and constantly badgered Bligh that the next ship to come out should bring further presents from King George—"large axes, files, saws, cloth of all kinds, hats, chairs, and bedsteads, with arms, ammunition, and in short every thing he could think of mentioning," Bligh grumbled.

Though Tu tried to prevent pilfering it still happened: Small metal items constantly disappeared, creating tension both with the islanders and among the crew. Bligh thought most incidents owed more to the negligence of his crew than to the Tahitians' love of thieving. When Tahitians extracted the metal gudgeon from the rudder of the *Bounty*'s large cutter under the nose of Alexander Smith, who was supposed to be guarding it, Bligh decided to make an example and sentenced him to a dozen lashes. Tu tried to intercede and Tahitian women wailed and slashed at themselves with sharks' teeth to reinforce his pleas, but Bligh would not relent. On December 1 a more serious theft occurred that Bligh again blamed squarely on his crew, writing that due to the "remissness of my officers and people at the tent, they suffered the boat's rudder to be stolen." He did not record whether he reprimanded Fletcher Christian and the shore party but it seems inconceivable that he did not.

The prickly Purcell then presented Bligh with yet another challenge to his authority. When a Tahitian to whom Bligh had presented a hatchet requested a whetstone on which to sharpen it, Bligh asked Purcell to fashion such a stone with his tools. The carpenter refused point-blank, insisting to a flabbergasted Bligh that "I will not cut the stone for it will spoil my chisel," which was his own property. Again, Bligh's options for punishing Purcell were limited. In his log he wrote, "This man having before shewn his mutinous and insolent behaviour, I was under the necessity to confine him to his cabin." It was light punishment for open defiance of a direct order from his commander and a sharp contrast to the twelve lashes Bligh awarded seaman Matthew Thompson the same day for "insolence and disobedience of orders."

If Bligh was growing dissatisfied with his men, they too had their grievances, especially about what they considered his profiteering at their expense by his prohibition of private trading. During the *Bounty*'s stay, Bligh set up by the ship's gangway an account book in which, after it had been counted or weighed, John Samuel, his clerk, noted every item of food brought aboard by the crewmen. Ninety percent went to the ship's stores. Morrison also alleged that

> the market for hogs beginning now to slacken, Mr. Bligh seized on all that came to the ship, big and small, dead or alive, taking them as his property and serving them as the ship's allowance at one pound per man per day. He also seized on those belonging to the master and killed them for the ship's use, though he had more than forty . . . on board of his own . . . When the master spoke to Mr. Bligh, telling him the hogs were his property, Mr. Bligh told him that "everything was his as soon as it was on board, and that he would take nine tenths of any man's property, and let him see who dared say anything to the contrary." Those of the seamen were seized without ceremony, and it became a favour for a man to get a pound extra of his own hog.

When the Tahitians discovered that Bligh was seizing all the hogs, they became "very shy of bringing a hog in sight of Lieutenant Bligh either on board or on shore." Instead they smuggled "provisions to their friends . . . cutting the pigs up, wrapping them in leaves, and covering the meat with breadfruit in the baskets, and sometimes with peeled coconuts." According to Morrison, Bligh never suspected their artifice and "by this means provisions were still plentiful."

With the western monsoon that runs from November to April fast approaching, the Tahitians warned Bligh of the risks to the *Bounty* in her current mooring. Though at other times the reef protected Matavai Bay from the pounding Pacific rollers, the bay was vulnerable to sudden violent seasonal storms. On December 5, wild seas surged over the reef, washing over the *Bounty* which, in Bligh's words, "rolled in a most violent manner." As the rain pelted, Bligh had no option but to release the defiant Purcell from his confinement to secure the hatches.

The next day, with the surf still running high, the *Bounty*'s men found it impossible to get ashore themselves but were astonished to see Tu and Iddeeah battling out to them in a canoe, bringing both food and news that the shore party and the precious breadfruit had nearly been washed away. The danger had come not from the sea but from a large river flowing down from the mountainous interior that disgorged into the bay close by the encampment. The rain-swollen river would have flooded the nursery but for the resourcefulness of Nelson and Brown, who dug out a channel to divert the water away.

A few days later, Bligh sent for his surgeon to treat a young Tahitian boy injured by one of the *Bounty*'s boats, only to be told that Huggan was in such a drunken stupor he could not stand. In fact, Huggan was dying. Later that day, Huggan's assistant, Ledward, informed Bligh that the surgeon had fallen into a coma and asked leave to move him into the great cabin to give him more air. Fryer, assisted by some seamen, descended to his tiny cubicle above the hold to fetch him, only to find that somehow Huggan had regained sufficient consciousness to struggle up on deck, where he had again collapsed. Though his colleagues laid him in the great cabin and tried to force coconut milk between his lips, he died that evening.

Bligh attributed Huggan's death to "drunkenness and indolence," adding that "exercise was a thing he could not bear an idea of . . . sleeping was the way he spent his time and he accustomed himself to breathe so little fresh air and was so filthy in his person that he became latterly a nuisance." They buried Huggan at Point Venus and affixed a board bearing an inscription to his memory to a nearby tree. Ledward, now appointed the *Bounty*'s Acting Surgeon, purchased his predecessor's instruments and medicine when, following naval custom, Bligh auctioned off Huggan's possessions, the proceeds going to the deceased's family.

To find safer mooring, Bligh contemplated sailing across to nearby Moorea but an anxious Tu urged an alternative: Oparre, the settlement just a few miles along the coast of Tahiti where Bligh had visited Tu's young son and where, he assured Bligh, a small deep bay would offer ample protection from waves and winds. After sending Fryer in one of the ship's boats to take soundings between Matavai and Oparre, Bligh agreed. On Christmas Eve, Nelson's nursery on Point Venus was dismantled and 774 healthy seedlings were taken aboard the *Bounty*, carefully protected from saltwater spray. Bligh sent Christian ahead to Oparre in the launch with all the equipment from the shore camp and orders to set up a fresh base there.

He was then to sail back to the reef at the harbor's mouth to help guide the *Bounty* safely in.

At ten thirty A.M. on Christmas Day, the *Bounty* set out for her new mooring, with Tu, Iddeeah, and a large entourage on board and Fryer on watch high in the rigging with orders to alert Bligh to any danger that "might be in our way." As the *Bounty* approached Oparre, Christian was, as ordered, waiting in the launch to show the way through the reef. However, he allowed the launch to fall into the *Bounty*'s lee, where suddenly losing the wind, it fell back so that, in Bligh's words, the *Bounty* "shot past" to ground on a part of the reef that, Morrison claimed, had escaped Fryer's sight. Bligh took some moments to realize what had happened. Then, with dark storm clouds rolling in, he sent the women aboard ashore and asked Tu's men to help free the ship while he himself clambered down into the launch. Ordering its crew to row close to the *Bounty*'s trapped bows, he succeeded in taking hold of the bower anchor and bringing it astern in an attempt to pull the *Bounty* off the reef. At the same time, he ordered Fryer, assisted by Christian—now back aboard the *Bounty*—to lower the kedge anchor, designed specifically for use when ships are aground, astern on the port side. Finally, as Bligh had hoped, the *Bounty* floated free.

Although probably embarrassed that Tu had witnessed the fiasco, Bligh at least had the satisfaction of seeing his ship safely moored in a bay that was everything Tu had promised—"vastly preferable to Point Venus . . . perfectly sheltered by the reefs, with smooth water, and close to a fine beach without the least surf." The plants—still "in a flourishing state"—were taken ashore to a fenced enclosure near a large hut provided by Tu and on December 28 the crew celebrated a delayed Christmas Day with a double ration of grog.

Oparre was no more immune to thieving than Matavai Bay. Soon a Tahitian stole his butcher's cleaver from the unfortunate Robert Lamb, who received twelve lashes for not guarding it better. The punishment was carried out in front of the Tahitian chiefs, whose own people, Bligh warned sternly, could expect the same punishment if caught stealing. He also gave cook's assistant William Muspratt twelve lashes for neglect of duty, an act that would help trigger the greatest challenge to his authority so far.

At four A.M. on January 5, at the change of the watch, the *Bounty*'s small cutter was found to be missing. Immediately mustering the ship's company, Bligh discovered that three of his crew—the recently flogged Muspratt, the master-at-arms Charles Churchill, and seaman John Millward had deserted, taking with them "eight stands of arms complete and eight cartouche boxes of ammunition." Midshipman Hayward had been in charge of the watch but had fallen asleep—such a dereliction of duty that Bligh raged: "Had the mate of the watch been awake no trouble of this kind would have happened. I have therefore disrated and turned him before the mast. Such neglectful and worthless petty officers I believe never was in a ship as are in this—No orders for a few hours together are obeyed by them, and their conduct in general is so bad, that no confidence or trust can be reposed to them. In short they have drove me to everything but corporal punishment and that must follow if they do not improve."

Bligh questioned the crew and, when no one volunteered any information about where the deserters might have gone, ordered a search of the three men's possessions. According to Morrison, a paper was found in Churchill's sea chest listing not only his own name but also those of three members of the shore party. Bligh immediately went ashore "and informed Mr. Christian of the business, calling the men and challenging them with being in league with Churchill and intending to desert. They persisted in their innocence and denied it so firmly that he was inclined from circumstances to believe them."

From Tu, Bligh learned that the cutter had been found in Matavai Bay, from where the deserters had been taken by canoe to Tetiaroa, a coral atoll north of Tahiti where they had misguidedly hoped to conceal themselves.* Bligh told Tu that he would not leave Tahiti without his men and asked for help in apprehending them. So intimidating was his manner that the chiefs asked whether, like Cook—who had always shown iron determination to recover deserters—he would hold them hostage. Bligh assured them he would not but waited impatiently for further news. Two weeks later, while Bligh was ashore testing the ship's chronometer, Fryer sent him a message asking what he should do with a Tahitian who had come on board, claiming he had taken the deserters to Tetiaroa in his canoe. Bligh was angry that Fryer had not locked the man up at once to be interrogated and was furious when he discovered that, before he himself could return to the *Bounty*, Fryer had allowed the man to leap overboard and escape.

The next day, Bligh had further cause to criticize the master when the *Bounty*'s spare sails were inspected and found to be mildewed and rotting—something that could never have happened had they been regularly aired as

---

*Marlon Brando purchased Tetiaroa after falling in love with Tahiti while on location for the 1962 film *Mutiny on the Bounty*.

he had ordered. Such neglect of duty, Bligh wrote in his log, was no less than "criminality" on the part of Fryer and William Cole, the bosun,

> for it appears that although the sails have been taken out twice since I have been in the island, which I thought fully sufficient and I had trusted to their reports. Yet these new sails never were brought out, nor is it certain whether they have been out since we left England, yet notwithstanding as often as sails were taken to air by my orders they were reported to me to be in good order . . . If I had any officers to supersede the master and boatswain, or was capable of doing without them considering them as common seamen, they should no longer occupy their respective stations.

All he could do was order sailmaker Lawrence Lebogue to do his best to repair the decaying sails.

Just before sunset on January 23, 1789, eighteen days after their desertion, Bligh finally received definitive news of the fugitives: They had been found only five miles away on Tahiti itself. Bligh at once set out in the cutter with a small armed party to apprehend them himself. Reaching the beach where he was told the deserters had taken refuge in a house, he went forward cautiously, pistols at the ready, "the night being very dark and windy," he wrote in his log. As he advanced, islanders emerged from the gloom. Suspecting they planned to attack and rob him, he brandished his pistol and they disappeared. In the event, he did not need to fire a single shot. The three deserters, who had learned of Bligh's arrival from the local people, emerged from the house without their weapons as Bligh approached, and surrendered. They claimed that they had been intending to return to the ship but, Bligh noted, "at the time they delivered themselves up to me it was not in their power to have made resistance, their ammunition having been spoiled by the wet" when their canoe had capsized on the return voyage from Tetiaroa.

Back on the *Bounty*, Bligh ordered the three to be placed in irons for one month and flogged. Morrison, who delivered the punishment, related that Churchill received two dozen lashes and Muspratt and Millward four dozen each—delivered at two separate punishment musters—after which they were allowed to return to duty. As the men well knew, Bligh could have had them hanged. They wrote Bligh a groveling letter, thanking him for his clemency in sparing them the "fatal consequences" of a court-martial. Bligh also allowed Hayward to return to duty as a midshipman but only after giving him a tongue lashing "for his neglect of duty" before the assembled crew each time the deserters were flogged. Bligh also punished American Isaac Martin with nineteen lashes for striking an islander—"such a direct violation of my orders, that I would on no account be prevailed upon to forgive it." Fryer further angered Bligh by failing to wind the chronometer as instructed while Bligh had been away, allowing it to run down.

Bligh now put his energies into readying his ship for departure, checking the re-caulking carried out by Purcell, the state of the rigging, and ordering the ship's interior to be thoroughly washed down with boiling water to kill the cockroaches with which the ship was swarming. Morrison described how even "the cables appeared alive with them, and they seemed to increase instead of diminish, though great quantities were destroyed every day." To get rid of rats and mice Bligh resorted to "traps and good cats"—the descendants, he thought, of those left behind by previous European ships.

Tu meanwhile continually expressed his nervousness that once his British protectors had departed, his enemies would rise up and overwhelm him. He proposed that he and Iddeeah should sail with Bligh to England to visit King George who, Tu was sure, would be pleased to see them. Bligh countered with promises that he would ask King George's permission for them to visit England and that if this was granted, he would come for them in a larger, more luxurious ship better fitted for the conveying of royalty. However, when Tu begged for arms and ammunition with which to defend himself after his British protectors had left, Bligh thought it only reasonable to agree, especially since Tu assured him he would only use the weapons to defend himself. Bligh readily believed him, considering Tu's disposition "neither active nor enterprising . . . If Tu had spirit in proportion to his size and strength, he would probably be the greatest warrior in Tahiti: but courage is not the most conspicuous of his virtues. When I promised to leave with him a pair of pistols . . . he told me that Iddeeah would fight with one." Bligh had already noted that the queen—a woman of "great bodily strength" befitting a champion wrestler—could load and fire a musket "with as much skill as any of us."

Bligh soon had concerns other than adding to the arms race developing among the Tahitians. At daybreak on February 6, he "discovered that the cable, by which the ship rode, had been cut near the water's edge, in such a manner that only one strand remained whole." Convinced an islander was responsible, he demanded that Tu identify and hand over the culprit. Unable to do so, Tu and Iddeeah suggested to Bligh that he might be from another part of the island intent on damaging their standing in Bligh's eyes. In fact, as later emerged, he was a *taio* of Hayward who, enraged by Bligh's punishment of his friend, had planned to kill Bligh if he had Hayward flogged.

On March 2, Bligh learned that during what had been a dark and rainy night part of an azimuth compass used for survey work, a water cask, and Peckover's bedding had been stolen from the shore camp. He at once went ashore "and rebuked the officers at the tent"—presumably Christian, Heywood, and Peckover—"for neglecting their duty." Their defense, according to Morrison, was that the night had been so black and the rain so heavy that they had been unable to see or hear a thing. This time Tu produced the thief, whom he cheerfully advised Bligh to kill. Bligh sent the man aboard to be punished "with a severe flogging"—one hundred lashes—after which he was placed in irons. The Tahitian later escaped under cover of darkness—he must have had help from one of the crew—and dived overboard. The man in charge of the watch that night was George Stewart, whom Bligh had no hesitation in blaming: "I had given in written orders that the mate of the watch was to be answerable for the prisoners . . . but I have such a neglectful set about me that I believe nothing but condign punishment can alter their conduct. Verbal orders in the course of a month were so forgot that they would impudently assert no such thing or directions were given." As a result he was having to issue written orders for routine activities that any "decent young officers" would carry out without needing to be told.

Bligh had also discovered that the ship's boats were in poor repair and the smallest—the jolly boat—was quite unseaworthy. Furthermore, teredo worm had entirely eaten away the wooden stock of the *Bounty*'s bow anchor. Again Bligh blamed his men. However, much of the responsibility was his own. Devoting so much time to being pampered and revered by the chiefs, he had left his men too much to their own devices. Though he had known that routine tasks needed to be performed and supervised, he had failed to establish routines to ensure this happened—an error his idol Cook would not have made. He had also persisted in taking too much for granted, failing to check personally the condition of such important items as sails and boats, until it was too late, whereupon he felt resentful and let down.

On March 25, Bligh issued his sailing orders. Among them were that his crew could only bring aboard those souvenirs they could stow in their sea chests; the ship was to be thoroughly searched for stowaways; all cats and dogs were—as ordered by Banks because of possible damage to the breadfruit plants—to be put ashore at once. As news of the *Bounty*'s departure spread, islanders gathered to witness the carrying aboard of the breadfruit plants. Bligh was delighted how well Nelson and Brown had tended them through baking sun and violent storms: "They were in excellent order; the roots had appeared through the bottom of the pots, and would have shot into the ground if care had not been taken to prevent it." Bligh was also pleased the strong westerlies that had been blowing constantly, bringing lashing rain, had died away, writing that "the rainy and bad season of the year" had ended.

By March 31, all the seedlings—1,015 in total—were on board "in 774 pots, 39 tubs, and 24 boxes." Nelson and Brown had also gathered a large collection of other fruit-bearing plants, including "a very superior kind of plantain" that Banks had specifically requested. Bligh had also embarked plants from which he had observed the islanders extract "a beautiful red colour" and "a root called peeah of which they make an excellent pudding."

Bligh presented his final gifts to Tu and his particular friends among the chiefs and also returned Captain Cook's portrait—which Tu had sent on board the *Bounty* soon after the ship's arrival as a mark of esteem—with the *Bounty*'s name, date of arrival and departure, and the number of breadfruit plants aboard noted on the back. His men prepared to part from their *taios*, who, Morrison described, "to show the last token of their friendship, loaded us with presents, and the ship became lumbered with hogs, coconuts, and green plantains for sea store." Even more painful for many was leaving their "wives," several of whom were pregnant.

On April 3, 1789, the eve of departure, Bligh recalled how "the ship was crowded the whole day with the natives." However, that night "there was no dancing or mirth on the beach, such as we had been accustomed to, but all was silent." Tu and Iddeeah dined with Bligh and slept aboard for one last night to postpone the distress of parting. At half past six the next morning, April 4, Bligh ordered his men to weigh anchor. In the absence of wind, the *Bounty*'s boats towed her through the narrow entrance of the bay. Soon after, a fresh sea breeze sprang up and Bligh wrote, with the salt air in their faces, "we stood off towards the sea," leaving the many canoes filled with flower-decked islanders that had escorted them in their wake.

Tu and Iddeeah were still aboard but the moment for final adieus had come. Bligh honoured his promise to give weapons to Tu, handing over "two muskets, a pair of pistols, and a good stock of ammunition." Amid what Bligh called "a vast excess of grief before going ashore," the weeping royal pair gave him a ritual blessing: *"Yourah no t'Eatua tee eveerah"*: "May the Eatua protect you, for ever and ever." It was, Morrison thought, "truly a tender scene." Tu asked to be saluted with a salvo from the ship's guns, which Bligh refused "for fear of disturbing the plants," but the assembled crew gave the departing chief and his wife three rousing cheers.

That evening, as the sun sank below the horizon and the outlines of Point Venus merged into the deepening shadow, the *Bounty*'s men, enjoying a double ration of grog, sailed from the island that for twenty-three weeks— considerably longer than any other European vessel—had been their home. There, Bligh later wrote, they had been treated with "utmost affection and regard"—indeed too much, in his view: "For to the friendly and endearing behaviour of these people may be ascribed the motives for that event which effected the ruin of an expedition that there was every reason to hope would have been completed in the most fortunate manner." Morrison presented a different picture: "Everybody seemed in high spirits and began already to talk of home, affixing the length of the voyage and counting up their wages. One would readily have imagined that we had just left Jamaica instead of Tahiti, so far onward did their flattering fancies waft them."

"THE PEOPLE ARE RIPE FOR ANYTHING"

$\mathcal{T}$oward noon the next day the *Bounty* anchored off the northwestern shores of Huahine where on his final voyage Cook had landed Omai after his visit to Britain. Bligh hoisted the red ensign "which all the islanders know perfectly well to be English." Before long canoes were pushing through the surf from the shore and the usual bartering and bargaining began. Bligh exchanged iron nails for coconuts and during the transaction learned that after Omai's death his house had been knocked down, his possessions looted, his muskets taken to another island, and nearly all his seeds and plants destroyed. Of his animals, only a mare that Omai had liked to ride survived. Bligh noticed that many islanders "had the representation of a man on horseback tattooed on their legs"—perhaps a representation of Omai since horses had previously been unknown on the island.

Sailing on, Bligh set a westerly course for the Friendly Islands (Tonga). In squally weather with dark clouds piling the sky, a tall waterspout whirled toward the ship. Bligh at once altered course and, with "a rustling noise," the spout passed harmlessly within ten yards of the *Bounty*'s stern. Bligh did not expect to make fresh discoveries in these now relatively well-charted waters but on April 11 was delighted to come upon a large, hilly, hitherto unknown island with lush, palm-crowned cays within its reef. Adverse winds prevented a landing, but four men paddled out to the *Bounty* in a canoe. Their leader "joined noses" with Bligh and presented him with a mother-of-pearl ornament on a necklace of braided hair and a long wooden spear. Bligh learned from them that the island was called "Whytootackee" ("Aitutaki" in the Cook Islands group). He noticed the men "were tattooed across the arms and legs, but not on the loins and posteriors, like the people of Tahiti." By April 17, the *Bounty* was passing another island—"Savage Island," so named by Cook after his men were attacked there in 1774, and Bligh did not attempt to land.

Bligh's accounts of this stage of the voyage focus on the *Bounty*'s progress, the direction of the wind, and sightings of cays and are silent on any tensions with his crew. However, according to sailmaker Lawrence Lebogue, two days after leaving Savage Island, with wet, windy weather buffeting the *Bounty*, Bligh berated Christian for neglecting to look after the *Bounty*'s sails. Fryer too described how "Mr. Bligh and Mr. Christian had some words" and Christian told Bligh, "Sir, your abuse is so bad that I cannot do my duty with any pleasure. I have been [in] hell for weeks with you"—the first incident during the entire voyage about which an eyewitness quoted Christian's words directly.

Further confrontations between Bligh and Christian followed when five days later, the *Bounty* anchored off Nomuka in the Friendly Islands—the ship's last halt before making for the feared Endeavour (Torres) Strait between New Holland and New Guinea. Bligh had helped chart the Friendly Islands in 1777 while master of Cook's *Resolution*. Recognizing one of the chiefs, a now lame and elderly man called Tepa, he entertained him aboard the *Bounty*. In return Tepa took Nelson and Bligh ashore to fetch breadfruit seedlings, since one plant in the *Bounty*'s great cabin had already died and several others were looking "a little sickly." Tepa also showed Bligh a flourishing plantation where Cook had planted pineapples. However, the condition of some of the island's people appalled Bligh. They had "dreadful sores on their legs, arms and breasts" while many bore the self-inflicted wounds of ritual mourning, "bloody temples, their heads deprived of most of their hair . . . almost everyone with the loss of some of their fingers. Several fine boys about 6 years old had lost both their little fingers."

Bligh's criticisms of his men meanwhile continued unabated. Some days before he had ordered seaman John Sumner twelve lashes for neglect of duty and, while anchoring the *Bounty* off Nomuka, he had lambasted master's mate William Elphinstone for allowing the bower anchor buoy to sink "for want of a little exertion." The atmosphere turned yet more sour when Bligh sent eleven men inland for water under Christian's command. He ordered them to keep well away from the locals and allowed them to take muskets but instructed them to leave them in the boat "considering [the men] much safer on shore without them." Perhaps Bligh was recalling what had happened to Cook in Kealakekua Bay after the ill-advised shooting in which he himself had been involved. However, his instructions must have seemed at least illogical to his men. As the party pushed inland, they could not avoid the islanders who crowded round, harassing and distracting them. In the confusion, an ax was stolen, which with Tepa's help was eventually recovered, as well as an adze, which was not.

When Christian reported the adze's loss, Bligh flew into a great rage, according to Morrison damning Christian "for a cowardly rascal, asking him if he was afraid of a set of naked savages while he had arms—to which Mr. Christian answered, 'the arms are no use while your orders prevent them from being used.'" Bligh himself was losing patience with officers who, he felt, continually let him down, writing: "As to the officers I have no resource, or do I ever feel myself safe in the few instances I trust them."

The next day, Bligh again dispatched the watering party under Christian to complete its task, but growing impatient sent Fryer to hasten its return. Mooring his boat near the shore Fryer headed inland to find stone- and club-wielding islanders menacing the watering party. He bravely distracted the attackers with gifts of iron nails to allow the watering party to get back to the beach. Meanwhile, however, those whom Fryer had left to guard his boat had allowed themselves to be distracted by children splashing in the water around them and, unseen by them, someone had made off with the grapnel—a small anchor.

Back on board, Fryer confessed the loss to Bligh, arguing that the grapnel was unimportant and that Coleman the armorer could easily replace it from shipboard stores, but Bligh was not to be mollified, thundering "the loss not very great, Sir, by God! Sir, if it is not great to you, it is great to me." As purser, he was responsible for bearing the cost of any missing equipment and was determined to get the grapnel back. Perhaps recalling tactics used by Cook, who had acted with uncharacteristic severity toward these same Nomuka islanders, Bligh decided to detain five chiefs including Tepa, then aboard, as hostages until the grapnel was recovered.

Since this would be the last place for weeks, if not months, where any serious trading could be done, Bligh allowed his men ashore for two hours to buy yams, coconuts, and whatever curios they wished. However, once all had returned, Bligh ordered the ship to sail with the still unsuspecting chiefs aboard. Fryer was overseeing the hoisting of the sails when, to his puzzlement, he heard Bligh call the men to arms and hurried to his captain's side. Bligh told him he intended to place armed guards over the detained chiefs who, as the ship began to sway and creak, were finally realizing their predicament. However, according to Fryer, Bligh was dissatisfied with the response to his call to arms: "while we were under arms as some of the people was rather awkward . . . Mr. Bligh made a speech to them, told them they were all a parcel of good for nothing rascals." Morrison recalled yet more graphically how Bligh dismissed all but two of them who were to act as guards over the chiefs, calling them "lubberly rascals" and claiming "that he would be one of five who would, with good sticks, disarm all of them." Pointing a pistol at William McKoy, he threatened to shoot him "for not paying attention."

As the hours passed and canoes of lamenting islanders, some slashing at themselves with sharks' teeth, followed in the *Bounty's* wake, the chiefs grew distraught, beating themselves "about the face and eyes." With no sign of the grapnel's return, Bligh eventually decided the chiefs were not privy to the theft and that their "distress was more than the grapnel was worth" and after making them some gifts let them go. Morrison, however, told a different story—how before releasing the chiefs Bligh forced them to "peel cocoa nuts for him . . . the greatest affront you can possibly offer to them." Other islanders who witnessed their chiefs' humiliation were so shocked that they "cut themselves with sharks' teeth and one would have cut his fingers off if he had not been prevented."

Toward nightfall on April 26 the *Bounty* was approaching the small island of Tofua, on the northwestern rim of the Friendly Islands, from which "vast columns of smoke and flame" could be seen rising from its volcano. The next day, while taking a turn on the quarterdeck, the pile of coconuts stored between the guns caught Bligh's eye. Staring harder he decided some had been stolen. Fryer suggested the pile had been flattened by people walking over it during the night but Bligh would not listen and ordered every man with coconuts aboard to produce them. Bligh interrogated every one of his officers and men about exactly how many they had bought and how many they had eaten. According to Morrison, he especially singled out Christian, who responded: "I do not know sir, but I hope you don't think me so mean as to be guilty of stealing yours," to which Bligh replied, "Yes, you damned hound, I do—You must have stolen them from me or you could give a better account of them." Then broadening his attack to include the other officers, he thundered, "God damn you, you scoundrels, you are all thieves alike, and combine with the men to rob me—I suppose you'll steal my yams next, but I'll sweat you for it, you rascals. I'll make half of you jump overboard before you get through Endeavour Strait."

Morrison recounted that Bligh called to his clerk, John Samuel, who acted as ship's steward and ordered, "Stop these villains' grog, and give them but half a pound of yams tomorrow, and if they steal then, I'll reduce them to a quarter." The result of this rant was that the officers "were heard to murmur much at such treatment, and it was discussed among the men that the yams would be next seized, as Lieutenant Bligh knew that they had purchased large quantities of them" so they therefore set about secreting as many as possible. Fryer confirmed Bligh ordered the yam ration cut but only to three quarters of a pound, which "was more than their allowance."

Some like Fryer and Purcell shrugged off Bligh's tantrums. Christian did not. Typically oblivious of the depths of his lieutenant's wounded feelings, Bligh invited him to dinner just after noon, but Christian excused himself on the grounds that he was unwell. Bligh, probably taking this at face value, instead invited Hayward who, despite the hisses of the other officers, accepted. Christian meanwhile seems to have reached a breaking point. Purcell found him with tears "running fast from his eyes in big drops." When the carpenter asked the cause, Christian replied, "Can you ask me, and hear the treatment I receive?" When Purcell responded, "Do not I receive as bad you do?" Christian said, "You have something to protect you— [Purcell's status as a warrant officer meant he could not be flogged, whereas Christian's substantive petty officer rank of master's mate allowed him to be derated and flogged]—and can speak again; but if I should speak to him as you do, he would probably break me, turn me before the mast, and perhaps flog me; and if he did, it would be the death of us both, for I am sure I should take him in my arms and jump overboard with him." Purcell tried to calm him, reminding him "it is but for a short time longer" but Christian would not to be comforted, saying, "In going through Endeavour Straits, I am sure the ship will be a hell." Another man heard him declare, "I would rather die ten thousand deaths than bear this treatment; I always do my duty as an officer and as a man ought to do, yet I receive this scandalous usage."

Such was Christian's distress that, according to Morrison and others, he planned "to quit the ship that very night" and "gave away that afternoon all his Tahiti curiosities; he was seen tearing his letters and papers, and throwing them overboard." Intending to make a plank raft in hopes of reaching land or at least of being taken up by a passing canoe, "he applied to the carpenter for nails, who told him to take as many as he pleased." Christian lashed two masts from the ship's launch to a plank and set about collecting provisions.

When Fryer's young brother-in-law, Tinkler, one of Christian's messmates, felt hungry that evening and "went below to get some pig which was left at dinner," he was surprised to find it missing. After searching he discovered it packed up with a breadfruit "in a dirty clothes' bag in Christian's cot."

At about ten thirty P.M. Bligh took a last turn around the deck before retiring for the night. In the pale light of a young moon and with a fresh breeze filling the sails, he instructed Fryer, taking the first watch of the night, on what course to follow, then went below. Fryer noted afterward that "we at that time was upon speaking terms"—a telling comment on the general state of relations between Bligh and his officers. At midnight Peckover took over what proved "a very pleasant watch" and was in turn relieved at four in the morning by Christian. Christian's flight from the ship may have been frustrated by crewmen being "upon deck in greater numbers than usual" during the night watching the spectacular pyrotechnics of Tofua's flaring volcano, or perhaps he had had second thoughts about taking such a dangerous step. No doubt emotionally exhausted, he had eventually gone to bed in the small hours. According to other crew members, he had not slept long and was "much agitated in mind" and "much out of order" when at four A.M. on Tuesday, April 28, George Stewart, coming off his own watch, roused him to go on duty.

Christian had clearly taken Stewart into his confidence and perhaps a chance remark from the young midshipman suggested an alternative way of solving his problems: Instead of removing himself from the ship, why not remove the source of all his anguish, Bligh? According to Morrison, Stewart told Christian he was glad he had not deserted for "the people are ripe for anything" and "this made a forcible impression on his mind." However, to attempt to seize a ship was a desperate undertaking, the consequences of which Christian, whose own surgeon brother Charles had been involved in a mutiny, was only too aware. He later told Peter Heywood that he might have drawn back even then had circumstances not conspired in his favor.

These "circumstances" were the neglect of duty of Hallett and Hayward, his fellow officers of the watch. Coming on duty Christian could see no sign of Hallett, while the perennially sleepy Hayward was alternately dozing or staring at a shark swimming astern of the ship. Others on Christian's watch were gunner's mate John Mills, carpenter's mate Charles Norman, and able seamen Isaac Martin, Thomas Burkett, Thomas Ellison, and Matthew Quintal. According to Morrison, the first men Christian told of his intentions were Quintal—the first man flogged on the expedition—and the recently flogged Martin. They in turn "called up Churchill and Thompson who put the business in hand." All the members of Christian's watch except Norman quickly decided to join the mutiny. The sheer speed with which others threw in their lot with Christian in what appears to have been an unpremeditated coup suggests not only the low morale on the ship and dislike of Bligh but also the trust and esteem in which Christian himself was held. The men would not have risked their lives and futures by following someone they thought incompetent or a fool.

While those whom he had recruited went quietly to rally others, Christian hurried below and, on the pretext of needing a musket to shoot at a shark, obtained from Coleman the armorer the key to the arms chest. Going to the chest, Christian found Hallett curled up asleep on it. Shaking him awake, he sent the guilty and unsuspecting midshipman up on deck and, opening the chest, began removing bayonets, muskets, and pistols. Hayward was presumably still dozing on deck when to his "unutterable surprise" he saw Christian, Churchill, Burkett, Sumner, Quintal, and others, all armed, coming along the deck toward him. Christian posted men to hold the upper deck and guard the hatchways, then led others back below.

Moments later a stupefied Hayward "heard the cry of murder from Captain Bligh," who woke as Christian and Churchill burst through the open door of his cabin and seized him. Burkett recalled Christian with "fury in his looks" and Churchill calling out for cord to bind the captain and yelling, "You infernal buggers, hand down a seizing or I'll come and play hell with you all." Someone brought cord and Christian and Churchill bound Bligh's hands tightly, assisted, according to Bligh, "by others who were also in the cabin, all armed with muskets and bayonets. I was now threatened with instant death if I spoke a word; I however called for assistance and wakened everyone; but the officers were in their cabins secured by sentinels at their doors so that no one could come to me."

The rumpus and Bligh's shouts had indeed woken Fryer in his cabin opposite Bligh's. Fryer was about to leap down from the locker on which, rather than his bed, he slept for coolness but "Sumner and Quintal laid their hands on my breast, and desired me to lay down, adding, 'Sir you are a prisoner.'" When Fryer tried to reason with them they told him he "was a dead man" if he did not hold his tongue. Through the open door Fryer saw Bligh, dressed only in shirt and night cap, being forced up the ladder to the quarterdeck, hands tied behind him and "Christian holding him by the cord." Bligh later wrote, "Our eyes met. He [Fryer] had a good pair of ship's pistols loaded. A

firm resolution might have made good use of them." The same thought obviously occurred to Churchill, who confiscated the pistols. Fryer later claimed
he had no ammunition for the pistols—something which Bligh disputed—
and therefore he could not have resisted.

When Fryer asked what the mutineers intended to do with Bligh, Sumner
replied, "Damn his eyes, put him into the boat, and let the bugger see if he
can live on three-quarters of a pound of yams per day." Fryer remonstrated
only to be told, "Hold your tongue, Mr. Christian is captain of the ship, and
recollect Mr. Bligh brought all this upon himself." He asked to join his captain
on the deck and Christian allowed him to do so. In the half-light of the
breaking dawn, Bligh was standing by the mizzenmast, hands tied tightly
behind him and "Christian holding the cord with one hand, and a bayonet
in the other." According to one report Christian himself had a plumb line
tied around his neck presumably so that the lead weight at its end would
cause him to sink faster and avoid the consequences if the mutiny failed and
he jumped from the ship. The rope binding Bligh's hands had caught in his
nightshirt, exposing his genitals, and in a gesture of humanity, Burkett darted
forward to twitch the nightgown down.

According to his own account, Bligh, "suffering great pain from the tight-
ness with which they had tied my hands," thought Christian "seemed to be
plotting instant destruction on himself and everyone, for of all diabolical
looking men he exceeded every possible description." Nevertheless, holding
his nerve when many others were losing theirs, Bligh demanded of Christian "the cause of such a violent act, but no other answer was given but 'Hold
your tongue, Sir; or you are dead this instant'; and holding me by the cord,
which tied my hands, he as often threatened to stab me in the breast with a
bayonet he held in his right hand." Fryer too tried to reason with Christian
only to be told, "Hold your tongue, Sir. I've been in hell for weeks past."
Reprising the words of his supporters, he added, "Captain Bligh has brought
all this upon himself."

Realizing Christian intended to cast Bligh adrift in the ship's smallest
boat, the cutter, the bottom of which was "almost eat out with worms," Fryer
pleaded for a better boat to give Bligh a chance of reaching land. Christian
refused. Meanwhile, Isaac Martin gave a shaddock fruit to the parched Bligh
to suck and Bligh managed to whisper to Fryer that Martin "was a friend."
Seeing this exchange, Christian put a bayonet to Fryer's chest and threatened,
"If you advance an inch further, I'll run you through." Then, as he had already

done with the two midshipmen Hayward and Hallett, he ordered the master to be taken back to his cabin and kept under guard. As he was about to go down the hatchway Fryer saw Morrison and asked whether he had had any hand in what was going on, to which Morrison assured him, "No, Sir; I don't know a word about it." But when Fryer told him to keep ready in case there was an opportunity to re-take the ship, Morrison replied, "Sir, go down to your cabin, it is too late now."

Below deck again, Sumner and Millward, who were guarding Fryer, allowed him to join Peckover and Nelson down in the cockpit above the hold where they slept. "A confused noise" followed by the sound of bayonets being fixed had woken Peckover. Jumping out of bed, thinking islanders might be attacking the ship, he had gone to his door to see Nelson, who told him the ship had been seized "by our own people, Christian at their head," adding, "but we know whose fault it is." Peckover had tried to go up but had been stopped by Sumner and Quintal wielding fixed bayonets down the hatchway.

Now Fryer, Peckover, and Nelson debated what to do. Fryer argued they should do all they could to remain on the *Bounty* rather than go with their captain, since if they stayed they could "restore the ship in a short time." Peckover disagreed, saying, "If we stay, we shall all be deemed pirates." Their conversation ended when—about two hours after the mutiny had begun—Christian ordered them out on deck. He had meanwhile changed his mind and decided that Bligh should have the launch, "not for his sake, but for the safety of those that were going with him."

Purcell claimed he was responsible for this change of heart. Quintal had woken him and told him bluntly, "We have mutinied and taken the ship; Mr. Christian has the command. Captain Bligh is confined, resistance is in vain, and if you attempt it you are a dead man." Rousing boatswain Cole, whose berth was nearby, Purcell went up on deck with him, passing the berths of Heywood and Stewart, who appeared to be under guard.

Out on the deck, which was now filled with most of the crew—many of whom, being confused and uncertain what to do, were doing little—Purcell saw Bligh, hands tied and naked bayonets and loaded cocked muskets trained on him. Learning that the plan was to put Bligh into the small cutter, Purcell said he had at once pointed out to Christian that the worm-eaten state of the boat meant it would sink long before it made land. Christian ordered him instead to prepare the large cutter but the carpenter, who should have repaired both vessels just as Bligh should have supervised him, argued that this boat was not seaworthy either. Making clear his intention to go with his captain, Purcell said that "if he meant to turn us adrift . . . to let us have the launch and not make a sacrifice of us."

Purcell's appeal worked and, though some mutineers like Quintal objected, Christian agreed. Purcell hurried back to his cabin to fetch whatever might be useful and told his assistants, Norman and Thomas McIntosh, to fill a bucket with nails and fetch a cross saw from the store room. Christian also allowed Purcell to have most of the contents of his tool chest despite, the carpenter recalled, cries of "They might as well give us a ship as to suffer me to have tools, for we should have another vessel in a month." Churchill clambered into the launch, wrenching open the chest and seizing a few larger items.

Some twenty men—mutineers, "loyalists," and some still undecided—were needed to lower the heavy launch into the water. Peckover asked to be allowed to go to his chest to fetch some of his things but Christian refused and the gunner could only scramble down into the launch, where a dozen men were already crouching. Burkett called down to Peckover to ask if he needed anything. The gunner replied that he had nothing "but what I stood in," at which Burkett hurried off, returning ten minutes later with a bundle "full of different clothes" which he threw down into the boat.

Bligh's servant, John Smith, had, on Christian's instructions, draped a jacket around his captain's shoulders after helping him into his trousers, Bligh still trying to make his erstwhile protégé see reason. Burkett heard him plead, "Consider what you are about, Mr. Christian, for God's sake drop it, and there shall be no more come of it." When Christian responded that it was too late, Bligh replied, "I'll forfeit my honour if ever I speak of it; I'll give you my bond that there shall never be any more come of it," but Christian was not to be moved. "*Mamoo*, sir. Not a word or you are dead* . . . You have treated me like a dog all voyage. I have been in hell this fortnight past and I am determined to suffer it no longer."

As well as Bligh, the mutineers were absolutely determined that Hallett, Hayward, and Bligh's clerk, John Samuel, whose doling out of the limited rations had won him few friends, should go. Others had made their intentions to accompany Bligh clear. Yet in these final fraught minutes, with people milling around, there was confusion about exactly who was leaving. Some

---

Mamoo means "be silent" in Tahitian.

who had not been involved in the seizure of the ship dazedly wondered whether to climb down into the small, heavily laden launch and take their chances or whether to remain on the *Bounty* and risk being branded pirates. Isaac Martin, among the first to join the mutiny, was having second thoughts and got down into the launch only to be spotted by Churchill, who ordered him out again at gunpoint. Among the "young gentlemen," Purcell later recalled seeing a confused-looking Heywood by the ship's booms, "resting his hand on a cutlass." His friend George Stewart was "dancing and clapping his hands in the Tahitian manner, and saying it was the happiest day of his life." An armed Edward Young was standing guard over Bligh. When Bligh reproached him, saying, "This is a serious affair, Mr. Young," he replied, "Yes, it is a serious matter to be starved. I hope this day to get a belly full."

Urged on by Bligh, Fryer tried to persuade Christian to allow him to remain but Christian, putting a bayonet to his chest, replied, "No, by God, Sir, go into the boat or I will run you through." Others wishing to go—like Coleman the armorer and Purcell's assistants McIntosh and Norman—were refused on the grounds that their skills were essential to the *Bounty*. For a while it had seemed doubtful whether Christian would allow the pugnacious Purcell himself to go, but perhaps he decided McIntosh and Norman would be easier to manage. For a while the mutineers debated whether to keep acting surgeon Ledward, who was adamant that he "would go with the captain . . . and not stay among the mutineers," but they concluded "they would have little occasion for doctors." In the confusion, Samuel, Bligh's clerk, before being put over the side, managed to collect together Bligh's "journal and commission, with some material ship's papers"—including his all-important "pursery" papers—without which Bligh would acknowledge gratefully "my honour and character might have been suspected."

Able seaman Ellison, himself among the mutineers, thought Christian "looked like a madman." Hoping the hard core of mutineers might yet be swayed, Purcell remembered making a last-minute plea, "desiring them to lay down their arms, asking them what they were about, and advising that, 'if the captain had done anything wrong, to confine him,'" to which Churchill replied, "You ought to have done that months ago." By now several mutineers, enflamed by the rum that Christian had ordered one of the cooks to serve to them, were abusing Bligh and shouting, "Shoot the bugger." Bligh himself made a very personal appeal to Christian: "Consider Mr. Christian, I have a wife and four children in England, and you have danced my children upon your knee," to which Purcell later testified Christian replied,

"Hold your tongue and I'll not hurt you; it is too late to consider now," adding yet again, "I have been in hell for weeks past with you." Morrison recalled Christian saying, "If you had any honour, things would not have come to this; and if you had any regard for your wife and family, you should have thought on them before, and not behaved so much like a villain."

Perhaps four hours after the mutiny had begun, Bligh was the nineteenth and last man into the overcrowded launch. Fryer begged for muskets but Churchill refused, saying, "Captain Bligh was well acquainted where he was going." However, on Christian's orders four cutlasses were handed down and Morrison threw in some pieces of pork and two large gourds of water. According to Morrison, Bligh pleaded for a sextant, at which Christian "took his own sextant, which commonly stood on the dripstone case, and handed it into the boat . . . saying, 'There, Captain Bligh, this is sufficient for every purpose, and you know the sextant to be a good one.'"

So aggressive were the catcalls from the *Bounty*—when quartermaster Norton asked for a coat to be thrown down to him a mutineer yelled back, "You bugger, if I had my will I would blow your brains out"—that boatswain William Cole said to Bligh, "We had better put off, or they will do us some mischief." While well-wishers on board threw down a few last provisions, and those in the launch rowed hastily astern to get clear of the ship's guns, Christian ordered the *Bounty*'s top-gallant sails to be unfurled. As she sailed away the cheers of those aboard could clearly be heard—a few, Bligh alone later alleged, shouting, "Huzza for Tahiti."

The mutineers were, as Bligh frankly stated, "the most able men of the ship's company." Of the twenty-five still on the *Bounty*, the wishes and behavior of several had been ambiguous. Four had clearly remained against their will: Purcell's assistants McIntosh and Norman, Coleman the armorer, and fiddler Michael Byrne who, prevented by his impaired eyesight from seeing what was going on, had mistakenly sat in the cutter, where he could be seen crying in distress. McIntosh and Norman were weeping at the rail and the latter was shouting, "Remember me to my wife and family, I am kept against my own will." In those final moments, as the *Bounty* sailed away, Bligh called out to them, "My lads, I'll do you justice."

XII

"RUN DOWN BY MY OWN DOGS"

I had scarce got a furlong on my way when I began to reflect on the vicissitude of human affairs . . . but in the midst of all I felt an inward happiness which prevented any depression of my spirits; conscious of my own integrity and anxious solicitude for the good of the service I was on I found my mind most wonderfully supported and began to conceive hopes not withstanding so heavy a calamity to be able to recount to my king and country my misfortune." So later wrote William Bligh of his feelings as the launch moved away from HMAS *Bounty* and the jeers and threats of the mutineers faded into the distance.

Few of the other eighteen men in the launch would have been likely to share his self-confident equanimity as they made toward the island of Tofua about thirty miles away on the horizon. Instead, according to Bligh, the sailors regarded their commander "with anxious looks," their minds probably still numb with shock at the scenes they had just witnessed and clouded with uncertainty as to what their future held.

The launch reached Tofua—only five miles long and four miles wide—just after dark the next evening. There Bligh hoped to find more fresh water and breadfruit to supplement their existing meager provisions. The coast appeared "so steep and rocky" that instead of landing he decided to stand off the shore for the night and to serve each man half a pint of grog to bolster their spirits. The next day, he succeeded in finding an anchorage about twenty yards off a stony beach. Bligh and some of his men ploughed through the surf pounding the shoreline and began to explore for food, hauling themselves up the precipitous cliffs using the long vine ropes local people had attached to them for the same purpose. But they could find little water or food except for a few plantains.

Over the next couple of days some islanders appeared and began to trade the small amounts of breadfruit and plantains they had for beads or for buttons the sailors cut from their coats. Even though there were few provisions to be obtained, Bligh decided not to put to sea again immediately because the weather was growing stormy. More islanders arrived and soon busied themselves examining closely what goods and weapons Bligh and his men possessed. Some asked who the launch party were and where their main vessel was. Bligh told them they were the only survivors of a shipwreck and were making for the larger island of Tongataboo (Tongatapu). Growing nervous at the number and demeanor of the islanders after some of them had attempted to pull the launch through the surf onto the beach, Bligh bartered successfully for two spears to supplement the two cutlasses he had brought ashore.

As May 3 drew on and he waited anxiously for the foraging parties he had sent out to return, more and more Tofuans surrounded Bligh and his shore party, and began clicking stones together. "I knew very well this was the sign of an attack," Bligh recalled. Memories of Kealakekua Bay must have again flooded back to him and those others who had been with Cook, since just such clicking had preceded the fatal attack there. Bligh began to get his men quietly to sneak what provisions and equipment they had back through the high surf to the launch, where Fryer had remained with some of the crew. The mate's young nephew, Robert Tinkler, proved particularly adept at this transfer, joking with the Tofuans, who let him move freely carrying small amounts of goods at a time.

The sun was nearly setting when, according to Bligh, "The chiefs asked me if I would not stay with them all night, I said, 'No, I never sleep out of my boat; but in the morning we will again trade with you, and I shall remain till the weather is moderate, that we may go . . . to Tongataboo.' . . .'You will not sleep on shore? then "Mattie" (which directly signifies we will kill you),' a chief replied." With the clicking of the stones growing ever more intense and rapid, Bligh reacted quickly. Perhaps instinctively thinking of Cook, he grabbed one of the chiefs "by the hand" and together "we walked down the beach, everyone in a silent kind of horror." Quickly letting the chief go and with Purcell—the only other Briton now remaining on the beach—at his side, Bligh splashed through the foaming surf hotly pursued by yelling islanders now busy throwing stones.

He just made it to the launch, which Fryer had brought in as close as he dared without grounding it. As Bligh scrambled over the side, some Tofuans grabbed hold of Purcell—who, according to Fryer, had stood by Bligh "longer than one in twenty would have done in that situation"—by the legs as he attempted to follow, trying to yank him away. Bligh struck out at them with his knife. They let go, whereupon Purcell fell into the boat. At the same time the hefty Liverpudlian quartermaster John Norton bravely jumped from the launch into the water and ran toward the beach to detach the shore line. Quickly islanders were all around him, knocking him down into the surf, beating out his brains among the rocks just as the Sandwich (Hawaiian) Islanders had done to Cook ten years before.

Realizing there was nothing they could do to help Norton, from whose bloodied body the islanders were already stripping the clothes, Bligh quickly cut the shore line but the small anchor, the grapnel, was still embedded among some rocks. Fortunately, as the desperate sailors pulled at its rope for all they were worth, one of its flukes broke and the launch was free. With two men bending to each of the six oars, the boat began to move away as several large stones hit Fryer and Bligh, both now standing in the stern. Another hit Peckover, one of the oarsmen, full in the face, producing an instant large swelling on his cut cheekbone, but he kept on rowing. With the islanders now pushing canoes into the surf and paddling furiously through the still high waves, Bligh and Nelson began to throw overboard spare clothes and even some provisions, anticipating their pursuers would stop to retrieve them, which they did, diving in the water to do so. Breasting the high seas, the launch soon began to outdistance the islanders.

The loss of Norton, a popular man whom Bligh described as the sole support "of an aged parent," shocked everyone, bringing home to them the reality of their perilous situation. However, from a practical, unsentimental point of view Norton's loss was a boon to the remainder since, as Bligh later acknowledged, "he was the stoutest man in the ship, which . . . would very materially have interfered with the boat's progress and the allowance of provisions."

As the sea began to calm, Bligh and his crew raised the two masts, one at the bow and one amidships, set the two sails, and began to take stock. In the launch, which was only twenty-three feet long and six feet nine inches at its widest, the eighteen men had 150 pounds of ship's biscuit, twenty-eight gallons of water, twenty pounds of salt pork, five quarts of rum, three bottles of wine, some coconuts, and whatever breadfruit from the island had not been squashed or trampled in their haste to depart. For protection, they had just four cutlasses and the two Tofuan spears. Navigation equipment included

Christian's sextant, an old quadrant, a watch belonging to Peckover to give some idea of time, an improvised logline to measure speed and distance, a copy of *The Practical Navigator*, and some nautical tables belonging to Hallett with which Bligh, and if necessary other experienced navigators such as Fryer, would be able to take the noon observations Bligh would often refer to in his accounts of the launch's voyage.

A debate ensued—instigated by Bligh, according to him, but by Fryer if his account is to be believed—about where their destination should be. Having decided that what happened at Tofua was, in Bligh's words, "a sample of the disposition of the natives," they determined "there was but little reason to expect much benefit by persevering in the intention of visiting [Tongataboo]; for I considered their good behaviour formerly to have proceeded from a dread of our firearms and which, therefore, was likely to cease, as they knew we were now destitute of them: and, even supposing our lives not in danger, the boat . . . would most probably be taken from us, and thereby all hopes precluded of ever being able to return to our native country." Therefore, they decided instead to head with the benefit of the prevailing easterly winds for the island of Timor 3,600 miles away in the Dutch East Indies. This would mean living on very short rations and Bligh wisely made each man swear "a sacred promise" that he would live on the daily ration Bligh would hand out of one ounce of bread and a quarter of a pint of water.

The next morning "the sun rose very fiery and red, a sure indication of a severe gale." Sure enough, the winds rapidly increased into a full easterly gale so that with foaming water frequently overtopping the stern, the sailors had to bail furiously to keep afloat the launch, which had no decking to protect it. Bligh ordered his men to throw overboard everything surplus to requirements, such as spare ropes and sails and pieces of clothing. They put the biscuit, some of it already moldy, into the carpenter's chest from which they had removed his tools, which they had laid in the bottom of the boat. Fryer couldn't help noticing the care which Bligh and Samuel were taking to preserve their account books and muster rolls despite the storm erupting around them, seemingly intent on retaining them in preference to other equipment, even if it meant "the boat would have been turned adrift without oar or sail."

After forty-eight hours the gales abated and the voyage began to settle into a routine of sorts, however harsh and uncomfortable. The weather nevertheless continued stormy with much thunder and lightning. Although frequent lashings of rain meant little respite from bailing, at least there was no lack of drinking water. On a particularly wet night the sailors trapped thirty-four gallons in a sail they had spread out. Sometimes the rain was so cold Bligh had his men dip their garments into the warmer seawater so that when they were wrung out and put back on, they felt a little warmer. He improvised scales from two coconut shells and used pistol balls as weights to measure out three times a day the scant rations, their paucity quickly leading to constipation and great "pains in their bowels."*

Occasionally Bligh served a teaspoonful of rum to warm their painful stomachs and raise their spirits. Sometimes they sang, but before long, the men's condition began to deteriorate, everyone "having almost lost the use of their limbs" because of the chill, wet, and cramped conditions. Day after day the words "wet and cold" recur in the notes Bligh was writing with numbed fingers. The crew failed miserably to catch any of the few fish or even dolphins they passed and many began to complain about the rations, begging for more. Bligh, however, resolutely passed through the Fiji Islands, refusing to land to look for food for fear of attack. Dedicated chart maker that he was, Bligh assiduously took sightings from the rocking launch and noted the positions of the twenty-three islands they passed by. Thinking much of the archipelago was undiscovered, he named the islands "the Bligh Islands."

On May 22, twenty-four days after being cast adrift, as Bligh later wrote, "The misery we suffered this night exceeded the preceding. The sea flew over us with great force, and kept us baling with horror and anxiety. At dawn . . . I found everyone in a most distressed condition, and I began to fear that another such night would put an end to the lives of several, who seemed no longer able to support their sufferings." Bligh's own thoughts turned to God. He composed a prayer asking God to "Grant unto us health and strength to continue our voyage, and so bless our miserable morsel of bread, that it may be sufficient for our undertaking. O Almighty God relieve us from our extreme distress, such as men never felt,—conduct us through thy mercy to a safe haven and in the end restore us to our disconsolate families and friends . . . Receive us this night into thy almighty protection."

This night, however, was the nadir of their fortunes and the sea quickly grew calmer and the sun began to shine. On May 25, "at noon some noddies

---

*Bligh's coconut scales and weights are in the National Maritime Museum in London's Greenwich.

came so near to us that one of them was caught by hand. This bird was about the size of a small pigeon. I divided it, with its entrails, into eighteen portions, and by a well-known method at sea of 'who shall have this?' it was distributed." Even this tiny supplement to their diet was welcome when, Bligh wrote, "[we] overhauled our bread and found 43 days bread at the weight of 2 musket balls, or 1/12 of a lb to each man per day," and their bowels had seized completely through lack of food and water—"most of us 18 days without an evacuation."

With the weather now "serene," "the heat of the sun was so powerful, that several of the people were seized with a languor and faintness which made life indifferent. We were so fortunate as to catch two boobies in the evening; their stomachs contained several flying fish and small cuttlefish, all of which I saved to be divided for dinner," wrote a grateful Bligh, who thanked "providence for refreshment in their great want and distress."

The presence of birds told everyone land—the northeast coast of New South Wales—was near. On May 28, a month after the mutiny, the exhausted sailors sighted the Great Barrier Reef. Fryer claimed that he first heard "a noise like the roaring of the sea against the rocks" at around one A.M. and immediately took action to furl the sails and back the oars to avoid the launch crashing into the razor-sharp coral. Bligh did not mention Fryer in his accounts of his own speedy action to avert disaster.

With the sun up, the crew eventually spotted a gap in the reef "half a mile wide" and safely negotiated it. Then, to their intense joy, islands appeared, together with a more distant shoreline. Heading toward an island that appeared deserted, the sailors grounded the launch on the beach and stumbled ashore. "We were like so many drunken men," Fryer wrote, "in setting [sic] so long in the boat and being so weak that when I first landed my head was so light that I fell down." Once slightly recovered, the men began to pull oysters and periwinkles from the rocks to eat raw, little caring if in the process they ripped their nails and fingers. Later they gathered more, adding them to an allowance of pork and bread to make "a fine dinner." "Much refreshed," they began to explore their surroundings and Bligh recorded finding the "skeleton of a snake 8 feet long hung on a tree."

The next morning, they began a more thorough search for food on what Bligh named Restoration Island, both because May 29 was the anniversary of the restoration to the English throne of Charles II in 1660 and because "the name was not inapplicable to our present situation (for we were restored to fresh life and strength)." He thought he detected "fresh marks of kangaroo" and decided there were many on the island. Bligh used the small magnifying glass he "always carried . . . to read of the divisions of my sextants" to make a fire on which they cooked a "dinner stew" of oysters and a small amount of salt pork in a copper pot they had brought with them. Bligh also found "among the few things which had been thrown into the boat and saved, a piece of brimstone and a tinderbox, so that I secured [the means of making] a fire for the future." Probably struck by the divine providence that had saved them, Bligh spent a lot of his time reading and annotating his prayer book. Afterward he gave "a new prayer night and morning" to his men.

With fruits plentiful, although even with Nelson's expert help it was difficult to identify which were edible, and a water source found, the sailors began to relax. As they did so, the relative harmony that had prevailed when they were at their greatest danger in the launch began to dissipate. Fryer and Bligh quarreled over the size and content of the oyster stew, Fryer wishing to add ship's biscuit to it. According to Bligh, Fryer "showed a turbulent disposition until I laid my commands on him to be silent." Subsequently some of the very small stock of salt pork went missing, but nobody admitted stealing it.

On another occasion, Bligh worked himself into "a sad passion, calling everybody [names] and telling them that if it had not been for him they would not have been there." According to Fryer, even the loyal Nelson, whom Fryer had "very seldom heard swear," when he heard of this said "yes, damn his blood it is his economy that brought us here."

Leaving Restoration Island behind, Bligh worked the launch north up the coast of New Holland, carefully avoiding "jet black" naked Aboriginals "running and hallooing to us" since he considered they might be hostile. He continued charting the "rather scorched" coastline and islands, noting currents and geographical features, observing "all the country is like Dampier's description of it" and deciding that kangaroos probably swam between the islands. On Sunday, May 31, they landed on another island Bligh named Sunday Island.* There a more serious dispute occurred between Bligh, Purcell, and Fryer, centered on the gathering and distribution of oysters and

---

*Consciously or not, Bligh echoed Cook's habit of naming geographical features after the day on which they were reached.

whether what was collected should be pooled or kept by the individual who gathered it. Purcell, who did not wish to share with "idlers," according to Bligh became "insolent to a high degree." According to Fryer, the latter stage of the altercation went as follows:

BLIGH: [You are] a damned scoundrel. I have brought you here when if I had not been with you, you would have all perished.

PURCELL: If it had not been for you, we should not have been here.

BLIGH: What's that you say, sir?

PURCELL: I say sir if it had not been for you we should not have been here.

BLIGH: You damned scoundrel what do you mean?

PURCELL: I am not a scoundrel, sir. I am as good a man as you in that respect.

Then, according to Bligh, "taking hold of a cutlass I ordered the rascal to take hold of another and defend himself when he called out that I was going to kill him . . . The master [Fryer] very deliberately called out to the bosun [William Cole] to put me under an arrest and was stirring up a greater disturbance when I declared if he interfered when I was in the execution of my duty to preserve order and regularity . . . I would certainly put him to death." Fryer later dismissed Bligh's account, writing, "I could not help laughing to see Captain Bligh swaggering with a cutlass over the carpenter's head—I said, 'no fighting here. I put you both under arrest.'" Peace was restored after a fashion, although Bligh was sufficiently concerned thenceforth always to keep a cutlass at his side and also to list those of his seventeen companions he thought he could rely upon. They numbered only ten and by implication the others (Fryer, Purcell, Lamb, Tinkler, Hall, Linkletter, and Simpson) were unreliable. Bligh certainly encountered problems with Lamb, the *Bounty*'s butcher, who when sent with two others to catch birds for the whole party slipped away and caught nine boobies, all of which he ate raw himself. Bligh gave him "a good beating" when he found out.

When at eight o'clock on the evening of June 4, 1789, Bligh ordered the launch to leave the shores of New Holland to cross the notoriously hazardous Endeavour Strait to Timor, Bligh thought his men were looking optimistic and refreshed: "So much confidence gave me great pleasure . . . for whoever had despaired would have been dead [even] before I got to New Holland." However, the weather turned foul again and they had to bale constantly. Bligh described his men's quickly deteriorating condition as "an extreme weakness, swell'd legs, hollow and ghastly countenances, great propensity to sleep and an apparent debility of understanding, [that] give me melancholy proofs of an approaching dissolution."

The sea life around the launch was tantalizingly prolific—porpoises, "yellow and spotted black or dark brown" sea snakes, flying fish—but they caught little. On June 6, the parched and starving men finally seized a booby, Bligh writing, "some of us ravenous even for the blood." By now, only nineteen days' allowance of bread remained assuming a ration of two ounces per man per day. "We now anxiously prayed to make the land," wrote Bligh on June 7, adding the following day, "begin to ship much water and [the] people become less and less able to bear it." On June 9 they caught a dolphin. Bligh allocated each man two ounces of raw offal, "a happy relief to us," and ordered the rest to be hung up to dry in the sun.

But by June 11, Bligh was again lamenting the extreme weakness of his men, writing repeatedly, "No sign of land." In fact, their journey was nearly over. The next day, "very weak and distressed," according to Bligh, "we discovered Timor." Fryer claimed that he and others had to stop Bligh heading away from it toward a smaller island and that Bligh in "a grand passion" told Fryer, "I suppose you will take the boat from me." Fryer denied it, suspecting that Bligh was enticing him to say something "that he could take hold of—which he had done numbers of times in the course of the voyage" so that he could charge him with an offense. With Bligh somehow convinced to return to the coast of Timor, they coasted "along a low shore, covered with innumerable palm trees" in search of the Dutch settlement at Kupang. Another confrontation between Bligh, Purcell, and Fryer occurred when the latter two asked to go ashore to look for supplies. Bligh after some debate agreed but ordered no one else was to follow them. Perhaps fearing marooning, Fryer and Purcell remained on board.

Eventually Bligh stopped at a shoreside village where, after he intimated "that I would pay him for his trouble," a local man agreed to guide the launch to their destination. At four A.M. on the morning of June 14 they arrived in the bay outside the Dutch harbor of Kupang, where two square riggers swung at anchor. Bligh, punctilious about protocol as always, relates, "I did not think it proper to land without leave . . . Among the things which the boatswain had thrown into the boat before we left the ship was a bundle of signal flags . . . with these we had, in the course of the passage, made a small [union] jack, which I now hoisted in the main shrouds as a signal of distress."

Duly invited to land, they were well received by the ailing Dutch governor and his deputy. Bligh penned a long letter home to his wife, Betsy, which showed his love for her, his concern to justify his conduct, and also the extreme importance he attached to his pursering profits:

My dear, dear Betsy,

I am now in a part of the world that I never expected, it is however a place that has afforded me relief and saved my life . . . What an emotion does my heart and soul feel that I have once more an opportunity of writing to you and my little angels, and particularly as you have all been so near losing the best of friends—when you have had no person to have regarded you as I do, and must have spent the remainder of your days without knowing what had become of me . . . All these dreadful circumstances I have combated with success and in the most extraordinary manner that ever happened, never despairing from the first moment of my disaster that I should overcome all my difficulties.

Know then my own dear Betsy, I have lost the *Bounty* . . . On 28 April at daylight in the morning Christian . . . with several others came into my cabin while I was asleep, and seizing me, holding naked bayonets at my breast, tied my hands behind my back, and threatened instant destruction if I uttered a word. I however called loudly for assistance, but the conspiracy was so well laid that the officers' cabin doors were guarded by sentinels, so that Nelson, Peckover, Samuel or the master could not come to me. I was now dragged on deck in my shirt and closely guarded—I demanded of Christian the cause of such a violent act and severely degraded him for his villainy but he could only answer— "not a word sir or you are dead." I dared him to the act and endeavoured to rally someone to a sense of their duty but to no effect. Besides this villain young Heywood was one of the ringleaders and besides him Stewart . . . Christian I had assured of promotion when he came home and with the other two I was every day rendering them some service—It is incredible! These very young men I placed every confidence in, yet these great villains joined with the most able men in the ship, got possession of the arms and took the *Bounty* from me, with huzzas for Tahiti. I have now reason to curse the day I ever knew a Christian or a Heywood or indeed a Manx man . . . Even Mr. Tom Ellison took such a liking to Tahiti that he also turned pirate, so that I have been run down by my own dogs . . .

My misfortune I trust will be properly considered by all the world—It was a circumstance I could not foresee—I had not sufficient officers and had they granted me marines most likely the affair would never have happened—I had not a spirited and brave fellow about me and the mutineers treated them as such. My conduct has been free of blame, and I showed everyone, that tied as I was, I defied every villain to hurt me. Hayward and Hallett were mate and midshipman of Christian's watch but they alarmed no one, and I found them on deck seemingly [unconcerned] until they were ordered into the boat—The latter has turned out a worthless impudent scoundrel . . .

I know how shocked you will be at this affair but I request of you my dear Betsy to think nothing of it, all is now past . . . Nothing but true consciousness as an officer that I have done well could support me . . . I have saved my pursing books so that all my profits hitherto will take place and all will be well . . .

Love, Respect . . .
Your ever affectionate friend and husband William Bligh

THE CALAMITIES OF CAPTAIN BLIGH

T he only way that Bligh could find to get himself and his men to Batavia (Jakarta), the Dutch headquarters on the island of Java whence ships sailed regularly to Europe, was to purchase a schooner, which he did for one thousand Dutch dollars, naming it the *Resource*. To pay for it, Bligh offered the governor bills of exchange drawn on the British government which, after some demur, he accepted. The apparent reasons for his hesitation were warnings from Fryer that Bligh might not be able to commit the Admiralty to expenditure in the way he claimed.

The friction between Bligh, Fryer, and Purcell had not dissipated, with Bligh denouncing Fryer in his log as "a vicious person" and Fryer accusing Bligh of disrespect for his status as master. Fryer was keeping a private account of the monies Bligh spent so that he could compare them with the accounts Bligh presented to him for formal countersignature. Purcell remained as stubborn and uncooperative as ever, for example refusing Bligh's order to give the Dutch authorities some chalk, which they had run out of, on the grounds that it was his own and not naval property. Sadly, while they were still waiting to depart, David Nelson, the quiet and universally popular gardener, died of "an inflammatory fever" after "imprudently leaving off warm clothing."

After five weeks at Kupang, Bligh and his party of sixteen set off in the *Resource* to Surabaya on Java en route to Batavia, taking the launch that had served them so well along with them. At Surabaya, a climactic confrontation between Bligh, Fryer, and Purcell occurred. It followed a drinking bout on shore in which Hallett and Elphinstone got "beastly drunk" and after reboarding the *Resource* said that they were too unwell to come on deck to attend to their duty. Bligh asked Fryer whether they were drunk or ill. "Am I a doctor?" Fryer responded. "Ask [them]." "What do you mean by this insolence?" Bligh asked. "It is no insolence," retorted Fryer. "You not only use me ill but every man in the vessel, and every man will say the same."

Other members of the crew backed Fryer up. "Yes, by God, we are used damned ill, nor have we any right to be used so." Purcell, "with a daring and vicious look," now "became spokesman," complaining that Bligh had left the men to pay for some goods to be brought out to the *Resource* at their own expense while he hobnobbed with the governor. There was "an open tumult" among "everybody on board." Bligh, never lacking physical courage, grabbed a bayonet and forced Fryer and Purcell to go below. Then he asked the Dutch governor to institute an inquiry into what had happened. From his confinement, Fryer presented his detailed document claiming Bligh was inflating his bills to the Admiralty for expenses incurred at Kupang and claimed that Bligh had also been profiteering from his men throughout the voyage by giving them short rations. No other of Bligh's men produced any substantive complaints except for Hallett, who claimed that Bligh had once beaten him in Tahiti for disobeying an order to enter a boat in water Hallett thought too deep.

Neither the Dutch authorities nor Bligh took any further action. There are some indications that around this time, perhaps mediated by the Dutch governor, Bligh and Fryer came to an agreement that Fryer would drop his charges of financial irregularity and apologize formally for his behavior, and in return Bligh would not attempt to have Fryer court-martialed as he would do Purcell.

Soon after this argument the *Resource*, with the *Bounty*'s launch in tow, put to sea again and on October 1 reached Batavia, a notoriously unhealthy port as Cook had discovered. By October 16, having sold the *Resource* at auction for 30 percent less than he had paid, as well as the *Bounty*'s never-named launch in which he had traveled 3,600 miles, Bligh was on a Dutch ship on his way home to Britain. With him were his clerk, John Samuel, and his servant, John Smith, but he left the rest of his men behind. He claimed that this was because he had been advised to sail as soon as possible by a Dutch surgeon, as he was suffering from intermittent violent headaches. Arguably he was right to hasten home to explain what had happened. Equally arguably he was looking to himself, abandoning his men, leaving them in the care of Fryer, whom he despised personally and professionally. Some of them were very ill and he could have taken them, rather than Samuel and Smith. Hall was already dead but master's mate William Elphinstone and Linkletter would die after Bligh's departure and before they could find a ship to return home. The *Bounty*'s butcher, Robert Lamb, would die aboard ship on his way back to Britain.

Before he left Batavia and despite his illness Bligh had been very busy. He wrote letters to Banks and others exculpating himself from any blame for the mutiny and the loss of his first Royal Navy command, which he put down to Tahiti and its women, consciously or not echoing so many others' views of the island paradise:

> It may be asked what could be the cause for such a revolution. In answer to which I have only to give a description of Tahiti, which has every allurement both to luxury and ease, and is the paradise of the world . . . The women are handsome and mild in their manners and conversation, with sufficient delicacy to make them admired and beloved, and the chiefs have acquired such a liking to our people that they . . . have encouraged their stay among them . . . and even made promises of large possessions to them . . . what a temptation it is to such wretches when they find it in their power (however illegally . . .) to fix them- selves in the midst of plenty in the finest island in the world, where they need not labour, and where the allurements of dissipation are more than equal to anything that can be conceived.

Bligh also drafted detailed descriptions of each of the mutineers so they could be apprehended if the Dutch came upon any of them. That of Chris- tian was: "Master's mate; aged twenty-four years [at the time of the mutiny]; five feet nine inches high; very dark complexion, dark-brown hair, strong made; a star tattooed on his left breast; backside tattooed; a little bow-legged; he is subject to a violent perspiration in his hands, so that he soils anything he handles."*

Bligh used some of the money from the sale of the *Resource* and the *Boun- ty*'s launch to advance the men a month's wages and other monies to pay for their passages but imposed strict terms on these advances, compelling anyone who received one to sign an affidavit that he, Bligh, was not to blame for the mutiny, which had been unprovoked. Thomas Ledward, the acting surgeon, however, disclosed in a letter to his uncle from Batavia some more surprising and onerous financial terms Bligh imposed upon him and others. Bligh would

---

*Christian's sweating palms are likely to have been a symptom of hyperhidrosis—a condition caused by problems with the part of the nervous system that controls sweating and is some- times related to anxiety.

not advance money "unless I would give him my power of attorney and also my will, in which I was to bequeath him all my property; this he called by the name of proper security. This unless I did, I should have got no money, though I showed him a letter of credit from my uncle and offered to give him a bill of exchange upon him. In case of my death I hope this matter will be clearly pointed out to my relations."*

Bligh was unimpressed by the Dutch ship on which he took passage back to Britain, complaining about the food and the dirty condition of both ship and crew. He also found Dutch navigation techniques wanting and claimed that had he been captain he could have got one and a half nautical miles an hour more out of the vessel. When the ship reached Cape Town, Bligh left a detailed description of the mutiny and the mutineers for onward transmission to the penal settlement at Botany Bay in case any of the mutineers should head for New South Wales.

Bligh reached England in mid-March 1790 after a five-month return voyage just over two years after he had set out on the *Bounty*, and at once became the hero of the hour. His romantic tales of sailors' love so strong it forced them into mutiny against a more dutiful captain so they could return to the welcoming arms of the fabled beauties of Tahiti, and his accounts of the bravery of the open-boat voyage on starvation rations through hostile islands and mountainous seas to safety, captivated all. Bligh was presented to the king. Newspapers burgeoned with breathless, sometimes exaggerated accounts of the mutiny and its aftermath. Bligh's *Narrative of the Mutiny on board His Majesty's Ship Bounty and the Subsequent Voyage of Part of the Crew in the Ship's Boat . . . to Timor* was published quickly, on July 1, 1790, and almost as quickly became a bestseller.

Just two months after he landed, a new play—a musical spectacular—was advertised to be performed at the Royalty Theatre in London called "The Pirates; Or the Calamities of Captain Bligh." It promised "a fact told in action, exhibiting a full account of [Bligh's] voyage . . . the captain's reception at Tahiti, and exchanging the British manufactures for the breadfruit—with a Tahitian dance—the attachment of the Tahitian women too, and their distress at parting from the British sailors—an exact representation of the seizure of Captain Bligh, in the cabin of the *Bounty* by the pirates, with the affecting scene of forcing the captain and his faithful followers into the

---

*Ledward was drowned when his ship was lost with all hands on his way back to Britain and it is believed Bligh did indeed profit from his will.

boat—their distress at sea . . . and their happy arrival in England." The publicity also claimed the play had been "rehearsed under the immediate instruction of a person who was on board the *Bounty*." (The truth of the latter and the identity of the anonymous playwright are lost in time.)

With no one to dispute his account, Bligh quickly won over Joseph Banks and other members of the establishment to his view of the mutiny. Banks, who had scarcely known Bligh when he set out, now became his firm patron and remained so for the rest of his life. Despite suffering increasingly from the gout that would later confine him for periods to a wheelchair, Banks retained great influence and energy and through his good offices obtained promotion for Bligh, first to commander and then, before the year's end, to the coveted status of post-captain.

The Admiralty was not, however, so entirely impressed by Bligh as to forego all financial prudence when dealing with him. Officials there refused out of hand his request to be paid £283, 1 shilling and 6 pence for the loss of his personal possessions on the *Bounty*. This sum, Bligh said, covered a wide variety of items from his library of forty-eight books (£47), port brandy and wine he bought at Tenerife (£59), down to 18 shillings for a dozen nightcaps and his box of pencils (2 shillings and 6 pence). The greatest loss was probably his *Resolution* log and charts, from his voyage with Cook, and similar material from the *Bounty* voyage up until the mutiny. He was, however, compensated, presumably on the basis of his lovingly preserved accounts, for provisions he had bought during the voyage but not, despite his claims, for the provisions he had obtained at Tahiti with the trade goods supplied by the authorities. However, the Jamaican House of Assembly more than made up for the monies denied him by the Admiralty by awarding him 500 guineas (£525) for his attempt—albeit unsuccessful—to bring the breadfruit to them to feed their slaves. With this reward and the increased pay from two promotions, Bligh's "poor little family" would be poor no more.

The families of all those named as mutineers would have been in shock, dismay, and quite possibly denial about their relations' activities. This was certainly the case with the only two families whose feelings were recorded— the Christians and the Heywoods. When Captain Taubman, husband of Fletcher Christian's cousin and the man who had advised him to contact Bligh for a position, asked Bligh to his face why Christian had acted as he did, Bligh replied simply, "insanity." In doing so, he probably came much closer to the truth than in anything he said about the charms of Tahitian women.

In a letter written a fortnight after his return to Britain in response to an inquiry from Heywood's widowed mother about her son, Bligh said that he understood "the extreme distress you must suffer from the conduct of your son Peter. His baseness is beyond all description but I hope you will endeavour to prevent the loss of him, heavy as the misfortune is, from afflicting you too severely." To one of Heywood's uncles he wrote, "His [Heywood's) ingratitude to me is of the blackest dye for I was a father to him in every respect and he never once had an angry word from me through the whole course of the voyage as his conduct always gave me much pleasure and satisfaction. I very much regret that so much baseness formed the character of a young man I had a real regard for and it will give me much pleasure to hear that his friends can bear the loss of him without much concern."

Charles Christian—perhaps remembering the mutiny in which he was involved on the East Indiaman *Middlesex*—wrote, "Fletcher when a boy was slow to be moved . . . [but] when men are cooped up for a long time in the interior of a ship there oft prevails such jarring discordancy of tempers and conduct that it is enough on many occasions by repeated acts of irritation and offence to change the disposition of a lamb into that of an animal fierce and resentful."

As is still the case with every Royal Navy captain who loses his ship and survives, Bligh faced a formal court-martial on the loss. This took place in Portsmouth on October 22, 1790, after all the survivors of the launch voyage had returned to Britain. Fryer appeared as a witness and confirmed Bligh's version of the mutiny, making no criticism of his commander. The court quickly concluded "the *Bounty* was violently and forcibly taken from the said Lieutenant William Bligh by the said Fletcher Christian and certain other mutineers." The court therefore honorably acquitted Bligh and the loyalists among his crew of any blame for the loss.

Keeping the agreement he seems to have made with the master in the Dutch East Indies, Bligh brought no charges against Fryer. However, he brought six charges against Purcell, who faced a court-martial two weeks before Bligh's own on the loss of the *Bounty*. The charges included Purcell's behavior at Adventure Bay and on Sunday Island. Fryer appeared and confirmed Bligh's version of events, admitting that he had heard Purcell "sometimes drop improper words." William Peckover, however, did add a detail or two to the story of Adventure Bay, when Purcell had told Bligh he had come on shore for nothing but to find fault. Sending him back to the ship, Bligh had yelled, "I'll put a rope about your neck!"

The court found the charges had been proved in part and sentenced Purcell to be reprimanded—the mildest punishment that could be awarded. The court no doubt did not wish to sully the heroic *Bounty* launch story in the public mind, just as the Admiralty had had no wish to sully the heroics of the HMS *Wager* survivors almost fifty years before. It is even possible Purcell was told that in return for not creating further trouble his sentence would be lenient. When Purcell was called to give evidence two weeks later at the court-martial investigating the loss of the *Bounty* he said he had no complaint against his captain. Bligh told Banks of the court's "exceeding great leniency . . . a great part of my evidence" had been held back "as it affected [Purcell's] life." In other words, Purcell could have been executed.

Neither Bligh nor the Admiralty had any intention that the mutineers should be allowed to live out their lives amid the pleasures of the South Seas. In early November 1790, the Admiralty dispatched Captain Edward Edwards aboard the twenty-four gun HMS *Pandora* to hunt them down. Edwards was a harsh disciplinarian. He had himself suppressed an incipient mutiny among his own crew aboard HMS *Narcissus* off the North American coast nine years earlier, following which five of the would-be mutineers had been hanged in New York and two others severely flogged, one receiving five hundred lashes and the other two hundred. Among the *Pandora*'s 140-man crew was Thomas Hayward, who had survived the open-boat journey with Bligh. Newly promoted from his previous rank of midshipman to third lieutenant, he was expected to be useful to the mission both for his knowledge of Tahiti— believed by Bligh to be the mutineers' destination—and his ability to iden- tify the individual mutineers.

Edwards's orders were to take HMS *Pandora* to the South Seas to endeavor to recover the *Bounty* and there hunt down "and bring in confinement to England . . . Fletcher Christian and his associates." The list of "mutineers" appended to Edwards's orders made no distinction between active mutineers, bystanders, and those detained against their will. All were to be "as closely confined as may preclude all probability of their escaping, having however proper regard to the preservation of their lives, that they may be brought home to undergo the punishment due to their demerits."

Specifically, Edwards was to sail first to Tahiti to see whether the muti- neers were still there. If not, he was to enquire discreetly of the islanders about the whereabouts of the *Bounty* and her crew without explaining his reasons until he had discovered whether the Tahitians knew Bligh had been dispossessed of his ship. If any mutineers were still on Tahiti, his orders included authority "to detain such of the chiefs as you may be able to get hold of" as hostages and to dispatch "a strong party well armed to go in quest of the mutineers." If he drew a blank at Tahiti, Edwards was to sweep the neighboring Society Islands before proceeding to the Friendly Islands and searching there. Then, "having succeeded or failed," before passing south of Java and heading home he was to sail through and survey the Torres Strait so that in future ships could take that route more confidently to Port Jackson.

Ever since Bligh's return with the news of the failure of the breadfruit expedition the West Indian plantation owners had been pressing Joseph Banks and the Admiralty for a second voyage to bring breadfruit plants to the Caribbean to feed their slaves. By early 1791 Bligh knew one was to take place and that he would command it, a mark of considerable trust and belief in him in the aftermath of the mutiny. In early February he wrote to Lieutenant Francis (Frank) Godolphin Bond, the son of his much older half-sister, offering him the post of first lieutenant on the voyage, which Bond accepted. Bligh helped select two ships for the expedition: the 420-ton HMS *Providence* and a one-hundred-ton brig named appropriately for its function HMS *Assistant*.

Bligh would this time have several other commissioned officers as well as Bond. His midshipmen included the son of John Gore, who had brought Cook's third expedition home, and seventeen-year-old Matthew Flinders. In later years, Flinders would command the first expedition to circumnavigate and produce detailed charts of the whole of New Holland, which in 1804 he would be the first to name "Australia."*

Of the loyal survivors of the *Bounty* voyage Bligh took only two—his servant, John Smith, and Lawrence Lebogue, the sailmaker. He refused William Peckover's request to join and to make a sixth visit to Tahiti. Bligh told Banks if anyone approached him about Peckover for any reason, Banks should say he was "a vicious and worthless fellow"—a surprising condemnation of someone who on Cook's voyages and on the *Bounty* and afterward had done little wrong except perhaps to repeat at Purcell's court-martial Bligh's threat to hang the carpenter. Some years later, when Bligh found

---

*Flinders was also the originator of the idea of using iron bars placed near a ship's compass to counteract the magnetic attraction of iron elsewhere in the ship and thus to keep the compass true. The bars were named Flinders Bars in his honor.

Peckover serving on a vessel he was to command he asked the Admiralty to get this "decayed" man off his ship.

To guard against any repetition of the *Bounty* mutiny, twenty marines would join the second voyage. As well as obtaining breadfruit plants from Tahiti and transporting them to the West Indies, Bligh's orders included the charting of the Torres Strait to facilitate the passage of British convict transports between Batavia and New South Wales. Two suggestions by Banks were not included in the orders: that Bligh should either visit Norfolk Island during the voyage to procure Norfolk pines and then take them to the New South Wales convict settlement for planting, or that he should visit New Zealand and find two local people skilled in working flax to take to the settlement to teach the convicts to make clothes for themselves.

Another proposal that did not in the end go ahead was made by the evangelical Dr. Thomas Haweis that Bligh should take with him to Tahiti two missionaries to convert the islanders to Christianity. He obtained the approval of both Bligh and Banks, even though the latter was "little inclined to conversions," partly by suggesting that a British presence on Tahiti would help the supply of pigs and other provisions to the convict colony. The scheme, however, foundered when the two young men, named Price and Waugh, refused to go after being declined ordination before departure.

XIV

"HURRAH FOR A BELLYFUL, AND NEWS OF OUR FRIENDS"

*W*hile the *Bounty* had still been at anchor in Tahiti and Bligh and his men were collecting breadfruit, three thousand nautical miles away Governor Phillip had continued to worry how to feed the new colony rising around Sydney Cove. In early November 1788, he set out with some officers to reconnoiter Port Jackson's eastern shores for further cultivable land. Following a river upstream they came to a hill that "free from that rock which everywhere covered the surface at Sydney Cove, well clothed with timber, and unobstructed by underwood," looked so promising that Phillip decided to establish another settlement there. He named it Rose Hill—not for its undoubted horticultural promise but in compliment to G. Rose Esquire, a treasury official in London—and ordered convicts to clear land ready for planting. Rose Hill soon returned to its Aboriginal name, Parramatta.

Phillip strove to improve the colony's relations with the Aboriginal people. Concluding that the only way to win their trust was through better communication, he decided—perhaps oddly, given that an act of violence would be unlikely to inspire confidence—to kidnap an Aboriginal man to act as an interpreter. On December 31, 1788, he dispatched two boatloads of marines, commanded by Lieutenant George Johnston of the marines and Lieutenant Ball of the *Supply*, "to seize and carry off some of the natives." They set out for Manly Cove, a bay on the north side of the harbor, so named by Phillip for the fine bearing of Aboriginal men he had observed there, where they spotted a group of men on the shore and by dint of "courteous behaviour and a few presents" lured two of them toward the boats.

As the marines tried to grab the pair, their companions ran off but returned quickly with reinforcements, all brandishing spears. One of the two men the marines were attempting to seize broke free and swam off. However, they managed to drag the second into a boat at which the Aboriginals "threw spears, stones, firebrands, and whatever else presented itself at the boats" and only retreated when "many muskets were fired over them." The marines bound their captive with rope to the thwarts of the boat, where for a while he "set up the most piercing and lamentable cries of distress," and set out for Sydney Cove.

As the boats arrived, curious people, Lieutenant Watkin Tench among them, hurried to the shore to witness the sight. He decided the captive was about thirty years old and that "under happier circumstances" his countenance "would display manliness and sensibility." Plainly and understandably terrified, the man was taken to Phillip's house where, to calm him, he was first served a meal of fish and duck before being bathed and having his hair—"filled with vermin," which his captors tried to discourage him from eating—cut short and his beard shaved. Next, to complete his transformation, Phillip had him dressed in a shirt, jacket, and trousers. Since he seemed reluctant to disclose his name—or perhaps did not understand what he was being asked—Phillip named him "Manly" after the place of his capture. To prevent him absconding, "a handcuff with a rope attached to it, was fastened around his left wrist" and a convict was assigned to stay with him night and day—"his keeper," as Tench called him.

Manly was given a hut in the grounds of Phillip's house and was fed well, astonishing Tench by his ability to devour at one sitting two kangaroo rats "each the size of a moderate rabbit" and three pounds of fish. Gradually, his dejection seemed to ease and he disclosed not only his name—Arabanoo—but also "much information relating to the customs and manners of his country."

From conversations with Arabanoo and later others, including in particular a young woman, Patyegarang, Tench's friend Lieutenant William Dawes would fill three notebooks with lists of Aboriginal words and phrases and attempt to analyze the language's structure. Among the many words he recorded were *biana*, "father"; *wiana*, "mother"; *garugal*, "a long time back"; and *berewalgal*, "people from a great distance off." He also noted Patyegarang's anger that the new arrivals had settled—unasked—on Aboriginal land and her fear of their firearms. Dawes's notebooks, unearthed in 1972 in the collections of London University's School of Oriental and African Studies, comprise the most extensive written record of the language spoken by Port Jackson's Aboriginal community to survive today.

Deprivation in the colony was growing daily more serious. In early February 1789, convict Joseph Paget informed on the colony's chief fisherman, William Bryant, for "secreting and selling large quantities of fish" above the amount he was allowed to keep and trading this surplus with other convicts for vegetables. This was a serious crime for which Advocate-General Collins sentenced him "to receive 100 lashes; to be deprived of the direction of the fish and the boat; and to be turned out of the hut he is now in along with his family." Bryant was bound by his ankles and wrists to the punishment triangle and, as marines drummed a rhythmic tattoo, whipped with a tarred and knotted cat-o'-nine-tails.

With the *Sirius* not yet returned from Cape Town, Phillip was again forced to reduce the rations. Soon after, sixteen convicts abandoned their work at the brick kilns posts, armed themselves with their work tools and some clubs, and headed to Botany Bay, intending to steal spears and fishing equipment from the Aboriginals. However, a group of Aboriginals attacked them, killing one and injuring seven more. Fleeing back to the camp, the survivors maintained they had been ambushed without warning while "quietly picking sweet tea." An incensed Phillip did not believe a word of this and forced them to admit they had been the aggressors. Each man was sentenced to 150 lashes and to wear leg irons for a year. Arabanoo was made to witness the floggings so he would "comprehend the cause and the necessity of it" and be able to assure his people justice had been done. However, he was as appalled as the Tahitians had been by such savage punishment, showing "symptoms of disgust and terror only."

Even more seriously from Phillip's point of view, on March 18 seven marines were found to have been stealing flour, meat, spirits, and tobacco from the public storehouses for eight months after duping a convict locksmith into making them duplicate keys. To save his own life, one marine informed against the others. On March 26 the remaining six—"the flower of our battalion" Tench wrote—were hanged from a gallows specially erected between the two storehouses with "hardly a marine present but what shed tears, officers and men." Aware from such episodes how easily hunger might destabilize the fragile colony, in early April Phillip put William Bryant—who as Collins observed "notwithstanding his villainy . . . was too useful a person to part with and send to a brick cart"—back in charge of the colony's fishing. He also allowed him, his wife, Mary, and her young daughter, Charlotte, to move back into their hut on the east side of the cove, but warned Bryant he would be closely watched.

To add to Phillip's anxieties, April brought what Tench called with justice "an extraordinary calamity": smallpox. The Aboriginal community, some already suffering from syphilis and gonorrhea courtesy of the new arrivals, were its chief victims. Tench wrote of the horror of "our boats finding bodies of the Indians in all the coves and inlets of the harbour." The reason for the outbreak puzzled Governor Phillip, Surgeon White, and others. As their pocked, pitted skin testified, many convicts had had smallpox in Britain, while some had been inoculated against it. During the voyage to New South Wales no one had contracted it. Tench wondered whether it might have spread from La Pérouse's ships or been introduced by Cook's expedition or even Dampier's a century earlier to the west coast. Another theory, dismissed by Tench as "so wild as to be unworthy of consideration," was that it had escaped from White's bottles of "variolous matter"—*variola* being the Latin name for smallpox—that he had brought from England in case he needed to inoculate anyone in the colony.

Collins hoped that treating suffering Aboriginal people at the hospital might help "do away the evil impressions they had received of us." Phillip, however, worried that the local people would blame him for the disaster which, according to one estimate, killed around two thousand Aboriginals. Arabanoo was among them. He helped bury victims, scooping out graves in the sand that he then lined with grass, until he too caught the disease, which he called *galgalla*, dying in May 1789. As a mark of special favor, Phillip had him buried in his own garden and attended his funeral.

Shortly before Arabanoo's death, there had finally been better news for the colony when toward sunset lookouts sighted the *Sirius* beating toward the harbor's distinctive sandstone Heads. By rounding Cape Horn, she had reached Cape Town in just thirteen weeks but it had not been an easy voyage. Encountering tumultuous seas and shrieking winds, she had lost the top of her foremast and her carved wooden figurehead of the Duke of Berwick. However, aboard were 127,000 pounds of flour—enough for four to six months—together with wheat and barley seed for planting, so that, Tench wrote "the day of famine was at least procrastinated."

The *Sirius*'s bounty allowed King George III's birthday on June 4, 1789, to be celebrated with genuine cheer. The program of "loyal festivity" included a performance by convicts of George Farquhar's comedy *The Recruiting Officer*, delivered with brio and a certain irony, according to Tench:

> The exhilarating effect of a splendid theatre is well known: and I am not ashamed to confess, that the distribution of three or four yards of stained paper, and a dozen farthing candles stuck in bottles around the mud walls of a convict-hut

failed not to diffuse general complacency on the countenances of sixty persons, of various descriptions, who were assembled to applaud the representation. Some of the actors acquitted themselves with great spirit, and received the praises of the audience: a prologue and an epilogue, written by one of the performers, were also spoken . . . contain[ing] some tolerable allusions to the situation of the parties, and the novelty of a stage representation in New South Wales.

Such escapism proved short-lived. A few weeks later a marine was convicted of raping an eight-year-old European girl. Though spared the death penalty, he was sent to Norfolk Island to serve there. A female convict—known variously as Ann Davis or Judith Jones—caught stealing from the huts of male convicts in November 1789, after Phillip had again cut the rations, did not receive such mercy. She tried to save herself by "pleading her belly"—the euphemism for being pregnant. However, "twelve of the discreetest women among the convicts, all of whom had been mothers of children, being impanelled as a jury of matrons," inspected her and concluded she was lying, and she was hanged—the first woman executed in New South Wales.

With, in Tench's words, "hardly a night passing without the commission of robbery," a prisoner named John Harris asked that a small group of trusted convicts be allowed to form a night watch. Phillip agreed. Collins regretted the necessity of appointing a guard comprising men "in whose eyes, it could not be denied, the property of individuals had never before been sacred," but had to acknowledge that many London streets "were not so well guarded and watched as the small, but rising town of Sydney." Indeed, so successful was the "convict watch" that another was introduced at Rose Hill.

Arabanoo's death had not deterred Governor Phillip from wishing to find another Aboriginal man to help him communicate with the locals and also to tell him "whether or not the country possessed any resources, by which life might be prolonged." In November, he dispatched Lieutenant Bradley of the *Sirius* to Manly Cove, where Arabanoo had been taken. There his men captured and shackled two Aboriginals, their kidnap triggering a cacophony of crying and screaming from those who witnessed it from the shore and from the captives themselves. Bradley thought it "by far the most unpleasant service I was ever ordered to execute."

Tench was again among those watching the two men—both scarred by smallpox—arrive in Sydney Cove. Also in the crowd was a young Aboriginal boy cured by Surgeon White of smallpox and since adopted by him, who greeted the older man as "Colby" and the younger as "Bennelong." Tench estimated Bennelong's age as about twenty-six, noting his strong build and "bold intrepid countenance which bespoke defiance and revenge." The captives were taken to Phillip, who again assigned each a "keeper." In Colby's case, the precaution was in vain. During the evening meal on December 12, he somehow managed to detach his leg shackle from its fastening and with "a small iron ring" still around his leg made a sudden and successful dash for freedom. His minder received one hundred lashes for his carelessness.

Focussing his attention on Bennelong, Phillip dressed him in a jacket and trousers and, on Sundays, a special suit of yellow clothes and taught him to toast King George; rapidly acquiring a taste for wine and brandy, he was happy to do so. According to Tench, "He acquired knowledge, both of our manners and language, faster than his predecessor had done. He willingly communicated information; sang, danced and capered, told us all the customs of his country . . . Love and war seemed his favourite pursuits."

As with Arabanoo, Phillip ensured Bennelong had plenty to eat—feeding him in one day the ration on which the colonists were expected to subsist for a week—to please and reassure him but also to camouflage the colony's increasingly precarious condition. Phillip feared that, "had he penetrated our state, perhaps he might have given his countrymen such a description of our diminished strength as would have emboldened them to become more troublesome." The food situation was indeed critical. By early 1790, so essential had fish become to the colonists' survival that Phillip agreed for the public good to allow William Bryant to use the governor's own cutter to catch fish three times a week. Since the cutter was larger and stronger than any other available boat, Bryant could range farther afield in search of the sometimes elusive shoals.

If hunger was taking its physical toll on the colonists, both captive and free, their growing sense of isolation was taking a mental one. Tench captured the increasing despondency, writing:

> Our impatience of news from Europe strongly marked the commencement of the year. We had now been two years in the country, and thirty-two months from England, in which long period no supplies, except what had been procured at the Cape of Good Hope by the *Sirius*, had reached us. From intelligence of our friends and connections we had been entirely cut off . . . Famine besides was approaching with gigantic strides, and gloom and dejection overspread every countenance. Men abandoned themselves to the most desponding reflections,

and adopted the most extravagant conjectures . . . every morning from daylight until the sun sunk, did we sweep the horizon, in hope of seeing a sail.

Another officer of marines echoed the thoughts of many: "Surely our countrymen cannot have altogether forgotten us?" But still no ship came.

In March 1790, Phillip dispatched Major Robert Ross—with whom he had been clashing with growing frequency over what Ross perceived as Phillip's over-lenient treatment of the convicts and unwarranted harshness toward the marines—aboard the *Sirius* to Norfolk Island. There he was to relieve Lieutenant Philip Gidley King, who was anxious to return to Britain and on whom Phillip thought he could rely to give the authorities an accurate picture of the colony's woes. After depositing Ross and nearly two hundred convicts at Norfolk Island, the *Sirius* was to sail on to China to buy supplies. The *Supply* would accompany her, carrying twenty-five more convicts and, after returning King to Port Jackson, follow the *Sirius* to China. Mary Broad's companion in highway robbery Mary Haydon was among the prisoners selected to sail to Norfolk Island, where she would soon be causing trouble, receiving fifty lashes "for being drunk and making a noise in the camp" and a further fifty for making fraudulent use of Ross's name.

Lieutenant Ralph Clark was horrified to learn that he was to accompany Ross. All he could do was pluck a few leaves of "sweet tea" to take with him and hope that at least Norfolk Island would have "more resources in it than this place . . . For I find there is no more from the first of next month than thirteen weeks of provisions left in store. God help us. If some ships do not arrive, I don't know what will." In fact, Norfolk Island was suffering as badly if not worse than Port Jackson, and King had been begging Phillip for more supplies, especially livestock. However, Clark could at least take with him the woman who, having finally put aside thoughts of his wife Betsey Alicia's perfections, he had taken as his mistress—nineteen-year-old Mary Branham, a former servant transported for stealing clothes. He would name the daughter they had Alicia.

Other officers had also by now formed lasting liaisons. Esther Abrahams, the young Jewish dressmaker from East London, was about to bear Lieutenant George Johnston of the marines a son. She would later marry Johnston and become one of Port Jackson's wealthiest, most influential women. On the other hand, Phillip—like Cook and Bligh during their expeditions—seems to have remained celibate throughout his stay in New South Wales.

Three weeks after the two ships sailed, Mary Bryant gave birth to a son who, on April 4, 1790, was baptized Emmanuel. The next day, the sight of a flag being raised on the South Head brought great excitement. Many thought supply ships had been sighted. Tench, going to Dawes's observatory to peer through his friend's powerful astronomical telescope, was less hopeful. The flag was indeed up but Tench "could see nobody near the flagstaff except one solitary being, who kept strolling around, unmoved by what he saw. I well knew how different an effect the sight of strange ships would produce."

Tench, together with Phillip, hurried down to the harbor and, Tench wrote, "We were surprised to see a boat, which was known to belong to the *Supply*, rowing towards us. On nearer approach, I saw Captain [Lidgbird] Ball make an extraordinary motion with his hand, which too plainly indicated something disastrous." Turning to Phillip he said, "Sir, prepare yourself for bad news!" Ball was indeed the bearer of bad tidings. He was hastening ashore from the *Supply* to report that shortly after reaching Norfolk Island the *Sirius* had been lost. Though the convicts and marines had disembarked safely on the island's north side, before supplies could also be landed, high winds had driven the *Sirius* out to sea. Hoping to find more sheltered conditions, the captain had sailed around to the island's south side and begun unloading provisions. However, further violent winds had forced the *Sirius* onto a reef and despite desperate attempts to free her by jettisoning her rigging and masts, she had foundered.

For Philip these were moments of "unspeakable consternation" as he realized that he would have to manage without the provisions the *Sirius* was to have brought back from China. He ordered an immediate inventory of the colony's remaining food stocks. Then, gathering his officers and officials, he told them that on current rations, the supplies of salt meat would run out on July 2, flour on August 20, and rice or peas on October 1. He had no option but again to reduce the food allowance to a mere "two pounds of pork, two pounds and a half of flour, two pounds of rice, or a quart of pease per week." What food remained was increasingly inedible. Tench described pork "salted between three and four years" and "so old and dry" that it shrank to half its size when boiled—instead, they toasted it on a fork over the fire—and maggoty rice of which every grain "was a moving body, from the inhabitants lodged in it."

With the *Sirius* sunk, the colony's only seagoing vessel was the *Supply*, which Phillip now dispatched to Batavia, where her captain was to purchase flour and also to charter an additional vessel to bring back provisions to Port

Buccaneer, naturalist, and hydrographer William Dampier, born in the west country of England—he and his pirate companions became the first Britons to set foot on Australia when, in 1688, they landed on the northwest coast. SHUTTERSTOCK

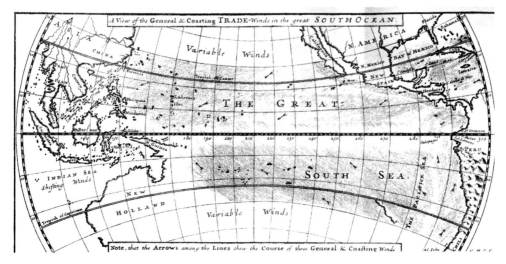

Dampier's wind map of the world—the first to include the wind patterns of the Pacific.

obereyau Enchantress

Purea, a Tahitian noblewoman who befriended Samuel Wallis, commander of the first British expedition to Tahiti, and subsequently Joseph Banks and James Cook. *OBEREYAU ENCHANTRESS* BY PHILIPPE JACQUES DE LOUTHERBOURG, NATIONAL LIBRARY OF AUSTRALIA, DIGITAL COLLECTION NUMBER 134414969

Omai, the first Polynesian to visit Britain—the need to return him to his homeland was the official explanation for Captain Cook's third and final expedition, but was in reality cover for Cook's search for the Northwest Passage. *OMAI OF THE FRIENDLY ISLES* BY SIR JOSHUA REYNOLDS, NATIONAL LIBRARY OF AUSTRALIA, DIGITAL COLLECTION NUMBER 135229180

CAPTAIN COOK TAKING POSSESSION OF THE AUSTRALIAN CONTINENT, ON BEHALF OF THE BRITISH CROWN, A.D. 1770,
UNDER THE NAME OF NEW SOUTH WALES.
FROM THE GREAT HISTORICAL PAINTING BY GILFILLAN, IN THE POSSESSION OF THE ROYAL SOCIETY OF VICTORIA.

Captain Cook on "Possession Island" on August 22, 1770, claiming Australia's eastern seaboard under the name of New South Wales for King George III. *CAPTAIN COOK TAKING POSSESSION OF THE AUSTRALIAN CONTINENT* BY SAMUEL CALVERT, NATIONAL LIBRARY OF AUSTRALIA, DIGITAL COLLECTION NUMBER 135699884

Joseph Banks, the gentleman naturalist who sailed on Cook's first expedition, became president of the Royal Society and was instrumental in the dispatch of the convict fleet to Botany Bay and of HMAS *Bounty* to Tahiti.

PORTRAIT OF SIR JOSEPH BANKS BY N. SCHIAVONETTI, NATIONAL LIBRARY OF AUSTRALIA, DIGITAL COLLECTION NUMBER 135980825

The great South Sea Caterpillar, transform'd into a *Bath Butterfly*.

Cartoonist James Gillray's satirical depiction of Joseph Banks metamorphosing from a caterpillar into a flaunting butterfly on his investiture with the Order of the Bath in 1795 by his friend and patron King George III, symbolized here by the sun.

A stone *marae*, scene of Tahitian rituals. PHOTO BY M. PRESTON

The monument erected
to Captain James Cook in
Kealakekua Bay, Hawaii
Island ("The Big Island"),
on the site where in 1779
he was clubbed to death.
PHOTO BY M. PRESTON

Arthur Phillip, who commanded the First Fleet carrying convicts to Botany Bay and was the first Governor of New South Wales.

William Bligh, who commanded the HMAS *Bounty* on its fateful voyage to Tahiti to fetch breadfruit seedlings.
PORTRAIT OF REAR-ADMIRAL WILLIAM BLIGH BY ALEXANDER HUEY, NATIONAL LIBRARY OF AUSTRALIA, DIGITAL COLLECTION NUMBER 136207002

FACING PAGE:
Captain Phillip raising the Union Jack in Sydney Cove, Port Jackson, on January 26, 1788, to mark the founding of the settlement there.
MITCHELL LIBRARY, STATE LIBRARY OF NEW SOUTH WALES, THE FOUNDING OF AUSTRALIA

THE FIRST FLEET

ENTERING PORT JACKSON, JANUARY 26, 1788.

The First Fleet sailing into Port Jackson after Captain Phillip decided this was a preferable place to found a settlement to the more exposed Botany Bay.

MITCHELL LIBRARY, STATE LIBRARY OF NEW SOUTH WALES, *THE FIRST FLEET ENTERING PORT JACKSON, JANUARY 26, 1788*

The Melancholy Loss of H.M.M.S. SIRIUS off Norfolk Island March 19 1790

Taken from the Flagstaff on Norfolk Island

HMS *Sirius*, Captain Phillip's flagship during the voyage from England of the First Fleet, foundering off Norfolk Island in 1790.

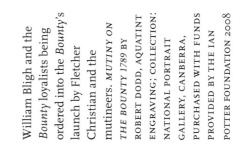

William Bligh and the *Bounty* loyalists being ordered into the *Bounty's* launch by Fletcher Christian and the mutineers. *MUTINY ON THE BOUNTY 1789 BY ROBERT DODD, AQUATINT ENGRAVING; COLLECTION: NATIONAL PORTRAIT GALLERY, CANBERRA, PURCHASED WITH FUNDS PROVIDED BY THE IAN POTTER FOUNDATION 2008*

Matavai Bay, where Wallis, Cook, Bligh, and Edwards anchored during their visits to Tahiti.
PHOTO BY M. PRESTON

Bennelong, the young Aboriginal man kidnapped on Captain Phillip's orders to act as interpreter and later brought to England by Phillip before returning to Port Jackson. Today, Sydney Opera House occupies the site of Bennelong's house.
MITCHELL LIBRARY, STATE LIBRARY OF NEW SOUTH WALES, PORTRAIT OF BENNELONG

Watkin Tench, an officer of the Royal Marines who sailed with the First Fleet and wrote sympathetically of the prisoners and of the early days of the settlement at Port Jackson.

James Boswell, friend and biographer of Dr. Samuel Johnson, who intervened to save Mary Bryant (née Broad) and her fellow escapees from Port Jackson after their arrest.

The font of the ancient church of St. Fimbarrus in the Cornish fishing village of Fowey where highwaywoman Mary Broad, who escaped from the convict settlement, was baptized.
PHOTO BY M. PRESTON

Fowey as it is today. PHOTO BY M. PRESTON

Elizabeth Farm Cottage in Rosehill, the oldest surviving private European dwelling in New South Wales and home to John Macarthur, who challenged William Bligh's authority as Governor of New South Wales, and his wife, Elizabeth. PHOTO BY M. PRESTON

The author with one of HMAS *Bounty*'s cannon salvaged by the mutineers after their arrival on Pitcairn Island. PHOTO BY M. PRESTON

HMAS *Bounty*'s anchor, Pitcairn Island. PHOTO BY M. PRESTON

Site where the burned wreck of HMAS *Bounty* lies off Pitcairn Island. PHOTO BY M. PRESTON

Grave of John Adams (alias Alexander Smith) on Pitcairn Island, where he was the last survivor of the *Bounty* mutineers who landed there. PHOTO BY M. PRESTON

Memorial HMAS *Bounty*, Point Venus, Tahiti. PHOTO BY M. PRESTON

Jackson. The *Supply* would also carry urgent dispatches from Phillip to the British government asking for their help, to be sent on from Batavia on other ships.

Meanwhile, the colony had to subsist as best it could. Like William Dampier a century before, the new arrivals still had no idea of how the Aboriginal community lived off the land and that sources of nutrition existed if they only knew where to look. Bennelong could no longer be of any assistance since—not long after Phillip had ordered the shackle on his ankle to be struck off and given him, as a mark of trust, a sword to wear—he had "nimbly leaped over a slight paling" in Phillip's garden "and bid us adieu." In the circumstances, the fish brought in under William Bryant's oversight were ever more important: David Collins noted every catch of two thousand pounds of fish allowed "a saving of 500 lbs of pork at the store, the allowance of thirty-one men for four weeks." To increase the supplies of fish, Phillip asked everyone from his officers to the Reverend Johnson to volunteer to go out with the boats. Phillip also chose the best marksmen from among the convicts and the marines and sent them "under the command of a trusty sergeant . . . to range the woods in search of kangaroos." As an incentive both the fishing and hunting volunteers received additional rations.

Despite these measures, people were fainting from hunger. A fishing party lost a full net because they lacked the strength to haul it in. The stomach of an elderly convict who collapsed and died while waiting for his rations was cut open and "found quite empty." Accepting that starving people could scarcely be expected to do a full day's work, Phillip decided they should work only in the mornings, leaving them free to cultivate their vegetable patches— if they had the energy—for the rest of the day. Many dreamed of escaping what had become a living hell, including Collins, who despaired at spending "the prime of my life at the farthest point of the world . . . under constant apprehensions of being starved."

Not until June 3, 1790, an unpromisingly wet and blustery day, did the people of Port Jackson learn that their homeland had not, after all, forgotten them, as a cry of "the flag's up resounded in every direction." Tench captured a moment of absolute exhilaration:

> I was sitting in my hut, musing on our fate, when a confused clamour in the street drew my attention. I opened my door, and saw several women with children in their arms, running to and fro with distracted looks, congratulating each other, and kissing their infants with the most passionate and extravagant

marks of fondness. I needed no more; but instantly started out, and ran to a hill, where by the assistance of a pocket glass, my hopes were realised. My next door neighbour, a brother-officer, was with me, but we could not speak. We wrung each other by the hand, with eyes and hearts overflowing.

Hastening down to the beach, Tench found Phillip preparing to board his cutter and asked to go with him. To their joy, ahead they saw "a large ship, with English colours flying, working in between the Heads." "'Pull away, my lads! She is from old England! A few strokes more, and we shall be aboard! Hurrah for a bellyful, and news from our friends!' Such were our exhortations to the boat's crew," Tench wrote. They soon discovered that the vessel was the *Lady Juliana* carrying more than two hundred female convicts and the forerunner of the "Second Fleet."

Relief that they were not after all to starve soon yielded to excitement about the letters the *Lady Juliana* was carrying—the first news from home for nearly three years. Tench described how he and his colleagues seized and ripped them open "in trembling agitation. News burst upon us like meridian splendour on a blind man. We were overwhelmed with it: public, private, general, and particular." As well as longed-for news from family and friends, the exiles learned of such dramatic events as King George's recent "dangerous and alarming illness"—(a severe bout in 1788–89 of the porphyria that would recur for the rest of his life)—and the outbreak of the French Revolution "with all the attendant circumstances of that wonderful and unexpected event," as the liberal Francophile Tench wrote.

The *Lady Juliana* also carried the first formal dispatches from London to reach Phillip. William Grenville, who had replaced Lord Sydney as Home Secretary, informed him that more ships were coming: "In the course of the autumn I expect that about 1000 more convicts of both sexes will be embarked from the several gaols and dispatched to Port Jackson," Grenville wrote. A newly constituted New South Wales Corps of three hundred men was also on its way to relieve the marines, who could choose to go home or, if they wished, stay on with a grant of land, to become farmers. Phillip discovered as well why resupply had taken so long. HMS *Guardian*, packed with provisions, seeds for planting, and farm animals and carrying twenty-five convict "artificers" including some experienced farmers and gardeners, had sailed in September 1789. However, in December of that year, after loading provisions at Cape Town, she had hit an iceberg with the loss of many lives and most of the stores. Only with a whaling vessel's help had the grievously damaged vessel limped back to Cape Town. There its disconsolate captain, Lieutenant Edward Riou, had met an acquaintance who had also suffered a recent disaster: Lieutenant William Bligh, returning to Britain to account for the loss of the *Bounty*.

As the initial euphoria at the *Lady Juliana*'s arrival wore off, certain realities came home, such as that she was only carrying provisions to feed the women she had brought: The provisions aboard the ill-fated *Guardian* had been meant to supply the colony's existing population. Collins probably expressed the feelings of many when he called the arrival of the additional female convicts "unnecessary and unprofitable." At least, though, the immediate threat of starvation had receded, a fact reinforced by the arrival several weeks later of the supply ship *Justinian*, carrying fifty thousand pounds of pork and beef, around five hundred thousand pounds of flour, together with pease, oatmeal, sugar, vinegar, bales of material for clothing, and, to Surgeon White's great satisfaction, a portable hospital. The next day the Reverend Johnson conducted a service of thanksgiving attended by the entire community.

On June 29 three further ships—the *Neptune*, *Scarborough*, and the *Surprise*—arrived with the additional convicts of whom Phillip had been forewarned. Like the convicts of the First Fleet, the *Lady Juliana*'s female prisoners had disembarked in relatively good health—only five women and two children had died on the voyage—but the condition of the latest arrivals was deplorable. William Hill, a captain in the newly formed New South Wales Corps who had arrived on the *Surprise*, later told William Wilberforce:

> The contractors had been in the Guinea [slave] Trade and had put on board the same shackles used by them in that trade, which are made with a short bolt, instead of chains that drop between the legs and fasten with a bandage about the waist, like those at the different gaols; these bolts were not more than three quarters of a foot in length, so that they could not extend either leg from the other more than an inch or two at most; thus fettered, it was impossible for them to move but at the risk of both legs being broken.

Like slaves, many had been kept in irons for the entire voyage and forced to lie in their own excrement, though Hill thought "the slave trade merciful compared with what I have seen in this fleet."

As the half-dying prisoners were landed—"some creeped upon their hands and knees, and some were carried upon the backs of others"—Phillip summoned the colony's women and many of the men to help. Collins thought the scene "truly distressing and miserable; upwards of thirty tents were pitched in front of the hospital, the portable one not being yet put up; all of which, as well as the hospital and the adjacent huts, were filled with people, many of whom were labouring under the complicated diseases of scurvy and the dysentery, and others in the last stage of either of those terrible disorders, or yielding to the attacks of an infectious fever." Some "died in the boats as they were rowing on shore, or on the wharf as they were lifting out of the boats;. . . on board the Neptune several had died in irons; and what added to the horror . . . was, that their deaths were concealed, for the purpose of sharing their allowance of provisions, until chance, and the offensiveness of a corpse, directed the surgeon, or some one who had authority in the ship, to the spot where it lay." The Reverend Johnson was the first to board the *Surprise* "and went down amongst the convicts, where I beheld a sight truly shocking to the feelings of humanity, a great number of them laying, some half and others nearly quite naked, without either bed or bedding, unable to turn themselves. Spoke to them as I passed along, but the smell was so offensive that I could scarcely bear it." Surgeon White tried to save his patients by feeding them as an antiscorbutic "a small berry like a white currant, but in taste more similar to a very sour green gooseberry" from a broom-like shrub.

The contractors responsible for this human misery—the company of Messrs. Camden, Calvert, and King—were the largest transporters of slaves in Britain. Though William Richards, contractor for the First Fleet, had supplied the *Lady Juliana*, Camden, Calvert, and King had won the contract for provisioning the other ships by undercutting him, receiving seventeen pounds seven shillings and sixpence a convict. As Collins observed, "This sum being as well for [the prisoners'] provisions as for their transportation, no interest for their preservation was created in the owners, and the dead were more profitable . . . than the living." Tench thought the contractors had "violated every principle of justice, and rioted on the spoils of misery" and hoped "a humane and liberal government would prevent such a thing ever happening again." By his calculations, of the 1,038 prisoners embarked, 273 had died at sea and 486 were landed sick, 450 being "so very emaciated and helpless that very few, if any of them, can be saved by care or medicine, so that the sooner it pleases God to remove them, the better it will be for this colony, which is not in a situation to bear any burden."

Phillip wrote frankly to William Grenville that clearing Britain's jails of the "disordered and helpless," not only unable to work but a burden to the rest, only added to the colony's woes since "we have many who are helpless and a deadweight on the settlement." What he badly wanted were a few industrious settlers. He also summoned the transports' three captains and told them he would do all in his power to see them punished for what he considered wholesale murder and he would recommend that thenceforth each transport carried a government official to ensure such a thing never happened again.

XV

"TO BRAVE EVERY DANGER"

*I*n late August, a sperm whale beached in Manly Cove. This was the signal for a massive feast for the Aboriginal community, Bennelong and Colby among them, who fell on the stranded animal, slicing off its blubber and meat with the sharp edges of shells and the blades of their spears. A small party including Surgeon White, traveling from Sydney Cove to Broken Bay, stumbled by chance on the festivities. Seemingly unabashed by his escape, Bennelong inquired after Governor Phillip and as the party was leaving gave them several large pieces of blubber, asking that the biggest be given to the governor, whom he was eager to see again.

Pleased at the prospect of reestablishing contact with Bennelong, Phillip set out at once with Collins for Manly Cove and the feasting Aboriginals. Bennelong indeed seemed pleased to see him, "inquiring by name for every person whom he could recollect at Sydney" and especially a lady—Phillip's housekeeper, Deborah Brooks—"from whom he had once ventured to snatch a kiss." Phillip offered Bennelong a glass of wine to see whether he retained his taste for it, which—after toasting the king—he drained. The atmosphere seemed friendly, though Phillip and his companions noticed that gradually their little group was being surrounded. A middle-aged man, "short of stature, sturdy, and well-set," approached Phillip but halted some twenty or thirty yards away. Phillip held out his hands in friendship and advanced slowly toward the man, who, Collins wrote, "not understanding this civility," began to look agitated. Perhaps thinking that Phillip was about to take him prisoner, the man "lifted a spear from the grass with his foot, and fixing it on his throwing stick, in an instant darted it at the governor." The twelve-foot-long barbed spear penetrated Phillip's right shoulder "just above the collar bone" with such force that "the point glancing downward, came out at his back."

As Phillip's attacker dashed into nearby woods, other Aboriginals threw more spears. One grazed the hand of one of Phillip's men, Lieutenant Waterhouse, as he tried to snap off the shaft of the spear in the governor's shoulder to make it easier to carry him back to the boat. Somehow Phillip's party managed to get him to the boat. He was bleeding profusely but his companions knew from experience that if they tried to pull out the barbed spear-tip this might prove fatal. They could only try to stanch the blood flow and row as hard as they could the seven miles back to Sydney Cove—a journey that took almost two hours. There in the hospital a young assistant surgeon named William Balmain succeeded in removing the barb and announced that though Phillip was "highly scorbutic," the wound was "not mortal."

Those who had been with the governor debated the reason for the attack. Collins thought Phillip had trusted in the Aboriginals too long and the attack should have taught him a lesson that "it might be presumed he would never forget." Phillip himself wondered whether the attack had been to settle a grievance and concluded it was not in itself significant to a people who settled disputes with their spears "as readily as the lower class of people in England stripped to box."

Phillip did not blame Bennelong personally and was eager to contact him again, though for the moment he had vanished. When a party led by Surgeon White eventually located him, he seemed pleased that Phillip had survived and claimed to have punished his attacker. However, he was wary of going to Sydney, insisting that Phillip should first visit him. Phillip did so several times until eventually Bennelong felt confident enough to take some companions to Sydney Cove, where he took great pleasure in demonstrating to them the use of candlesnuffers—or "nuffers" as he called them. Thereafter, Bennelong became a regular visitor to Government House, indeed a man of "so much dignity and consequence, that it was not always easy to obtain his company," according to Tench. When he asked for a brick house to be built for him on the eastern shores of Sydney Cove, Phillip agreed.*

However, Phillip's patience with Bennelong began to wear thin because of his increasingly erratic behavior and violence toward his two wives, whom he beat regularly and savagely, on one occasion attacking the younger one with a sword. When Phillip ordered her to be carried to the hospital so White

*Today the Sydney Opera House stands on the site of Bennelong's house, on land known as Bennelong Point.

could treat her wounds, Bennelong threatened to go after her there and kill her. When Phillip warned he would be shot, Bennelong "treated even this menace with disdain." The relationship between the two men deteriorated further when Bennelong led a group of spear-wielding Aboriginals to relieve a fishing party of convicts and soldiers of their catch. Summoned to explain himself to Phillip in Government House, Bennelong argued angrily that the fish belonged to his people. When the governor proved unsympathetic, he stormed out and Phillip ordered that thenceforth he be barred from Government House. Collins understood perhaps better than the governor the gulf that still lay between the area's traditional owners and the new arrivals: "We had not yet been able to reconcile the natives to the deprivation of those parts of the harbour which we occupied. While they entertained the idea of our having dispossessed them of their residences, they must always consider us as enemies."

Phillip's relationship with the Aboriginal community was tested further when, in December 1790, a group of men attacked convict John McEntire, the colony's chief hunter. McEntire and some companions had been lying in wait for kangaroos when a small group of Aboriginal people approached them. Recognizing one of them, McEntire had told his companions not to be alarmed. Then quite suddenly—in something of a repetition of the attack on Phillip—the man had hurled his spear into the side of McEntire, who crumpled to the ground, crying out, "I am a dead man."

Until now, according to Tench, Phillip had believed that "in every former instance of hostility"—including the attack on himself—the Aboriginals had acted "either from having received injury, or from misapprehension." However, in the case of McEntire—who did indeed die, though not for some days—he was convinced the attack had been unprovoked, though in fact a group of Aboriginals had singled out McEntire for punishment for the crime, in their eyes, of killing a dingo, an animal significant in initiation rituals. Ignorant of this and deciding an example had to be made, Phillip ordered Tench to take armed marines and track down those responsible, executing ten of them immediately—cutting off their heads "for which purpose hatchets and bags would be furnished" and capturing two more for public execution in Sydney Cove. A horrified Tench argued that Phillip could make his point equally well by capturing just six Aboriginals, some of whom could be held hostage as a guarantee of future good behavior. Phillip agreed, saying he would hang two and send the rest to Norfolk Island.

Lieutenant Dawes was ordered to go with Tench but, after consulting the chaplain, refused to have anything to do with what he regarded as a punitive mission, holding firm even when Phillip taxed him with "unofficerlike behaviour" and threatened to court-martial him. Setting off with fifty men, Tench spent futile days tramping about in the heat, beating off mosquitoes and sand flies and, probably to his relief, encountering almost nobody except Colby, whom it seemed inconceivable to him to behead or arrest, before returning to Sydney Cove without a single prisoner. Phillip immediately dispatched Tench on a second equally fruitless expedition. When he again returned to Sydney Cove empty-handed, Phillip abandoned his plans for bloody reprisals.

Phillip anyway had other matters to think about. In early December 1790, the *Supply* returned with provisions from Batavia, followed on December 17 by a vessel that, in accordance with Phillip's instructions, the *Supply*'s captain had chartered to bring further supplies—a three-hundred-ton Dutch cargo vessel—a "snow"—named *Waaksamheyd*, or "Vigilance." Her cargo—staples like beef, pork, rice, sugar, and flour—was more welcome to Phillip and his senior officers than her captain, a Dutchman named Detmer Smith, who had sold the *Waaksamheyd*'s services to the struggling colony at what they thought an exorbitant price. Furthermore, the rice on board was light by some 43,000 pounds compared with the amount contracted and paid for. Smith claimed this was nothing to do with him and offered to sell some of his own stocks of rice and flour at a high price, which the commissary had reluctantly to agree to. When Phillip asked to charter his vessel again—this time to take Captain Hunter and some of his crew back to England to face the customary court-martial for the loss of their ship, the *Sirius*—Smith further annoyed Phillip by his "frantic and extravagant behaviour" in demanding another exorbitant sum. However, as Smith well knew it was a seller's market. Eventually, if acrimoniously, a contract was agreed for the continued use of the *Waaksamheyd*.

With Smith frozen out of "official" circles, Mary Bryant and her fisherman husband, William Bryant, befriended him. They had a particular purpose in doing so as he discovered when, in early February 1791, they revealed to him their scheme for escaping from Port Jackson with Mary's daughter, Charlotte, now three and a half years old, and their eight-month-old son, Emmanuel. The vessel in which they planned to make their bid was nothing less than the governor's own cutter, well equipped with six oars and two sails.

Venturing across largely uncharted waters in an open boat was a terrible risk, particularly with two small children. Smith must have wondered why William Bryant, whose sentence would expire in a few months, and Mary, who had only two years left to serve, would even contemplate it. Mary may have convinced her husband to do so because she suspected that once he had served his time he would return to England, abandoning her and the children. He was known to take his New South Wales wedding vows lightly: Collins wrote that he had often been heard to express "what was indeed the general sentiment on the subject among the people of his description, that he did not consider his marriage in this country as binding." If leaving Mary had indeed been Bryant's plan, the irony is that on learning of Bryant's comments about marriage Phillip had ruled that no one "who had wives or children incapable of maintaining themselves and likely to become burdensome to the settlement" would be allowed to leave—a pronouncement that Mary could deploy in arguing for escape.

More likely, and with echoes of today's refugee families prepared to hazard all to the sea, is that the deprivation and disease in the colony had convinced the couple that if they remained they would not long survive. An open-boat journey into the unknown was the lesser of two evils. Also, even when Bryant's term expired, there was no guarantee he would be set free. Phillip was still awaiting records from London that he should have been given when he first sailed confirming the respective lengths of the convicts' sentences. Several convicts were already claiming their terms had expired and that they should be freed but were unable to prove it, leaving them, as Collins noted with sympathy, "most peculiarly and unpleasantly situated. Conscious in their own minds that the sentence of the law had been fulfilled upon them, it must have been truly distressing to their feelings to find that they could not be considered in any other light . . . than that in which alone they had been hitherto known in the settlement." Also, the Bryants may have been encouraged by what Collins described as "a desertion of an extraordinary nature" when in September five convicts had stolen a boat from the lookout post on the South Head, intending to make for Tahiti, and seemed to have got safely away.*

---

*The escapees did not reach Tahiti. Five years later four of them were found living farther up the coast, where they had survived with the help of the Aboriginal people. The fifth man had died.

Though the Cornish-born William Bryant was a skilled boat handler—as was probably Mary, the daughter of a fisherman—they knew they could not make the journey alone. In fact, their final escape party would include seven other convicts. Two of these were friends—James Martin and James Cox had been transported with the Bryants aboard the *Charlotte*. Of the remaining five, two were also First Fleeters: gray-eyed, sandy-haired, forty-nine-year-old John Butcher—alias Samuel Broom—convicted at Shrewsbury of stealing three small pigs, and Samuel Bird—also known as John Simms—convicted of stealing thirty pounds' worth of saltpeter. The remaining three—fifty-four-year-old Yorkshireman William Allen, transported for stealing twenty-nine handkerchiefs in Norwich; dark-haired, sallow-skinned thirty-eight-year-old Irish-born Nathaniel Lilley, convicted of stealing a fishing net, a watch, and two spoons; and William Morton from Northumberland—were new arrivals on the Second Fleet. The Bryants may have selected some for their skills: Morton, at least, knew something about navigation, and other members of the group would refer to him as their "navigator"; while Allen is described in official records as "a mariner." Possibly others had learned of the plan and threatened to betray the Bryants if they were not allowed to join. Of the escape party, only Lilley and Cox had been transported for life.

Whatever the reasons behind the composition of the escape party, befriending Detmer Smith, who had no reason to love the colony's rulers, was certainly part of the plan. The escapees managed to raise enough cash to buy a quadrant and compass from him, together with fourteen pounds of salt pork and a hundredweight apiece of rice and flour, which they hid, together with whatever extra food they could obtain, beneath the floor of the Bryants' hut. Smith also gave or sold them two muskets, ammunition, a large barrel of water, and a chart showing the route to Batavia through the notorious Torres Strait. The latter, together with Smith's own advice, was probably what persuaded them to attempt what Bligh had done when put overboard at Tofua and make for the Dutch East Indies. They may also have learned specifically from Smith or others about Bligh's successful open-boat journey.

They knew they had to make the attempt before the southern hemisphere winds began to gust—usually by April—so time was running out. Then on February 28, all the scheming came close to collapse. William Bryant was returning in Phillip's cutter from fishing with some fellow prisoners and

Bennelong's sister, Karangaran, and her two children, when a fierce gale blew up and the boat capsized. Bennelong's sister swam to safety with her children while Bryant and others struggled to right the vessel. Several Aboriginals, including Bennelong, saw that the cutter was being driven onto some rocks and leapt into the sea to help. Captain Hunter witnessed their efforts: "After clearing the boat, they collected the oars and such articles as had been driven on shore in different places . . . The natives then towed the boat up to the cove." Hunt was convinced that without Bennelong's help some of the crew would have drowned. So vital to the colony was the governor's cutter that carpenters were soon laboring in suffocating heat of more than one hundred degrees Fahrenheit to fit a fresh mast, sails, and planking.

At the same time the final preparations were being made to the *Waaksamheyd*, which by March 28 was ready to sail. As well as Hunter and his men and several officers of marines whose tours of duty in the colony had ended, the ship was to carry the usual numerous dispatches and letters. These included one from Phillip to Nepean asking for a second time to be allowed to return to England (Phillip had first requested this a year earlier from Lord Sydney), and again citing his need to attend to his financial affairs but also his deteriorating health: He was suffering sharp pains in his left kidney, probably the result of prolonged eating of highly salted food. To William Grenville, who had succeeded Sydney as Home Secretary, he expressed his belief that the colony was "now so fully established, that the great labour may be said to be past" and again asked for permission to return home. To Banks he wrote, "I am sorry I cannot send you a [Aboriginal] head. After the ravages made by the smallpox . . . the natives burned the bodies."

The excitement and activity surrounding the *Waaksamheyd*'s departure provided useful camouflage for the escapees as they made their final preparations, and not coincidentally chose the evening of her sailing, March 28, to leave. At about eleven P.M. on what was a moonless night, the convicts crept along the shore with all the goods and equipment they had accumulated, including a bag of "sweet tea" leaves that Mary had gathered. As well as the items Detmer Smith had sold or given them they had a new seine net for fishing and carpenter's tools. In their haste, they dropped "a handsaw, a scale and four or five pounds of rice."

The governor's newly repaired cutter was moored out in the cove, and someone swam out, cut the rope, and towed it closer to the shore. As silently as they could, the escapers climbed in. Using the oars was too risky in case anyone on shore picked up the sound of their splash. Instead, they allowed the current to carry them past tiny Pinchgut Island and out past the South Head, where in the darkness the sentry on duty—Sergeant James Scott— failed to see them. As the Pacific swells moved beneath them, they raised their sail and their voyage began.

The escape was not discovered until around dawn the next day, when it roused surprise but also some sympathy. Watkin Tench could easily understand why people should wish "to brave every danger and every hardship rather than remain longer in a captive state." He also thought that the colony's rulers had failed them: "I every day see wretches pale with disease and wasted with famine, struggle against the horrors of their situation . . . toil cannot be long supported without adequate refreshment. The first step in every community . . . should be to set the people above want."

Knowing some of the group to be "competent navigators," Tench had no doubt that "a scheme so admirably planned, would be adequately executed . . . After the escape of Captain Bligh which was well known to us, no length of passage or hazard of navigation seemed above human accomplishment." Private John Easty thought it a "very desperate attempt to go in an open boat for a run of about 16 or 17 hundred leagues and in particular for a woman and two small children the oldest not above three years of age. But the thoughts of liberty from such a place as this is enough to induce any convicts to try all schemes to obtain it as they are the same as slaves all the time they are in this country."

Following the departure of the *Waaksamheyd*, there were no seagoing vessels in the harbor: the *Supply* had left for Norfolk Island a few days earlier. Impotent to undertake a serious pursuit, Phillip and his officers could only try to reconstruct what had happened. From a source he did not name, Advocate-General Collins wrote, "we learned that Detmer Smith . . . had sold [Bryant] a compass and a quadrant and had furnished him with a chart, together with such information as would assist him in his passage to the northward." A search of the Bryants' hut revealed "cavities under the boards" where they had concealed items. What puzzled many was how the convicts had kept their escape bid secret. Collins wrote that most of the escapers "were connected with women; but if these knew anything, they were too faithful to those they lived with to reveal it."

Some clearly had not known. The next morning, Sarah Young, partner of James Cox, discovered a letter he had left for her "conjuring her to give over the pursuit of the vices which, he told her, prevailed in the settlement, leaving to her what little property he did not take with him, and assigning as a reason for his flight, the severity of his situation, being transported for life, without the prospect of any mitigation or hope of ever quitting the country but by the means he was about to adopt."

Collins, whose own intention was "to embrace the first opportunity that offers of escaping from a country that is nothing better than a place of banishment for the outcasts of society," may, like Tench, have felt some empathy with the fugitives. The general assumption was, he wrote, that "they would steer for Timor, or Batavia, as their assistance and information were derived from the Dutch snow." With their boat "a very good one, and in excellent order," and provided "no dissension prevailed among them, and they had but prudence enough to guard against the natives wherever they might land," like Tench he did not doubt their succeeding. But he thought "what story they could invent on their arrival at any port, sufficiently plausible to prevent suspicion of their real characters, it was not easy to imagine."

XVI

"WE MUST HAVE STARVED"

$\mathcal{F}$or two days, the fugitives bore north-northeast until, two degrees north of Port Jackson, they reached a little bay where the land looked decidedly more fertile than in Sydney Cove. According to James Martin, who later wrote an account of the voyage, they decided to risk going ashore for more supplies to augment their rice, salt pork, and flour. They were so relieved to find "a great many cabbage trees some of which we cut down and procured the cabbage [for food]" and "a great many fishes"—gray mullet—as well as "a quantity of fine burning coal," the first found by Europeans in Australia, that they named their landing place Fortunate Creek. They had anxious moments when some Aboriginals approached but after the fugitives gave them clothes and other items they "went away very well satisfied."

Early on March 31, the escapers set out again, following the coast northward until two days later they reached a fine bay with a deep inlet running into it with abundant fresh water, which William Bryant described as "superior to Sydney."* With Governor Phillip's cutter already leaking badly, the group hauled it onto the beach and, turning it over, started to caulk the bottom as best they could with beeswax and resin, of which they had a small quantity. However, as darkness fell some Aboriginals who must have been watching drove them away. Fearing they meant "to destroy us," Martin wrote, they hastily put back to sea. The next day, when they again landed nearby to finish repairing the boat's seams, more Aboriginals—"quite naked, of a copper colour, shock hair"—appeared, this time "in great numbers with spears and shields." Hoping to frighten them off, the fugitives fired one of the muskets they had obtained from Detmer Smith over their heads, but

---

*This was possibly Port Stephens, where the Myall and Karuah Rivers converge.

they took "not the least notice." The escapers could only right their boat, push off, scramble in, and "get out of their reach as fast as we could."

Having twice been driven off, the Bryants and their companions decided to probe farther around the bay. After about ten miles they saw "a little white sandy island" ahead where, finally untroubled by hostile visitors, they caulked their boat "with what little materials we had," Martin wrote. On April 6, sailing across to the mainland and finding an uninhabited spot to go ashore, they refilled their water casks and harvested further chunks of cabbage tree before continuing their journey northward. Soon strong offshore winds drove them out of sight of land however hard they battled against them. When finally they succeeded in approaching the shore again, the surf was "running so very hard" that penetrating it was impossible. For three weeks as they sailed along the four hundred-nautical-mile expanse of coast between modern-day Port Macquarie and Brisbane, adverse winds delayed them and relentless surf frustrated any attempt to land. At last, "much distressed for water and wood" and thinking the surf was starting to abate a little, two of the group swam ashore with a cask but, seeing a large number of Aboriginals on the beach, abandoned their attempt.

By April 28—a month after leaving Sydney Cove—the cutter was leaking so badly that, as Martin recalled, "it was with great difficulty we could keep her above water." Reaching a river mouth, Bryant maneuvered the boat over shoals at its entrance where the water was barely six feet deep—a feat Bligh would commend, when he read of it, for doing so "without receiving any damage"—to sail upriver. Eventually, they found a spot to pull the cutter from the water and again attempt to plug the seams. With no wax or resin left, they resorted to soap, "which answered very well," Martin thought.

However, they could find no food—"no fish of any kind"—so that after two nights they put back to sea, only to find themselves buffeted by high waves that threatened to swamp them. Desperate to lighten the cutter, which, like Bligh's launch, was open with no decking to keep the water out, they threw all their precious spare clothing overboard just as Bligh and his men had done when caught in storms after leaving Tofua. Reaching another bay, they searched for somewhere to land but again pounding surf thwarted them. Deciding to moor offshore, they dropped a grappling anchor, which suddenly broke, so that they were swept into the boiling surf, "expecting every moment that our boat would be staved to pieces and every soul perish," Martin wrote. However, "as God would have it," they finally made the shore, although they lost one of their oars. The date was May 1. Hauling the cutter up onto the beach once more, the sodden group lit a fire "with great difficulty, everything that we had being very wet." Shellfish and fresh water were plentiful but suddenly "the natives came down in great numbers." One of the fugitives hastily discharged a musket over their heads and this time it worked: "They dispersed immediately and we saw no more of them."

On May 3, revived, refreshed, and having dried their clothes over the fire, they set out once more but soon ran into new danger. For nearly three days, the seas were so heavy and the cutter shipping so much water that one of the group had to bale constantly "to keep her up." On May 6, reaching another inlet, which they named White Bay, they spotted a place where the surf was less fierce and they could land and where two Aboriginal women and two children were sitting by a fire on the beach. As the Bryants and their companions came ashore the women took fright and backed away until the Britons managed to make them understand by signs that all they wanted was a brand from their fire to light their own, which the women gave them, "crying at the same time in their way," Martin wrote. What the Aboriginal women and their two children made of Mary and her two children and whether their presence reassured them he does not say.

Finding two rough huts, the convicts removed their belongings from the boat, took them inside, and prepared for the night. However, news of their arrival had spread because by eleven the next morning "a great number of the natives" appeared. By again firing over their heads, the Bryants and their companions managed to drive them away and felt safe enough to remain another night before putting to sea again toward evening on the third day. Almost immediately "a heavy gale of wind" and strong currents drove them way out to sea so that, Martin wrote, they expected "every moment to go to the bottom." The next morning, with the sea still "running mountains high," they kept their mainsail close-reefed but there was no respite. As darkness came, a heavy rain began to fall and with the sea "coming in so heavy upon us" two people again had to keep bailing. Of these hours, Martin, usually spare and factual, wrote: "I will leave you to consider what distress we must be in. The woman and the two little babies were in a bad condition, everything being so wet we could by no means light a fire. We had nothing to eat except a little raw rice at night." William Bryant paid tribute in his journal to his wife and children, who "bore their sufferings with more fortitude than most among them."

The next day, to their relief, the group sighted a small island ahead ringed by reefs.* With the surf "so very high," they hesitated whether to attempt a landing on a sandy beach they could see but, as Martin noted, they knew they had to try since "if we kept out to sea we should every soul perish." Again, William Bryant needed all his skill to thread the cutter through the reefs toward the beach. Reaching it safely, the exhausted occupants hauled their boat out of the water "without much damage." Their priority, Martin wrote, was to light a fire, "which with great difficulty we did and being almost starving we put on a little rice to cook." By now they had only a gallon of fresh water left and a search of the island revealed not a single spring; but at least it appeared uninhabited. At low tide, they picked their way out to the reefs to look for shellfish and were overjoyed to find "a great quantity of very fine large turtles."† They caught five and, killing one immediately, "had a noble meal," Martin recalled. They also had fresh water to drink since that night it began to rain and, just as Bligh's men did, they spread their mainsail to collect the drops.

During the convicts' stay on the island, they caught seven more turtles, curing the flesh by smoking it over their fire to take with them. They would have liked to take live ones with them but decided reluctantly that "our boat would not admit of it." Further welcome additions to their diet were the "great quantity of fowls" they found living in burrows in the ground and "a kind of fruit which grew like a bell pepper" and, Martin thought, "tasted very well." After six days of eating, recuperating, and re-soaping the seams of their boat, they set off again around May 18, navigating through a maze of islands where they searched in vain for turtles but found only shellfish, which were "none of them very fit to eat but being very hungry we were glad to eat them and thank God for it." Without the shellfish and the turtle meat they had cured, Martin thought, "we must have starved."

Indeed, they would find nothing else edible until they rounded Australia's northern tip, Cape York. Passing through the Torres Strait, the fugitives entered the shallow Gulf of Carpentaria—320 nautical miles wide at its mouth, bounded by Cape York to the east, Cape Arnhem to the west, and the Arafura Sea to the north—to find themselves among a mass of islands. In urgent need of food and water, cautiously they approached one. However,

*This was possibly Lady Elliot Island at the southern edge of the Great Barrier Reef.

†Probably green sea turtles, which breed on Australia's northeastern and northern coasts and can grow to 1.5 meters (5 feet) in length.

a group of local men who had just landed from their canoe at once took up "a posture of defence against us," Martin wrote, at which the convicts took their now customary precaution of firing a musket over their heads. Instead of fleeing, the islanders immediately unleashed from their bows a storm of arrows, whereupon the convicts hastily rowed away. Though the arrows— about eighteen inches long—dropped into the sea all around the cutter, they hit no one. Martin thought their attackers "very stout and fat and blacker than those we saw in other parts . . . one which we took to be the chief with some shells round his shoulders."

In desperation, the fugitives made for the mainland where they saw on the shore a cluster of bark-walled, grass-roofed huts, seemingly uninhabited and temptingly close to a stream. Quickly they landed and filled their water casks but, Martin wrote, "afraid of staying ashore for fear of the natives," pushed off again and only dropped anchor when a safe distance of some three or four miles from the shore. The next morning, they again landed for more water but saw to their horror "two very large canoes coming towards us. We did not know what to do for we were afraid to meet them. There seemed to be about 30 or 40 men in each canoe. They had sails [which] seemed to be made of matting. One of the canoes was ahead of the other a little way. It stopped till the other came up and then she hoisted her sails and made after us. As soon as we saw that we tacked about . . . as God would have it we outrun them. They followed us till we lost sight of them."

After four and a half days with "but little fresh water and no wood to make a fire" the convicts finally reached the western shores of the Gulf of Carpentaria, which they sailed anxiously along, seeking fresh water but finding none until finally they reached a small river where they replenished their supplies. Setting off again and with heavy swells threatening "to have swallowed us up," Martin wrote, "we concluded the best way to shape our course would be [to make] for the Island of Timor [to the northwest] with what little water we had, which we made in thirty-six hours. We ran along the island till we came to the Dutch settlement." With these matter-of-fact words, Martin described the end of an epic 3,254-nautical-mile open-boat voyage north along Australia's eastern seaboard and the Great Barrier Reef, westward through the feared Torres Strait, and across the largely uncharted Arafura Sea during which nine adults and two children had overcome hunger and thirst, notoriously hazardous seas, and hostile locals to reach safety. They arrived on June 5, 1791—sixty-nine days after their escape from Port Jackson. The settlement was Kupang, where, almost exactly two years before, on June

14, 1789, Bligh and the ragged, skeletal survivors of his open-boat journey had tottered ashore.

As David Collins foresaw, the convicts needed a plausible story to tell the Dutch authorities and during their anxious days at sea they had clearly devised one. Conducted to his house they told the governor, Timotheus Wanjon—deputy governor when Bligh arrived but who had succeeded the previous governor, his father-in-law William Adrian van Este, on his death—that they were survivors from a wrecked whaling vessel, the *Neptune*, and that "the captain and the rest of the crew would probably follow in another boat." According to Martin, the governor "behaved extremely well to us, filled our bellies and clothed us." Here they would remain for two months recuperating in a place celebrated for its lush, hilly beauty and climate so healthy that, a British naval surgeon noted, it was "the favourite resort of valetudinarians and invalids from Batavia and other places." So confident were the new arrivals that they even "drew bills on the British Government" in order to be "supplied with every necessary they stood in need of" which—borrowing his wife's maiden name—William Bryant signed as "William Broad."

XVII

"MR. CHRISTIAN WAS BELOVED"

*O*n becoming "master" of the *Bounty* on April 28, 1789, Fletcher Christian had ordered the breadfruit seedlings to be thrown overboard and he moved into William Bligh's cabin. He also divided those on board into two watches with his friend George Stewart commanding one and himself the other. His immediate plan was to return to Tahiti, but first to call in at Tubuai, a small island about three hundred miles south of Tahiti that had been charted without landing by Cook aboard the *Resolution*.

James Morrison later claimed that he still hoped "that the ship might yet be recovered if a party could be formed and . . . I fixed on a plan . . . to take the opportunity of the night when the ship anchored at Tahiti, when we could easily get rid of those we did not like by putting them on shore. In all probability, our design might be favoured by an extra allowance of grog." Christian learned of the plot and, suspecting armorer Coleman—detained on board against his will—of being among the plotters, confiscated the keys of the arms chest from him and gave them to Churchill, who thenceforth slept on the chest. Christian also took the precaution of arming himself and those crewmen he trusted with pistols, keeping Bligh's own weapon tucked permanently into his pocket.

As the *Bounty* sailed toward Tubuai, Christian had old sails cut up to make uniforms, giving his own blue naval jacket to use as edging, "observing that nothing had more effect on the mind of the Indians as a uniformity of dress." On May 28, 1789, as Tubuai came in sight, Christian sent Stewart and some sailors ahead in the large cutter to seek a gap through the reef described by Captain Cook. Almost at once a canoe filled with islanders wielding eighteen-foot-long spears attacked them, boarded the cutter, and stole a jacket and other items. Trying to defend himself, Stewart discharged a pistol. Though it misfired, the report was enough to frighten off his assailants, who could not use their long spears in the confined space of the boat. Continuing in the cutter, Stewart located and marked the path through the reef and the next day the *Bounty* sailed safely into the lagoon to anchor in a sandy bay.

More proof that Tubuai was no friendly Tahiti came as islanders massed on the shore "armed with clubs and spears of a shining black wood," blowing conch shells and dressed in red and white, which Morrison thought "gave them a formidable appearance." More conch-blowing warriors pushed off from the shore in canoes and soon surrounded the ship but did not attack. Finding that the Tubuaiians understood Tahitian, the mutineers tried to coax some on board and eventually persuaded a venerable-looking old man—a chief, they presumed—onto the *Bounty*. He appeared terrified by the hogs and goats penned on deck and Christian sought to soothe him with gifts. However, the crew soon realised that their visitor was carefully "counting our number" and "the arms were therefore got to hand."

The next day, more canoes put out from the shore, among them this time "a double canoe, full of neatly dressed women, their heads and necks decorated with flowers and pearl shells. As they approached . . . they stood up and beat time to a song given by one of them . . . They were all young and handsome, having fine long hair that reached their waists in waving ringlets." The young women—eighteen in all—came readily on board while twenty canoes each carrying fifteen to twenty warriors circled the *Bounty*. Realizing the women were "a snare to catch us," the *Bounty* men kept a close eye on the canoes. The few men they did permit to board at once started to pilfer. Christian caught one "stout fellow" stealing part of a compass, which he only retrieved, damaged, after striking the man smartly with the end of a rope. He then put him back over the side to be followed by the other Tubuaiian men and women, whereupon all the canoes departed.

As the Tubuaiians rowed away "they began to show their weapons, which till now they had kept concealed, brandishing them with many threatening gestures." One man tried to make off with an anchor buoy, at which point Christian fired his musket and also ordered one of the ship's four-pounder cannon to be fired, loaded with grapeshot. Hoping they had overawed the islanders, several crewmen climbed into the *Bounty*'s boats and headed for the shore but, as they tried to land, the islanders threw stones at them. Again the mutineers fired their muskets, killing eleven men and a woman, and the rest ran off. Inspecting the canoes drawn up on the beach, they discovered cords "which we supposed were intended for binding us." They christened the spot Bloody Bay.

Christian still hoped to make peace with the islanders, having by now, as Morrison wrote, "formed a resolution of settling on this island." Setting out with the ship's boats the next day—a white flag of truce fluttering in the bow of one and a Union Jack in the bow of the other—he explored as far as Tubuai's eastern tip, landing several times and leaving gifts of axes in empty huts, but meeting no one. The following day, May 31, Christian weighed anchor and sailed north-northeast for Tahiti.

According to Morrison, despite their reception by the islanders Christian still thought Tubuai might ultimately provide a suitable home. It was a reasonable size—"about six miles in length from east to west"—and while it had no livestock, not even pigs, breadfruit, coconuts, and plantains were plentiful. Though the islanders appeared hostile, Christian concluded they must be few in number and that he could forge a friendship with them, just as he had with the Tahitians. "As the anchorage . . . was not enticing" few ships would call. Thus he could "live . . . in peace . . . all he now desired, knowing that he had taken such steps as had forever debarred him from returning to England or any civilised place."

If this was Christian's dream, not all his shipmates shared it. Morrison thought it a thoroughly bad plan and that the Tubuaiians' "savage aspect and behaviour could not gain favour in the eyes of any man in his senses." However, Christian clearly had enough support on the *Bounty* to impose his will. On the voyage to Tahiti he announced that any man who disclosed to the Tahitians the plan to settle on Tubuai would be severely punished and that he would personally shoot any deserter "as soon as he was brought back." Morrison's account suggests a clear division on the *Bounty* now between unequivocal "Christian loyalists" and those who had not supported the mutiny or were now regretting their actions. When the clothes and other possessions of Bligh and those put over the side with him were divided by lot, Morrison claimed "Mr. Christian's party was always better served than those who were thought to be disaffected."

On June 6, the *Bounty* was back in Matavai Bay, scene of such affecting farewells just two months earlier. The Tahitians were surprised to see the ship and "flocked on board in great numbers." The mutineers had ready their answers to the inevitable questions. According to Morrison, "Mr. Christian answered that we had met Captain Cook, who had taken Mr. Bligh and the others, with the plants and the longboat [the launch], and had sent us for hogs, goats, etc., for a new settlement that the king had sent him to make, which he described to be on New Holland." This account "passed very well," though

Morrison thought it might not have mattered had they simply told "our old friends" the truth since, "Mr. Christian was beloved by the whole of them. On the contrary, none liked Mr. Bligh."

While he entertained the chiefs on board, plying them with wine and arrack, Christian sent Churchill and Morrison ashore to buy livestock: They acquired 460 hogs, 50 goats, chickens, dogs, cats, and also the bull and cow Cook had left on the island ten years before and by which the islanders "set little store." To pay for all this, Christian set Coleman to hammering out iron objects to use as currency for trading. On June 16, Christian and his men left Tahiti for Tubuai to found their new colony. Also on board were, Morrison noted, "9 men, 8 boys, 10 women, and a female child, some of which hid themselves below till we were at sea." Some of the women, like Christian's Isabella, Quintal's Sarah, and McIntosh's Mary, were "wives" of the *Bounty* men and eager to stay with them. Others had effectively been kidnapped to help populate the new colony. Able seaman Alexander Smith later recalled that one reason for returning to Tahiti had been because they lacked women and each wanted to obtain one.

After a rough passage during which the bull, four pigs, and a goat died, on June 23 the *Bounty* again dropped anchor in Bloody Bay on Tubuai. At first Christian's hopes appeared likely to be fulfilled. The islanders seemed to welcome them, "without weapons or conch shells or the least appearance of hostility." The ruler of this northwestern part of the island, a chief named Tummotoa, helped Christian search for a site to build his settlement. However, finding nowhere suitable, Christian crossed into the adjoining territory of another chief, Taroatchoa, where he found a spot he thought ideal. Tummotoa, no friend to Taroatchoa, was "jealous" and deeply offended. Ignoring Christian's attempt to placate him with gifts, he forbade his people to have any further contact with the *Bounty*. A chief named Tinnarow, whose people had been those killed at Bloody Bay, made common cause with Tummotoa against the foreigners.

Determined to start building a fortress, Christian moved the *Bounty* close to his chosen site. The passage was "beset by patches of coral rock" and so shallow that with the *Bounty* only halfway there, he had to lighten the ship, removing the ship's boom and spars and mooring them to a grapnel anchor. Soon, though, as Morrison wrote, "it started to blow fresh and they went adrift, and we saw them no more." Christian thought it "no great loss, as he never intended to go to sea anymore." During this period, according to Heywood, disobedience to orders, "drunkenness, fighting and threatening each other's life" were common until Christian with Churchill's help persuaded the crew formally to forgive each other's past misdemeanors.

With the *Bounty* safely anchored off Tubuai's easternmost point, Christian went ashore to choose the exact spot for his fort. On his return, he discovered that John Sumner and Matthew Quintal had gone ashore without leave. When they returned the next day and he challenged them, they replied, "The ship is moored, and we are now our own masters," at which Christian put his pistol to the head of one, saying, "I'll let you know who is master" and ordered both to be put in irons. Morrison thought Christian's "resolute behaviour" showed "he was not to be played with." The next day, Sumner and Quintal apologized, whereupon Christian freed them. However, realizing that the men had gone looking for women, Christian wisely announced that from then on two men could sleep ashore each night and on Sundays any man who wished might go ashore.

On July 18, an event echoing Phillip's possession ceremony in Sydney Cove—on a more modest scale but no less patriotic—took place when the *Bounty* men gathered where they intended to start building: "The ground was measured out for the fort and possession of the land taken by turning the turf and hoisting the Union Jack on a staff. On this occasion an extra allowance of grog was drunk and the place named Fort George," presumably after the king. Also like the New South Wales colonists, the *Bounty* men lacked the necessary skills for the task ahead. Morrison wrote that "not a man knew anything of fortification." However, "some cut stakes, others made battens, some cut sods . . . The carpenters made barrows and cut timber for the gates and drawbridge. The work began to rise apace. Nor was Mr. Christian an idle spectator, for he always took part in the most laborious part of the work."

The "colonists" made good progress on their square fort with its twelve-foot-high walls and twenty-foot-wide dry moat until, in late August, a series of incidents began to render their position on Tubuai untenable. The first occurred when women from Tinnarow's district lured some of the *Bounty* men into his territory, where islanders attacked, stripped, and robbed them, holding Alexander Smith prisoner for a few hours before releasing him clad only in his shirt. When Christian demanded the return of the stolen items, Tinnarow refused, upon which Christian burned down his house after removing two "curious carved images of their household gods . . . decorated with pearl shells, human hair, teeth, and nails," which he suspected might prove useful bargaining counters. Tinnarow indeed tried to get the images back, arriving with baskets of gifts on an ostensible peace mission. However, some of the Tahitians from the *Bounty* alerted Christian that Tinnarow's men had secreted their spears nearby intending to attack the foreigners once they were off guard. Realizing his scheme had been detected, Tinnarow withdrew in a rage.

More damaging to Christian's plans were the growing divisions among the *Bounty* men themselves, some of whom grew alarmed when he "began to talk of taking the masts out and dismantling the ship when he intended to erect houses and live on shore." Morrison, who "had some hope that I could reach Tahiti in the large cutter," spoke to George Stewart, "who told me that he and Peter Heywood had formed the same plan." The cutter was the same leaking, unseaworthy vessel in which Captain Bligh and his companions had so nearly been set adrift. Yet so eager were Morrison, Stewart, and Heywood to get away they decided to risk it, despite knowing that if they hit rough weather "our crazy boat would certainly have made us a coffin."

However, friction between Christian's men about the shortage of available women made this desperate venture unnecessary. Morrison wrote that, unlike the Tahitians, "the natives still kept their women from living among us" and therefore some of the *Bounty* men insisted "that Mr. Christian would heed them and bring the women in to live with them by force" and refused to work "until every man had a wife." Christian, whose "desire was to persuade rather than force them," refused to accede to "such an absurd command," prompting three days of argument during which the men demanded more grog and when he refused "broke the lock of the spirit room and took it by force." His authority under threat, Christian tried to mollify them with a double ration each day but "all to no purpose."

In desperation, on September 10 he gathered all hands to discuss what to do. One suggestion—Morrison does not say from whom—was "that we should go to Tahiti, where they might get women without force and there separate." The idea was at first "overruled"—presumably by Christian—but the next day "on a call for a show of hands, sixteen appeared for Tahiti." They then agreed that those who chose to remain on Tahiti "should have arms, ammunition and part of everything on the ship," while the *Bounty* "would be left in charge of Mr. Christian, in a proper condition to go to sea, with her sails, tackle, and furniture."

Tubuai, though, had not quite done with the *Bounty* men. Christian sent out a party to round up the livestock—hogs, goats, and, in particular, the cow—they had turned loose. However, islanders attacked and robbed them and sent back word to Christian "that they would serve him the same way." The next day Christian led twenty men, Morrison among them, to collect the stock and punish the attackers. They set out taking with them thirteen Tahitian men and boys, one carrying the Union Jack. According to Morrison, after only a mile, seven hundred men "all armed with clubs, spears and stones" surrounded them but, as the *Bounty* men fired their muskets, fell back.

Weapons at the ready, the group rounded up some animals, only to be warned by friendly islanders that their old enemy Tinnarow planned to take the stock from them. Shortly afterward, Tinnarow's men ambushed them while they were passing through some thickets, spearing Burkett in his left side. Dragging Burkett with them and firing on their assailants, the *Bounty* crew retreated under volleys of stones, helped by their Tahitian comrades who "behaved manfully," grabbing some of their enemies' long spears. Several Tahitians were wounded but eventually the attackers fell back. The sailors got Burkett into a boat while the Tahitians gathered "such spoils as they thought proper," including Tubuaiian spears and clubs. One man begged "to cut out the jawbones of the killed, to hang round the quarters of the ship as trophies"—a request that was denied. Back on board, Burkett's wound was dressed; the spear had glanced off a rib and he recovered. Heywood estimated fifty Tubuaiian men were killed. Morrison thought sixty, together with six women "supplying them with spears and stones."

On September 17, 1789, carrying several Tubuaiians "who were now very fond of Mr. Christian" and feared what might happen to them at the hands of their fellow islanders if they remained, the *Bounty* cleared the reef and set sail. Five days later she anchored in Matavai Bay where, as Morrison says simply, "everything being settled," the sixteen men who wished to remain began landing their chests, hammocks, and the equipment Christian had agreed they could have. This included carpenter's and armorer's tools, iron for an anvil, a grindstone, iron pots, a copper kettle, "two spy glasses and an old azimuth compass," "sails and canvas that he thought he would not want," and "about three gallons of wine per man."

In addition to Morrison, those choosing to remain were, unsurprisingly, the four men detained on the *Bounty* against their will—carpenter Purcell's assistants Thomas McIntosh and Charles Norman, the armorer Joseph Coleman, and the partially blind fiddler Michael Byrne—but also master-at-arms Charles Churchill, the two midshipmen George Stewart and Peter Heywood, the cooper Henry Hillbrant, and able seamen John Millward, William Muspratt, Matthew Thompson, Richard Skinner, Thomas Burkett,

John Sumner, and young Thomas Ellison. When they told the Tahitians they intended to remain with them, they were relieved to find "our old friends ready to receive us with open arms." Christian had also agreed to let them have weapons: "for each man (except Byrne) a musket, pistol, cutlass, bayonet, cartridge box, seventeen pounds of powder, a quantity of lead to make ball." The reason for excluding Byrne was not only his poor eyesight but also his "very troublesome disposition" because of which "we thought that arms put into his hands would only help him to do some mischief." Christian gave Morrison the Tubuaiian images he had taken "as a present for the young king."

At nightfall, after everything had been taken ashore, Morrison related that Christian told those who were to remain "that he intended to stay a day or two. He hoped that we would assist him to fill some water, as he intended to cruise for some uninhabited island where he would land his stock (of which the ship was full, together with plants of all the kinds that are common in these islands) and set fire to the ship. He hoped to live the remainder of his days without seeing the face of a European other than those who were already with him." The faces he would have to live with were those of midshipman Edward Young, five able seamen—the American Isaac Martin, William McKoy, John Williams, Matthew Quintal, who seems to have put his argument with Christian on Tubuai behind him, and Alexander Smith, as well as Scottish gunner's mate John Mills and gardener's assistant William Brown.*

After all Christian had said, that same night, September 22, 1789, Morrison and his companions were amazed to see the *Bounty* standing out to sea and could only suppose "that he either was afraid of a surprise"—that those remaining on Tahiti might try to seize the *Bounty* from him—or "had done it to prevent his companions from changing their minds." Also on board were six Polynesian men, including two Tubuaiians, and nineteen women, some voluntarily but others who had no idea the *Bounty* was putting to sea until they felt the shiver and creak of her timbers as she cleared the reef.

---

*According to an account given late in his life by Heywood, that day Christian took him aside and entrusted him with a message to pass on to Christian's family describing circumstances that, though they could not justify his actions, would extenuate them. Heywood never disclosed what Christian said and it has been the subject of much speculation ever since.

XVIII

"THE STRANGE COMBINATION OF CIRCUMSTANCES"

Shortly after dawn on March 23, 1791, five days before the Bryants and their companions escaped from Sydney Cove, HMS *Pandora* sailed into the wide arc of Matavai Bay. The Admiralty's instructions to Captain Edwards to enquire with discretion about the *Bounty* proved unnecessary. According to the ship's surgeon, Northumberland-born George Hamilton, an islander immediately paddled out to the ship, joyfully embraced the new arrivals, and told them that Fletcher Christian and nine others had "long since" sailed off in the *Bounty* but that other crewmen were still on Tahiti. He also insisted that Cook was still alive and that Bligh had gone to live with him on Aitutaki.* When Lieutenant Hayward, who had purposely kept in the background, stepped forward, the Tahitian was astonished.

Even before the *Pandora* had anchored, the *Bounty's* armorer, Joseph Coleman, swam out to the ship. He confirmed that others were indeed on the island, of whom some had sailed the previous day in a boat they had built to Papara in the south of Tahiti to join another group settled there. Coleman also reported that the *Bounty's* master-at-arms Charles Churchill had been murdered by able seaman Matthew Thompson, and Thompson himself subsequently had been "killed by the natives and offered as a sacrifice on their altars for the murder of Churchill, whom they had made a chief." Though Bligh had identified Coleman, like Norman and McIntosh, as having been detained on the *Bounty* against his will, Edwards had him put in irons.

Bligh's "young gentlemen," Peter Heywood and George Stewart, arrived soon afterward. Any hopes that Hayward would intercede for them were

---

*Aitutaki is in the archipelago discovered by Cook southwest of Tahiti named by him the Hervey Islands, later renamed the Cook Islands.

quickly dashed. According to Heywood, "Knowing from one of the natives that our former messmate, Mr. Hayward, now promoted to the rank of lieutenant was on board, we asked for him, supposing he might prove our assertions. But he (like all worldlings when raised a little in life) received us very coolly, and pretended ignorance of our affairs . . . Appearances being so much against us, we were ordered in irons and looked upon . . . as piratical villains!" Learning that another *Bounty* man—able seaman Richard Skinner—was at Matavai, Edwards asked a chief to apprehend him. Skinner arrived before nightfall, whether like Heywood and Stewart of his own accord or because the chief had coerced him, Edwards was unsure. It made no difference. He too was immediately put in irons.

In the eighteen months since the *Bounty* had left Tahiti, life among those remaining had not been harmonious and cliques had formed. Peter Heywood had lived quietly, amusing himself by compiling a Tahitian dictionary. George Stewart had settled down with his Tahitian wife, Peggy, and had been laying out a fine garden. James Morrison had soon begun to wonder whether "it would be possible to build a small vessel in hope of reaching Batavia, and from thence to England." He had persuaded McIntosh and Millward to join his endeavors. A sign of the divisions on the island was that the trio kept their real motive secret, maintaining that the boat —a schooner— was for "pleasuring about the island." They began assembling materials at Matavai Bay. When Norman, Hillbrant, Burkett, Sumner, Ellison, and Churchill joined them, Morrison maintained the fiction that the purpose was only "to cruise about the island."

On November 12, 1789—two months after the *Bounty*'s departure—they laid the thirty-foot-long keel, assisted by Tahitians intrigued by their methods of boatbuilding. They made swift progress, only interrupted by events such as a festival to which they were invited and which opened with the veneration of Cook's portrait: "The cloth with which it was covered being removed, every person present paid the homage of stripping off their upper garments . . . The master of the ceremonies then made the oodoo (or usual offering) making a long speech to the picture, acknowledging Captain Cook to be chief of Matavai . . . The speech ran 'Hail, all hail Cook, Chief of Air Earth and Water. We acknowledge you chief from the beach to the mountains, over men, trees and cattle, over birds of the air and fishes of the sea.' "

However, February 1790 brought a rift in the workforce when Matthew Thompson—at the time living with Coleman at Point Venus—assaulted a young girl whose brother knocked him down before fleeing. Enraged,

Thompson vowed revenge "on the first [Tahitian] person who offended him," which happened to be a Tahitian family who, curious to see Englishmen, visited his house. He broke the mother's jaw and shot the father and a child—an act, Morrison thought, of plain murder. Churchill, who Morrison suspected "had always been aspiring at command," offered to become the *Bounty* men's leader and organize their defense in case the Tahitians sought retribution, which they did not. When the others rejected his proposal, Churchill and Thompson took themselves off to another part of the island, where local chiefs appointed Churchill their sovereign. As Coleman told Captain Edwards, his "reign" was short. During a quarrel, Thompson shot Churchill, only to have his brains dashed out by islanders angrily avenging their leader.

Morrison and his team doggedly continued with their boatbuilding, making pitch from breadfruit to caulk the seams. On July 1 four hundred singing Tahitians helped haul her down to the beach where, christened *Resolution*, she was launched. She proved watertight but much was still to be done, from cutting masts and making casks to assembling rope. Sometimes Morrison and his helpers had to stop work when Tu asked the *Bounty* men's help in quelling risings on the island, which they agreed to give. This was the first time Europeans, with their western weapons like the muskets with which they armed themselves and some of their Tahitian allies, intervened directly in island affairs. Morrison described how once "as we entered the enemy's country they fled to the mountains, and our party on shore pursued them, burning the houses and destroying the country . . . rooting up the plantains and taro, notching the bark round the breadfruit trees to stop their growth, and laying all in ashes."

Whenever he could, Morrison returned to finishing his schooner. Short voyages around the island and across to Moorea, Tahiti's northwestern neighbor, confirmed her seaworthiness but Morrison realized that her sails—improvised from woven matting for lack of canvas—would not withstand the battering of a voyage to the Dutch Indies. Reluctantly he abandoned his plans to leave Tahiti but still sailed the *Resolution* around the island, which is what he was doing when on March 23, 1791, Captain Edwards and the *Pandora* arrived. Morrison had taken Norman, Ellison, Byrne, McIntosh, Millward, and Hillbrant to visit Burkett, Sumner, and Muspratt, who were living at Papara on the south coast. They had barely arrived when, to their shock, an islander told them "that a ship had anchored at Matavai since we had left it," that Heywood, Stewart, Coleman, and Skinner had already gone on board and that armed boats had been dispatched to catch the rest of them. These were the *Pandora's* launch and pinnace, commanded by Hayward and another lieutenant, Robert Corner. Edwards's hope was to seize the *Bounty* men before they learned of his arrival.

Edwards had quickly acquired a useful informant—a sailor, John Brown, whose ship *Mercury* had put in at Tahiti while Christian and the *Bounty* had still been at Tubuai. On Tahiti Brown had slashed the face of another sailor with an old razor and been clapped in irons. When the *Mercury* sailed he had voluntarily remained behind. On the *Pandora's* arrival he had hastened aboard to assure Edwards that he had only associated with "the pirates" "for his own safety." Deciding Brown would be useful as "guide, soldier and seaman," Edwards entered his name on the *Pandora's* muster.

Morrison and his companions agreed to "avoid the boats" until they had decided what to do. Therefore they spent an entire day evading their pursuers until Corner and Hayward returned exhausted to the *Pandora*. When Morrison finally put in to the shore, Burkett, Sumner, Muspratt, Hillbrant, McIntosh, and Millward departed to hide in the mountains, leaving Morrison, Norman, and Ellison behind with the boat. Morrison concluded they must turn themselves in, though a Tahitian friend warned him that "Hayward will kill you, for he is very angry" and urged him to "go into the mountains" as well. When Morrison refused, Tahitians put Morrison, Norman, and Ellison under guard in a house on the shore to prevent them leaving.

The next evening to their surprise John Brown arrived bringing them a pistol, two hatchets, a knife, and a bottle of gin. His purpose in coming has never been clear and Morrison, who had long thought him "a dangerous kind of man," evidently did not trust him though he did tell him their intention was to reach the *Pandora*. Later that night, Morrison, Norman, and Ellison escaped from the house, leaving Brown behind, and set out by canoe. After paddling six miles along the shoreline, they landed and approached Matavai Bay and the *Pandora* on foot. At about four in the morning they saw the *Pandora's* launch, commanded by Lieutenant Corner, lying at anchor.

Events now turned somewhat farcical. Finding Corner and his crew soundly asleep, Morrison and his companions "waked him and delivered ourselves up to him, telling him who we were." At daybreak, Corner set off overland to Papara with eighteen men to seek the remaining "pirates," leaving his three captives under guard to await the arrival in another boat of their former shipmate, Lieutenant Hayward. When Hayward appeared in the early afternoon he had the prisoners' hands bound and dispatched them to the *Pandora* while he continued to Papara, where Corner had been struggling over tumbled basalt rocks, through dense foliage, and across fast-flowing waterfalls. Hayward eventually located the last six *Bounty* men, who surrendered peacefully.

Edwards set guards with pistols and bayonets over the prisoners, ordering them, according to Morrison, "not to suffer any of the natives to speak to us, and to shoot the first man that spoke to another in the Tahiti language." At first the *Bounty* men were kept in irons below deck where sympathizers among the *Pandora's* crew gave them "plenty of coconuts" to quench their thirst, though "any who looked pitifully towards us were ordered out of the ship." However, to secure his prisoners during the long voyage home and prevent "their having any communication with, or to crowd and incommode the ship's company," Edwards ordered the construction of what Morrison called "a kind of poop on the quarterdeck for our reception."

Edwards himself described it as a "round house . . . airy and healthy." The fourteen men confined within would soon call it *"Pandora's* Box." According to Morrison,

> The poop, or roundhouse, being finished we were conveyed into it and put in irons as before . . . the entrance being a scuttle on the top, eighteen or twenty inches square, secured by a bolt . . . two scuttles of nine inches square in the bulkhead for air with iron grates; and the stern ports barred inside and out with iron. The sentries were placed on the top . . . The length of this box was eleven feet . . . and eighteen wide . . . and no person was suffered to speak to us but the master-at-arms . . .
>
> The heat of the place . . . was so intense that the sweat frequently ran in streams to the scuppers and produced maggots . . . The hammocks, being dirty when we got them, we found stored with vermin . . . which we had no method of eradicating . . . though our friends would have supplied us with plenty of cloth, they were not permitted to do it, and our only remedy was to lay naked . . . the two necessary tubs . . . helped to render our situation truly disagreeable.

When the officer of the watch discovered that McIntosh had managed to free one of his legs from the heavy shackles, Edwards had all the prisoners' leg irons tightened. A lieutenant also tested the fit of their handcuffs by "setting his foot against our breasts and hauling the handcuffs over our hands with all his might, some of which took the skin off with them. All that could be hauled off by this means were reduced, and fitted so close, that there was no possibility of turning the hand in them. When our wrists began to swell, he told us that 'they were not intended to fit like gloves.'"

Morrison also related how at first, "the women with whom we had cohabited on the island came frequently under the stern (bringing their children, of which there were six born, four girls and two boys; several of the women were big with child). They cut their heads till the blood discoloured the water about them." They included George Stewart's wife, Peggy, and their young daughter. Though "always driven away by the captain's orders," they stubbornly continued "to come near enough to be observed and there performed their mourning rites."

Captain Edwards questioned "different people" and sifted through "journals kept on the *Bounty* . . . found in the chests of the pirates at Tahiti" hoping for clues about the *Bounty*'s destination. All he learned was that Christian had frequently declared "he would search for an unknown or uninhabited island in which there was no harbour for shipping." Since this information "was too vague to be followed in an immense ocean strewed with an almost innumerable number of known and unknown islands," Edwards decided to sail to Aitutaki, where the *Bounty* men had told the islanders that Bligh was living with Cook, searching other islands on the way. He also decided to refit and take with him as a tender Morrison's *Resolution*—"decked, beautifully built, and the size of a Gravesend boat," Hamilton wrote approvingly in his later account.

While at Matavai, Tahiti's legendary charms were at work on Edwards's crew, if not the captain himself. To Surgeon Hamilton it was "the Cythera of the southern hemisphere . . . what poetic fiction has painted of Eden and Arcadia, is here realised, where the earth without tillage produces both food and clothing, the trees loaded with the richest of fruit, the carpet of nature spread with the most odoriferous flowers, and the fair ones ever willing to fill your arms with love." He perceived a natural nobility, devoid of selfishness and self-interest, in the islanders' way of life that, he thought, made even the "generous, charitable" British seem "stingy": "A native of this country divides everything in common with his friend, and the extent of the word friend, by them, is only bounded by the universe, and was he reduced to his last morsel of bread, he cheerfully halves it with him . . . The king and beggar relieve each other in common."

Like others, Hamilton also reflected, "Happy would it have been for those people had they never been visited by Europeans; for, to our shame be it spoken, disease and gunpowder is all the benefit they have ever received from us, in return for their hospitality and kindness. The ravages of the venereal disease is evident, from the mutilated objects so frequent amongst them, where death has not thrown a charitable veil over their misery . . . A disease of the consumptive kind has of late made great havoc amongst them; this they call the British disease."

On May 8, 1791, "filled with cocoa-nuts and fruit" and "as many pigs, goats and fowls, as the decks and boats would hold," the *Pandora* sailed for Aitutaki. Hamilton called it a "dismal day" on which hearts aboard were "heavy . . . Every canoe almost in the island was hovering round the ship; and they began to mourn." To the prisoners, squinting through the tiny scuttles of *Pandora*'s Box, the cries of their women were enough to "melt the most obdurate heart."

Six days into the voyage Henry Hillbrant—perhaps hoping for better treatment—claimed that, the night before the *Bounty* had finally left Tahiti, Christian had told him that he intended to seek out an uninhabited island discovered by Captain Byron where, if it proved suitable, he intended to settle after running the ship onto a reef and wrecking her. Edwards identified the island as probably the Duke of York's Island.* He thought the suggestion "plausible" but decided to go first to Aitutaki. Finding no trace of the *Bounty* there, he set course for the Duke of York's Island.

En route there he called at Palmerston Island (in the Cook group) where Lieutenant Corner made a promising discovery—"a yard and some spars marked 'Bounty.'" Edwards landed a shore party "to advance with great circumspection, and to guard against surprise" and sent the *Pandora*'s cutter to circumnavigate the island. However, neither found any trace of the mutineers. The only "surprise" to the shore party, exhausted by having to swim ashore through the surf in cork jackets, was when a coconut they had thrown on their fire and forgotten "burst with a great explosion." Believing themselves under attack they all jumped up and grabbed their muskets. In fact, the mutineers had never landed here. The spars found on the beach were those lost while the *Bounty* was in Tubuai and had drifted with the prevailing winds. As "the weather became thick and hazy, and began to blow fresh," the *Pandora*'s jolly boat and her crew of five vanished among the island's reefs.

*Atafu in the western Pacific.

Though Edwards searched, neither boat nor men were ever seen again and Edwards could only sail on.

On June 6, the *Pandora* reached the Duke of York's Island where, despite Hillbrant's claim, there was no sign of the *Bounty* either. A frustrated Edwards continued onward, stopping to search other islands, including one where islanders naked except for "a girdle of leaves round their middle" and garlands of sweet-smelling flowers came aboard to trade spiced puddings and bright-feathered birds. Hamilton admired a naked woman "six feet high, of exquisite beauty, and exact symmetry . . . Many mouths were watering for her but Captain Edwards . . . had given previous orders that no woman should be permitted to go below," as some of the crew had not recovered from the venereal disease encountered on Tahiti.

A few days later, in strong winds the *Pandora* lost contact with the *Resolution*. Edwards had guns fired and fires lit on the *Pandora*'s deck to help the schooner's nine-strong crew find their way back, but to no avail. Eventually Edwards set sail for Nomuka in the Friendly Islands (Tonga) which, after the loss of the jolly boat, he had designated as the rendezvous if any vessel became separated. Bligh and his men had been attacked on Nomuka during their open-boat journey and while the *Pandora* waited there for news of the *Resolution* her crew also received a hostile reception: "The second lieutenant was knocked down on shore . . . and some of the men were stripped stark naked," Morrison wrote. Islanders climbed into Edwards's cabin and stole some of his books.

However, they were as eager as the Tahitians to trade for metal. Surgeon Hamilton described how "the quarter-deck became the scene of the most indelicate familiarities" as mothers bartered their daughters' virginity for as little as "an old razor, a pair of scissors, or a very large nail." Among the male traders were some who had attacked Bligh's party and looked much abashed when they recognized Lieutenant Hayward. Edwards could not punish them since, if the *Resolution* did eventually arrive, the islanders might avenge themselves on her crew.

In early July, Edwards embarked on a sweep of neighboring islands, searching for clues to the *Bounty*'s whereabouts but, discovering nothing, returned to Nomuka where there was still no news of the *Resolution*. On August 2, leaving a letter for the *Resolution*'s crew with the islands' chiefs, he sailed away.

In the humid heat and heavy tropical rain, conditions for the prisoners cooped up in *Pandora*'s Box worsened. Morrison described how "when any rain fell we were always wet . . . Our miserable situation soon brought sickness on amongst us." Though "the surgeon [Hamilton], a very humane gentleman . . . informed us that Captain Edwards had given such orders that it was out of his power to be of any service to us . . . between him and the second lieutenant, a copper kettle was provided to boil our cocoa . . . This and Divine Providence kept us alive."

By August 8, having still discovered nothing of the *Bounty*, Edwards set course westward for the Torres Strait and home. On August 13, through the heat haze, lookouts sighted an island on which, Edwards wrote, "we saw smoke very plain, from which it may be presumed that the island is inhabited." The island was Vanikoro in the Solomon Islands and the smoke may have been from fires lit by survivors of La Pérouse's expedition, which Phillip and the First Fleet had encountered in Botany Bay. La Pérouse's ships the *Boussole* and *Astrolabe* had subsequently foundered on Vanikoro's reefs three years before. Had Edwards sent a landing party it might have rescued any survivors.

Four days later, the *Pandora* almost grounded on shoals—a warning that she was approaching Cook's "insane labyrinth"—the Great Barrier Reef. On August 28, Edwards sent Lieutenant Corner in one of the ship's yawls to seek an opening through the reef. At five o'clock that afternoon Corner signaled that he had found a safe passage but, with night falling, Edwards ordered him back to the ship. The yawl only regained the *Pandora* with difficulty, guided through the "exceeding dark, stormy night" by flashes from muskets fired on the mother ship's deck. Shortly afterward, the *Pandora* suddenly hit the reef so violently that Morrison "expected at every surge that the masts would go by the board."

Within five minutes the hold was flooded to a depth of eighteen inches. Fifteen minutes later the water was nine feet deep. Surgeon Hamilton recalled, a "dreadful crisis . . . it blew very violently; and she beat so hard upon the rocks, that we expected her, every minute, to go to pieces . . . the gloomy horrors of death presented us all round, being everywhere encompassed with rocks, shoals and broken water." Edwards set hands—including Coleman, Norman, and McIntosh, whom he released from *Pandora*'s Box—to pumping and baling. Even so the *Pandora* was listing. To lighten her, Edwards ordered the guns to be thrown overboard but in the process one careered over the deck, crushing a sailor. A spare topmast crashed down, killing another.

By dawn, Edwards and his officers knew the *Pandora* could not be saved. He ordered the ship's boats, moored astern, to be loaded with provisions, rafts to be built, and, Hamilton wrote, "spars, booms, hen-coops and every-thing buoyant" cut loose. The ship "now took a very heavy heel, so much that she lay quite down on one side." An officer told Edwards that "the anchor on our bow was under water; that she was then going; and, bidding him fare-well, jumped over the quarter into the water. The captain then followed his example, and jumped after him. At that last instant, she took her last heel; and, while everyone were scrambling to windward, she sunk in an instant. The crew had just time to leap overboard, accompanying it with a most dreadful yell." Those who could swam to the ship's boats to be hauled aboard by their comrades but the cries of others "drowning in the water was at first awful in the extreme; but as they sunk, and became faint, it died away."

Hamilton also wrote that before the *Pandora* took her final great list, "the prisoners were ordered to be let out of irons." Inmates of *Pandora*'s Box recalled a more complex and frightening picture. Morrison recounted how, when the ship hit the reef, realizing the ship "would not hold long together" and "as we were in danger at every stroke of killing each other with our irons we broke them so we might be ready to assist ourselves." They "informed the officers what we had done," assuring Lieutenant Corner that "we should attempt nothing further, as we only wanted a chance for our lives." Corner promised they had nothing to fear. However, as soon as Edwards learned his prisoners had broken free of their irons "he ordered us to be handcuffed and legs ironed again . . . We begged for mercy and desired leave to go to the pumps but to no purpose." Ignoring their pleas, Edwards placed additional guards over them armed with a brace of pistols apiece and "with orders to fire among us if we made any motion." The prisoners decided "there was no remedy but prayer, as we expected never to see daylight. Having recom-mended ourselves to the Almighty's protection, we lay down."

At daybreak on August 29, realizing from what they could either hear or glimpse through the scuttles that the crew were preparing to abandon ship, according to Morrison, the prisoners "begged that we might not be forgotten, when by Captain Edwards's order Joseph Hodges, the armourer's mate . . . was sent down to take the irons off Muspratt and Skinner, and send them and Byrne (who was then out of irons) up. But Skinner, being too eager to get out, got hauled up with his handcuffs on, and the other two followed him closely. The scuttle was shut and barred before Hodges could get to it." Morrison and Stewart, whose irons Hodges had meanwhile struck off, begged the master-at-arms guarding them "to leave the scuttle open" to which he replied, " 'Never fear, my boys, we'll all go to hell together.' The words were scarcely out of his mouth when the ship took a sally, and a general cry of 'there she goes' was heard. The master-at-arms and the other guards . . . rolled overboard." Peering through the small air scuttle at the stern, Morrison saw Edwards swimming toward the ship's pinnace. There seemed little hope for the men locked in *Pandora's* Box: "Burkett and Hillbrant were yet handcuffed, and the ship under water as far as the main mast."

Then "Divine Providence" sent bosun's mate William Moulter to their aid. Hearing their desperate cries, he paused to release the scuttle's bolt before himself leaping into the sea. All except Hillbrant managed to scramble out, including Hodges the armorer's mate. But with the ship sinking beneath them and loose debris surging about in the water, they were still in danger. Morrison described how

> observing one of the gangways come up, I swam to it and had scarcely reached it before I perceived Muspratt on the other end. It had brought him up, but it fell on the heads of several others, sending them to the bottom . . . The top of our prison had floated and I observed on it Mr. Peter Heywood, Burkett and Coleman . . . Seeing Mr. Heywood take a short plank and set off to one of the boats, I resolved to follow him. I threw away my trousers, bound my loins up in a sash . . . after the Tahitian manner, got a short plank and followed.

An hour and a half later Morrison was hauled into a boat where he also found Heywood. The crew made for a sandy key about four miles from the ship, where other survivors were already gathering. When the muster was taken it showed that "89 of the ship's company and 10 of the pirates . . . were saved and that 31 of the ship's company and 4 pirates were lost." The dead *Bounty* men were Hillbrant, trapped in *Pandora's* Box, Skinner, who had still been in handcuffs, and Stewart and Sumner, who had been struck by debris.

Edwards ordered the *Pandora's* sailors to ready the ship's four boats for a voyage that he hoped would take them, like Bligh, to Kupang and safety. They had some stocks of ship's biscuit but only a small barrel of water and a larger amount of wine that had been thrown into one of the boats in the *Pandora's* dying moments. For the moment they drank wine in preference to the water they knew they had to preserve. Hamilton described how "by a calculation which we made, by filling the compass boxes, and every utensil we had, we could admit an allowance of two small wine glasses of water a-day to each man for sixteen days." One sailor was already behaving so erratically his comrades thought him drunk until they realized "the excruciating torture he suffered from thirst" had led him to drink saltwater.

If the *Bounty* prisoners hoped for less harsh treatment now they were disappointed. Though tents were erected for the *Pandora's* officers and crew, the mutineers were warned not to approach either. When they begged for a sail to shelter their nearly naked bodies, pallid from confinement in semi-darkness for five months, from the blistering sun, Edwards refused. He also restricted them to a small area of the key—soon nicknamed "Wreck Island"—with orders to speak to no one but each other. Morrison recalled how "we had our skin flayed off from head to foot, though we kept ourselves covered in the sand during the heat of the day."

The day after the disaster, Edwards sent the *Pandora's* master to see what he could salvage from the wreck, which was protruding from the water. He returned with some timbers and the ship's cat, which he had found clinging to a mast. The next day, August 31, the convoy of four boats—a pinnace, a launch, and two yawls—set out, the *Bounty* prisoners divided among them. Each boat carried an improvised set of wooden scales, similar to Bligh's coconut apparatus, so that "a musket-ball weight" of biscuit could be weighed out for each man at mealtimes. Morrison, McIntosh, and Ellison had the misfortune of being in Edwards's boat where, as Morrison recalled, "As I was laying on the oars talking to McIntosh, Captain Edwards ordered me aft, and without assigning any cause ordered me to be pinioned with a cord and lashed down in the boat's bottom. Ellison, who was then asleep in the boat's bottom, was ordered to the same punishment." When Morrison asked why they were being treated "thus cruelly," Edwards replied, "Silence, you murdering villain, are you not a prisoner? You piratical dog, what better treatment do you expect?" When Morrison continued to remonstrate, Edwards "in a violent rage" grabbed a pistol and threatened to shoot him.

All the time they searched for watering places. Sometimes they were lucky but on one occasion they were chased away by canoes paddled by Aboriginal men of such "very savage aspect . . . we judged it prudent to avoid them." Reaching an island, they tried to trade knives and buttons from their coats with the locals for water, only to be suddenly attacked by men loosing "a shower of arrows amongst the thick of us."

On the evening of September 2, Edwards recorded that "we saw the northernmost extremity of New South Wales." His "little squadron" continued west across the top of the Gulf of Carpentaria, then skirted the northern coast of New Holland searching for watering places. When on Edwards's boat a booby was caught, "the blood was eagerly sucked." Landing on an island, they heard what they thought was the "hideous growling" of wolves—probably dingoes—but digging deep in a hollow "had the ecstatic pleasure to see a spring rush out," enabling them to gorge "our parched bodies . . . till we were perfectly water-logged." As Bligh's party had done, they searched for oysters to quell the hunger that wracked them once their thirst was satisfied.

Striking out due west toward Kupang, a heavy swell threatening to capsize them, sometimes the boats became separated. Their occupants became so thirsty that few ate their daily allowance of biscuit, meager though it was, and some drank their own urine. "As their sufferings continued," Hamilton wrote, "they became very cross and savage in their temper." One seaman went insane.

On September 13, they sighted land. A prodigious surf at first frustrated their attempts to land but eventually they sailed safely into a creek where they could drink their fill and sleep on the grass. Local people soon arrived bringing chickens, pigs, milk, and bread to sell. One man "offered to traffic with us for the charms of his daughter, a very pretty young girl. But," Hamilton acknowledged with his customary frankness, "none of us seemed inclined that way, as there were many good things we stood much more in need of." He also wrote that they were nervous of the local people since, "From Bligh's narrative and others we had been warned of the danger of landing in any other part of the island of Timor but Kupang, the Dutch settlement, as [the inhabitants] were represented hostile and savage." A sudden noise made them "all panic-struck . . . Most . . . scrambling upon all fours down to the river, and crying for Christ's sake to have mercy."

When sufficiently recovered, they set out for Kupang and on September 15, 1791—three months after the Bryants' arrival and after a journey of sixteen days and 1,200 nautical miles—sailed into its harbor under the gaze of a population growing used to such arrivals. After presenting his credentials to Governor Wanjon, Edwards handed over the *Bounty* prisoners, who were taken to the fort and put into stocks in a cell. On being given proper food after so long, their clogged bowels began to move but they were "forced to ease nature where we lay." A Dutch surgeon sent to examine them refused to enter their cell until slaves had scrubbed it. They received greater kindness from the fort's commander, who six days later, "being informed of our distress," visited them and "ordered irons to be procured and linked us two and two, giving us liberty to walk about the cell." Being nearly naked, they wove hats from palm leaves that they were allowed to sell to raise money to buy clothes.

The *Bounty* prisoners discovered they were not the only British prisoners in the fort: The escapees from Botany Bay were also confined there. For a while the Bryants and their companions had succeeded in living quietly in Kupang under their assumed identities as shipwrecked whalers. According to James Martin they had even found employment—"We remained very happy at our work for two months"—until "William Bryant had words with his wife, [and] went and informed against himself, wife and children and all of us . . . We was immediately taken prisoners and was put in the castle." Martin should have known what had precipitated the convicts' arrest, though other accounts tell slightly different stories. Morrison was told that "not being able to keep within bounds, they were discovered to be cheats and confined in the castle till they should pay the debt they had contracted." On a later visit to Kupang, Bligh was shown the journal kept by William Bryant and wrote that "one of the party informed through pique at not being taken so much notice of as the rest." Another report suggested that William Bryant betrayed their secret while drunk.

Hamilton believed the arrival of the *Pandora* survivors was the convicts' undoing: "The captain of a Dutch East Indiaman, who spoke English, hearing of the arrival of Capt. Edwards . . . run to them with the glad tidings of their captain having arrived; but one of them, starting up in surprise, said, 'What Captain! Dam'me, we have no Captain;' for they had reported that the captain and remainder of the crew had separated from them at sea in another boat. This immediately led to a suspicion of their being impostors; and they were ordered to be apprehended . . . One of the men, and the woman, fled into the woods but were soon taken." However, remarks by James Martin that until Edwards's arrival Governor Wanjon allowed them out of the fort "two at a time for one day, and the next day two more" suggest that they had been arrested before the *Pandora* party arrived.

Whatever the precise circumstances of their arrest, Edwards questioned them closely, "to know who we were." "We told him we was convicts and had made our escape from Botany Bay. He told us we was his prisoners," Martin later wrote. William Bryant and James Cox tried to convince Edwards that their sentences had expired but, he wrote to the Admiralty, even if that were true, the fact of their stealing a boat "to enable themselves and others to escape" made them "liable to punishment."

On October 6, Edwards embarked his entire party—*Bounty* prisoners, Botany Bay escapees, and *Pandora* survivors—on the Dutch Indiaman *Rembang*, bound for Batavia. Morrison described how the *Bounty* men—arms pinioned behind their backs "as almost to haul them out of their sockets"— were "tied two and two by the elbows" and taken by longboat out to the *Rembang*, though "before we reached her some of us had fainted, owing to the circulation of the blood being stopped by the lashings." He also recorded how "the Botany Bay men were now brought on board by a party of Dutch soldiers and put in irons with us, in the same manner." How Mary Bryant and her children were treated he did not say.

A week later off the island of Flores a severe storm "attended with the most dreadful thunder and lightning we had ever experienced" broke over them. Hamilton described with chauvinistic scorn how "the Dutch seamen were struck with horror, and went below; and the ship was preserved from destruction by the manly exertion of our English tars, whose souls seemed to catch redoubled ardour from the tempest's rage." On October 30, the battered *Rembang* and her no less battered occupants limped into Samarang on the north coast of Java where, Edwards and his men discovered, the lost schooner *Resolution* had arrived six weeks before. After losing contact with the *Pandora*, her crew had mistaken an island in Fiji for the agreed rendez-vous of Nomuka. After waiting in vain for the *Pandora* they had made their own perilous way through the Torres Strait in stark contrast to the *Pandora*'s fate—and in a tribute to Morrison's shipbuilding skills. Edwards's arrival was timely since the Dutch authorities, suspecting the *Resolution*'s crew might be "the *Bounty* pirates" of whom they had received reports, had placed them under guard.

Sailing on with the *Resolution*, on November 7 the *Rembang* arrived in Batavia, where Edwards transferred his prisoners to a Dutch prison hulk on which they were held in irons. Cook had called Batavia the cause of "the death of more Europeans than any other place upon the globe." Several survivors of Bligh's open-boat journey had died there. Hamilton, disturbed by the sight of corpses floating in the water and bumping against the ship, thought it a "Golgotha." He blamed not the climate but the Dutch passion for canal building: "All the mortality of that place originates from marsh effluvia arising from their stagnant canals and pleasure-grounds."

To ward off the miasma of "pestilential vapours" and "thick stinking fog," the new arrivals smoked tobacco continuously; but many were already ill or soon became so. There was little option but to dispatch them to the hospital—in Hamilton's view "a cadaverous stinking prison"—where their chances of survival "surrounded by poor wretches whose pallid faces and emaciated bodies plainly indicated their approaching dissolution" were slim. Among those sent to this charnel house were the Bryants' twenty-month-old son, Emmanuel, who, James Martin wrote, "we lost" on December 1 and William Bryant himself, who, "taken bad," died three weeks later.

Edwards found passage for all his prisoners and crew on Dutch ships bound for Holland via the Cape of Good Hope. He embarked with the ten surviving *Bounty* men on the *Vredenburg*. Of the convicts, Mary Bryant and the last remaining member of her family, her four-year-old daughter Charlotte, were put aboard the *Horssen* together with William Allen and James Cox, while James Martin, John Butcher, William Morton, Samuel Bird, and Nathaniel Lilley sailed on the *Hoornwey*. During the three-month voyage of frequent "heavy gales" and "mountainous sea" Morton and Bird died, while James Cox leapt overboard. Edwards recorded simply that he drowned. Surgeon Hamilton thought he managed to swim ashore which, given that he was in irons, seems unlikely.

At Cape Town, Edwards found HMS *Gorgon*, returning home after carrying convicts to Port Jackson with the Second Fleet, and he embarked all his prisoners on her. By a quirk of fate, among those already aboard were Watkin Tench, now a captain, and a number of other marines, including Lieutenant Ralph Clark, returning to Britain after completing their service in the colony. Tench was impressed when he heard the story of the Bryants' party, which had escaped the colony a year before:

> It was my fate to fall in again with part of this little band of adventurers. In March 1792, when I arrived in the *Gorgon*, at the Cape . . . six of these people, including the woman and one child, were put on board of us to be carried to England . . . The woman and one of the men had gone out to Port Jackson in the ship which had transported me thither. They had both of them been always distinguished

for good behaviour . . . I confess that I never looked at these people without pity and astonishment. They had miscarried in a heroic struggle for liberty after having combated every hardship, and conquered every difficulty . . . I could not but reflect with admiration at the strange combination of circumstances which had again brought us together to baffle human foresight and confound human speculation.

As well as the marines who had once guarded them, aboard the *Gorgon* were other reminders to the Botany Bay prisoners of the land they had fled. According to Mrs. Parker, the captain's wife, the ship was "crowded with kangaroos, opossums, and every curiosity that country produced. The quarter deck was occupied with shrubs and plants, while the cabin was hung around with skins of animals," many destined for Joseph Banks.

On April 6, 1792, the *Gorgon* sailed in weather soon so stiflingly hot that Ralph Clark noted how belowdecks, where the prisoners were confined, "there is hardly any living for the heat." Four days later, he noted that "this hot weather is playing the devil with the children." By May 2, the children were "going very fast": Five young children of the marines had already died and another followed on May 4. Then on Sunday, May 6, Clark recorded, "Squally weather with a great deal of rain all this day. Last night the child belonging to Mary Broad, the convict woman who went away in the fishing boat from Port Jackson last year, died about four o'clock. Committed the body to the deep."*

On June 18, 1792, the *Gorgon* anchored at Portsmouth and all the prisoners on board, including the trebly bereft Mary Bryant, prepared to face whatever justice lay in store.

---

*Lieutenant Ralph Clark did not long survive his service in Port Jackson, dying aboard ship in 1794—possibly killed in action. Soon after, his eight-year-old son, Ralph, a midshipman aboard the same ship, died of yellow fever. Clark's wife, Alicia, had died earlier that year after giving birth to a stillborn child. The island in Sydney Harbour where Clark cultivated a vegetable garden is named after him. What became of convict Mary Branham and Alicia, the daughter she bore Clark, appears unknown.

XIX

"THIS AMAZON"

*J*ames Morrison, Peter Heywood, and the other alleged mutineers were disembarked at Portsmouth and conveyed to HMS *Hector* to await trial while the *Gorgon* continued to London with Mary Bryant and her four surviving male companions. Later in June the latter were brought before magistrate Nicholas Bond of the Public Office in Bow Street. Captain Edwards identified them and Bond committed them to Newgate Prison. According to the *London Chronicle*, "they declared they would sooner suffer death than return to Botany Bay. His Majesty who is ever willing to extend his mercy surely never had objects more worthy of it. These poor people being destitute of necessities, several gentlemen gave them money." These gifts were typical of the widespread sympathy for their plight. According to the *Evening Mail*, Bond "declared he never experienced so disagreeable a task as being obliged to commit them to prison and assured them that as far as lay in his power he would assist them." A later edition of the *Chronicle* stated that the five found Newgate "a paradise compared with the awful suffering they endured on their voyage."

If this was the case, their voyage must have been truly terrible since conditions in Newgate Prison were very poor, even though it was less than ten years old, having been completely rebuilt following a fire. Prisoners were kept in irons if they could not pay the keeper "for easement." Anything more than the most basic food had to be purchased. Gin was so prevalent and cheap that many prisoners were perpetually drunk, and other poor creatures were insane. The collection taken up for the Port Jackson fugitives would, however, have helped them considerably to buy better food and better conditions.*

---

*Newgate was finally demolished in 1902 to make way for the Central Criminal Court (the rebuilt Old Bailey), although a single wall of the old Newgate survives.

The ultimate penalty for returning to Britain after escaping from transportation was death (the fate Magwitch feared in Dickens's *Great Expectations*). The commutation of Mary's original death sentence had also been formally revoked by her escape. She was therefore in double jeopardy and must have been more than a little apprehensive as she stood at the bar of the Old Bailey on July 7, 1792. The judge did not, however, pronounce a sentence of death on either Mary or any of her four companions but ordered them to "remain on their former sentence until they should be discharged by due course of law"—this being an indeterminate sentence.

Around this time the fifty-two-year-old James Boswell began to take an interest in Mary's case. In 1782, Boswell had inherited his family estate in Scotland together with the title "Laird of Auchinleck." Dr. Johnson had died two years later, in 1784. (Joseph Banks was one of his pallbearers.) Boswell's wife, Margaret, had died of consumption in 1789. His life of Dr. Johnson had been published in 1791 to popular if not always critical acclaim. Boswell was now living in Great Portland Street in London with two of his daughters while struggling to make a living at the London bar. He had not given up either his drinking or his whoring, although the latter, which brought him nineteen cases of venereal disease in his lifetime, was growing more infrequent.

However, Boswell had another side. From the beginning of his career as a lawyer he had always shown great interest in the fate of poor criminals, taking on cases when no one else would. He also hated public executions. The hanging of a highwayman and a female thief he had attended many years before had made a deep impression on him. He had gone to Tyburn, then London's place of public execution, having read so much about it that "I had a sort of horrid eagerness to be there." The hanging of the highwayman went smoothly but the female thief somehow freed her hands and struggled with the executioner before being hanged. The spectators jeered and catcalled but Boswell vomited and was "most terribly shocked" so that he went to the house of his friend Erskine because "gloomy terrors came upon me so much as night approached that I durst not stay by myself; so I went and had a bed (or rather half a one) from honest Erskine."

The execution in 1774 for sheep stealing of John Reid, whom Boswell had defended at the courts in Edinburgh and believed innocent, led him to a deep questioning of the nature of mortality. "We are all condemned to die. But what is it like to know the hour of one's death? How does a man die? What is it to pass from the known to the unknown? How will I die?"* Boswell's anxiety and concern about Reid's fate were so acute that he devised a scheme to obtain Reid's body after his execution and have it taken to some pseudo-doctors who claimed to be able to raise the dead. In the end, he thought better of it.

Now, in the summer of 1792, he took up the case of Mary Broad—as Boswell's accounts show, she appears to have used that name rather than Bryant after her return to Britain—and the four men with Evan Nepean, the Undersecretary at the Home Office and friend of Governor Phillip. Nepean told him, "Government would not treat them with harshness, but, at the same time, would not do a kind thing to them, as they might give encouragement to others to escape." Despite having recently fallen out with him, Boswell petitioned his old university friend and fellow mason Henry Dundas, Secretary for the Home Department, for a pardon for Mary and her companions.

Meanwhile, further details of the convicts' case, their escape and current situation, appeared frequently in the press. The *Dublin Chronicle* declared,

> This escape was perhaps the most hazardous and wonderful effort ever made by nine persons (two were infants [sic]) to regain their liberty which they declared they should not have ventured on but from the dread of starving and the certainty that if they did survive the period for which they were transported they should never again see their native country. They said that Governor Phillip used them very well, but the soil did not return half the quantity of grain which had been sown on it. Their cattle had been destroyed by the natives and a famine was the consequence . . . they therefore seized the first opportunity of throwing themselves upon the mercy of the sea rather than perish upon this inhospitable shore.

Boswell succeeded in getting an appointment to see Dundas in mid-August, which he kept, putting off a visit to Cornwall to do so, but Dundas did not appear, whereupon Boswell wrote to him, "The only solution you can give me for this unpleasant disappointment is to favour me with two lines directed Penrhyn, Cornwall, assuring me that nothing harsh shall be done to the unfortunate adventurers from New South Wales for whom I interest myself and whose very extraordinary case will not find a precedent."

---

*He had previously asked Dr. Johnson whether fear of death was natural. Johnson answered, "So much so, Sir, that the whole of life is but keeping away the thoughts of it."

Dundas replied almost immediately that he would give Boswell's plea due consideration.

Boswell's visit to Cornwall lasted about six weeks. As far as is known he did not take up Mary's case while he was there or visit Fowey. Dundas took no action on Mary's case until on May 2, 1793, he gave her a full pardon, but at that point he did nothing for her four companions. Boswell supplied the freed Mary with clothes, a bonnet, shoes, and a prayer book, gave her some funds, and helped her find accommodation in Little Titchfield Street in London. He also sought contributions for her from his friends and acquaintances, keeping rough notes of his expenditure on her. He described how he called uninvited upon Lord Thurloe, a former Lord Chancellor, for breakfast: "I asked him to give something to Mary Broad. He exclaimed, 'Damn her blood, let her go to a day's work.' But when I described her hardships and heroism he owned I was a good advocate for her and said he would give something if I desired it."

Boswell's good works for Mary were interrupted in early June 1793 when, reeling home drunk, he was mugged. According to the *London Chronicle*, "Mr. James Boswell was knocked down and left lying in the street stunned. He was found by a passing gentleman who called the watch. He suffered a severe cut to the back of his head and a contusion on both his arms."

Once he recovered, Boswell continued to exert himself on Mary's behalf. He received a letter from Mary's cousin Elizabeth and then one from Elizabeth's husband, Edward Puckey, a tailor, confirming she would be welcome back in Fowey where her father and mother were still alive. The newspapers continued to feature Mary's story. One praised her courage and determination without revealing its source: "The resolution displayed by the woman is hardly to be paralleled. At one time their anchor broke and the surf was so great that the men laid down their oars in a state of despair, and gave themselves up as lost; but this Amazon, taking one of their hats, cried out, 'Never fear!' and immediately began to exert herself in clearing the boat of water. Her example was followed by her companions and by great labour the boat was prevented from sinking."

Boswell's journal, missing for the period in which he began to interest himself in Mary's case, starts again in August 1793 and on August 18 he wrote,

This morning there called on me Mr. Castel at No. 12 Cross Street, Carnaby Market, a glazier, who told me he was a native of Fowey and knew all the relations of Mary Broad very well, and had received a letter from one of them directing him to me; that he wished to see her and inform them about her, and also to introduce her sister Dolly to her who was in service in London. He mentioned that a large sum of money had been left to Mary Broad's father and three or four more—no less than three hundred thousand pounds. I had a suspicion that he might be an impostor. However, I carried him to see her, and from his conversation it appeared that he really knew her relations. She did not recollect him, but he had seen her in her younger days. I was pleased with her good sense in being shy to him and not being elated by the sound of the great fortune. He said he would bring her sister Dolly to her in the evening. I walked away with him nearly to Oxford Street and then returned to Mary and cautioned her not to put any trust in any thing he said till he had brought her sister. I sauntered restlessly . . . Called on Mary in my way home, and found that Castel had actually brought her sister Dolly to her, a fine girl of twenty [sic] who had been in great concern about her, and shewed the most tender affection.*

A week later Boswell wrote,

In the evening I went to Mary Broad's to meet her sister Dolly, who was very desirous to see me and to thank me for my kindness to Mary. I found her to be a very fine, sensible young woman, and of such tenderness of heart that she yet cried and held her sister's hand. She expressed herself very gratefully to me, and said if she got money as was said, she would give me a thousand pounds. Poor girl, her behaviour pleased me much. She gave me, on my inquiring, her whole history since she came to London, from which it appeared that she had most meritoriously supported herself by good service. She was now cook at Mr. Morgan's in Charlotte Street, Bedford Square; but the work was much too hard for her, a young and slender girl, I resolved to exert myself to get her a place more fit for her. It was now fixed that Mary should go by the first vessel to Fowey to visit her relations, her sister [presumably cousin Elizabeth Puckey] there having written to me that she would be kindly received. She had said to me as soon as she heard of the fortune that if she got a share she would reward me for all my trouble.

---

*Unknown to Mary, she might soon have been reunited with another person intimately bound up with her past—Catherine Prior, with whom she had been convicted for highway robbery and who had married fellow convict John Arscott. With both their sentences having expired, the two had taken ship to England in April but Catherine died en route to Batavia. Mary Shepherd, the third member of their "gang," married a marine she met on Norfolk Island and did not return to England until 1810.

Boswell next wrote about Mary in his journal on October 12:

I had fixed that Mary Broad should sail for Fowey in the Ann and Elizabeth, Job Moyse, Master, and it was necessary she should be on board this night, as the vessel was to be afloat early next morning. Having all along taken a very attentive charge of her, I had engaged to see her on board, and in order to do it, I this day refused two invitations to dinner . . . I went to see her in the forenoon and wrote two sheets of paper of her curious account of the escape from Botany Bay.* I dined at home and then went in a hackney coach to her room in Little Titchfield Street and took her and her box. My son James accompanied me, and was to wait at Mrs. Dilly's till I returned from Beal's Wharf, Southwark, where she was to embark.

I sat with her almost two hours, first in the kitchen and then in the bar of the public house at the wharf, and had a bowl of punch, the landlord and the captain of the vessel having taken a glass with us at last. She said her spirits were low; she was sorry to leave me; she was sure her relations would not treat her well. I consoled her by observing that it was her duty to go and see her aged father and other relations; and it *might* be her interest in case it should be true that money to a considerable extent had been left to her father; that she might make her mind easy, for I assured her of ten pounds yearly as long as she behaved well, being resolved to make it up to her myself in so far as subscriptions should fail; and that being therefore independent, she might quit her relations whenever she pleased. Unluckily she could not write. I made her leave me a signature "M. B." similar to one which she carried with her, and this was to be a test of the authenticity of her letters to me, which she was to employ other hands to write. I saw her fairly into the cabin, and bid adieu to her with sincere good will . . . I paid her passage and entertainment on the voyage, and gave her an allowance till 1 November and five pounds as the first half year's allowance per advance, the days of payment to be 1 November and 1 May.

Boswell and Mary never met again but before parting she gave him a few dried leaves of the "sweet tea" she had gathered in Sydney Cove.† No one knows whether Mary and Boswell, with his penchant for women from poor or

---

*The two sheets are now unfortunately lost.

†The tea leaves were discovered in 1937 in a packet on which Boswell had written in his own hand, "leaves from Botany Bay used as tea." Some of the "sweet tea" leaves are now preserved at Yale University and ten are in the Mitchell Library in Sydney, Australia.

working-class backgrounds, ever became lovers. Some of his friends suggested his interest in Mary was more than friendly. One penned a poem in which Mary wrote from Cornwall to her "Apollo of Auchinleck," pining for him:

> tho' every night the Strand's soft virgins prove
> on bulks and thresholds thy [Boswell's] Herculean love

She even dreams that they die together on the scaffold:

> Embracing and embraced, we'll meet our fate:
> A happy pair whom in supreme delight
> One love, one cord, one joy, one death unite!
> Let crowds behold with tender sympathy
> Love's true sublime in our last agony!

Boswell had continued to press Henry Dundas for the release of Mary Broad's four companions. In a petition of May 1793 he argued that if freed they could find work with the help of friends and family. He detailed for each man what they would do when released, stating about Irishman James Martin that he was "by trade a bricklayer and mason. Had worked in England seven years before the misfortune happened to him. Has a wife at Exeter, from whom he has heard several times, also one child, a son. Could get a guinea a week, being a very good workman as he proved when at Botany Bay, where he worked a great deal for the settlement. Is willing either to return to his own country, where his mother, brother and sister are—and he has heard from them—or he will get work in London."

One of the men, John Butcher, alias Samuel Broom, had petitioned Dundas in January 1793 saying that he was well versed in agriculture, understood what crops grew in New Holland, and, although he had suffered a great deal in going and coming from Botany Bay, "yet he was willing to go back" to apply his farming expertise and knowledge of the area to improve the agriculture of the settlement. Dundas did not take up his offer. However, the four men were pardoned and released on November 2, 1793, and went to Boswell's house to thank him for his efforts on their behalf. Nothing further is known of any of them except that after his release Butcher did enlist in the New South Wales Corps and on September 5, 1795, received a grant of twenty-five acres "on the River Hawkesbury."

No evidence has been found of any inheritance by Mary's family or indeed of any legacy of the size mentioned by Castel anywhere in Cornwall at this time, although Mary's family may just possibly have received a part of the legacy of mariner Peter Broad, who left two to three thousand pounds, a large sum for the time.

Mary Broad fades from sight soon after her return to Cornwall. Edward Puckey wrote to Boswell on Mary's behalf in February 1794 thanking him for his help and Mary signed the letter "M. B." A letter from the local vicar to Boswell around this time confirmed Mary's good behavior since her return. Another from him, endorsed "M.B." by Mary that May, confirmed she had received her five-pound half-yearly payment. In October 1794 a letter from Boswell authorized the next payment and in November the vicar again wrote confirming she had received it and Mary signed "M. B." Boswell died in May 1795 having been taken ill in early April and there are no records of any further payments to Mary.

The names Mary Broad and Mary Bryant—both common in Cornwall— occur quite frequently in parish records across Cornwall but much less so in the records of Fowey itself and the adjacent parishes. If Mary did remarry, there is no record of it in or near the place of her birth. When her annuity from Boswell dried up, she may have left Fowey. Some writers have suggested that a Mary Bryant who married a Richard Thomas in October 1807 at Breage, near Helston, forty miles from Fowey, might be her. However, this woman only made her mark on the register, while Mary would surely have managed "M. B." as she had on the letters to Boswell. This woman too gave birth to children in 1811 and 1812. Mary Broad would have been forty-seven in 1812— very old for a mother at that time. Other documents in Helston record the voluntary examination in 1810 of a Mary Bryant described as a "single mother" and her testimony under oath that she was pregnant by one Thomas Turner, a cutler from Sheffield. But again it seems unlikely this could be Boswell's protégée.

The most likely reason why hard evidence of Mary's later life is missing— there are no references in contemporaneous letters and diaries to a woman who must have been something of a celebrity—is that she did not long survive Boswell. The records of the parish of Lanteglos-by-Fowey on the eastern shores of the Fowey River—just a short ferry ride from Fowey itself—note the burial of a Mary Broad on December 23, 1799. No age is given.

XX

"ALL ARROGANCE AND INSULT"

*E*ven before the arrival of HMS *Gorgon* in June 1792, the British press had begun alerting its readers to Captain Edwards's capture of the suspected *Bounty* mutineers, reporting that Peter Heywood and the armorer Joseph Coleman had swum out to the *Pandora* even before its boats had gone ashore but were so heavily tattooed that they had been mistaken for Tahitians. Although relieved to hear that Peter was alive and would soon return home, the Heywood family began to realize from Bligh's letters to them and what they had learned of his condemnation of Heywood to others that Peter Heywood would be put on trial for his life for mutiny. Consequently, they immediately began to call upon whatever influence, or "interest" as it was then known, they could to preserve his life.

Entirely convinced of her "beloved brother's" innocence, Peter's twenty-four-year-old sister Nessie took a leading role. Among the first of the many people she contacted was her and Peter's uncle by marriage, Commodore Thomas Pasley, commander of HMS *Vengeance*. Pasley warned the family correctly that under naval law "the man who stands neuter is equally guilty with him who lifts his arm against his captain" and that showing he had not stood idly by would be the problem for young Heywood as it would for others. He promised to do what he could for his nephew and this proved to be a considerable amount.

By the time HMS *Gorgon* arrived in England and Peter Heywood had the chance to protest his innocence to his family in letters, Pasley had already approached several of those who had made the open-boat journey with Bligh and found that they had little evidence to implicate Heywood in active mutiny. He also discovered from his Admiralty contacts that in his official reports Bligh had not named Heywood as a mutineer, as he had in his private correspondence. Heywood's task would indeed, therefore, be to show that due to his youth and inexperience he had been confused and uncertain how to react when roused from sleep during the mutiny, rather than that he had acquiesced in what was going on. Obvious to Heywood's supporters—as indeed to other defendants—was that it would be in their best interest for the court-martial to take place while the unforgiving, unforgetting, not to say vengeful William Bligh was away on the *Providence* on the second bread-fruit expedition. Accordingly, Heywood's advisers drafted a letter, which Heywood duly submitted, petitioning the Admiralty for "a speedy trial."

The Admiralty agreed to this request and on the morning of September 12, 1792, the court-martial assembled in the great cabin that spanned the width of the stern of HMS *Duke*. Among the eleven naval captains acting as judges under the presidency of Vice-Admiral Lord Hood, commander-in-chief Portsmouth, was one—Captain Bertie by name—who was a distant relation by marriage to the Heywoods and had already helped Peter by advancing him some money to buy necessities in his confinement, and at least one other who was a particular friend of Pasley. The ten defendants—Peter Heywood, James Morrison, William Muspratt, Thomas McIntosh, Michael Byrne, Charles Norman, John Millward, Thomas Ellison, Thomas Burkett, and Joseph Coleman—were rowed in squally weather under marine guard across Portsmouth Harbour to HMS *Duke* from HMS *Hector*, where they had been confined in the gun room and although shackled by the leg treated well in the circumstances by the *Hector*'s captain, another friend of Pasley. As the boat rose and fell in the choppy water they must have felt highly apprehensive about what lay ahead, even if some (Coleman, Norman, and McIntosh) knew that Bligh had himself stated they had been held aboard the *Bounty* by force.

Many of those waiting to give evidence—Fryer, Cole, Purcell, Peckover, Hallett, and Hayward, as well as Captain Edwards and two of his lieutenants from the *Pandora*—must have felt some apprehension too. The quarrels that Fryer and the previously court-martialed and rebuked Purcell had had with Bligh were becoming known. Neither Hallett nor Hayward had been anything but passive or "neuter" during the mutiny. Both had been asleep on duty at various times—Hayward at Tahiti when Muspratt, Millward, and Churchill had deserted, whereafter Bligh had confined him in irons for a month. He had also been dozing when on duty at the time of the mutiny. Hallett had been asleep below in the crucial minutes of the mutiny when as a member of the duty watch he should have been on deck. Bligh had roundly criticized both for their general conduct during the voyage, calling Hallett a "worthless impudent scoundrel" in his letter to his wife from Batavia. Captain Edwards's harsh treatment of the mutineers on the *Pandora* was being heavily criticized. The *Times* wrote, "The sufferings of the unhappy mutineers of the *Bounty* were greater than it could be imagined human nature is capable of bearing. They have been upwards of nineteen months in irons, fastened to a bar, five months of which time both legs and hands were secured, when they were entirely without clothing, till the natives of a friendly island procured them such articles as they could part with."

While defendants would need to present their own actions and the reaction of others to them in the best light to preserve their lives, the witnesses would have to take only slightly less care to show their own—often equally ambiguous—behavior in a way that would preserve their careers in the navy and just possibly prevent them being court-martialed themselves. Being asleep on duty, for example, was a capital offense.

During their time on the *Hector* both Heywood and Morrison had busied themselves writing. Each had produced an account of the mutiny and their part in it, both to aid them in presenting their case to the court and for prior circulation to any who might be sympathetic to their cause. Heywood, of course, had his family and its wide circle of influence to help him spread his version of events. Morrison had no such ready-made route. However, he, like Heywood, seems to have turned to religion during his ordeal on the *Pandora*. This perhaps helped him to win the support of Reverend Howell, the vicar of a Portsmouth church who acted as an unofficial chaplain to the prisoners in their confinement. Howell circulated Morrison's "memorandum" among his numerous naval contacts. Morrison's main purpose was to explain why the warrant officers and crew had done little to support Bligh during the mutiny. His answer was "that the officers were not on such good terms with their commander, as to risk their lives in his service." In addition to writing their memoranda and Heywood writing his letters of exculpation to his family and friends, Heywood was continuing to work on a Tahitian vocabulary while Morrison was starting an account of Tahitian culture.

Both Morrison and Heywood and their supporters would have taken some comfort that, in its leniency toward Purcell at his 1790 court-martial, and willingness to allow their own court-martial to go ahead with the key prosecution witness, Bligh, absent, the navy seemed to be showing itself as reluctant to press with full rigor against participants in dubious activities in distant waters as it had in not proceeding against the *Wager* mutineers half a century earlier. However, they may also have worried what effect the latest blood-curdling news from France might have on the minds of the judges and their willingness to countenance any defiance of authority.

When the French Revolution had broken out with the storming of the Bastille in July 1789 and the subsequent Declaration of the Rights of Man, creation of a constituent assembly, and abolition of feudalism, many in Britain had approved. They included Fletcher Christian's old schoolmate William Wordsworth. In his "Prelude, or Growth of a Poet's Mind," Wordsworth recorded the thoughts of his formative years and wrote how the Utopia previously found only in distant islands was now emerging in Paris and everyone, not just the authorities, would shape the future:

> *Bliss was it in that dawn to be alive,*
> *But to be young was very heaven!—Oh! times,*
> *In which the meagre, stale forbidding ways*
> *Of custom, law and statute, took at once*
> *The attraction of a country in romance! . . .*
> *Now was it that both found, the meek and lofty*
> *Did both find, helpers to their hearts' desire . . . ,*
> *Were called upon to exercise their skill.*
> *Not in Utopia, subterranean fields,*
> *Or some secreted island, Heaven knows where!*
> *But in the very world, which is the world*
> *Of all of us,—the place where in the end*
> *We find our happiness, or not at all!*

Others were less impressed with the revolution as an expression of Utopia. Despite having supported the American colonies in their bid for independence, the statesman Edmund Burke dismissed arguments about the benefits of a state of nature without artificially imposed hierarchies and regulations: "We have not yet subtilised ourselves into savages. We are not the converts of Rousseau; we are not the disciples of Voltaire . . . Atheists are not our preachers; mad men are not our law givers . . . we fear God; we look up with awe to kings; with affection to parliaments; with duty to magistrates; with reverence to priests."

By the summer of 1792, Burke's fears appeared to be increasingly justified, with the French King and Queen, Louis XVI and Marie Antoinette, already imprisoned in the Tuileries and many antireligious and antiproperty measures enacted by authorities who were finding it increasingly difficult to control the hotheads and zealots among the populace. Then in August 1792, while the *Bounty* defendants were preparing their cases, Parisian mobs had attacked the Tuileries, massacring more than five hundred of the king's Swiss bodyguards, mutilating their bodies, and parading their heads on pikes. Soon afterward, the provisional assembly removed all his powers from the prisoner king. By the time the *Bounty* court-martial assembled, news of further massacres was reaching Britain with the arrival of many terrified refugees from Paris.

In the first week of September 1792, a mob of about two hundred, both men and women, attacked Paris's prisons, which were full of aristocrats, priests, and their supporters and servants as well as criminals. They began torturing, murdering, and mutilating indiscriminately in an orgy of violence in which they killed some twelve hundred people. Half-drunk and roused to hatred by agitators, they cut throats and stripped bodies, the latter partly to humiliate the victims and partly to profit from selling their expensive garments. They soaked a countess and her two children in cooking oil and threw them onto a bonfire and burned priests in their prison cells. One of those they treated the most savagely was the Princess de Lamballe, friend of Marie Antoinette and, some said, her lover. She was raped, her breasts and genitalia cut off, her heart cut out and "roasted on a cooking stove in a wine shop" and then eaten; some of her limbs were fired from a cannon and her head was impaled on a pike and paraded before Marie Antoinette's window. The *Bounty* defendants could only hope that these bloody events might serve to underline the bloodless and insignificant nature of the mutiny rather than demonstrate the need to suppress incipient dissent at its outset.

Only Peter Heywood and more surprisingly William Muspratt had legal representation. Heywood in fact had two advisers, both with excellent contacts in naval circles. Unlike the rest of the defendants, who were poorly dressed in tattered clothes, his supporters had provided Heywood with a new suit of clothes for the occasion. The first witness to enter the great cabin was the *Bounty*'s master, John Fryer. In addition to the judges, the defendants, and their representatives, a crowd of onlookers was already present, including off-duty officers from the warships in the harbor and for much of the time England's Attorney-General. Fryer gave his evidence hesitantly, perhaps through nerves, and on occasion contradicted himself, to the annoyance of the judges. He confirmed that Norman, Coleman, and McIntosh had been held on the *Bounty* against their will and that Byrne too, alarmed, blind, and crying, had been unable to join the loyalists in the launch. Fryer had seen only Millward and Burkett under arms and Heywood not at all. When asked why Fletcher Christian might have exclaimed he was "in hell," Fryer answered succinctly, "from the frequent quarrels that they had, and the abuse which he received from Mr. Bligh."

Boatswain William Cole was the next witness. He remembered Heywood had appeared on deck before going below again. Coleman, Norman, McIntosh, and Byrne had been detained against their will, the last three weeping at their fate. Asked by the judges whether any other prisoner had been detained against his will, Cole responded, "I believe Mr. Heywood was. I thought all along he was intending to come away . . . he had no arms and he assisted to get the boat out and then went below." Questioned as to whether he had seen any one of the prisoners make an attempt to put an end to the mutiny he answered, "None." William Peckover's evidence added little. The only defendant he had seen armed was Burkett. Purcell succeeded Peckover and stated he had seen Ellison, Burkett, and Millward under arms. Also in response to a question he said he had seen Heywood "leaning the flat part of his hand on a cutlass on the booms. When I exclaimed 'in the name of God Peter, what do you do with it,' he instantly dropped it." Under further questioning from the judges he explained he had regarded Heywood "as a person confused and that he did not know that he had the weapon in his hand, or his hand being on it for it was not in his hand." Shortly afterward Heywood had gone below. Purcell was more helpful to Morrison, whom he confirmed had desired him "to take notice in the face of the whole of the mutineers that he was prevented from coming into the boat."

Midshipman—now Lieutenant—Hayward came next and was less supportive of Morrison. Morrison had been unarmed but as he helped launch the boat he had looked "rejoiced," not "depressed." Hayward had told Heywood to get into the launch. Asked whether he thought him to be one of the mutineers he said, "I should rather suppose [him] after my having told him to go into the boat and he not joining us, to be on the side of the mutineers." However, Hayward admitted his view "must be only understood as an opinion as he was not in the least employed during the active part of it." Hayward also stated that he had seen both Muspratt, who had scarcely been mentioned previously, and Millward carrying arms. Hallett followed Hayward. During his brief appearance, he did not mention—and no one asked—why he was asleep when he should have been on duty.

He did, however, much damage to both Morrison's and Heywood's cases, stating that Morrison had been armed and that when Heywood was standing by Bligh, who had his arms tied behind his back and a bayonet to his throat, "Captain Bligh said something to him but what I did not hear, upon which he laughed, turned round and walked away."

Captain Edwards and his junior officers added little, confirming that Coleman, Heywood, and Stewart had come aboard immediately of their own accord when the *Pandora* anchored off Tahiti. Their appearance concluded the prosecution case, which left Coleman, McIntosh, Norman, and Byrne almost certain of acquittal; the lives of Millward, Burkett, Ellison, and probably Muspratt in grave danger; and those of Morrison and Heywood seemingly hanging in the balance. Both Morrison and Heywood had secured permission to put opening statements to the court, which in their similarities suggest that the two might have sensibly put their heads together in their confinement.

In his, Morrison denied he had been armed, suggesting that Hallett had been confused and mistaken him for someone standing near him. He ably answered the allegations as to his apparent cheerfulness during the mutiny and failure to join the loyalists in the boat: "My countenance has been compared with that of another employed on the same business. This . . . court knows that all men do not bear their misfortunes with the same fortitude . . . and that the face is too often a bad index to the heart. If there were no sorrow marked in my countenance, it was to deceive those whose act I abhorred that I might be at liberty to seize the first opportunity . . . favourable to the re-taking of the ship." He asked the court to put themselves in his place in considering why he had not got into the boat. It had been "already crowded, those who were in her crying out she would sink and Captain Bligh desiring no more would get in." He had realized that with a small stock of food those in the overcrowded boat would have little chance of escaping "the lingering torments of thirst and hunger . . . the murderous weapons of cruel savages or being swallowed up by the deep."

Heywood's defense was presented by one of his advocates. He denied sneering at Bligh, citing Bligh's comment in his published narrative that no one had been allowed near him while he was under guard and, using words similar to Morrison's, stated the countenance was no index to the heart. He suggested that both Hayward and Hallett had been alarmed and agitated throughout and sometimes in tears, which had added to the confusion he was already suffering due to his youth and inexperience. For most of the time his "faculties were benumbed." After he had gone below to his berth, Thompson had prevented him coming back onto the deck to get into the launch. Getting into the overloaded launch would in any case have been "a kind of an act of suicide." As for his view of Captain Bligh, from Bligh's "very kind treatment of me personally I should have been a monster of depravity to have betrayed him."

One can imagine Heywood crossing his fingers as the following concluding statement was read on his behalf—that the absence of Captain Bligh had deprived him "of an opportunity of laying before the court much that would have been grateful to my feelings, though I hope not necessary to my defence." Bligh would have "exculpated me from the least disrespect." In his cross-examination of witnesses, which he had with the court's permission delayed until after his statement, he drew glowing testimonials to his character from several of them, Purcell, for example, stating his conduct had been "in every respect becoming the character of a gentleman and such as merited the esteem of everybody."

The court's verdict, read on Tuesday, September 18, 1792, was that Coleman, McIntosh, Norman, and Byrne were acquitted but that the remaining six defendants were guilty and sentenced to hang. The court, however, recommended both Morrison and Heywood to the royal mercy and five nervous weeks later, on October 24, they were pardoned. William Muspratt, profiting from the help of his lawyer, immediately petitioned that the court had prevented him from calling defendants who had been found innocent to give evidence on his behalf as would have been permitted in a civil court. He too was eventually pardoned.

On the morning of October 29, 1792, Burkett, Ellison, and Millward were led out onto the deck of HMS *Brunswick*. Sailors placed nooses attached to ropes swinging from the yardarms around their necks. Rather than receiving final benedictions from a cleric, their old shipmate James Morrison—who had remained with them while Heywood left for the bosom of his family—blessed them. At 11:26 A.M. sailors pulled on the ropes and the three men were left swinging from the yardarms.

After the verdict supporters of Captain Bligh would allege that Heywood's supporters had gone beyond the legitimate use of "interest," claiming "Heywood's friends have bribed through thick and thin to save him and from public report have not been backward in defaming [Captain Bligh]." These alleged defamatory activities included feeding stories to the press that Bligh had suffered a second mutiny on the *Providence* in the East Indies as well as a report that Heywood had inherited the vast sum of thirty thousand pounds. The latter rumor was presumably intended to engender the thought that he might be generous to any who supported him.

In November 1792, Fletcher Christian's brother Edward, professor of law at Cambridge University, received a letter from "an officer late of the *Bounty*" that read, "If it would not be disagreeable to you I will do myself the pleasure of waiting upon you and endeavour to prove your brother was not the vile wretch, void of all gratitude, which the world had the unkindness to think him; but on the contrary, a most worthy character; ruined only by having the misfortune . . . of being a young man of strict honour and adorned with every virtue; and beloved by all (except one whose ill report is his greatest praise), who had the pleasure of his acquaintance." The letter, which was dated November 5, was in fact from the newly pardoned Peter Heywood and suggested to his fellow Manx-man a very different view of Bligh than the favorable one he had presented at his own court-martial. Edward Christian passed the letter to the *Cumberland Packet*, which quickly published it on November 20, as did several London papers afterward, as confirmation of the evidence from the court-martial that Bligh's behavior had had much to do with the outbreak of the mutiny.

Encouraged by Heywood's letter, the press response to it, and quite possibly by contacts among the extended Heywood and Christian families, Edward, who like the rest of his family had kept silent since news of his brother's mutiny broke, now began to use the family's influence to press their side of Fletcher Christian's story. His vehicle was an unofficial committee of inquiry he established into the circumstances of the mutiny. Its eleven members were influential and well-known men such as the celebrated legal reformer Samuel Romilly; four ministers of religion, among them a canon of Windsor and a chaplain to the Bishop of London; and William Wordsworth's old tutor at St. John's College, Cambridge University, which Edward Christian had also attended. John Wordsworth, cousin of William Wordsworth's father and a captain of an East Indiaman, added a dash of nautical knowledge. Several other members of the inquiry had connections with St. John's College and with Cumberland and the Wordsworth family. Several too had links with William Wilberforce, who had also attended St. John's College. Most agreed with his antislavery views, which had led him to bring bills for the abolition of slavery before Parliament in 1791 and 1792.

Both had been defeated but marked the beginning of his ultimately successful parliamentary campaign.

The members of Edward Christian's committee of inquiry would therefore have been out of sympathy from the start with Bligh and his relationship with slave plantation owner and West Indian trader Duncan Campbell and more generally with the concept of the breadfruit voyage—itself intended as it was to bolster the economy of the plantations by producing cheap food for the slaves. Most, too, were liberals, if not radicals, and initially at least, like Wordsworth, would have had considerable sympathies with the French revolutionaries rather than the rigid hierarchies of the ancien régime. Many would also have sympathized with the views expressed by Thomas Paine in his *Rights of Man*, published in two parts and several editions in 1791 and 1792. Therein he defended the French Revolution against the attacks of Burke and others and advocated a republic with a representative government and social reforms designed to help the poor and oppressed—which led to his exile from Britain.

Only Edward Christian attended all witness interviews, several of which took place in the Crown and Sceptre public house in London's Greenwich, the rest in Edward Christian's London legal chambers. Among those *Bounty* crewmen interviewed were Fryer, Purcell, Byrne, Peckover, Hayward, Morrison, Smith, Coleman, Lebogue, and McIntosh. What the committee members learned from their witnesses was that no one had a bad word to say about Fletcher Christian's character. This, somewhat surprisingly, had also been true at the court-martial, where the defendants could easily have heaped blame on Christian to excuse themselves. Christian was variously praised: "a gentleman, every inch of him and I would still wade up to the armpits in blood to serve him"; "he was adorned with every virtue and beloved by all, as good and generous a man as ever lived." He had been a reluctant mutineer and afterward "always sorrowful and dejected." Bligh, on the other hand, had been a tyrant, verbally abusing and humiliating his men, and Fletcher Christian in particular, calling them "scoundrels, damned rascals, hounds, hell-hounds, beasts and infamous wretches."

Morrison too was continuing his work on his own account of the mutiny, which would in the end amount to some 380 folio pages and be in two parts—the first based on his memorandum circulated before his court-martial and dealing with the *Bounty* voyage, the mutiny, and its aftermath; the second providing an excellent description of Tahiti and Tahitian culture. Many of Morrison's criticisms of Bligh concerned profiteering and pilfering for his own benefit from food supplies, thus depriving his men of their proper rations. For example, the work contains Morrison's allegations that while the *Bounty* was still in the Thames, Bligh had had a cask opened and two cheeses sent to his home, according to the cooper Henry Hillbrant and the sailor John Williams. Morrison also accused Bligh of coercing crewmen into signing false bills of purchase for nonexistent goods so he could falsely claim money from the Admiralty to meet them.

The Reverend Howell continued to support Morrison in his efforts to make public his alleged truths about Bligh. At the end of November 1792, a month after Morrison's pardon, Howell wrote to Captain Molesworth Phillips, then working for Sir Joseph Banks, telling him about the progress of Morrison's volume and advising him, "It is very natural for Sir Joseph Banks not to think so unfavourably of Bligh as you or I may—there was a time when no one could have an higher opinion of an officer than I had of him—so many circumstances, however, have arisen up against him attended with such striking marks of veracity that I have been compelled to change that idea of him into one of a very contrary nature."

Captain Phillips had, as a lieutenant, commanded the marine shore party in Kealakekua Bay when Cook was killed. Bligh had blamed him for Cook's death rather than, as most others had done, praising him as a hero while damning for cowardice Bligh's friend and fellow Mason Lieutenant John Williamson for deserting the shore party in the launch. Given Bligh's outspoken nature, Molesworth Phillips would certainly have known of Bligh's hostility and already be no friend to him. At some point, Phillips passed a copy of the draft of Morrison's work to Banks. Thereupon, Banks, disinclined to see criticism of Bligh and by implication of himself as responsible for Bligh's appointment, seems to have used his influence to obtain Morrison an appointment as a naval gunner as a way of at least postponing his proposed publication. Nevertheless, drafts of Morrison's work continued to circulate. Together with the reports emerging from Edward Christian's not yet published inquiry, it began to change the public view of both Bligh and Fletcher Christian and also the Admiralty's perception of Bligh.

Accordingly, when Captain Bligh and HMS *Providence* and HMS *Assistant* arrived home in early August 1793, Bligh found his reception only lukewarm despite his second breadfruit voyage having proved successful. The ships had arrived in Tahiti in early April 1792, having traveled via the Cape of

Good Hope and Adventure Bay in Tasmania. On this, his third visit to the island, Bligh had found it once more greatly changed. George Vancouver, a midshipman on Cook's last two voyages, had visited the island at the beginning of 1792 in command of an expedition in HMS *Chatham* en route to complete the charting of the Northwest coast of the American continent. Vancouver had proved a harsh captain, having twenty-four of his crew flogged—some with forty-eight lashes—by the time he reached Tahiti. By comparison, Bligh had had only four of his men flogged on his voyage to Tahiti on the *Bounty*. Vancouver had also had one of his midshipmen, Thomas Pitt—a sixteen-year-old cousin of Prime Minister William Pitt and his brother Lord Chatham, the current First Lord of the Admiralty—publicly beaten three times.

In his five weeks on Tahiti, Vancouver had alienated Tu and other of the island's chiefs and insulted one of the god of war Oro's chief priests, as well as having young Pitt whipped again for contravening his order not to offer iron for sex. Although his subsequent charting of the Northwest coast of America was highly successful, by his return to Britain Vancouver had had almost half his men flogged (double the usual proportion for a Pacific voyage) and had discharged Thomas Pitt from the ship in the Sandwich (Hawaiian) Islands, thereby alienating the whole Pitt family. When Thomas Pitt, a somewhat unbalanced young man, returned he even challenged Vancouver to a duel, which Vancouver declined. The burden of the Pitts' displeasure, which resulted in legal disputes, combined with illness that had dogged Vancouver throughout the voyage, bought about his early death at age forty, less than three years after his return.

After Vancouver's visit an epidemic had swept through Tahiti, which the islanders blamed on the wrath of the god Oro for allowing Vancouver to insult his priest. As a result of European diseases and epidemics, Tahiti's population had declined substantially from the two hundred thousand perhaps overestimated by Johann Forster on Cook's second voyage to the thirty thousand estimated by Morrison. As a consequence of Vancouver's visit, Bligh had some difficulty initially in reestablishing good relations with the ruling family. However, he succeeded because the family recognized the now frequent British visitors as potential allies in the island's power struggles. These were becoming increasingly bloody because rival factions had now succeeded in obtaining muskets from some of the *Bounty* mutineers and also from visiting whaling ships. One day Bligh was surprised to receive from a local chief his own copy of Dampier's *Voyages*, which had been taken ashore

from the *Bounty* by the mutineers. The chief suggested that he would
exchange further volumes from Bligh's library if Bligh would provide him
with the proper paper to make powder cartridges for the muskets he had
obtained—the pages he tore from Bligh's volumes apparently being ill-suited
for the purpose.

Bligh left Tahiti after three months, his ships loaded with 2,126 breadfruit
plants as well as five hundred other plants of different varieties. He had still
found much to appreciate in Tahiti including the verdant, prolific vegetation,
the islanders' hospitality, and the beauty and disposition of their children,
even if in praising the latter he displayed prejudice, writing, "Few more
engaging and pretty children are to be met with, could we divest ourselves
of the dislike to the colour." However, he thought contact with Europeans
had done little to improve the Tahitians, writing, "Our countrymen have
taught [the Tahitians] such vile expressions . . . the quantity of old clothes
left among these people is considerable, they wear such rags and dirty things
as truly disgust us . . . It is rare to see a person dressed with a neat piece of
[bark] cloth which formerly they had in abundance and wore with much
elegance. Their general habiliments are now a dirty shirt and an old coat
and waistcoat; they are no longer clean Tahitians, but in appearance a set of
ragamuffins with whom it is necessary to have great caution."

Bligh successfully led his ships through the Torres Strait, producing
detailed charts and again demonstrating his undoubted abilities as a navigator and mapmaker. Calling in at Kupang in October 1792, this time in more
favorable circumstances, Bligh learned for the first time of Captain Edwards's
arrest of some of the *Bounty* mutineers, the subsequent wreck of the *Pandora*,
and Edwards's own open-boat journey to Kupang. Though Edwards had left
a written account of the loss of the *Pandora* with Timotheus Wanjon, the
governor, he had since lost it, leaving Bligh disappointed "at having no written
account to judge Captain Edwards' misfortune."

Bligh was also very interested to hear of the arrival in Kupang of the fugitives from Port Jackson and, when the governor told him he possessed a
"very ingenious account of their misfortunes" written by William Bryant,
Bligh "teased" him to show it to him and was impressed: "This journal was
very distinctly kept and entitled 'Remarks on a Voyage from Sydney Cove,
New South Wales, to Timor.' It gave the account of everything as it really
happened . . . The woman and children bore the fatigue wonderfully well
and not one person died. The latitude and distances were not regularly kept

up, so it is impossible to ascertain the different places stopped at, but the journal is clear and distinct, and shows the writer must have been a determined and enterprising man." He also noted that the fugitives had found coal north of Port Jackson.*

Eager to have a copy of William Bryant's account, but feeling too ill to write it out himself—he was suffering "violent headache and touches of fever"—Bligh employed a man "but he did not get a fourth part through it" before Bligh had to leave.† The *Providence* and the *Assistant* sailed onward to the West Indies, where Bligh delivered breadfruit plants to St. Vincent and Jamaica. The grateful planters of St. Vincent presented him with a piece of silver plate worth one hundred pounds and those of Jamaica awarded him a bounty of £1,050 (1,000 guineas).

While in Jamaica, Bligh and his men learned that, following the execution of King Louis XVI by the revolutionaries in January 1793, France had declared war on Britain. The British authorities detained Bligh and his ships for a time until they could both reinforce Jamaica's defenses and assemble a convoy of ships to return to Britain. In the interim Bligh succeeded in obtaining some prize money for himself and his crew, though not by directly capturing an enemy ship. Instead he claimed it for being the first naval commander to encounter and take possession of enemy vessels worth £2,500, already seized by a local Jamaican commander named Bartholomew James, who lacked the official documents (letters of marque) to establish him as a privateer entitled to keep the proceeds from enemy shipping he had captured. Bligh's action was strictly legal if not entirely admirable and James's reaction can only too easily be imagined.

---

*As Bligh's praise goes some way to indicate, the Port Jackson escapees' open-boat journey deserves comparison with his own after the loss of the *Bounty*. Both certainly rank among the greatest such journeys ever made, being comparable to the voyage by Shackleton and his five companions from Elephant Island to South Georgia in the twenty-three-foot-long boat *James Caird*, which was of shorter duration (seventeen days) and distance (eight hundred miles) though through worse conditions. Yet Google "open boat voyages" and it is Shackleton's and Bligh's voyages that always come up, rather than the convicts', which merits greater recognition in maritime history. Shackleton, like Bligh, had a curmudgeonly carpenter, in his case Henry McNeish, to deal with.

†The original Bryant manuscript has been lost. The Dutch National Archives have suggested it may have been destroyed between 1811 and 1817 when the British occupied Timor and, finding themselves short of ammunition, plundered the Kupang archives for paper from which to make cartridges.

When Bligh returned to Britain with his two vessels in early August 1793, although he had not come close to facing another mutiny, he had not enjoyed a happy relationship with most of his crew, who had nicknamed him "the Don," suggesting his pride and arrogance were equal to those of the notorious Spanish nobility. He had derated Matthew Flinders from midshipman to seaman following an argument remarkably similar to his own after the *Resolution* voyage about the authorship of charts. According to Flinders's journal, Bligh reduced the armorer Henry Smith to ordinary seaman and "deprived" him of his warrant, after which Smith jumped overboard—an apparent suicide. In subsequent years, when Banks mooted the possibility to Flinders of serving under Bligh when charting Australia, Flinders told Banks he did not wish to be subordinate to Bligh "since the credit, if any, [which] would be due to my labours would be in danger of being monopolised [by Bligh]." In another letter he complained to Banks "of the injustice of [Bligh] considering me with an unfavourable eye." Later still, when Flinders was writing a book about his own voyages and Bligh asked him to dedicate it to him, Flinders declined.

Bligh's nephew and first lieutenant Frank Bond had also found the experience of serving under his uncle not a pleasant one. In a letter to his brother he wrote,

> Yes, Tom, our relation had the credit of being a tyrant in his last expedition, where his misfortune and good fortune have elevated him to a situation he is incapable of supporting with decent modesty. The very high opinion he has of himself makes him hold everyone of our profession with contempt, perhaps envy; nay, the navy is but a sphere for fops and lubbers to swarm in without one gem to vie in brilliancy with himself. I don't mean to depreciate his extensive knowledge as a seaman and nautical astronomer but condemn that want of modesty, in self-estimation . . .
>
> He has treated me, (nay, all on board), with the insolence and arrogance of a Jacobs and notwithstanding his passion is partly to be attributed to a nervous fever with which he has been attacked most of the voyage, the chief part of his conduct must have arisen from the fury of an ungovernable temper. Soon after leaving England I wished to receive instruction from this imperious master, until I found he publicly exposed any deficiency on my part in the nautical art.
>
> Every dogma of power and consequence has been taken from the lieutenants, to establish as he thinks, his own reputation—what imbecility for a post captain! One of his last and most beneficent commands was, that the

carpenter's crew should not drive a nail for me without I would first ask his permission—but my heart is filled with the proper materials always to sustain this humiliation.

. . . My messmates have remarked he never spoke of my possessing one virtue—though by the by he has never dared to say I have none. Every officer who has nautical information, a knowledge of natural history, a taste for drawing or anything to constitute him proper for circumnavigating becomes odious."

Bond's son would later remember his father condemning Bligh for "a dictatorial insistence on trifles, everlasting fault-finding, slights shown in matters of common courtesy, condemnation of little errors of judgement—all these things stung the hearts of his subordinates and worked them up to a state of wrath which would probably have much surprised Bligh himself had he known . . . Bligh was all arrogance and insult, despotic insistence without explanation, advice or show of kindness; often an hauteur and distance . . . utterly ignored the nephew as well as the rank of his first lieutenant."

And yet, not all his officers on the *Providence* felt so hostile to Bligh. Young Lieutenant George Tobin wrote to Bond in later years:

I am sure, my dear friend that in the *Providence* there was no system of tyranny exercised by him likely to produce dissatisfaction. It was in those violent tornadoes of temper when he lost himself, yet, when all, in his opinion, went right, when could a man be more placid and interesting. For myself I felt that I am indebted to him. It was the first ship in which I ever sailed as an officer—I joined full of apprehension—I soon thought he was not dissatisfied with me—it gave me encouragement and on the whole we journeyed smoothly on. Once or twice indeed I felt the unbridled licence of his power of speech yet never without soon receiving something like an emollient plaister to heal the wound.

These differing reactions may in part be explained by the differing positions of those possessing them. Tobin as a young officer of average abilities was prepared to humor Bligh as Christian had done on his voyages with Bligh on Campbell's merchant ships. Consequently, he found him easier to deal with than did Bond, Bligh's immediate deputy in a similar position to that of Christian on the *Bounty*, or Flinders, an able potential rival to Bligh as a chart maker.

One symptom of the new coolness Bligh found the Admiralty displayed toward him on his return to Britain was his discovery that it had docked two shillings per day from his pay to take account of his profits as the *Providence's* purser. Bligh complained that he had not been told this before setting out and stated disingenuously that, not being a professional purser, he had made little profit: "Of those profits I shall not receive sufficient to clear my expenses which have been occasioned in contributing to the comfort of every individual who was under my command on what were necessary for the outfit of such a voyage." The Admiralty was unmoved.

Another major sign of the Admiralty's disfavor was Bligh's inability to secure an interview with Lord Chatham, the First Lord of the Admiralty, despite going in person to the Admiralty on several occasions and waiting. He told Banks he was "astonished at this . . . His Lordship not seeing me is certainly a slight." Banks himself was delighted that Bligh had returned with one thousand trees, shrubs, and plants, according to Banks the largest ever collection of living plants brought back to Britain: "Never before [have I] seen plants brought home by sea . . . in so flourishing state."

The much-leaked report on Edward Christian's committee of inquiry was not published until early 1794, and then as an appendix to a transcript produced by William Muspratt's lawyer Stephen Barney of the prosecution case at the mutineers' court-martial. Publication only served to deepen criticism of Captain Bligh's behavior. As a lawyer, Christian may have wished to provoke Bligh to sue him for libel, whereupon the mutiny could have been raked over in public in the fullest detail. To protect those who had given evidence, Christian listed the names of each of his witnesses but did not attribute any statement to a particular one.

Although he wisely decided not to sue, Bligh felt obliged to respond. In private correspondence and a short published document, he reiterated that the cause of the mutiny was not his own behavior but the wish of Fletcher Christian and the other mutineers to return to a lotus-eating life on Tahiti. He pointed out that he had disciplined or criticized several of Edward Christian's witnesses. He also included statements by three of them—Coleman, Smith, and Lebogue—that they had not been responsible for allegations made in the report. Bligh also tried to procure a similar statement from Michael Byrne, turning to Frank Bond, now serving on the same ship as Byrne, for help. In seeking the help of his nephew, who had considered Bligh a tyrant on the *Providence*, Bligh again demonstrated his insensitivity and failure to understand what others thought of him and his behavior, just as he had when he had asked Fletcher Christian to dine with him on the *Bounty* after the coconut incident on the eve of the mutiny. Bond must have felt some pleasure in replying to Bligh that Byrne would not change his evidence, whereupon Bligh told Bond, "As to the blind scoundrel, I can only beg of you to make the best of him, and get him flogged nobly whenever he deserves it for he is certainly a very great villain."

Bligh, however, correctly pointed out the discrepancies between Peter Heywood's laudatory description of him at the court-martial and the derogatory remarks subsequently attributed to him in the press. He also refuted one of Morrison's most serious allegations: his attempting to defraud the Admiralty. He demonstrated that one of the documents he had asked his men to sign was part of a private transaction in Cape Town whereby he had bought from a merchant at a discount a bill for goods legitimately provided to the Admiralty. He had then forwarded the same bill to Duncan Campbell in London, who secured payment in full from the Admiralty, furnishing the habitually money-conscious Bligh with a profit.

Edward Christian had the last word, however, publishing his own brief response to Bligh, including statements by Purcell and Peckover that "every part [of the report] within [their knowledge] was correctly stated." With this final exchange, which probably changed little in the minds of either supporters or opponents of Bligh, the story of the mutiny began slowly to fade from press and public prominence, overtaken by the revolutionary wars with France, into which nearly all of the *Bounty*'s crew who had returned to Britain were drawn.*

---

*After his pardon, Peter Heywood had joined his uncle Thomas Pasley's ship as a midshipman and by 1794 was a lieutenant, becoming captain in 1803 and retiring after a successful career in 1816. James Morrison drowned as a master gunner in the wreck of HMS *Blenheim* in 1807 off Madagascar. Hallett and Hayward were both dead by 1796. Hallett, invalided from the service after a paralyzing illness, died ashore; while Hayward drowned when a sloop he was commanding foundered in the South China Sea. By 1798 when his will was proved, William Muspratt too was dead, cause unknown. Sailmaker Lawrence Lebogue died aboard HMS *Jason* in harbor aged forty-eight and George Simpson in his hammock on HMS *Prince of Orange* as early as 1793.

XXI

"NO ONE BUT CAPTAIN BLIGH WILL SUIT"

*C*aptain Bligh did not return to sea until, in April 1795, he was appointed to command HMS *Calcutta*, a twenty-four-gun armed transport. In early 1796 he was given command of the sixty-four-gun HMS *Director*. On both occasions he offered the post of First Lieutenant to his nephew Frank Bond. Each time Bond turned him down. Later Bond wrote on the back of a letter from Bligh suggesting that he, Bond, only had himself to blame for an unattractive appointment he had taken, rather than sailing on his uncle's ship: "I impute no blame; as any situation would be preferable to that of first lieutenant with the blamer. I know the choice I had. If I had acted contrary to my former sentiments, I should have been unworthy of the approbation of those who know the truth."

While captain of the *Director*, in the early summer of 1797, Bligh was caught up in the great naval mutiny at the Nore, a fleet anchorage off Sheerness on Britain's southeast coast. Sailors with genuine grievances about poor and overdue pay and bad conditions mutinied, removing their captains and other unpopular officers from their posts and dispatching them on shore while declaring their ships "floating republics." Bligh was one of the captains removed but the mutineers did not single him out for special criticism. The authorities sent ships and troops to blockade the mutinous vessels, which eventually surrendered. In the aftermath, using his contacts with Evan Nepean, now Secretary to the Navy, Bligh protected several of his men from the harsh punishments inflicted elsewhere.

With order again restored, HMS *Director* fought under Bligh's command at the Battle of Camperdown on October 11, 1797, against the Dutch ships of the Batavian Republic—a client state of the revolutionary French republic formed after the French defeat of the Dutch in early 1795. By 1801, with the

Director decommissioned, Bligh was commanding the fifty-six-gun HMS *Glatton*. On March 29 that year, Bligh and his ship took part in Admiral Horatio Nelson's great victory at Copenhagen—the occasion when his superior, Admiral Parker, hoisted a signal ordering Nelson to withdraw, and Nelson put his telescope to his blind eye and claimed not to see it, before going on to a great victory. Bligh was either so confident of his ship's achievements in the fight, or fearful others might attempt to denigrate them, that he sought and received a commendation from Nelson: "Captain Bligh . . . has desired my testimony to his good conduct, which although perfectly unnecessary, I cannot refuse; his behaviour . . . can reap no additional credit from my testimony."

After the battle, Bligh was transferred to the command of the larger HMS *Monarch*, a seventy-four-gun ship of the line, in which he was ordered to return to Britain with two other damaged ships containing many wounded. The crew of the *Monarch* did not warm to their new captain. A midshipman wrote of Bligh, "His manners and disposition were not pleasant, and his appointment to the Monarch gave very general disgust to the officers. This they expressed among themselves without reserve, and even in his presence behaved but with distant civility." Other officers complained about his high-handedness, bad language, and disdain for their abilities. Afterward, Bligh was again transferred, this time to command HMS *Irresistible*. One lieutenant on the ship, John Putland, cannot have found Bligh an unsupportable commander since he later became his son-in-law, marrying Bligh's daughter Mary.

Bligh returned to half-pay during the brief period of peace between the end of the French Revolutionary wars and the outbreak of the Napoleonic wars, and later spent short periods on surveying and hydrographic work for the navy. In May 1804, with the French armies beginning to mass on the other side of the English Channel, preparing to invade, Bligh was placed in command of HMS *Warrior*, another seventy-four-gun ship of the line. His abrasive command style again brought him into conflict with his crew. Almost as soon as he took command, one of his lieutenants wrote to the Admiralty the first of four letters requesting a transfer, finding himself "uncomfortably situated," and later described how Bligh's behavior toward his officers "frequently hurt my feelings and I undoubtedly thought it lessened the officers in the eyes of the ship's company."

A more serious clash occurred with another of his lieutenants, John Frazier, who, according to Bligh, had joined the *Warrior* with "an habitual lameness in his ankle" following an accident while in the merchant service. Frazier then claimed he had injured his ankle further during the voyage in an incident aboard a ship's launch. The *Warrior's* surgeon put him on the sick list but Bligh, convinced he was malingering and seeking a medical discharge, took him off it. Bligh ordered Frazier back to duty but Frazier several times refused to stand watch. Bligh had him arrested and on the *Warrior's* return to port from patrol formally charged him with a refusal to obey orders.

Frazier alleged in turn that Bligh did "publicly . . . grossly insult and ill treat me in the execution of my office by calling me a rascal, scoundrel and shaking his fist in my face . . . at various times he behaved himself towards me and other commissioned, warrant and petty officers . . . in a tyrannical and oppressive and un-officer-like behaviour contrary to the rules and discipline of the navy and in open violation of the articles of war." Frazier requested that Bligh should himself be court-martialed and his request was granted.

Frazier's court-martial took place on November 23, 1804. The *Warrior's* surgeon testified that he had placed Frazier on the sick list with a leg "very much swelled." He had removed him from the list only after a written order from Bligh. Other officers confirmed Frazier had seemed unable to walk. The court-martial speedily acquitted him.

Bligh's own court-martial did not begin until February 25, 1805. The prosecution witnesses demonstrated Bligh's explosions of anger, aggression, and abuse: He had called his gunner "a damn'd long pelt of a bitch" and told the boatswain he was "a scoundrel and a villain" and threatened that if he got him in a dark corner he would do for him and one of his lieutenants. The master of the *Warrior* said that Bligh's conduct to him was so bad and "so much the effect of passion" that he had contemplated seeking "public redress." None of the evidence, however, seemed serious enough to justify charges of tyranny. Bligh himself admitted, "I am not a tame and indifferent observer of the manner in which officers placed under my orders conducted themselves in the performance of their several duties. A signal or any communication from a commanding officer have ever been to me an indication for exertion and alacrity . . . and peradventure I may occasionally have appeared to some of those officers as unnecessarily anxious for its execution."

The court decided that the charges were "in part proved" and, therefore, ordered Bligh to be "reprimanded," as Purcell had been at his court-martial in 1790, and "admonished to be in future more correct in his language." Bligh was returned immediately to the command of the *Warrior*, where he had to live with and oversee those who had given evidence against him, unsurprisingly complaining that they were "a very bad set of men as I ever heard of" and that the surgeon was "the most designing wicked man ever came into a ship."

Then on March 15, 1805, not long after the court martial hearing, Sir Joseph Banks wrote to Bligh, offering him the post of governor of New South Wales. His letter began:

> An opportunity has occurred this day which seems to me to lay open an opportunity of being of service to you; and as I hope I never omit any chance of being useful to a friend whom I esteem, as I do you, I lose not a minute in apprising you of it.
>
> I have always, since the first institution of the new colony at New South Wales, taken a deep interest in its success, and have been constantly consulted by His Majesty's Ministers . . .
>
> At present, [Philip Gidley] King, the Governor, is tired of his station; and well he may be so. He has carried into effect a reform of great extent, which militated much with the interest of the soldiers and settlers there. He is, consequently, disliked and much opposed, and has asked leave to return.
>
> In conversation, I was this day asked if I knew a man proper to be sent out in his stead—one who has integrity unimpeached, a mind capable of providing its own resources in difficulties without leaning on others for advice, firm in discipline, civil in deportment and not subject to whimper and whine when severity of discipline is wanted to meet [emergencies]. I immediately answered: As this man must be chosen from among the post captains, I know of no one but Captain Bligh who will suit . . .

Banks went on to say that he would double King's salary of one thousand pounds for Bligh, even though King had been able to put much of his salary aside for his return. He produced some detailed calculations indicating Bligh could expect a pension of perhaps one thousand pounds. He also suggested Bligh's unmarried daughters would find it easier to find suitable husbands in New South Wales than in Britain.

Bligh was tempted but concerned about another long separation from his wife, Betsy, whom he undoubtedly loved. She would not be able to accompany him because, as he told Banks, "her undertaking the voyage would be her death, owing to her extreme horror of the sea, the sound of a gun or thunder." However, ambitious and always eager to improve his finances, Bligh eventually accepted "to procure a little affluence" for himself, on the basis that he would take his daughter Mary to function as his hostess and her husband, Lieutenant Putland, to be his aide.

As Banks's letter had hinted, the home government was concerned about the administration of the colony. Much had changed in Port Jackson since the escape of Mary Bryant and her companions. The men of the Marine Corps had been fully replaced as the colony's guards by the newly formed army regiment, the New South Wales Corps, which Mary's companion John Butcher had joined to return to New South Wales after his pardon. Those marines who preferred to stay in the colony rather than to return home, as most of their officers like Watkin Tench did, had transferred as a unit into the new corps under the command of marine officer George Johnston, who became a captain in the corps.

Governor Arthur Phillip had left Port Jackson in December 1792. On his return to Britain at the age of fifty-three after a period of recuperation he resumed his naval service, becoming a rear admiral in 1799. Retiring in 1804, he died in 1814. In 1796 he had remarried—this time a forty-year-old spinster who again brought him considerable wealth. What very few indications there are suggest that, like his first, his second marriage was neither particularly close nor happy. Perhaps the self-restraint and lack of emotion that had helped him in his public life proved disadvantages in his private one.

Two Aboriginal men—Bennelong and his kinsman, a handsome youth called Yemerrawannie, whom Tench praised as "a good tempered lively lad"—had, at Phillip's request, accompanied him on his return to Britain. The *London Packet,* reporting their arrival, was unimpressed: "That instinct which teaches to propagate and preserve the species, they possess in common with the beasts of the field, and seem exactly on a par with them in respect to any further knowledge of, or attachment to kindred. This circumstance has given rise to the well founded conjecture that these people form a lower order of the human race."

As Omai from the Tahitian islands had been, Yemerrawannie and Bennelong were presented at court to King George III, in their case dressed in identical green coats, blue and beige striped waistcoats, and silk stockings. They lodged in Mayfair's Mount Street at the home of William Waterhouse— father of the lieutenant who had snapped the shaft of the spear that had wounded Phillip at Manly Cove. They entertained their host by beating sticks together and singing. A neighbor, Edward Jones, harpist to the Prince of Wales, transcribed the words and notes, later publishing them in his *Musical Curiosities*—the oldest known published music from Australia.

Bennelong and Yemerrawannie had a servant to attend them and a tutor to teach them to read and write since Phillip hoped that, having mastered these skills, they could give valuable details about the Aboriginal way of life. For entertainment, they visited the Tower of London, the theater to see Italian comic opera and ballet, the Parkinson Museum housing artifacts from Cook's voyages, and swam in the chilly Serpentine.

However, London life did not agree with them, unlike Omai, who had pleaded to be taken to Britain and flourished under the attentions of Joseph Banks, Samuel Johnson, Fanny Burney, and others. According to the Scottish naturalist Robert Jameson, the pair seemed "constantly dejected, and every effort to make them laugh has for many months past been ineffectual." On September 29, 1793, the *Observer* noted that they seemed now both to need the aid of walking sticks and that Yemerrawannie "appears much emaciated." By May 1794, after months of painful and ineffectual medical treatment, from laxatives to hot plasters, Yemerrawannie was dead aged only nineteen. The *Morning Post* wrote that "his companion pines much for his loss."*

In February 1795 Bennelong sailed back to Port Jackson, which he reached safely. In a letter to an acquaintance in England he wrote: "I am very well. I hope you are very well. I live at the Governor's. I have every day dinner there. I have not my wife; another black man took her away . . . he speared me in the back, but I better now . . . Not me go to England no more." Bennelong's experiences and treatment seem to have left him stranded between the two societies. Sometimes he would remove his European clothes, leaving them neatly folded in Government House, to return to his people in the bush. He took increasingly to alcohol and sometimes became violent. He died at Kissing Point in 1813, the year before Phillip. An unsympathetic obituary in the *Sydney Gazette*, echoing the tone of the *London Packet*, referred to him as "this veteran champion of the native tribe" but added that the "benevolent treatment" he had received in Britain "produced no change whatever in his manners and inclinations, which were naturally barbarous and ferocious."

---

*Yemerrawannie was buried in the churchyard of St. John the Baptist at Eltham. However, his bones were later removed to make room for further burials. Attempts to locate his remains to return them to Australia to be reinterred with due Aboriginal rites have failed.

Francis Grose, the senior local military officer and commander of the New South Wales Corps, replaced Phillip as the colony's governor on a temporary or acting basis. The new permanent governor, John Hunter—Phillip's former deputy who had previously returned to Britain—did not arrive until 1795. Grose in the meantime introduced several measures to bolster the power of the New South Wales Corps. In particular, he secured permission from the British government to allocate land to the officers of the corps, something Phillip had not been permitted to do for the marine officers, much to the latter's disappointment. Soon some officers had amassed tracts of five hundred or more acres of land. Grose also allocated each estate a labor force of convicts who worked unpaid. Unsurprisingly the officers prospered. Because there was little coin or other cash in the colony, a barter economy naturally and quickly developed in Port Jackson even before Phillip's departure.

The New South Wales Corps came to dominate it because of their regular pay in cash, which they used to purchase commodities. In particular, they secured a virtual monopoly on the supply of rum—much desired and consumed by guards and convicts alike—and soon became known as the Rum Corps. Contracts quickly came to be written specifying payment of a sum of cash or an equivalent value of rum, or less often another commodity or sometimes solely in rum. Officers soon became wealthy enough to begin to charter vessels to bring in supplies of rum and other provisions and equipment. Quickly, by agreeing not to compete with each other, they put themselves in a position to dictate prices at which they bought—low ones—to any independent ship's master who sailed into Port Jackson and then to sell the goods, whether provisions or scarce farm equipment, at inflated prices to others.

These high prices often proved too much for time-served convicts attempting to farm land granted to them by government at the conclusion of their sentences, forcing them to sell their land to the New South Wales Corps' officers at low prices, further increasing the latter's land holdings. The dispossessed obtained what compensation they could by demanding high wages from the officers for working the land, since labor was in short supply. In turn the Rum Corps officers increasingly switched to less labor-intensive farming such as cattle and in particular sheep raising, rather than crop farming, exacerbating grain shortages and enabling the Rum Corps to charge even higher prices for what was available. The officers also contributed most of the judges and magistrates to the civil and criminal courts, even though most were unqualified. Courts therefore rarely found against the Rum Corps' interests.

The Rum Corps officers themselves were not in general men of high ability or elevated moral standards. One from an aristocratic family had been tried and only acquitted through family influence on a charge of being a highwayman, before being bundled off to New South Wales where he served as a surgeon. Others had less aristocratic backgrounds but were equally predatory when pursuing their own interests. Prime among them was the charismatic, clever, and calculating John Macarthur, known behind his back as either "Jack Bodice," because his family had been in the clothing business, or "the Great Perturbator" for his abilities to stir matters up to his own advantage. After arriving in the colony in 1790 as an officer, he swiftly became not only one of the most successful traders but also a leader of the Rum Corps officers in protecting their mutual interests against Governor Hunter and his successor in 1800 Philip Gidley King, who struggled manfully but by no means entirely successfully to curtail their influence.

On one occasion Macarthur went over Governor Hunter's head, directly complaining to the Secretary of State in Britain about his behavior. Hunter himself wrote of Macarthur to King, "There is not a person in this colony whose opinions I hold in greater contempt than I do this busybody's, because I have ever observed that under the most specious and plausible of them there has always been . . . a self-interested motive." King was equally scathing: "His employment during the eleven years he has been here has been that of making a large fortune, helping his brother officers make small ones (mostly at the public expense) and sowing discord and strife . . . Many and many instances of his diabolical spirit had shown itself before Governor Phillip left . . . and since . . . in many instances he has been the master worker of the puppets he has set in motion."

When Governor King refused to implement some harsh sentences Rum Corps officers, acting as magistrates, had passed, Macarthur orchestrated a boycott of the governor. When his commanding officer Colonel William Paterson—a Fellow of the Royal Society and a frequent correspondent with Joseph Banks, on botanical matters—opposed his action, a duel resulted in which Macarthur, a veteran of two previous duels—one with the captain of the ship taking him to New South Wales and another with a fellow Rum Corps officer—wounded Paterson. Thereupon Governor King seized the opportunity to be rid of Macarthur, sending him to London for court-martial. When he reached Britain in 1802, he was never brought before a court since there was no one in the country to give evidence against him. He sold his commission, thereby freeing himself of any possibility of further action against him for the duel. He then spent the next two years lobbying adroitly for a scheme he had devised to produce large quantities of fine-quality wool in New South Wales, where he considered the conditions were favorable. Part of his plan was to import merino sheep to improve the quality of existing flocks. One of the first people he contacted was Joseph Banks, who was not only the government's New South Wales expert but also their sheep expert, having retained his interest in the merino breeding program since he had introduced the breed to the United Kingdom and founded the royal flock at Kew fifteen years previously.

Banks was distinctly lukewarm to Macarthur's proposal, perhaps instinctively suspicious of a man who had wounded a fellow member of the Royal Society or simply because he did not believe the breed would prosper in New South Wales where he thought "luxuriant pastures" were lacking and the grass "tall, coarse, reedy and very different from the short and sweet mountain grass" upon which merinos thrived. It is testimony to Macarthur's persuasive powers that, despite the opposition of the government's much-favored and lauded expert, by bringing together commercial investors and convincing certain officials of the Colonial Office who had recently taken over responsibility for the colony from the Home Office, he eventually secured permission for his project and in principle agreement to a land grant of five thousand acres, with more to follow if he were successful. The only concession to Banks's continuing opposition was that the land granted to Macarthur could be varied at any time to meet Banks's point that a large permanent land grant near the settlement might inhibit its scope for expansion.

Well satisfied, Macarthur returned to New South Wales in a ship he had purchased, taking with him a number of merino sheep for which Joseph Banks seems to have ensured he paid a very high price. Approached by Macarthur to implement the land grant, Governor King decided after some investigation that this potentially contentious matter should be one for the successor he had requested.

The whole question was no doubt one upon which Joseph Banks briefed his protégé, William Bligh, before he sailed. Bligh himself was however more concerned with sorting out the detail of the financial arrangements surrounding his appointment. In particular, as it stood, he would lose his captain's pay when he left the *Warrior* and not receive his governor's pay until he reached New South Wales. Eventually a compromise was reached. To preserve his naval pay during the voyage the Admiralty would award him a sinecure as co-captain of HMS *Porpoise*, the naval vessel escorting the commercial convoy on which he would sail to New South Wales. The very fact that he would travel not on the *Porpoise* but on one of the merchant vessels emphasized the nominal nature of the appointment.

This fudge would have worked smoothly had it not been for the character of both Bligh and his co-captain of the *Porpoise*, Commander Joseph Short, who had his family with him and was intending to retire and settle with them at the end of the voyage in New South Wales, where he had been promised a government grant of land. In his last naval appointment he wanted to preserve his authority as the *Porpoise*'s commander. Bligh too wanted to be in sole charge. During the voyage neither Short nor Bligh showed any restraint or judgment in their constant quarrels and recriminations. At one point Short ordered Lieutenant Putland, Bligh's son-in-law—serving on the *Porpoise* to avoid forfeiting his own naval pay prior to taking up his appointment as Bligh's aide in the colony—to fire two shots across the bows of the ship on which Bligh and his daughter—Putland's wife—Mary were traveling to ensure it took what he considered its proper place in the convoy and not, as Bligh wished, the lead. When Bligh's vessel did not respond, Short threatened to have Putland, his officer of the watch, fire one shot directly at it.

Reaching New South Wales, Bligh refused to make a land grant to Short and returned him to Britain with his family. There he faced a court-martial at which he was acquitted—the incident of the firing of the shots apparently considered too ludicrous to figure among the charges. One fellow captain offered an unvarnished view of the two men's arguments: "They were both wrong, both had acted intemperately and foolishly, both had laid themselves open to censure." The dispute, however, did Bligh no favors, reinforcing his reputation in both New South Wales and Britain as a quarrelsome leader whose actions were sometimes ill-considered and often put him at variance with his subordinates. Back in Britain, Bligh's sensible wife, Betsy, and Joseph Banks had to use their influence to quash demands from his detractors for his recall.

When Bligh arrived in August 1806, New South Wales had a population of some ten thousand—the great majority convicts and ex-convicts—and was beginning to thrive. The port was serving as an entrepôt, particularly for the whaling vessels now starting to exploit the mammals of the southern ocean. A good market had developed in cured pork imported from Tahiti, which was deemed particularly flavorsome by the ships' crews to whom it was sold. Spices from the East Indies were also being traded. These new activities had already somewhat diminished the dominance of the Rum Corps in the colony's affairs before Bligh's arrival, and Governor King had already removed their monopoly in rum, at least in name. However, Bligh was clear that his instructions from the home government were to reduce the corps' influence further and to make the colony a more open and fairer society.

One of his first actions did nothing to convince anyone that this would be the case. Governor King was still in New South Wales when Bligh arrived and the two men concocted a corrupt deal entirely unauthorized by government to enrich themselves at public expense. While King was still in post, he made three land grants totaling 1,245 acres to Bligh. Once Bligh had taken office from him and while King was still in the country, he in return made a land grant of 790 acres to King and his wife for a farm that King gratefully, if injudiciously, named "Thanks." The mutual illegal grants quickly became known and did much to undermine the new governor's moral authority as an agent for change for the better. What's more, the well-documented evidence of the corrupt land deal gives credence to some of the allegations of financial and commissary irregularity leveled against Bligh by Morrison and others earlier in his career.

Bligh's first meeting with John Macarthur, who approached him to lobby for an immediate confirmation of the land grant for his sheep project, did not go well. According to Macarthur, they were walking alone when:

> I enquired if he had been informed of the wishes of government . . . I particularly alluded to the sheep, and the probable advantages that might result to the colony and the mother-country from the production of fine wool . . . Bligh thereupon burst out instantly into a most violent passion, exclaiming, "What have I to do with your sheep, Sir; . . . Are you to have such flocks of sheep . . . as no man ever heard of before?—No, Sir! . . . I have heard of your concerns, Sir, you have got 5,000 acres of land in the finest situation in the country; but, by God! you shan't keep it." I told him that as I had received this land at the recommendation of the Privy Council and by the order of the Secretary of State, I presumed that my right to it was indisputable. "Damn the Privy Council! and damn the Secretary of State too!" he says; "What have they to do with me?—You have made a number of false representations respecting your wool, by which you have obtained this land."

Macarthur's account, part of his testimony in a subsequent court case and perhaps partial, nevertheless reflects previous accounts of Bligh's explosive language and temper.

Bligh's first moves to put trade on a sound footing were to ban the use of rum as a barter commodity and to rule that no contract could be written solely in terms of barter but had to contain a monetary equivalent. Both decisions were entirely consistent with his orders and were, unsurprisingly, deeply resented by the Rum Corps. They should, however, have been welcomed, and Bligh lauded, by those in the settler community without Rum Corps affiliations, whether time-served convicts or those who had come out to the colony as free settlers. However, Bligh failed to convert these people into a solid support base. Unlike his two predecessors Hunter and King, who had served with Phillip on the First Fleet, he lacked knowledge of the origins of the colony and its internal dynamics. His aggressive manner and lack of empathy, intuition, and insight regarding people alienated those who could have supported him, as it did most of his fellow naval officers, who might have been expected to support him against their army colleagues.

Bligh's daughter Mary was of little help to her father in building good relationships, quickly gaining a reputation for an aloof snobbishness and a temper almost as explosive as that of her father. Her disposition cannot have been helped by the illness of her husband, Lieutenant Putland, who had contracted tuberculosis and was clearly dying, and, as a consequence, was also unable to offer Bligh much support. Nonetheless, Bligh wrote to Banks in early October 1807—as so often before either self-deluding or vaingloriously ignorant of the truth—"the colony is recovered from a most deplorable state, indeed, I can give you every assurance of its now raising its head to my utmost expectation . . . The discontented are checked in their machinations whilst the honest settler feels himself secure, and the idler no encouragement."

In truth, a showdown with the Rum Corps could not be much delayed and when it began in late October was the result not of a dispute with one of the serving officers but with the former officer John Macarthur. The early skirmishes centered on two spirit stills allegedly illegally imported by Macarthur. Then in December he and Bligh clashed over a merchant schooner named the *Parramatta* owned by Macarthur and a business partner. After the escape of Mary Bryant and her companions, the guard on small ships in the harbor had been so strengthened that the opportunity to steal one sufficiently large to have a realistic chance of escape by sea was almost nil. Therefore, most would-be escapers had instead attempted to stow away on the trading vessels visiting the harbor. As a result, the authorities demanded of each ship's owner a large bond to be forfeited if a convict escaped on their vessel. Consequently, smoke could often be seen rising from the portholes and hatches of ships about to depart as saltpeter was used to smoke out any stowaway who had eluded physical searches.

However, a notorious convict serving life, John Hoare, had earlier defeated whatever measures the *Parramatta*'s crew had instituted to detect him, successfully stowed away among some firewood, and escaped ashore when the vessel reached Tahiti. Some of the British missionaries now on the island immediately complained to the British authorities about the danger of such a man being loose in their islands. When the *Parramatta* eventually returned to Sydney in November 1807, the captain and some of his crew admitted under questioning by Bligh that Hoare had indeed stowed away on the schooner. Bligh therefore declared that the bond Macarthur and his partner held against stowaways—in this case for the large sum of nine hundred pounds—should be forfeited.

Probably with the intention of discrediting or embarrassing the authorities either in court or more generally in the public eye, Macarthur and his partner declared they were abandoning the *Parramatta*, worth probably ten thousand pounds, to the authorities, who had refused the crew and the ship landing rights and put guards aboard to prevent her unloading. Macarthur and his partner claimed they were neither responsible for paying the forfeit bond nor for maintaining the crew aboard the ship. After a while the crew came ashore illegally and the authorities, refusing to accept Macarthur's abandonment of them, held him legally accountable for their actions. Formally asked to visit Bligh at Government House to explain what had happened, Macarthur refused what he treated as a private invitation, not a summons. Thereupon Judge-Advocate Richard Atkins, a long-time and well-known adversary of Macarthur, issued a warrant for Macarthur's arrest, later claiming Bligh had approved it. For his part, Bligh had previously described Atkins with some justice as "accustomed to inebriety . . . the ridicule of the community . . . [and] a disgrace to human jurisprudence."

MacArthur defied the warrant, which he called "horrid tyranny," and was subsequently arrested for doing so. During almost a month on bail Macarthur claimed vociferously that he should not face a court headed by Atkins as would normally be the case, as Atkins was known to be prejudiced against him and indeed owed him money. He began mustering support among not only the Rum Corps but also others disconcerted by Bligh's questioning of certain Sydney-center leases. His final stratagem was to have his son host a party in his absence, on the night before the trial, at which the commander of the Rum Corps, George Johnston, now a major, got so drunk he fell out of his gig on his way home to his long-term mistress, former convict Esther Abrahams, and injured himself.

The next morning at the opening of his trial, which, despite his protests, was to be held before Atkins and six officers of the Rum Corps serving as usual as members of the court, Macarthur again inveighed against Atkins's involvement. Thereupon the six officers effectively expelled Atkins from his position and wrote to Bligh backing Macarthur's view. Bligh, in turn, replied there could be "no court without the Judge Advocate." After further exchanges with the officers, Bligh attempted to involve Major Johnston. Johnston's response was to claim he was too bruised and shaken by his accident after the party to attend. The following morning Bligh had Macarthur arrested and imprisoned and accused the six officers of treasonable behavior. He also again summoned Johnston. The major knew he could no longer avoid taking sides, and chose to back Macarthur.

About six thirty on the evening of January 26, 1808—the twentieth anniversary of the founding of the colony—Major Johnston led between three and four hundred members of the New South Wales Corps from their barracks toward Government House, where Bligh and some of his followers were dining, to depose the governor. They were marching in closed ranks. Their band was playing "The British Grenadiers," their colors were flying, and their muskets were loaded. The only resistance they met was from Mary Putland, whose husband had died only a few days previously. According to an eyewitness, with parasol gripped firmly in her hand, "she hastened to the gates and gallantly opposed their entrance, setting the bayonets at defiance and exclaiming, 'You traitors, you rebels, you have just walked over my husband's grave and now come to murder my father.' She continued until forcibly dragged away—but again escaped nor would she be opposed."

Bligh himself was initially nowhere to be found and the search for him lasted between one and two hours—accounts differ. Bligh's several versions of events vary a little but in essence he claimed to have "retired" upstairs to think about his next move. There he was eventually discovered. According to the accounts of the two men who found him, he was hiding under a bed and when they pulled him out "some dirt . . . from the bottom of the bed

[was] hanging to his epaulets and skirts." Bligh's version was that he was "stooping" by a bed while destroying confidential papers.

What is beyond a doubt is that just as on the *Bounty*, the mutiny was bloodless. No one other than Mary Putland physically opposed the Corps' entrance, which would in any case have been futile given the number of soldiers involved. By nine P.M., two and half hours after they had begun their march from the barracks, the mutineers had left Bligh and his daughter in Government House under a version of house arrest guarded by just five sentries, showing how little they feared any rescue attempt. Elsewhere Bligh's effigy was being paraded and defaced and drunken celebrations were beginning. According to one eyewitness, "the soldiers and mob placed Macarthur in a chair and carried him about the town in a disorderly triumphant manner." Macarthur himself wrote to his wife, "I have been deeply engaged all this day in contending for the liberties of this unhappy colony, and I am happy to say I have succeeded beyond what I expected . . . The tyrant is now no doubt gnashing his teeth with vexation at his overthrow. May he often have cause to do the like!" Order restored, Macarthur and some others petitioned Johnston to take the role of Lieutenant Governor. He agreed to do so, rewarding those who had supported the coup and removing from office those such as Atkins who had not. The quashing of charges against Macarthur was a mere formality.

A considerable period of standoff between the rebel administration and Bligh, in isolation in Government House, persisted until fourteen months after the mutiny when Bligh, his daughter, and some of his supporters boarded HMS *Porpoise*, Bligh having sworn on "his honour as an officer and a gentleman" to proceed directly and without stopping to Britain. Bligh, however, immediately reneged on the agreement. Although the *Porpoise*'s captain refused Bligh's command to train the ship's cannon on Sydney, Bligh and the *Porpoise* lingered outside the Heads for some while before sailing not for Britain but for the British penal colony established in Tasmania in 1803. There he unsuccessfully sought support for his reinstatement from the colony's Lieutenant Governor and veteran of the First Fleet, David Collins, with whom he was soon at loggerheads.

News of the rebellion reached a British government preoccupied with the Napoleonic wars in September 1808, to be followed by correspondence from both factions laying out their positions. The government took a little time before deciding on the recall and replacement by another regiment of the entire Rum Corps and the recall of Bligh and his replacement by a new governor. Their first candidate fell ill, whereupon their choice fell upon his deputy Lachlan Macquarie.

Macquarie arrived in Sydney at the end of December 1809 to find that both Macarthur and Major Johnston had already sailed for Britain to state their cases. Two weeks after Macquarie landed, Bligh arrived on the *Porpoise* from Tasmania to meet his successor. Macquarie, who would serve as governor for eleven years and put the colony on a sound and prosperous footing, found Bligh "revengeful in the extreme and I am sure he would be delighted to hang, draw and quarter all those who deprived him of his government." He later described Bligh as "certainly a most disagreeable person to have any dealings, or public business to transact with; having no regard whatever to his promise or engagements however sacred, and his natural temper is uncommonly harsh, and tyrannical in the extreme. He is certainly generally detested by high, low, rich and poor . . ."

In May 1810, Bligh sailed for Britain in a small convoy also carrying the members of the recalled New South Wales—or Rum—Corps whose power he had effectively broken at great cost to himself. Just before his departure, he had had another surprise, which in a benign way again demonstrated his insensitivity to and ignorance of the emotions and feelings of others. He described to his wife, Betsy, how a few days before he and his now twenty-seven-year-old daughter Mary were due to embark, Macquarie's deputy, Lieutenant Colonel O'Connell, approached him and asked for Mary's hand. "I gave him a flat denial for I could not believe it. I retired with her, when I found she had approved of his address and given her word to him." He therefore consented and before Bligh left the couple were married and he embarked alone.

On his arrival in Britain, Bligh was reunited with his loving Betsy, only to find her "not well, her nerves being very much broke" by her husband's latest tribulations and her lobbying on his behalf. When he met Joseph Banks, the latter surprised him with news at last of Fletcher Christian and the rump of the mutineers who had left Tahiti aboard the *Bounty* two decades before, and whose fate until then had remained unknown.

XXII

"WHY DOES THE BLACK MAN
SHARPEN AXE?"

*O*n February 6, 1808, an American sealer—the *Topaz*, commanded by Captain Mayhew Folger—came upon Pitcairn Island. As he and some of his men set out for shore in a small boat they were first surprised to see smoke rising from what they thought was an uninhabited island. They were even more surprised when an outrigger canoe containing three tawny-skinned young men came out to meet them and its occupants hailed them in English. In response to Folger's questions, they told the sealers, "We are Englishmen" born "on that island which you see." When Folger asked, "How are you Englishmen, if you were born on that island, which the English do not own and never possessed?," they replied, "We are Englishmen because our father was an Englishman." Folger asked their father's identity and the following exchange took place:

CANOERS: "Aleck."
FOLGER: "Who is Aleck?"
CANOERS: "Don't you know Aleck?"
FOLGER: "How should I know Aleck?"
CANOERS: "Well then, did you know Captain Bligh of the *Bounty*?"

Thereupon Folger realized with "a shock of mingled feelings, surprise, wonder and pleasure not to be described" who the young people must be—descendants of the mutineers who had left Tahiti on the *Bounty* with Fletcher Christian in 1789 and disappeared. When Folger told the three youths that he and his crew were American not English, the three did not know where America was, concluding it might be "in Ireland."

After Folger and his men landed they were introduced to the white-haired, corpulent sole survivor of the mutineers "Aleck"—Alexander Smith, real name John Adams—who appeared relieved they were not British and so not going to return him to Britain for court-martial. Slowly and in response to their questions, Folger and his men learned that nine mutineers, six Polynesian men, twelve women, and a baby girl led by Fletcher Christian had reached the island in 1790, the community had lived in harmony until, "a great jealousy arising," the Polynesian men had killed all the mutineers but Adams and Edward "Ned" Young, and then in turn been killed the following night by the Tahitian women. Thereafter Adams and Young had lived with the women until Young had died of a chest complaint. As for the mutiny itself, it had been led by Fletcher Christian because of "the overbearing and tyrannical behaviour of the captain." According to what he told Folger, Adams himself had been asleep when the mutiny began until, awoken and bewildered, "arms were put in his hands," whereas all other accounts of the mutiny had him taking a leading role in the seizure and guarding of Captain Bligh. Throughout Adams was undoubtedly keen to minimize his role, both in the mutiny and in the Pitcairn violence of which he was the sole European survivor.

When, after "five or six hours," Folger and his crew left the island and its thirty-five inhabitants—all but Adams, youths, women, and children—Folger had been impressed by the order and piety of the little settlement. He was carrying with him presents from Adams, which included the *Bounty's* Kendall chronometer and the ship's azimuth compass. An account of Folger's visit did not reach Britain until some two years later via a British naval officer stationed in Valparaiso in Chile. It appeared in *The Quarterly Review* with the following comment: "If this interesting relation rested solely on the faith that is due to Americans, with whom we say with regret truth is not always considered as a moral obligation, we should hesitate in giving it this publicity." The editors, however, continued that they had made several checks, including that the *Bounty* had indeed been equipped with a Kendall chronometer and that Adams had appeared as he claimed on the *Bounty's* muster roll as Alexander Smith. The report generated less interest than might perhaps have been expected, even given Britain's involvement in the Napoleonic Wars.

This first account in *The Quarterly Review* contained some discrepancies, in particular about how and when Fletcher Christian had died, recording that the second mate of the *Topaz* had been told that shortly after arriving on the island Christian had become insane and thrown himself off rocks into the sea, rather than being killed in the general massacre reported by Adams to Folger. Folger himself later gave a friend a third version of Christian's fate: that Adams had said Christian died from natural causes before the massacre.

Further major discrepancies, contradictions, and ambiguities arose in the story of events on Pitcairn following visits to the island by two British naval ships in 1814 and subsequently by American and British vessels, including one of sixteen days in 1825 by Captain Frederick Beechey in HMS *Blossom*. Beechey took some time to record Adams's testimony and was given a copy of a journal by Ned Young starting after the massacre.* A particularly valuable account—because it gives the sometimes ignored women's and Tahitian point of view and because it was made away from John Adams's influence—came from one of the Tahitian women, Teehuteauaonba known to the mutineers as Jenny, after she left the island in 1817 and returned to Tahiti. After Adams's death in March 1829 at age sixty-six, the younger inhabitants of Tahiti continued to pass on to visitors stories they had heard from their parents and older islanders.

Adams had changed his own account several times, becoming more open about what had actually happened as his fear of being taken to Britain for court-martial receded. Nevertheless, he continued to promote himself and his actions in as positive a light as possible. At this distance in time, and with the evidence available, no one can be certain about the precise detail of events, but, balancing all the accounts, what follows accords with what seem the more reliable sources.

The *Bounty* left Tahiti for the last time in late September 1789. In addition to the nine mutineers—Fletcher Christian, Edward Young, John Mills, William Brown, John Adams/Alexander Smith, William McKoy, Isaac Martin, Matthew Quintal and John Williams—there were six Polynesian men. Two of the latter, Oha, a chief, and his nephew Titahiti, had left Tubuai with the mutineers when they abandoned their settlement there, believing they had been too friendly with the mutineers to be safe any longer on the island. Three others, Menalee, Timoa, and young Nehow, came from Tahiti while the sixth, Tararo, had lived in Tahiti but was of Raiatean stock. Nineteen Tahitian women and one child were also on board.

Most of the women had effectively been kidnapped, having been invited to dine on the *Bounty* and told when the anchor was raised that the ship was

---

*He copied some extracts but the diary itself is now lost.

only shifting anchorage. One brave woman dived overboard and swam ashore and six were subsequently so vociferous that they were put off on Moorea, leaving twelve women ranging from the willing—such as Christian's partner, Isabella, and Ned Young's partner, Susannah—to others who had been more or less abducted. Jenny, who had been the partner of John Adams/Alexander Smith and had "AS 1789" tattooed on her arm, and who became during the voyage the partner of Isaac Martin, could perhaps be seen as semi-willing. The names of the remaining nine women were Mary, Sarah, Vahineatua (Mills's partner), Mareva, Pashotu, Paurai, Prudence, Teatua-hitea, and Toofaiti. The baby was Mary's and was also named Sarah.

After discarding the idea of going to the Marquesas, Christian first headed the *Bounty* toward Tonga before traversing what are now known as the Cook Islands, all the time looking for an uninhabited or at least very sparsely inhabited isolated island for their refuge. After a little time, in one of the remaining books from Captain Bligh's library he found Philip Carteret's description of his discovery and naming of Pitcairn in 1767. Thinking it likely to be a good choice of hideaway he, with the other mutineers' consent, headed for it. Because the Admiralty charts had misplaced it by 180 nautical miles, they found it difficult to locate but on January 15, 1790, they sighted its surf-pounded cliffs. Jenny later related how after two months' voyage without seeing land they came upon the island and Christian led a party of six men ashore including Brown, Williams, and McKoy. On their return, they reported, "there were no natives on the island; that it abounded with coco-nuts and sea-fowl and that they had found traces of its having been once inhabited. Charcoal, stone axes, stone foundations of houses with a few carved boards were discovered." There was also fresh water.

The mutineers agreed that the small, oblong island two miles by one mile with only one landing place—a difficult one in a small bay—was suitable for habitation and sufficiently isolated. Thereupon, according to Jenny,

Christian got the vessel under a rocky point and came to anchor. The mutineers began to discharge the ship by means of the boat and a raft made out of the hatches. The property from the ship was landed principally on the raft by means of a rope fastened to the rocks. When all they wanted was brought on shore they began to consider what they should do with the vessel. Christian wished to save her for a while. The others insisted on destroying her, and one of them went off and set fire to her in the fore part. Shortly after two others went on board and set fire to her in different places. During the night all were in tears at seeing her in flames. Some regretted exceedingly they had not confronted Captain Bligh and returned to their native country instead of acting as they had done.

Later, Jenny identified Matthew Quintal as the man primarily responsible for the burning.

The group at first lived in tents made from the *Bounty*'s sails, while they set about clearing the bush and building shelters on the plateau about three hundred feet above their landing place. They were careful to leave a screen of trees to prevent the settlement being seen from the sea. They landed the pigs, goats, and chickens they had brought with them and the cats, but no dogs, fearing they might give away their presence by barking. The nine mutineers then divided the cultivable land among themselves, whether with or without the consent of the others is unknown. They planted yam and sweet potato seeds that they had brought with them. The mutineers also each took a Tahitian woman as their partner, clearly with consent if they had been previous partners, but how much choice the other women had is unknown. This left only three women for the six Polynesian men. Tararo took Toofaiti for his own, Oha and Titahiti shared Prudence and the remaining three the third woman, Mareva. Tahitian culture allowed women to share partners but how far the women acquiesced in this arrangement is again unclear.

One Thursday in October 1790, Isabella gave birth to her and Christian's first child, whom they named Thursday October Christian in honor of the day of his birth. Not long afterward, Pashotu, Williams's partner, died of a scrofula-related throat disease. He demanded one of the Polynesian men's women but his fellow mutineers would not allow this. However, when John Adams's partner, Paurai, fell to her death from a cliff face about a year later while collecting birds' eggs and he—probably a much stronger character than Williams—demanded one of the Polynesians' women, the mutineers took all three women from the Polynesians and, according to Jenny, simply "cast lots for them." Adams took Prudence from Oha and Titahiti while Williams took Toofaiti from Tararo, leaving the one remaining woman to the six Polynesians.

Some of the Polynesian men found this behavior intolerable and in autumn 1791 planned to attack the mutineers. Their plot was betrayed by some of the women. According to one account, Isabella overheard Toofaiti, who was doing chores, singing quietly, "Why does the black man sharpen axe? To kill white man." She told Christian, who confronted those he thought responsible in their hut, firing a musket "humanely loaded with powder only" at them to show the seriousness of his intent. Three of the Polynesian men—Oha, Tararo, and Titahiti—fled. Tararo was later joined willingly or not by Toofaiti, whom Williams had taken from him.

The mutineers persuaded the remaining three Polynesian men that the only way they could demonstrate their loyalties was by hunting their compatriots down and killing them. They succeeded in killing both Oha and Tararo—though the latter in most accounts was actually said to have been battered to death with a stone by Toofaiti, while struggling with another of his fellow islanders. Titahiti, after being kept in confinement in irons for a while, was reintegrated into the little community. Toofaiti returned to Williams again.

The identification of Adams as the second man who lost his partner and precipitated these first murders is perhaps the greatest uncertainty of this part of the story. Some sources say it was Christian who had lost his wife, but Isabella was still alive and introduced to visitors well into the 1800s. Others say that only Williams had lost his wife, but that does not tally with what is known of the numbers and fates of the women on the island. Only after Adams's death did islanders acknowledge that he was the second man. Adams would clearly have had good reason to conceal his role in the first killings on the island.

According to Jenny, "After this the mutineers lived in a peaceful manner for some years." In this period, many children were born to the mutineers and their Tahitian partners and the remaining four Polynesian men seem to have been turned into virtual slaves, working for McKoy, Quintal, Mills, Martin, and Brown. Sometimes they were beaten, McKoy and Quintal being particularly savage. Quintal is said to have literally rubbed salt into their bleeding wounds and also to have been violent to his partner, Sarah.

Jenny related what happened next:

> The natives again concerted among themselves to murder the English and went about from day to day with their muskets on a pretence of shooting wildfowl. The mutineers did not suspect their intentions. Williams was the first man shot, while putting up a fence around his garden . . . [Next] they found Christian clearing some ground for a garden and while in the act of carrying away some roots they went behind him and shot him between the shoulders—he fell. They then disfigured him with an axe about the head and left him dead on the ground. [They] next proceeded to another enclosure, where they found Mills and McKoy;

the former was shot dead, but McKoy saved himself by flight. They now went to Martin's house and shot him; he did not fall immediately, but ran to Brown's house, which was not far off. He was there shot a second time, when he fell; they beat him on the head with a hammer till he was quite dead; Brown at the same time was knocked on the head with stones and left for dead. As the murderers were going away, he rose up and ran. One of them pursued and over-took him. He begged hard for mercy. They promised they would spare his life; however one with a musket got behind him and shot him dead. John Adams was next fired at in his own house; the ball grazed his neck and broke two of his fingers. He was saved by the women . . . [They] threw themselves on his body; and at their entreaties his life was spared.

Quintal fled to join McKoy in the mountains. All accounts agree that Ned Young was not attacked, and many state this was because he was a particular favorite of the women, who protected him. Over the next days, the Polynesian men apparently quarreled among themselves over the distribu-tion of the dead mutineers' women and in their arguments one, Timoa, was killed by Menalee, seemingly the most aggressive of the Polynesians. Subse-quently, with the help of some of the women the surviving mutineers killed Menalee and then the two remaining Polynesian men, Nehow and Titahiti.

Many questions about this bald account remain. In particular was the rising simply along racial lines by the Polynesian men, or had it been orches-trated with the help of some of the women by certain of the mutineers—in particular Ned Young, perhaps with Adams as his accomplice? Indeed, after Adams's death, one of the islanders who suggested that Young had been implicated in the massacre said that he had given orders to the Polynesians that Adams should be spared, but they had "forgot."

Ned Young recorded in his diary that after this massacre the women became dissatisfied with their lot on the island and begged for a boat to be built to enable them to leave. Eventually the men agreed. Jenny in partic-ular took a lead in the boatbuilding, "in her zeal" tearing planks from her home to help in its construction. However, when launched in mid-August 1794 the boat "upset," as Young wrote, "according to expectation"—perhaps because the men had put little effort into its building.

Three months later, according to what Adams told Captain Beechey, "A conspiracy of the women to kill the white men in their sleep was discovered upon which they were all seized." They were pardoned on promising not to repeat their behavior. In his account, Beechey quoted from Young's diary:

"We did not forget their conduct and it was agreed among us that the first female who misbehaved should be put to death." The men also concealed two muskets in the bush

> for the use of any person who might be so fortunate as to escape, in the event of an attack being made . . . On the 30th November the women again collected and attacked them but no lives were lost and they returned on being once more pardoned but were again threatened with death the next time they misbehaved. Threats thus repeatedly made, and as often unexecuted, soon lost their effect and the women formed a party whenever their displeasure was excited and hid themselves in the unfrequented parts of the island carefully providing themselves with firearms. In this manner, the men were kept in continual suspense, dreading the result of each disturbance as the numerical strength of the women was much greater than their own.

Slowly relations between the outnumbered men and the spirited women improved and six more children were born. Some of the mutineers took to drinking heavily. According to the varying accounts, spirits had either begun to be distilled earlier by Young, using his knowledge of rum production in the West Indies, or at this time, 1798, by McKoy, who knew from employment in a distillery in his native Scotland how to produce whisky. For his feedstock he used the sweet syrup from the root of the ti tree. Whatever the case, according to what Adams told Beechey, McKoy frequently became "intoxicated" and "[liquor eventually] produced fits of delirium in one of which he threw himself from a cliff and was killed."

A little afterward, Quintal lost his much-suffering and abused wife, Sarah, whose ear he had bitten off on one occasion when she failed to catch sufficient fish to satisfy him, when she fell to her death from a cliff, again while collecting birds' eggs. Although there were other women on the island, Quintal set his mind on taking Young's partner to replace her or—if not her—Adams's partner. According to Beechey, "Of course, neither of them felt inclined to accede to this unreasonable indulgence; and he [Quintal] sought an opportunity of putting them both to death. He was fortunately foiled in his first attempt but swore he would repeat it. Adams and Young having no doubt he would follow up his resolution and fearing he might be more successful in the next attempt, came to the conclusion, that their own lives were not safe while he was in existence and that they were justified in putting him to death, which they did with an axe."

Young died of "an asthmatic complaint under which he had sometime laboured" in 1800, after spending much of his final months teaching Adams to improve his writing and reading skills, using the *Bounty*'s Bible as the basis for doing so. After Young's death, Adams, as the last surviving mutineer on the island and having renounced alcohol, set himself up as Pitcairn's patriarch so successfully that everybody who visited praised his piety, moral rectitude, and leadership. All, whether British naval officers or not, agreed that he should be left to rule over his little community and not be returned to Britain for trial.

Whether Adams was really as benign and the community as well ordered and contented—a paradise—when visitors departed can only be a matter of conjecture. Some islanders later suggested that he had been cruel to one of his partners and had insisted on his religious observances being carried out "even to severity of discipline." However, Beechey was typical in praising how Adams had set about the task of establishing a moral community:

> The loss of his last companion was a great affliction to him . . . his reformation could not perhaps have taken place at a more propitious moment. Out of nineteen children upon the islands, there were several between the ages of seven and nine years, who, had they been longer suffered to follow their own inclinations, might have acquired habits which it would have been difficult, if not impossible, to eradicate . . . His laudable exertions were attended by advantages both to the objects of his care and to his own mind, which surpassed his most sanguine expectations. He nevertheless had an arduous task to perform. Besides the children to be educated, the Tahitian women were to be converted; and as the example of the parents had a powerful influence over their children, he resolved to make them his first care. Here, also, his labours succeeded; the Tahitians were naturally of a tractable disposition and gave him less trouble than he anticipated; the children also acquired such a thirst after scriptural knowledge that Adams in a short time had little else to do than to answer their enquiries and put them in the right way. As they grew up, they acquired fixed habits of morality and piety; their colony improved; intermarriages occurred and they now form a happy and well-regulated society, the merit of which, in a great degree, belongs to Adams, and tends to redeem the former errors of his life.

POSTSCRIPT

The People

After his return from New South Wales and the death of his wife, William Bligh never again received an active appointment ashore or afloat, though the navy's system of progression by seniority led to him becoming a vice admiral. He collapsed and died on London's Bond Street on December 7, 1817, aged sixty-four. He was buried in St. Mary's Church, Lambeth, his stone tomb topped appropriately by a breadfruit finial. Equally suitably the church is now the Garden Museum, created to celebrate British gardeners and their work and the burial place of John Tradescant, Britain's first great gardener and plant hunter, who died in 1638.

What were the achievements and character of William Bligh? He was certainly more than the bullying, blustering, pint-size turkey-cock or pantomime villain sometimes represented. He was an outstanding navigator, surveyor, and chart-maker, persisting in surveying even in the most challenging circumstances. He was brave, confronting the *Bounty* mutineers, the dissidents during his great open-boat voyage, and opponents encountered later during more conventional naval actions. He inflicted fewer than the average number of floggings for Pacific voyages. He had a supreme self-confidence and belief in his own abilities and their superiority to those of others. Such characteristics were an advantage in times of crisis. During the launch voyage his certainty that he would deliver his men safely to Kupang encouraged weaker characters. However, in less challenging times his narcissistic self-regard contributed to Bligh's poor relations with others, leading him to be what his nephew Frank Bond called "a blamer." Never at fault himself, errors were always someone else's.

Bligh's tongue could be lacerating and his language foul and ill-considered. He was oblivious to the effect of his words and behavior on others, for example inviting Christian to dine with him after their last quarrel. Despite the lessons of the *Bounty* mutiny, such insensitivity was probably too well ingrained in his character for him to change, as Frank Bond's experiences and the testimony at Bligh's HMS *Warrior* court-martial, among many other instances, show. Indeed, Bligh spent the remainder of his life in denial that his behavior had, in any way, contributed to the mutiny. Possibly he may also just have enjoyed mentally wounding people who were his subordinates or owed him something and watching their reaction to his goads.

Bligh was status-conscious and ambitious, keen to exert any influence he had and to ingratiate himself with those who had it. However, his inability to understand other people's thoughts, feelings, motivations, and ambitions, allied to his own self-confidence and self-belief, short temper, and bad language, were grave disadvantages both as a naval commander and colonial governor and in society in general. Consequently, unlike Cook, who flogged more of his men, Bligh failed to inspire loyalty and admiration among his crew, just as he failed to win supporters in his role as a colonial governor among those who should have been his natural allies. Neither on the *Bounty* nor in New South Wales did anyone, with the exception of his daughter Mary in the latter case, risk themselves to support him in his moments of crisis.

As is sometimes the case among people brought up in genteel but relatively impecunious circumstances, Bligh was highly conscious of the value of money and did everything he could to obtain it, as witnessed by his disputes with the Admiralty over his pay and expenses for all his voyages and his governorship of New South Wales. His desire for money led him at least once—the occasion of his swapping of land grants with his predecessor King in New South Wales—into downright illegality and corruption and most probably colored his behavior when acting as both commander and purser, as alleged by Morrison and other *Bounty* crew members.

Overall Bligh, despite his undoubted gifts, was a man with whom many preferred to avoid dealing, which raises questions when trying to identify the causes of the *Bounty* mutiny. Since Fletcher Christian, its instigator, left no known written records of his thoughts either before or after the mutiny, no one can be sure of the precise cause. However, Christian's oral remarks, relayed by others, indicate both considerable mental turmoil—"I am in hell"—and an unwillingness to tolerate any more of what he considered undue abuse from Bligh.

As Fletcher Christian's brother Charles observed of his own experience on the *Middlesex*, dissent easily arose among sailors living for extended periods in confined circumstances in hostile or uncertain environments. Magellan, Drake, Hudson, Dampier, and some of the *Wager* survivors all faced mutiny or incipient mutiny. Bligh, though, always maintained that the exotic allures of Tahiti had caused the mutiny—a claim no one else, loyalist or mutineer, advanced and one that, of course, removed all blame from Bligh. Morrison suggested conversely that on leaving Tahiti "everyone was in high spirits and began to talk of home . . . counting up their wages."

The character of Fletcher Christian and the reasons why his former closeness to Bligh evaporated are key to understanding what happened. In complete contrast to Bligh, in no surviving record does any of the *Bounty* crew—again whether mutineer or loyalist—criticize Christian's behavior before the mutiny. Given that it appears to have been an almost unpremeditated spur-of-the-moment decision by Christian, he must have been sufficiently well regarded as a potential leader—and sufficiently charismatic—for men to join him in an action punishable by death, however great their dissatisfaction with Bligh.

Christian's near-suicidal plans to escape the *Bounty*, even gathering stores, indicate deep desperation. He seems to have contemplated suicide itself—at one stage threatening that if Bligh did not stop persecuting him he would grab him and leap into the sea with him. Clearly Christian preferred death to capture if the mutiny failed, hanging a lead weight around his neck to help him sink if he had to jump overboard. His determination at all costs to avoid capture later led him to rugged, isolated Pitcairn.

Yet Bligh and Christian were once close. Some have suggested they had a homosexual relationship and that their quarrel had its roots in Christian refusing to return to it after his heterosexual relations on Tahiti. If usual ratios are applied, there are likely to have been one or more homosexuals among the *Bounty*'s crew. However, no evidence suggests either Christian or Bligh was among them. Had they been, some crew member would surely have hinted at this in the aftermath. Bligh's relationship with his wife, Betsy, appears to have been strong and truly loving. His apparent celibacy on Tahiti probably reflects his desire to emulate his idol Cook, who undertook no such relationships, and perhaps his own seemingly buttoned-up, fastidious, somewhat joyless nature.

Yet Bligh's and Christian's early relationship might have had some elements of a mutually admiring if sexless "bromance"—stronger on Bligh's side, and on Christian's influenced by his ambition. Christian's father had died when he was very young. Bligh had no brothers and his only half-sibling, a sister, was considerably older. Also, he had no surviving sons. Perhaps each fulfilled an emotional need in the other. Bligh certainly tried to mentor other aspirant young officers. Yet, as with Christian, the relationships eventually foundered. Bligh resented it when his juniors asserted their own influence or personalities and was especially harsh on any he considered a potential rival. He was also quick to condemn what he perceived as ingratitude from those he believed he had tried to develop, as shown by his relations with his nephew Frank Bond, Matthew Flinders, Peter Heywood, and Christian.

Christian's regard for Bligh had begun to wither over the course of the *Bounty's* voyage to Tahiti. Once there, Christian enjoyed a great deal of independence as shore commander as well as a loving relationship with Isabella, both of which may have matured him and made him ever less tolerant of Bligh's domineering, quasi-paternal, hectoring guidance. On April 28, 1789, Christian finally snapped. The consequence was mutiny.

Bligh's patron and protector Sir Joseph Banks died aged seventy-seven on June 19, 1820, still President of the Royal Society. Though confined to a wheel-chair for many years, he had continued to be the hub for a vast system of plant collection, distribution, and commercial exploitation throughout Britain's colonial possessions and beyond.

Banks's reputation in history rests on several pillars, firstly, his youthful work in botany and biology particularly during Cook's first expedition. He became a plant collector and major figure in descriptive botany and zoology—the methodical, objective, and detailed recording and description of plants and animals; he was a field worker rather than a theorist. (The large and renowned genus Banksia is named after him, as are some eighty species of plants.) Secondly, he created Kew Gardens and developed it into the world's most renowned plant center and entrepôt at the time. Thirdly, he became the British government's expert on New South Wales, promoting its use as a penal colony and advising on its subsequent development.

More generally Banks was a great facilitator, communicator, and patron, roles in which his genial, outgoing character proved a great asset. A voluminous and assiduous correspondent, his letters are believed to have numbered at least fifty thousand and perhaps one hundred thousand before being dispersed and some lost. His correspondents included Benjamin Franklin, Erasmus Darwin, the astronomer William Herschel, the chemist Humphrey Davy, Samuel Taylor Coleridge, and the King of Haiti. Among other expeditions, he facilitated the South American explorations of Alexander von Humboldt and his friend Aimé Bonpland, and of Matthew

Flinders's surveys of Australia. He was also a founding member of the African Association, which sent young Mungo Park on his quest to discover the course of the Niger. Banks can truly be said to have been the epitome of an Enlightenment man.

Arthur Phillip also stands out in the early history of the British in the Pacific. He proved a good choice as commander of the First Fleet and as governor of the penal colony. Calm, reasoned, and efficient, his persistent complaints to his superiors led to the First Fleet setting out better provisioned than it might have been. His insistence on the buying of fresh food en route and on the equal sharing of what was available among convicts, sailors, and marines, as well as his requirement on all three for cleanliness, brought the fleet to New South Wales in a much better state than that in which most of its successors would arrive. Once arrived, he quickly took the wise decision to move the settlement from Botany Bay to Port Jackson.

Phillip did his best to establish the colony on a sound footing and, not always successfully, to secure good relations with the Aboriginal people. His even-handed, disciplined, and comparatively humane approach to the convicts and their misdemeanors prevented the uprisings that many had feared, and that might well have occurred under another more combative, more partial, and less restrained governor. He did not allow the more hard-line views of some of his officers and marines, who thought he was unduly lenient and sympathetic to the convicts and Aboriginals alike, to sway him from his balanced and humane policies. Yet his relative aloofness and inability to delegate contributed to his failure to build a team strong and committed enough to continue his work after he left New South Wales.

THE PLACES

On leaving Tahiti for the last time, Captain James Cook wrote that it might have been better for the people of Tahiti if they had not encountered Europeans but that, now they had, there could be no going back to their previous lives. Several others, including William Bligh and surgeon George Hamilton of the *Pandora*, expressed similar views.

Even at the time of Cook's voyages, well before the planning of the penal colony or the breadfruit voyage, the reactions to the arrival of the newcomers differed on both sides in Tahiti from those in New Holland. In Tahiti, the British generally found a people who welcomed them and were as curious about them as they were about the islanders. They found a hierarchy, rulers and classes, that they could equate to their own. In praising Tahitian society initially as a Utopia, they overlooked or were ignorant of the customs of human sacrifice and infanticide. Yet even when Cook, Bligh, and others learned of them, they still found much to admire in the islands.

Similarly, the Tahitians could identify with the chain of command on the British ships and Cook's undisputed position as leader. Just as the British sought new natural products from them, they were eager to benefit from the encounter by acquiring new knowledge and new materials, such as iron. More hard-headed than sometimes suggested, they also saw the Europeans' friendship and access to gunpowder weapons as valuable in their internal power struggles.

By contrast, the British found the simpler, more communal structure of Australia's Aboriginal society far more difficult to understand, being so different from their own. Captain Cook sensed this, commenting that his expedition found it difficult "to form any connection" with the indigenous people and that "all they seemed to want was for us to be gone." The British in general failed to understand the complexity of the Aboriginal relationship to the land, including that the actual landscape was not barren, as it appeared to them, but had been shaped and managed, including by thousands of years of planned burning.

The arrival of the First Fleet signaled a significant difference between eighteenth-century Britain's approach to Australia compared with Polynesia. The First Fleet brought settlement on a scale never contemplated by the British in Tahiti, significantly exacerbating conflict with the Aboriginal people over the land and the sea and their products. The settlement exposed the Aboriginal communities to European diseases such as smallpox and tuberculosis, against which they had no resistance, causing perhaps even greater population loss than they occasioned in Tahiti.

Despite initial attempts by Captain Phillip, Lieutenant Dawes, and others to understand Aboriginal people and society, the expansion of transportation to Tasmania and other parts of the continent together with the spread of settlements—initially along the coast but soon extending inland along river valleys—proved equally disastrous for the original inhabitants. Transportation to New South Wales did not cease until 1850 and not until

1853 to Tasmania. The last convict transport—the *Hugouemont*—reached western Australia on January 10, 1868. The 269 convicts aboard were the last of the approximately 162,000 people transported in total from Britain to Australia.*

Perhaps the most important early and long-lasting change to Tahitian society brought by the British was in religion. When Mary Broad/Bryant returned to Fowey at the end of October 1793, she would have found many of the little port's inhabitants caught up, like much of Cornwall, in the Evangelical Revival. So strongly did two brothers from the extensive Puckey family, into which Mary's cousin Elizabeth had married, feel about the evangelical cause that fewer than three years after Mary's return they left Fowey for the Pacific as missionaries to preach "the pure, powerful, unadulterated Gospel of our great God and Saviour, Jesus Christ."

The inspiration behind the first British mission to Tahiti was the same Cornishman, the Reverend Dr. Thomas Haweis, who in 1791 had persuaded Captain Bligh and Joseph Banks to agree to take two missionaries on the second breadfruit expedition to Tahiti, only to be thwarted when the chosen men had refused to sail while still unordained. He had now achieved sufficient support to found in 1795 the Missionary Society, later known as the London Missionary Society. Haweis concluded that Tahiti remained his chosen territory: "No region of the world which I have yet observed . . . affords us happier prospects in our auspicious career of sending the Gospel to the heathen lands; nowhere are the obstacles apparently less or the opportunities greater, for the admission of the truth as it is in Jesus. No persecuting government, no Brahminic castes to oppose, no inhospitable climate to endure, a language of little difficulty . . . with free access and every prejudice in our favour."

---

*The intrusion of western arms into the South Pacific culminated in the testing of nuclear weapons. With the agreement of the Australian government, the British undertook nuclear tests there between 1952 and 1963, mainly at Maralinga in South Australia, where the tests were almost the first contact the local Aboriginal people had had with white people. France, as the colonial power in French Polynesia, tested nuclear weapons at Mururoa in the Tuamoto Archipelago, 780 miles southeast of Tahiti, from 1966 to 1996 without seeking the agreement of the Polynesian people.

Haweis strongly believed that the Gospel could best be explained by working men who could also apply their practical skills to benefit "the heathen": "A plain man with a good natural understanding, well read in the Bible, full of faith and of the Holy Ghost, though he comes from the forge or the shop would, I own, in my view, as a missionary to the heathen, be infinitely preferable to all the learning of the schools and would possess, in the skill and labour of his hands, advantages which barren science could never compensate."

Although the Tahitians were as soon as possible to be deflected from what he saw as their public prostitution, Haweis also believed from his conversations with Bligh and others that the Tahitian women would be quickly converted and make good wives for his "godly mechanics." Among the artisans selected from many applicants were the Puckey brothers—William, age twenty-two, and James, who was five years older—both carpenters. Thirty members of the mission party embarked on a vessel named the *Duff* in the summer of 1796. Four were ordained, while the remaining twenty-six, with the exception of a surgeon, were all tradesmen—a hatter, tailors, weavers, cobblers, coopers, and carpenters among them. Four men were accompanied by their wives, and three of the group's children were aboard, including a sixteen-week-old boy, Samuel Otoo Hassell, apparently named Otoo after Tu (Otoo being the British spelling of his name) to honor the man the parents understood to rule the island.

None of the missionaries had ever been abroad before. Each had been given a book listing the 1,400 contributors to the mission's funds, who included Joseph Banks, and containing as its only information on their destination James Morrison's account of Tahiti. It seems inconceivable that before setting out on their daunting journey the two Puckey brothers did not consult their relation by marriage—and almost certainly the only person in Fowey to have visited the Pacific—Mary Bryant, about her experiences in the South Seas.

After a voyage full of prayer services and Bible discussion meetings, sometimes punctuated by intense theological disputes, the *Duff* reached Tahiti on what the missionaries thought was Sunday, March 5, 1797, although they in fact were a day out—it was Saturday, March 4. Thereafter, for a long time they held their "Sunday" services on Saturday.

On arrival, they were greeted by the usual canoes, and a party of *arioi*, led by Manne Manne, high priest of Oro, god of war, came on board. Although somewhat put out by their visitors' refusal to trade on what they believed to be Sunday, the Tahitians stayed on to witness the evangelical service. According to the missionaries, "during sermon and prayer the natives were quiet and thoughtful but when the singing struck up, they seemed charmed and filled with amazement; sometimes they would talk and laugh, but a nod of the head brought them to order." Some of the missionaries commented that the Tahitian women were not as beautiful as they had heard. The *Duff*'s captain lightened the mood by producing a wooden cuckoo clock, which amused some and frightened others of the Tahitians, one of whom tried to feed the cuckoo with pieces of breadfruit.

In following days, the missionaries met both Tu and his wife, Iddeeah, as well as Tu's son, the titular ruler. The Tahitians allowed the missionaries to live in Matavai Bay in Bligh's old house from the second breadfruit expedition. After a while the *Duff* sailed off as planned to land ten of the missionaries on one of the Tongan islands and two others on the Marquesas. There, one reembarked immediately after he was "offered the wife of a chief as his bedmate for the night, refused to sleep with her, and was investigated as to his sex by a party of women while asleep alone." The missions in both Tonga and the Marquesas were eventually abandoned.

On Tahiti, the missionaries were shocked when Iddeeah had a child she had conceived with a member of the *arioi* killed at birth, and then resented their condemnation of her act. They found their well-meant naming of young Samuel Otoo Hassell after Tu unwelcome, since it was taboo to give the king's name to any but a king. They were also appalled by the effeminate *maku*, a male group little commented on by previous visitors but whose favors the missionaries found the male chiefs coveted. The Tahitians were equally disappointed in their visitors, who had few trade goods and none of the weapons they desired to impose their dominance on the island. Manne Manne told the missionaries, "You give me much paraow [talk] and much prayers but . . . very few axes, knives, scissors or cloth."

After twelve months of uneasy coexistence, the arrival in March 1798 of an American ship, the *Nautilus*, brought the Tahitians and the missionaries into conflict. The *Nautilus*'s crew were happy to barter firearms for provisions they badly needed and to accept the favors of Tahitian women in return for other goods. Horrified, four of the missionaries, including William Puckey, went to remonstrate with Tu and his chiefs. The account of one describes the result: "The brethren attempted to deliver their message to [Tu] but all in vain, for the king was wrath and intoxicated." On their way to protest to another chief, "they were overtaken by a large mob . . . who took and separated the brethren from each other and ill treated them all. William Puckey they took and stripped naked, dragging him to the water and most cruelly beat him. After which they held his head under the water till the blood gushed out of his nose. After they had gone this length, they let him go being naked and almost dead."

Although Tu quickly restored order and punished the attackers, eleven of the missionaries decided "all hopes of usefulness was cut off for the present" and prepared to leave on the *Nautilus*, which was bound for Port Jackson. This group included the two Puckey brothers.* Although four of Haweis's missionaries chose to remain in Tahiti, their influence could not compete with that of European weapons and mercenaries. In 1806 Joseph Banks wrote, "Tahiti is said to be at present in the hands of about one hundred white men, chiefly English convicts [from New South Wales] who lend their assistance as warriors to the chief whoever he may be, who offers them the most acceptable wages payable in women, hogs etc; and we are told that these banditti have by the introduction of diseases, by devastation, murder and all kinds of European barbarism, reduced the population of that one interesting island to less than one tenth of what it was when the Endeavour visited it in 1769."

Gradually, though, with the help of reinforcements, the missionaries converted the Tahitians to Christianity. Tu's son, known to the missionaries as Pomare II—(Tu had died in September 1803)—was baptized in 1812. With the missionaries' support, he gradually took control of Tahiti from all other contending factions, bringing stability and peace. When the Russian explorer Baron Fabian von Bellingshausen arrived in 1820 he found some elements of the Utopia described by previous visitors: "They [the Tahitians] find fresh food almost all the year round ready to hand on the trees; and they pluck it when needed. There is no necessity to lay in stores or provide for the future."

Much else, though, had changed. The sacred *maraes* had been destroyed after the conversion to Christianity and were "just a heap of stones." The *arioi* had been disbanded and of course infanticide prohibited. The missionaries had translated the Bible and set up a printing press. They had drawn up a code of laws to which they had secured the agreement of the Tahitians and their rulers. These included: "In punishment for theft, the guilty person

---

*James died in Cape Town in 1803 on his way home to Britain. William went back to Cornwall and married before returning to Sydney in 1815 and then going as a missionary to New Zealand. He died in 1824. His son William Gilbert Puckey became a celebrated missionary in New Zealand.

should be forced to pave the area around the church or should work at shore defences against . . . the sea; those convicted of adultery should be condemned to work as servants for distinguished natives." Tattooing was heavily discouraged. Long hair for woman was prohibited as sinful and unclean. According to Bellingshausen, "since their conversion . . . the islanders regard it as a sin to sing their former songs because they recall their idolatrous habits and have of their own free will abandoned not only their old songs but also their former dance." Alcohol was banned. Having agreed to its prohibition, both Pomare II and his queen asked the Russians for it when the missionaries weren't looking. Bellingshausen recounts how, when told a bottle would be sent to the king for her, the queen replied, "He always drinks the whole bottle and never leaves a drop for me." Thereupon one of the Russians sent two bottles directly to her.

The Tahitians were now rigorous in their Christian worship and Sunday observance. A member of the London Missionary Society noted how on the Sabbath, "not a fire is lighted, neither flesh nor fruit is baked, not a tree is climbed nor a canoe seen on the water, nor a journey by land performed, on God's holy day; religion—religion alone—is the business and delight of these simple-minded people." Another visitor was somewhat less polite: "The inhabitants of Tahiti were celebrating Sunday, on which account they do not leave their houses, where they lay on their bellies, reading the Bible and howling aloud."

When Charles Darwin visited on the *Beagle* in 1835, he called Tahiti "that fallen Paradise," although he admired the "mildness in the expression of their countenances which at once banishes the idea of a savage; and an intelligence which shows that they are advancing in civilisation." Tattooing was making a comeback and alcohol, though prohibited, was still in demand. Darwin related how on an expedition with two Tahitian guides, "unwittingly, I was the means of my companions breaking, as I afterwards learned, one of their own laws and resolutions. I took with me a flask of spirits, which they could not refuse to partake of; but as often as they drank a little, they put their fingers before their mouths and uttered the word 'Missionary.'"

The British missionaries' rigid rules and intolerance of any other branch of the Christian faith proved the nemesis of the island's independence. The British authorities had never put into effect Captain Wallis's claiming of the island by establishing any official government settlement or presence on the island. In 1835 and 1836, the British missionaries persuaded the ruler, by then Queen Pomare, not to allow some French Roman Catholic missionaries to settle on the island. France used this as a pretext for the annexation of the islands in 1843. The British did not react to the loss of Wallis's "Paradise Island." Tahiti remains French. Like the rest of French Polynesia, in 2004 it became a Pays d'Outremer, "overseas land," of France. The inhabitants are full French citizens.

By 1831, the descendants of the *Bounty* mutineers on Pitcairn numbered 135. With so many young people numbers would be bound to expand rapidly. This aroused fears of overpopulation among the community leaders, so that when Queen Pomare of Tahiti offered them the opportunity to settle there they agreed to evacuate Pitcairn, which they did in February 1831. The Pitcairners, however, failed to settle on Tahiti and many quickly fell victim to diseases unknown on Pitcairn to which they had no resistance. Six died in the first six weeks of their stay and another eleven, including Thursday October Christian, before the remainder returned to Pitcairn in September 1831.

Increasing numbers, isolation, and poor harvests again tempted the people of Pitcairn to leave their small island in May 1856. This time the entire population of 194 embarked for Norfolk Island, abandoned as a penal colony the year previously and nearly ten times the size of Pitcairn. The new arrivals used many of the penal colony's buildings and facilities. Again, however, not all the Pitcairners could settle. Two and a half years later, two brothers, Moses and Mayhew Young, returned to Pitcairn with their wives and twelve children to be followed in 1864 by twenty-seven more of the original islanders. In 1887 the Pitcairn islanders all converted to Seventh-Day Adventism under the influence of American missionaries. Since Seventh-Day Adventists do not eat pork—the favored meat of the islanders' Tahitian ancestors—the Pitcairners killed all the pigs on the island.

Life on Pitcairn continued seemingly tranquilly throughout the next century, with the numbers of inhabitants fluctuating, but diminishing in more recent times as young people moved to New Zealand and Australia for education and did not return. Today around fifty islanders live there, together with a few professionals such as a doctor, policeman, and teacher. The cost to the British government of maintaining the remote community for the financial year 2016–17 was some £3.5 million.

A welcome development has been the British government's establishment in 2015 of the world's largest continuous marine protection zone around Pitcairn and the other three islands—all uninhabited—in the group with the aim of protecting what is one of the world's most pristine ocean habitats from illegal fishing. Satellite surveillance to enable enforcement is undertaken from Harwell in Oxfordshire in the United Kingdom, showing how far the world has contracted since the likes of Wallis, Cook, and Phillip set out from Britain and changed the South Pacific irrevocably.

At the end of the twentieth century, British police began to investigate allegations of child sexual abuse on the island, resulting in the trial on Pitcairn of defendants still resident there and in New Zealand of others. The case caused friction within the close-knit island community. Some of the defendants' supporters erroneously claimed that the offenses had their roots in the island's inherited liberal Tahitian sexual culture. Six men living on the island were convicted, including a former mayor. Three of these were imprisoned in a newly built facility on the island, where they were joined by two others convicted in New Zealand. When arranging for the transport of the latter two men, the New Zealand Court Registrar, Graham Ford, drafted an order "to convey two convicted prisoners in custody from Papakura [New Zealand] to Pitcairn Island by direct sea voyage." He likened his order to the transportation orders used to take British convicts to New South Wales in 1788.

ACKNOWLEDGMENTS

I wrote this book with my husband, Michael. We would like to acknowledge with grateful thanks the knowledgeable, friendly, and efficient help of the staff of the Bodleian Library in Oxford, the Cornwall Record Office in Truro, the British Library, London Library and the UK National Archives in London, the Mitchell Library and the Rocks Discovery Museum in Sydney, and finally of the James Norman Hall Museum in Tahiti.

We also are most grateful to Kim Lewison and Neil Munro for their reading of the draft text and their insightful comments upon it, and to Clinton Leeks for his advice on freemasonry. As always we much appreciate the helpful advice and encouragement of our agents, Bill Hamilton in London and Michael Carlisle in New York, of our editor George Gibson, and of the team at Bloomsbury, especially Anton Mueller, Grace McNamee, and Jenna Dutton.

BIBLIOGRAPHY

PRIMARY SOURCES: PRINTED AND/OR DIGITIZED

Anon. *An Epistle from Mr Banks, Voyager, Monster-Hunter and Amoroso to Oberea Queen of Tahiti*. London: John Swan and Thomas Axtell, 1773.

———. *An Historic Epistle from Omiah to the Queen of Tahiti*. London: T. Evans, 1775.

Banks, Joseph. *The Endeavour Journal of Joseph Banks*. Edited by J. C. Beaglehole. 2 vols. London: Angus and Robertson, 1962.

———. *Indian and Pacific Correspondence, 1768–1820*. Edited by Neil Chambers. 4 vols. London: Pickering and Chatto, 2008–2011.

———. *The Letters of Sir Joseph Banks: A Selection 1768–1820*. Edited by Neil Chambers. London: The Royal Society/Imperial College Press, 2000.

———. Sir Joseph Banks Electronic Archive Project, National Library of Australia. https://www.nla.gov.au/selected-library-collections/joesph-banks-collection.

Beechey, F. W. *Narrative of a Voyage to the Pacific and Beering's Strait*. 2 vols. London: Henry Colburn and Richard Bentley, 1831.

Bellingshausen, Thaddeus. *The Voyage of Captain Bellingshausen to the Antarctic Seas, 1819–21*. Vols. 1 and 2, series 2, xci-xcii, London: Hakluyt Society, 1945.

Bligh, William. "Answer to Certain Assertions Contained in the Appendix to a Pamphlet Entitled 'Minutes of the Proceedings of the Court Martial . . . on Ten Persons Charged with Mutiny on Board . . . Bounty.'" London, 1794. Widely reproduced in print, for example in *A Book of the "Bounty"* (see below), and digitally.

———. *A Book of the "Bounty" and Selections from Writings of William Bligh and Others*. Edited by George Mackaness. Everyman's Library, No. 950. London: J. M. Dent and Sons, 1952.

———. *Log of the Bounty*. An authoritative printed version is edited by O. Rutter, 2 vols. London: Golden Cockerell Press, 1937. Minorly differing versions exist in the Mitchell Library, Sydney, Australia; and the United Kingdom's National Archives, Kew, London. Both have been reproduced in print and digital form.

———. *Log of the Proceedings of HM Ship Providence* (Vol. 2, July 20, 1792 to September 6, 1793), State Library of New South Wales, and reproduced in William Bligh, *Return to Tahiti: Bligh's Second Breadfruit Voyage*, edited by Douglas Oliver. Honolulu: University of Hawaii Press, 1988.

———. *Mutiny on the Bounty*. Mineola, New York: Dover Publications, 2009 (reproducing the text of Bligh's *A Voyage to the South Sea*, see below).

———. *A Narrative of the Mutiny on board His Majesty's Ship Bounty and the Subsequent Voyage of Part of the Crew in the Ship's Boat . . . to Timor*. London, 1790.

———. Notebook used by William Bligh to record his open-boat launch voyage to Timor. (Original in the National Library of Australia [MS 5393] but available in print and digital form).

———. *A Voyage to the South Sea, Undertaken for the Purpose of Conveying the Bread-fruit Tree to the West Indies*. London, 1792. This includes a slightly modified and amended version of Bligh's 1790 material. The work has been frequently reproduced, for example under the title *Mutiny on the Bounty* (see above).

Boswell, James. *Boswell: The Great Biographer, 1789–1795*. Edited by M. K. Danziger and F. Brady. London: Heinemann, 1989.

———. *Letters Addressed to the Rev. W. J. Temple*. London: Richard Bentley, 1857.

———. *Letters*. Vol. 2, 1778–1795, edited by C. B. Tinker. Oxford: Clarendon Press, 1924.

Bowes Smyth, Arthur. *Journals, Lady Penrhyn 1787–89*. Edited by P. G. Fidlon. Sydney: Australian Documents Library, 1979.

Burney, Fanny. *The Early Journals and Letters of Fanny Burney*. Vol. 2, 1774–1777, edited by L. E. Troide. Oxford: Clarendon Press, 1990.

Byron, John. *John Byron's Journal of his Circumnavigation 1764–66*. Edited by Robert E. Gallagher. Cambridge: Hakluyt Society, 1964.

Campbell, James. "Letters of James Campbell." *First Fleet Collection of Journals, Correspondence and Drawings 1786–1802*. Mitchell and Dixon Libraries (State Library of New South Wales; see online acms.sl.nsw.gov.au).

Christian, Edward. "A Short Reply to Captain Bligh's Answers." Widely reproduced, for example on the Fateful Voyage website at http://archive.is/fatefulvoyage.com.

Clark, Ralph. *Journal and Letters, 1787–1792*. Edited by P. Fidlon and R. J. Ryon. University of Sydney Library and reproduced in full on setis.library.usyd.edu.au.

Collins, David. *An Account of the English Colony in New South Wales*. Vols. 1 and 2. Project Gutenberg Australia, gutenberg.net.au.

Cook, James. *The Journals of Captain James Cook: The Voyage of the Endeavour, 1768–1771*. Edited by J. C. Beaglehole. Cambridge: Cambridge University Press for the Hakluyt Society, 1955; reprinted in Sydney: Boydell Press, 1999.

———. *The Journals of Captain James Cook: The Voyage of the Resolution and Adventure, 1772–1775*. Edited by J. C. Beaglehole. Cambridge: Cambridge University Press for the Hakluyt Society, 1961 (reprinted 1969).

———. *The Journals of Captain James Cook: The Voyage of the Resolution and Discovery, 1776–1780*. Vols. 1 and 2. Edited by J. C. Beaglehole. Cambridge: Cambridge University Press for the Hakluyt Society: 1967.

———. *The Three Voyages of Captain James Cook Around the World*. 7 vols. London: Printed for Longman, 1821.

Dampier, William. *Voyages. Dampier's Collected Works*. Vols. 1 and 2. Edited by J. Masefield J. London: E. Grant Richards, 1906.

Darwin, Charles. *Voyage of the Beagle*. London: John Murray, 1913.

Duyker, Edward, and Per Tingbrand, eds. *Daniel Solander: Collected Correspondence, 1753–82*. Oslo: Scandinavian University Press, 1995.

Easty, John. *Memorandum of the Transactions of a Voyage from England to Botany Bay, 1787–1793. A First Fleet Journal.* Sydney: Trustees of the Public Library of New South Wales with Angus and Robertson, 1965.

Forster, John. *The Resolution Journal of Johann Reinhold Forster 1772–1775.* Cambridge University Press for the Hakluyt Society: 1982.

Fryer, John. *Narrative of the Mutiny on HMS Bounty.* Original held by the Mitchell Library, Sydney; reproduced both in print, for example by the Golden Cockerel Press, London, 1934, and digitally, for example on http://archive.is/fatefulvoyage .com.

Hamilton, George. *A Voyage Round the World in His Majesty's Frigate Pandora.* Berwick, UK: W. Phorson, B. Law and Son, 1793.

Historical Records of New South Wales, vols. 1–6. Sydney: Charles Potter, 1892.

Journals of the *House of Commons,* vols. 37 and 40.

King, Philip Gidley. *Journal 1787–1790.* Vols. 1 and 2. Australian Digital Collections, adc .library.usyd.edu.au.

Lansdown, R., ed. *Strangers in the South Seas: The Idea of the Pacific in Western Thought.* Honolulu: University of Hawaii Press, 2006.

Mackaness, George, ed. *Fresh Light on Bligh, Being Some Unpublished Correspondence of Captain William Bligh with Lieutenant Bond's Manuscript Notes Made on the Voyage of HMS Providence.* Sydney: D. S. Ford, 1953.

———. *Some Correspondence of Captain William Bligh, RN, with John and Francis Godolphin Bond, 1776–1811.* Sydney: D. S. Ford, 1949.

Martin, James. "Memorandoms" [sic] (Original Version and Fair Copy). Edited by Tim Causter. Bentham Project, University College London, 2014. www.ucl.ac.uk.

Heywood, Mary. Letter Book. MSS 5719. Mitchell Library, Sydney, Australia.

Minutes of the Proceedings of the Court Martial held at Portsmouth on Ten Persons Charged with Mutiny on Board the *Bounty,* published by Stephen Barney, 1794, with an appendix by Edward Christian containing the report of his committee into the mutiny. These are widely reproduced in print, for example in *A Book of the "Bounty,"* edited by George Mackaness, see above. Everyman's Library, No. 950. London: J. M. Dent and Sons, 1952.

Morrison, James. "Memorandum and Particulars Respecting the *Bounty* and Her Crew," October 10, 1792. The manuscript is in the Mitchell Library, Sydney, Australia; and reproduced on https://archive.is/www.fatefulvoyage.com.

———. "Journal." An extended version of his "Memorandum," completed after his release, reproduced in *After the Bounty,* edited by D. A. Maxton. Washington, D.C.: Potomac Books, 2010.

Oliver, Douglas. *Return to Tahiti.* Honolulu: University of Hawaii Press, 1988.

Parkinson, Sydney. *A Journal of a Voyage to the South Seas in His Majesty's Ship, The Endeavour.* London: Caliban Books, 1984.

Rickman, John. *Journal of Captain Cook's Last Voyage to the Pacific Ocean.* London: E. Newbery, 1785.

Robertson, G. *The Discovery of Tahiti: A Journal of the Second Voyage of H.M.S. Dolphin.* London: Hakluyt Society, 1948.

Tench, Watkin. *A Complete Account of the Settlement at Port Jackson, Including an Accurate Description of the Situation of the Colony; of the Natives; and of Its Natural Productions.* First published 1793. adc.library.usyd.edu.au.

———. *A Narrative of the Expedition to Botany Bay: With an Account of New South Wales, Its Productions, Inhabitants etc.* First published 1789 and sent back to England on *Alexander* in July 1788. Before he sailed, Tench had agreed with J. Debrett of London to record and publish impressions of the colony. adc.library.usyd.edu.au.

Tobin, George. *Captain Bligh's Second Chance: An Eyewitness Account of His Return to the South Seas.* Edited by R. Schreiber. London: Chatham Publishing, 2007.

Edwards, Edward, and George Hamilton. *Voyage of H.M.S. "Pandora" Despatched to Arrest the Mutineers of the "Bounty" in the South Seas, 1790–91: Being the Narratives of Captain Edward Edwards, R.N., the Commander, and George Hamilton, the Surgeon.* Edited by Basil Thomson. London: Francis Edwards, 1915.

White, John. "Journal of a Voyage to New South Wales." Project Gutenberg Australia, gutenberg.net.au.

Worgan, George. "Journal Kept on Voyage to New South Wales and Letter to Brother." Accessible at www2.sl.nsw.gov.au.

Zimmermann, H. *Reise um die Welt mit Capitain Cook.* Published Mannheim 1781 and reproduced in F. W. Howay, ed. *Zimmermann's Captain Cook.* Toronto: Ryerson Press, 1930.

LIBRARIES AND RECORD OFFICES (ORIGINAL DOCUMENTS)

United Kingdom National Archives (UKNA), Kew, London:

ADM/1/1509

ADM/1/1692

ADM/1/5328 Pt. 2 (Purcell's court-martial)

ADM/1/5262

ADM/1/5330 (*Bounty* court-martial papers)

ADM/1/5367

ADM/1/5368

ADM/2/1322

ADM/51/4373 (log of the *Fishburn*)

ADM/51/4541

ADM/55/103 vol. 1 (Clerke's Journal)

ADM/106/3315

CO/201/20

HO/7/1 (Banks's testimony to 1785 House of Commons Committee)

HO 47/5/28

British Library:

Draft of William Dampier's New Voyage, BL/Sloane/MS 3236

Cornwall Record Office:

1147047 (Baptism record Dolly Broad)

1147129 (Baptism record Mary Broad)

2907912 (Burial record Mary Broad, Lanteglos-by-Fowey)

Mitchell Library:

MLMSS A85, 10/10/1807.

MLMSS 5366, 12/07/1788

MLMSS 5393 (Bligh's launch notebook)

MLMSS 5719 (Mary Heywood's letter book)

MLMSS 7241 3/07/1788

WEBSITES

adb.anu.edu.au (Australian Dictionary of Biography)

adc.library.usyd.edu.au

fellowshipfirstfleeters.org.au

foundingdocs.gov.au (archive of documents on early history of settlement of Australia)

gutenberg.net.au

http://archive.is/fatefulvoyage.com (extensive electronic archive of original sources on *Bounty* mutiny)

http://www.slnsw.gov.au/Banks (Banks electronic archive)

setis.library.usyd.edu.au.

winthrop.dk (for information on the Bounty's chronometer)

SECONDARY SOURCES

Alexander, C. *The Bounty*. London: HarperCollins, 2003.

Becke, Louis, and Walter, Jeffery. *Admiral Phillip: The Founding of New South Wales*. London: T. Fisher Unwin, 1899.

Brady, F. *James Boswell: The Later Years, 1769–1795*. London: Heinemann, 1984.

Boswell, James. *The Life of Johnson*. London: Penguin, 1979.

British, Museum. *Indigenous Australia: Enduring Civilisation*. London: British Museum, 2015.

Burke, Edmund. *Reflections on the Revolution in France*. Edited by J. C. D. Clark. Stanford: Stanford University Press, 2001.

Christian, Glynn. *Fragile Paradise: The Discovery of Fletcher Christian, Mutineer*. London: Hamish Hamilton, 1982.

Cobley, John. *The Crimes of the First Fleet Convicts*. Sydney: Angus and Roberston, 1970.

Cook, Judith. *To Brave Every Danger*. Truro, Cornwall: Dyllansow Truran, 1999.

Currey, C. H. *The Transportation, Escape and Pardoning of Mary Bryant*. Sydney: Angus and Robertson, 1963.

Danielsson, Bengt. *What Happened on the Bounty*. London: George Allen, 1962.

Delano, Amasa. *A Narrative of Voyages and Travels in the Northern and Southern Hemispheres*. Boston: Published for the author, 1817.

Dening, Greg. *Mr. Bligh's Bad Language*. Cambridge: Cambridge University Press, 1992.

Fara, Patricia. *Sex, Botany and Empire*. London: Icon Books, 2003.

Frost, Alan. *Botany Bay: The Real Story*. Collingwood, Victoria, Australia: Black Inc., 2012.

———. *First Fleet: The Real Story*. Collingwood, Victoria, Australia: Black Inc., 2011.

Garrett, John. *To Live Among the Stars: Christian Origins in Oceania*. Geneva, Switzerland: World Council of Churches in association with the Institute of Pacific Studies, 1982.

Gillen, Mollie. *The Founders of Australia: A Biographical Dictionary of the First Fleet*. Sydney: Library of Australian History, 1989.

Guttridge, Leonard F. *Mutiny*. Annapolis, MD: Naval Insititute Press, 1992.

Hawkesworth, John. *An Account of the Voyages Undertaken by the Order of His Present Majesty for Making Discoveries in the Southern Hemisphere*. Vols. 1, 2, and 3. London: W. Strachan and T. Cadell, 1773.

Hobbes, Thomas. *Leviathan*. Oxford: Clarendon Press, 1909.

Hibbert, Christopher. *The French Revolution*. London: Penguin, 1982.

Holmes, Richard. *The Age of Wonder*. London: Harper Press, 2008.

Hough, Richard. *Captain Bligh and Mr. Christian*. London: Cresset Library, 1988.

———. *Captain James Cook*. London: Coronet, 1995.

Hughes, Robert. *The Fatal Shore*. London: Pan, 1988.

Johnson, Paul. *The Birth of the Modern*. London: Orion, 1992.

Keneally, Thomas. *The Commonwealth of Thieves*. London: Chatto and Windus, 2006.

Kennedy, Gavin. *Captain Bligh: The Man and His Mutinies*. London: Cardinal, 1989.

King, J. *Mary Bryant*. Pymble, New South Wales, Australia: Simon and Schuster, 2004.

Lovett, Richard. *The History of the London Missionary Society, 1795–1895*. Vol. 1. London: Oxford University Press, 1899.

Mackaness, George. *The Life of Vice-Admiral Bligh*. Vols. 1 and 2. Sydney: Angus and Robertson, 1931.

———. *Sir Joseph Banks: His Relations with Australia*. Sydney: Angus and Robertson, 1936.

Marks, Kathy. *Trouble in Paradise*. London: Harper Perennial, 2008.

Maton, W. G. *Observations of the Western Counties of England*. Vol. 1. Salisbury: J. Easton, 1797.

McKay, John. *The Armed Transport Bounty*. London: Conway Press, 1989.

McLynn, Frank. *Captain Cook: Master of the Seas*. New Haven and London: Yale University Press, 2011.

Moorehead, Alan. *The Fatal Impact*. London: Reprint Society, 1967.

O'Brian, Patrick. *Joseph Banks*. London: Harvill Press, 1989.

O'Shaughnessy, Andrew. *The Men Who Lost America*. London: One World Publications, 2013.

O'Sullivan, Daniel. *In Search of Captain Cook*. London: I. B. Tauris and Co, 2008.

Parker, Derek. *Arthur Phillip*. Warriewood, New South Wales, Australia: Woodslane Press, 2009.

Pottle, F. A. *Boswell and the Girl from Botany Bay*. London: William Heinemann, 1938.

Rodger, N. A. M. *The Wooden World: An Anatomy of the Georgian Navy*. London: Folio Society, 2009.

Salmond, Anne. *Aphrodite's Island*. London: Penguin Viking, 2009.

———. *Bligh*. Berkeley: University of California Press, 2011.

———. *The Trial of the Cannibal Dog*. London: Penguin, 2004.

Schreiber, R. *The Fortunate Adversities of Captain Bligh*. Lincoln, NE: iUniverse, 2000.

Shankland, P. *Byron of the Wager*. New York: Coward, McCann and Geoghegan, 1975.

Skevington Wood, Arthur. *Thomas Haweis: 1734–1820*. London: SPCK, 1957.

Walker, Mike. *A Long Way Home*. Chichester, UK: John Wiley and Sons, 2005.

Wilkinson, C. S. *The Wake of the Bounty*. London: Cassell, 1953.

Woodman, Richard. *A Brief History of Mutiny*. London: Constable Robinson, 2005.

Wulf, Andrea. *The Brother Gardeners*. London: Heinemann, 2008.

JOURNALS

Gould, R. T. "Bligh's Notes on Cook's Last Voyage." *Mariner's Mirror* 14 (1928): 371–385.

Quarterly Review 3 (1810): 23–24.

United Service Journal 2 (1829): 581–93.

Usherwood, S. "'The Black Must Be Discharged': The Abolitionists' Debt to Lord Mansfield." *History Today* 31, no. 3 (March 1981).

EIGHTEENTH- AND EARLY NINETEENTH-CENTURY NEWSPAPERS AND JOURNALS

Annual Register for 1792 (London)

Cumberland Packet

Diary, or *Woodfall's Register* (London)

Evening Mail (London)

Gazeteer and New Daily Advertiser (London)

Gentleman's Magazine (London)

London Chronicle

London Packet

Morning Post (London)

Observer (London)

Quarterly Review (London)

Sherborn Mercury (Dorset, UK)

Sydney Gazette

Times (London)

NOTES AND SOURCES

The sources for the stories of Captain Cook's voyages, the mutiny on the *Bounty*, and the early days of the New South Wales penal colony are numerous. Many are reproduced in full both in published works and online as well as existing in their original form in libraries and archives such as the British Library, the David Scott Mitchell Library at the State Library of New South Wales in Sydney, and the United Kingdom's National Archives at Kew in London. The most important editions and websites consulted are listed in the bibliography. Among the most useful websites (see bibliography) are the Fateful Voyage (http://archive .is/www.fatefulvoyage.com), which reproduces the key documents for the *Bounty* mutiny; the digitized version of the Historical Records of New South Wales; and the Project Gutenberg versions of the published accounts of officers of the First Fleet. Where the digital versions lack formal pagination, the relevant chapter number or date is given.

The sources for the Mary Bryant story are less extensive. With the noteworthy and valuable exception of works by Pottle and Currey, some rely considerably on conjecture or incorporate elements of "faction," which I've tried to eliminate.

For brevity the following abbreviations are used:

BCM—*Bounty* court-martial papers

BJB—Joseph Banks's *Endeavour Journal* edited by Beaglehole

BL—British Library, London

CJB—James Cook's journals edited by Beaglehole

CRO—Cornwall Record Office, Truro

HRNSW—Historical Records of New South Wales

ML—Mitchell Library, State Library of New South Wales, Sydney, Australia

UKNA—UK National Archives, Kew, London (formerly the Public Record Office)

INTRODUCTION

x "Oh Tempora! . . . the Governor": Salmond, *Bligh*, p. 461.

CHAPTER ONE

1 "amazing phenomenon . . . floating island . . . wonder and fear": Quoted in Salmond, *Aphrodite's Island*, p. 46.

1 "filled . . . Europeans": Robertson, *The Discovery of Tahiti*, p. 135.

1–2 "one . . . man . . . a gold-laced hat": Ibid., pp. 136–7.

2 "to be . . . surly": Ibid., p. 137.

2 "fine . . . land . . . like . . . barns": Ibid., p. 139.

2 "this land . . . outrigger": Quoted in Salmond, *The Trial of the Cannibal Dog*, pp. 39–40.

3 "to trade . . . regard": UKNA/ADM/ 2/1322.

3 *pupuhi* . . . "distance": Quoted in Salmond, *The Trial of the Cannibal Dog*, p. 42.

3 "a great . . . tricks": Robertson, *Discovery*, p. 154.

3 "so well-proportioned": UKNA/ADM/51/4541 (comments of F. Wilkinson).

4 "to see . . . to perform . . . some . . . transgressions": Robertson, *Discovery*, p. 156.

4 "all . . . happened": Ibid., p. 167.

5 "a strong . . . on board": Ibid., p. 206.

5 "my breast . . . hair": Ibid., p. 211.

5 "This . . . lovers": Ibid., p. 212.

5 "This . . . children": Ibid., p. 227.

6–7 "crying . . . than then": de Bougainville from J. Forster's translation quoted in Lansdown, ed., *Strangers in the South Seas*, p. 76.

7 "more . . . alive . . . he . . . body . . . desiring . . . shore": Ibid., p. 77.

7 "hellish . . . reign": Quoted in Salmond, *Aphrodite's Island*, p. 91.

7–8 Despite his mistress's . . . of his own: All quotes in this paragraph are from Philibert Commerson, "Postscript: On the Island of New Cythera or Tahiti," 1769, translation based on that in *Strangers in the South Seas*, Lansdown, ed., pp. 77, 81–85, and the author's own translation.

Commerson was the first European to identify the beautiful tropical plant Bougainvillea. He did so in South America during his voyage with de Bougainville, after whom the plant was subsequently named.

8 "the true Utopia": Quoted in Salmond, *Aphrodite's Island*, p. 109.

8 "almost . . . are": Quoted in Moorehead, *Fatal Impact*, p. 42.

9 "no knowledge . . . brutish and short": Hobbes, *Leviathan*, chapter 13.

10 "Here is . . . overthrow": Quoted in Woodman, *A Brief History of Mutiny*, pp. 29–30.

A few survivors of a Spanish expedition originally led by Garcia Jofre de Loaísa straggled home, completing a circumnavigation in eleven years (1525–36), having been shipwrecked and imprisoned and having traveled in a number of ships.

10–11 "which I never . . . like bread": All quotes in this paragraph are from Dampier, *Voyages*, vol. 1, ed. Masefield, p. 357. Dampier and his companions were possibly but not probably the first Europeans to land on the Australian mainland. In January 1623 Jan Carstensz probably landed briefly in the Gulf of Carpentaria believing himself to be in New Guinea. Dirk Hartog had landed in 1616 for two nights on the large island off the west coast that now bears his name and there had been Dutch shipwrecks on outer islands.

11 "bore . . . berries . . . shaped . . . cutlass": Dampier, *Voyages*, vol. 1, pp. 452–53.

11–12 The *New Voyage* . . . "throat": All quotes in this paragraph are ibid., p. 453.

12 "of good . . . lean . . . want of food . . . matted-up . . . negroe's . . . for . . . combs": BL/Sloane/MS 3236.

12 "the earth . . . do so . . . very . . . fish": Dampier, *Voyages*, p. 454.

12 "for the . . . nation": UKNA/ADM/1/1692.

12–13 For what . . . "my men": All quotes in this paragraph are from UKNA/ADM/1/5262.

In Bahia Dampier continued his natural history researches. The four types of "long-legg'd fowls" he saw wading in the swamps were, he decided, as "near a-kin to each other, as so many sub-species of the same kind"—the first ever use of the term and concept "subspecies."

14 "He . . . hunger": Quoted in Woodman, *A Brief History of Mutiny*, p. 77.

John Byron, a handsome young man, clearly had some of the characteristics of his grandson the poet, enjoying much success with the ladies of Santiago who had "a strong disposition to gallantry."

With hindsight, perhaps John Byron's most lasting achievement was landing on the Falkland Islands and claiming them for Britain. He was not the first to land: Captain John Strong was the first recorded to do so in 1690.

15 "We saw . . . continent": Byron, *Journal*, p. 105.

CHAPTER TWO

16 "safe, spacious . . . harbour": Quoted in Hough, *Captain James Cook*, p. 51.

16 "at a cost . . . tons": UKNA/ADM/ 106/3315.

17 "the South Sea . . . science": Banks to his friend Penin, quoted in Salmond, *The Trial of the Cannibal Dog*, p. 30.

18 "so odious . . . support it": S. Usherwood, " 'The Black Must be Discharged'— The Abolitionists' Debt to Lord Mansfield," *History Today* 31, no. 3 (March 3, 1981).

18 "in pursuance . . . continent": Secret instructions to Captain Cook, June 30, 1768, www.foundingdocs.gov.au.

18–19 The *Endeavour* . . ."an arcadia": All quotes in this paragraph are from BJB, vol. 1, p. 252.

19 "almost everything . . . worst": CJB. vol. 1, p. 76n.

19 "for the . . . body": BJB, vol. 1, p. 258.

19 Cook soon . . ."Indians": All quotes in this paragraph are from Parkinson, *A Journal of a Voyage to the South Sea*, p. 15.

20 "Our . . . young . . . but . . . left": BJB, vol. 1, p. 266.

20 "fine . . . flame": Ibid., p. 270.

20 "stripped myself": Ibid., p. 281.

20 "the chief . . . ease": Quoted in O'Brian, *Joseph Banks*, p. 91.

20 "I was . . . myself": BJB, vol. 1, p. 289.

21 "most of . . . globe": Parkinson, *Journal*, p. 25.

21 "the first . . . sister": Quoted in McLynn, *Captain Cook*, p. 126.

21 "it was . . . meat": CJB, vol. 1, p. 103.

21 "Their chief amusement . . . and opposing . . . half way": BJB, vol. 1, p. 283.

21 "with . . . times . . . a profusion of blood": Ibid., p. 265.

21 "These people . . . frequent in Europe": Ibid., p. 339.

22 "I shall . . . of age": Ibid., pp. 335–36.

22 "That thieves . . . Tahiti": Hawkesworth, *An Account of the Voyages*, vol. 2, p. 149.

22–23 "the captain . . . put me to": BJB, vol. 1, p. 312.

23 "At 10 . . . of sand . . . the appearance . . . fertility": BJB, vol. 2, p. 49.

23 "capacious . . . bay": CJB, vol. 1, p. 310.

23 "Isaac . . . first": Ibid., p. 305n.

23 "The great . . . 'Botany Bay' ": Ibid., p. 310.

23 "in general . . . relator": BJB, vol. 2, p. 111.

23 "lank . . . crisped . . . at all . . . negroes . . . naked . . . his fall": Ibid., p. 124.

23 "appeared . . . anchorage": CJB, vol. 1, p. 312.

23 " 'Cape Tribulation' . . . begun": Ibid., p. 343.

23 "a dark chocolate . . . soft and tunable": Ibid., p. 358.

23–24 "far happier . . . of Condition": Ibid., p. 399.

24 "content with . . . necessaries": BJB, vol. 2, p. 130.

24 "strong liquors . . . tea etc.": Ibid.

24 "Providence . . . a leveller": Ibid.

24 "Quadrupeds . . . killed only one": BJB, ibid., p. 116.

24 "once more . . . New South Wales": CJB, vol. 1, pp. 387–88.

24 "men . . . of people": Quoted in Fara, *Sex, Botany and Empire*, p. 117.

The Earl of Sandwich is the subject of one of the eighteenth century's most famous "put downs." He once said to the liberal John Wilkes, "You will either die on the gallows or of pox," to which Wilkes replied,

"That depends on whether I embrace your Lordship's principles or your mistress."

25 "The women . . . commodities": Quoted in O'Sullivan, *In Search of Captain Cook*, p. 168.

25 "motions . . . conceive": Hawkesworth quoted in Holmes, *The Age of Wonder*, p. 44.

26 "I own . . . produce to thee!": Anonymous, *An Epistle from Mr Banks*.

26 Such double entendres . . . "botany": The quotes in this paragraph come from Fara, *Sex, Botany and Empire*, pp. 38, 43, and 39, respectively.

The exchange between Boswell and Dr. Johnson comes from Boswell, *Life of Samuel Johnson*, May 1, 1772.

27 "must . . . leisure": Quoted in O'Shaughnessy, *The Men Who Lost America*, p. 323.

27 "how immense . . . the study": Joseph Banks to Sir James Smith, December 25, 1817, in N. Chambers, ed., *The Letters of Joseph Banks*.

27 "By God . . . heard of": CJB, vol. 2, p. xxx.

27 "swore . . . mad man": Ibid.

28 "I flatter . . . all ages": Quoted in McLynn, *Captain Cook*, p. 264.

29 "Mr. Kendall's . . . advocates": www.winthrop.dk/the Bounty chronometer.

29 "The Paradise . . . those Seas . . . the grassy groves . . . the blessed . . . If we fairly . . . felt at Tahiti": J. Forster, Hakluyt Soc., vol 2, p. 336.

29 "If the knowledge . . . restless inhabitants": Quoted in Lansdown, ed., *Strangers in the South Seas*, pp. 71–72.

29 "to our shame . . . with Europeans": CJB, vol. 2, p. 175.

30 "to make . . . own country": Quoted in Salmond, *Bligh*, p. 335.

On the advice of King George, Banks arranged for Omai to be inoculated against smallpox, a disease unknown in Tahiti and to which he would have had no resistance. Dr. Edward Jenner would first introduce

vaccination against smallpox in 1796. Unlike inoculation, which gave the patient a small dose of smallpox itself and carried a risk of developing the full-blown disease, vaccination gave the patient a dose of the less dangerous but related cowpox to produce immunity against smallpox.

30 "How do King Tosh": Quoted in Hough, *Captain James Cook*, p. 323.

30 "the daring . . . resistance": Quoted in Salmond, *Aphrodite's Island*, p. 394.

30 "He rose . . . foreign Court": Fanny Burney, *The Early Journals and Letters*, vol. 2, p. 60.

30 "He was . . . for the other": Boswell, *Life of Samuel Johnson*, April 3, 1776.

CHAPTER THREE

33 "could be . . . anchor": *The Three Voyages of Captain James Cook Around the World*, vol. 5, p. 72.

33 "the singular . . . last century": CJB, vol. 3, pt. 1, p. 7n.

33 "of an . . . whiteness": Quoted in Alexander, *The Bounty*, p. 48.

34 "What . . . pure nature": Boswell, *Life of Samuel Johnson*, late April 1776.

35 "The overflowing plenty . . . handsome": Quoted in Salmond, *Bligh*, p. 96.

35 "In these . . . Vauxhalls": Rickman, *Journal of Captain Cook's Last Voyage*, p. 149.

35 "bespoke an . . . to conceal": Ibid., p. 140.

35 "cruel ravages": Quoted in Salmond, *Bligh*, p. 87.

36 "executed . . . the Europeans": F. W. Howay, ed., *Zimmermann's Captain Cook*, p. 57.

36 "my real . . . years ago": *Cook's Voyage to the Pacific Ocean, Critical Review* (July 1784), p. 14.

37 "perceived . . . blink": CJB, vol. 3, p. 148.

37 "a very . . . tyrant": Quoted in Salmond, *Bligh*, p. 81.

39 "C. Clerke . . . proper": Gould, "Bligh's Notes on Cook's Last Voyage," *Mariner's Mirror* 14 (1928), p. 384.

39 "a pretty . . . story . . . whenever . . . ill": Ibid., p. 383.

39 "bribing . . . England": Quoted in Salmond, *Bligh*, p. 43.

40 "None . . . my works": Gould, "Bligh's Notes," p. 371.

There is no evidence that Campbell's ships engaged in the slave trade, although he later owned plantations on which slaves worked.

CHAPTER FOUR

43 "declined . . . down . . . soon . . . out": Quoted in Frost, *Botany Bay*, p. 65.

44 "fetters . . . other": Ibid., pp. 68–69.

45–46 In 1779 . . . suggestion: Banks's evidence is given in *Journal of the House of Commons* 42 (1779).

46 "Let it . . . remarked . . . that [the convicts] . . . work or starve": HRNSW, August 23, 1783, vol. 1, pt. 2, p. 7.

46 "cause a . . . the whole": Ibid.

46 "that very remarkable plant": Ibid., January 13, 1785, p. 11.

46 "no doubt . . . Europeans": UKNA/HO/7/1 and JHC vol. 40 (1784–5).

46–47 "house . . . building . . . very few inhabitants . . . like the Arabs . . . which . . . can show . . . From the fertility . . . of Europe": UKNA/HO/7/1 and BJB, vol. 2, p. 128.

47 "too trivial . . . with Government": Enclosure to letter to Lord Sydney, August 18, 1786, HRNSW, vol.1, pt. 2, p. 19.

47 "for effectually . . . the metropolis": Ibid., p. 17.

47 "a further number . . . without difficulty": Ibid., p. 18.

47 "gross irregularities": Ibid.

48 By the end . . . settlers: The newspapers referred to in this paragraph are quoted in Frost, *First Fleet*, pp. 21, 23, and 27.

48 "the languages": Quoted in Parker, *Arthur Phillip*, p. 2.

49 "great . . . honour": Ibid., p. 25.

49 "As regards . . . respect": Quoted in Becke and Jeffery, *Admiral Phillip*, pp. 319–20.

There is no surviving evidence to substantiate the story current at the time of his appointment that while serving in the Portuguese navy Phillip had commanded a convict transport.

49–50 "In the article . . . down": BJB, vol. 1, p. 341.

50 "If a man . . . return": Hawkesworth quoted in Hough, *Captain Bligh*, p. 61.

50 "universally . . . the world": Letter D. Solander to J. Ellis, May 4, 1776, in Duyker and Tingbrand, eds., *Daniel Solander: Collected Correspondence*, pp. 363–64.

50 "the captain . . . person . . . the true . . . vegetation": Quoted in Alexander, *Bounty*, p. 41.

50 "six . . . state": Quoted in Hough, *Captain Bligh*, p. 61.

51 "more likely . . . successful": Letter to Lord Liverpool, March 30, 1787, quoted in Alexander, *Bounty*, p. 42.

51 No detailed . . ."plant": The quotes in this paragraph are from Mackaness, *The Life of Vice-Admiral Bligh*, vol. 2, pp. 49–50.

52 "I have . . . such a trust": Ibid., p. 50.

CHAPTER FIVE

Today, Sydney Harbor ferries bear the names of the First Fleet ships. Watkin Tench's account of the First Fleet and the early days of the New South Wales settlement are contained in his *Narrative of the Expedition to Botany Bay: With an Account of New South Wales, Its Productions, Inhabitants* and his *Complete Account of the Settlement at Port Jackson*. For brevity, in this and subsequent chapters, his remarks are only sourced where they are politically significant, not clearly attributed to him, or considerably out of time sequence. Similarly, Ralph Clark's accounts of the fleet in his journal and letters are only referenced in the same circumstances. As there are online versions, quotes are sourced to chapters or dates, not page numbers.

53–54 "very strong . . . nails . . . across . . . convicts": Philip Gidley King, *Journal 1787–1790*, pt. 1, adc.library.uyd.edu.au (digital text sponsored by University of Sydney Library).

54 "The situation . . . fatal to themselves": Phillip to Nepean, March 18, 1787, HRNSW, vol. 1, pt. 2, p. 59.

54 "Let me repeat . . . very little": Ibid.

54 "no kind . . . instruments . . . very difficult . . . confined": Phillip, January 11, 1787, HRNSW, vol. 1, pt. 2, p. 46.

The contractor appointed to supply the First Fleet was a London merchant, shipbroker, and evangelical Christian, William Richards Jr.

54 "By some mistake . . . that number": Phillip, April 11, 1787, HRNSW, vol. 1, pt. 2, p. 77.

54–55 "the confinement . . . full allowance": Charles Middleton to Nepean, April 1787, ibid., p. 92.

56 "the flash . . . language . . . unnatural jargon": Tench, *Complete Account*, ch. 18.

57 "feloniously . . . £11.11s": Judith Cook, *To Brave Every Danger*, p. 41.

58 "forest dweller": Ibid.

58 "the fish . . . to eat": See W. G. Maton, *Observations of the Western Counties of England*, vol. 1, pp. 139–46, for detailed account of late-eighteenth-century Fowey. Visitors to Fowey, with its narrow streets descending the steep hillsides to the river, were struck by "the height of the rocks, the boldness of the hills and the wildness of the distant landscape" that were its backdrop.

59 "the Royal mercy": UKNA/HO 47/5/28.

59 "transported . . . may be": Transportation Order Book 1771–1789, UKNA/HO/47/5/28.

59 "feloniously . . . Cary": Quoted in Judith Cook, *To Brave Every Danger*, p. 38.

59 "You . . . Bodmin jury": Ibid., p. 8.

60 "most respectable . . . Chester": Australian Dictionary of Biography.

60 "to enforce . . . obedience . . . for the defence . . . the natives": Lord Sydney to Lords of the Admiralty, August 31, 1786, HRNSW, vol. 1, pt. 2, p. 21.

60–61 "An opportunity . . . desperate a measure . . . the behaviour . . . their conduct": Tench, *Narrative*, ch. 1.

61 "the necessity . . . port . . . a scorbutic taint": UKNA/CO/201/20.

61 "voluntarily . . . expedition . . . indispensably . . . our lives . . . without which . . . hardships . . . change of climate . . . extreme fatigue": Memorial from the Marines, May 7, 1787, HRNSW, vol. 1, pt. 2, pp. 100–01.

61 "gentleman's gentleman": Quoted in Parker, *Arthur Phillip*, p. 69.

63 "the seamen . . . their side": King, *Journal*.

64 "to render . . . beds": *Gentleman's Magazine*, November 1786.

64 "Each . . . happen": Quoted in Johnson, *The Birth of the Modern*, p. 250.

64 "to be rewarded . . . public": Quoted in Keneally, *The Commonwealth of Thieves*, p. 63.

CHAPTER SIX

David Collins's two-volume *Account of the English Colony in New South Wales* and John White's *Journal of a Voyage to New South Wales* are, like Tench's and Clark's accounts, only specifically referenced in this and subsequent chapters where politically significant, not obviously attributed to them, or considerably out of time sequence. Again, because an online version was used, volume and section numbers are given.

65 "The usual . . . cheers": King, *Journal 1787–1790*, May 20, 1787.

65 "who had . . . indulgence . . . on the least . . . irregularity . . . with . . . security": Collins, *Account*, vol. 1, section 1.

65 "Of a design . . . ship": Ibid.

65–66 The fleet . . . "gundeck": The quotes in this paragraph come from King, *Journal*, June 4, 1787.

66 "in general . . . villains": Phillip to Nepean, June 5, 1787, HRNSW, vol. 1, pt. 2, p. 108.

66 "had the address . . . rowed off": Tench, *Narrative*, ch. 3.

66 "heavily ironed": Collins, *Account*, vol. 1, section 1.

67 "preventatives . . . frequent . . . tar": Tench, *Narrative*, ch. 4.

67 "to keep . . . wholesome": White, *Journal*, July 18, 1787.

69 "musket balls . . . in repair . . . we shall . . . distressed": Phillip to Sydney, June 5, 1787, HRNSW, vol. 1, pt. 2, p. 107.

69 "nearly naked": Phillip to Nepean, September 2, 1787, Ibid., p. 112.

69 "'Russia' . . . be used . . . convicts": Ibid.

69 On September 4 . . . reach him: All quotes in this paragraph are White, *Journal*, September 8 and 19, 1787.

69 "the Cape . . . not excepted": Collins, *Account*, vol. 1, section 2.

69 "like another Noah's Ark": George Worgan, letter to brother Richard, page 1.

70 "the rarest . . . seed . . . one pound . . . vegetables": Collins, *Account*, vol. 1, section 2.

70–71 With strong . . . "mechanics": All quotes in this paragraph are from Tench, *Narrative*, ch. 7.

71 "just as we . . . this night": Bowes Smyth, *Journals*, January 1, 1788.

71 "irregular liaisons": Quoted in Judith Cook, *To Brave Every Danger*, p. 90.

72 "a perfect hurricane . . . a sea . . . snow": Bowes Smyth, *Journals*, January 10, 1788.

73 "in a menacing tone": Quoted in Keneally, *The Commonwealth of Thieves*, p. 87.

73 "pretty extraordinary . . . together": Bowes Smyth, *Journals*, January 20, 1788.

73 "open . . . natives . . . amity and kindness": April 25, 1787, HRNSW, vol. 1, pt. 2, p. 89.

73–74 "halloo'd . . . execution . . . desired . . . gone": King, *Journal*, January 20, 1788.

74 The new arrivals . . . "shout": All quotes in this paragraph are from King, *Journal*, January 20, 1788.

74 "very good . . . trees": Quoted in Keneally, *Commonwealth*, p. 86.

74 "very open . . . swell": Tench, *Narrative*, ch. 8.

75 "the finest . . . world . . . a thousand . . . security": HRNSW, vol. 1, pt. 2, p. 122.

75–76 Returning from . . . "contemplation": All quotes in these two paragraphs are from Tench, *Narrative*, ch. 8.

77 "natives . . . approach": ADM/51/4375 (log of the *Fishburn*)

Chapter Seven

Unless stated otherwise, Bligh's comments come from his own *Voyage to the South Sea*, 1792, reproduced in *Mutiny on the Bounty*, Dover Publications, 2009, and from Fryer's short *Narrative of the Mutiny*.

78 "one of . . . nature": Clerke to Banks, October 23, 1776, quoted in Alexander, *Bounty*, p. 56.

78 "fully sufficient": Quoted in Alexander, *Bounty*, p. 50.

78 "pretty . . . riding-habit": enclosure to Bligh's letter to Banks of October 13, 1789, reproduced in Mackaness, ed., *A Book of the "Bounty"*, p. 311.

78 "his pay . . . widows": Ibid.

79 "no more . . . souls": Alexander, *Bounty*, p. 50.

79 "my little ship": Bligh's letter to Campbell, December 23, 1787, reproduced in Mackaness, ed., *A Book of the "Bounty"*, p. 299.

79 "Government . . . a voyage": Betham's letter to Bligh, September 21, 1787, ibid., p. 295.

79 "poor . . . family": Bligh's letter to Campbell, December 22, 1787, ibid., p. 299.

79 "a rum . . . captain": Quoted in Salmond, *Bligh*, p. 104.

80 "dark . . . pursery": Quoted in Rodger, *Wooden World*, p. 70.

80 "I'm . . . past": Betham's letter to Bligh, September 21, 1787, reproduced in Mackaness, ed., *A Book of the "Bounty"*, p. 295.

80–81 "very   deserving . . . little . . . voyage . . . unless . . . sail . . . I had . . . of it": Bligh's letter to Sir George Young, quoted in Kennedy, *Captain Bligh*, p. 16.

81 "He . . . choice": Banks to Sir George Younge, quoted in Mackaness, *The Life of Vice-Admiral Bligh*, vol. 1, p. 53.

81 "too . . . bottoms": Bligh, *Voyage*, p. 13.

81 "the difficulty . . . inter-tropical countries": Banks to William Pitt the Younger, February 1787, Letter 114, in N. Chambers, ed., *Indian and Pacific Correspondence of Sir Joseph Banks*, vol. 2, p. 166.

82 "no dogs . . . unpleasant smell": Ibid.

83 "A   quadrangular . . . farmstead": Quoted in Christian, *Fragile Paradise*, p. 15.

83 "allowed . . . scholar . . . longer . . . navy": Edward Christian's committee report reproduced in Mackaness, ed., *A Book of the "Bounty"*, p. 263.

84 "ruled . . . manner": Quoted in Christian, *Fragile Paradise*, p. 45.

84 "it was . . . worse for it": Edward Christian's committee report reproduced in Mackaness, ed., *A Book of the "Bounty"*, p. 264.

84 "so experienced a navigator": Ibid.

84 "wages were . . . officers . . . We . . . common man": Ibid.

85 "very passionate": Ibid., p. 265.

85 "seemed to . . . humour him." Ibid.

85 "blind to his faults": Lamb to Bligh, October 28, 1794, reproduced in Mackaness, *Life of Vice-Admiral Bligh*, vol. 1, p. 46.

85 "a very great obligation": Reproduced in Mackaness, ed., *A Book of the "Bounty"*, p. 265.

86 "a favourite . . . everybody . . . a great . . . distress": Quoted in Kennedy, *Captain Bligh*, p. 19.

86 "my surgeon . . . voyage": Bligh's letter to Banks, November 5, 1787, reproduced in Mackaness, ed., *A Book of the "Bounty"*, p. 297.

87 "how to . . . powder . . . capable . . . sea . . . sobriety . . . command": Report on Morrison's examination for master gunner reproduced on the Fateful Voyage website, http://archive.is/www.fatefulvoyage.com.

87 "a severe scald": Bligh's description of the mutineers, HRNSW, vol. 1, pt. 2, p. 705.

Bligh's complement of twenty-three able seamen included the four "young gentlemen" and assistant surgeon Ledward.

87 "of poor . . . parents . . . me and . . . orphans": Quoted in Dening, *Mr. Bligh's Bad Language*, p. 331.

88 "seaman . . . rivers": Rodger, *Wooden World*, p. 129.

88 "being . . . drowned . . . a   man . . . company": Boswell, *Life of Samuel Johnson*, p. 86, 1759.

88–89 As the final . . . "the officers": All quotes in those four paragraphs are from the Manx National Heritage Library, Douglas, Isle of Man, MS 09381, widely reproduced in, for example, G. Christian, *Fragile Paradise* and C. Alexander, *The Bounty*.

89–90 With the *Bounty* . . . "at Kew": All quotations in these two paragraphs are from the Admiralty's orders to Bligh of November 20, 1787, in Bligh, *A Voyage*, pp. 17–18.

90 Bligh knew . . . "per day": All quotes in this paragraph are from Bligh's letter to Campbell, December 10, 1787, reproduced in Mackaness, ed., *A Book of the "Bounty"*, pp. 298–99.

90–91 "I have . . . Mr. Nepean": Bligh's letter to Campbell, November 24, 1787, quoted in Mackaness, *Life of Vice-Admiral Bligh*, vol. 1, p. 64.

91 "would make . . . to me": Bligh to Banks, December 6, 1787, Letter 184, N. Chambers, ed., *Indian and Pacific Correspondence of Sir Joseph Banks*, vol. 2, p. 268.

91 "a violation . . . to me": Bligh to Banks, December 10, 1787, Letter 186, Ibid., p. 269.

91 "Everything . . . hand . . . Seaman's . . . prices": Quoted in Alexander, *Bounty*, p. 72.

91 As contrary . . . "risk": All quotes in this paragraph are from Bligh, *Voyage*, p. 25.

92 "The object . . . discoveries": Ibid., p. 16.

CHAPTER EIGHT

All unreferenced quotes from Bligh in this chapter are from his 1792 *Voyage to the South Sea*, reproduced in *Mutiny on the Bounty*, Dover Publications, 2009. All quotes from James Morrison in this and subsequent chapters are from his forty-two-page "Memorandum and Particulars Respecting the Bounty and Her Crew" and his extended "Journal" based on his "Memorandum."

93 On December 29 . . . salute: All quotes in this paragraph are from Bligh, *Voyage*, p. 26.

93 "plants and natural curiosities": Ibid.

93 "two hogsheads . . . Madeira": Bligh to Banks, January 9, 1788, Letter 204, in Chambers, ed., *Indian and Pacific Correspondence of Sir Joseph Banks*, vol. 2, p. 286.

93 "for the ship's use": Morrison, "Journal," p. 12.

93 "miserable . . . for the . . . mule": Ibid.

94 "Seamen . . . like children": Bligh, *Log of the Bounty*, May 24, 1788.

95 "as the . . . spent . . . at all . . . try": Morrison, "Journal," p. 12.

95 "cheerfully": Ibid.

95 However . . . their due: All quotes in these two paragraphs are from Morrison, "Journal," p. 12.

95 "brutal and inhuman": Quoted in Alexander, *Bounty*, p. 85.

96 "they . . . bread . . . on Mr. Bligh's . . . with you . . . everyone . . . pumpkin . . . including . . . against it:" Morrison, "Journal," p. 13.

96 The supply . . . "table": All quotes in this paragraph are from Morrison, "Journal," and "Memorandum," March 1788.

96 "content . . . at night": Bligh's letter to Campbell, February 17, 1788, reproduced in Mackaness, ed., *A Book of the "Bounty"*, p. 301.

96 "we are . . . offenders": Bligh to Banks, February 17, 1788, Letter 211, in Chambers, ed., *Indian and Pacific Correspondence*, vol. 2, p. 296.

97 "the calms . . . sickness": Bligh, *Voyage*, p. 33.

97 "insolence . . . behaviour": Ibid., p. 35.

97 "until . . . anyone": Bligh log, March 10, 1788.

97 "has not . . . navigators . . . I have . . . time": Bligh, *Log of the Bounty*, March 23, 1788.

97 "most difficult . . . passage": Ibid., March 25, 1788.

97–98 "the quantity . . . 'have this?'": Morrison, "Journal," p. 15.

98 "nothing . . . bones . . . some . . . dinner": Morrison, "Memorandum," March 23, 1788.

98 "a storm . . . stiffness": Bligh, *Log of the Bounty*, April 1, 1788.

98–99 As great . . . "violence": All quotes in these three paragraphs are from Bligh, *Voyage*, pp. 38–39.

99 "on whom . . . fell . . . much . . . fatigued . . . I had . . . time": Bligh to Banks, May 24, 1788, Letter 219, in Chambers, ed., *Indian and Pacific Correspondence*, vol. 2, p. 305.

99 "to the . . . board": Bligh, *Voyage*, p. 40.

99 "had I . . . greatest ease": Bligh, *Log of the Bounty*, May 24, 1788.

Kendall Larcum, who had also made K1, completed work on K2 in early 1771 after promising the Board of Longitude that he "could construct a timekeeper upon Harrison's principles but leaving out any unnecessary complication and yet achieve similar results for the sum of £200" (www.withrop/dk) rather than the five hundred pounds K1 had cost. Before being given to Bligh, K2 had been taken on a voyage in quest of the Northwest Passage and then used on the North American station.

100   "frequently remind . . . when any . . . private obligations": Beechey, *Narrative of a Voyage to the Pacific and Beering's Strait*, vol. 1, pp. 70–71.

100   "some of . . . to remove": Bligh, *Log of the Bounty*, June 30 to July 1, 1788.

100–101   "I am . . . good health . . . I might . . . friends there . . . Should any . . . with them": Bligh to Banks, June 28, 1787, Letter 223, in Chambers, ed., *Indian and Pacific Correspondence*, vol. 2, p. 310.

While in the Cape, Bligh dined with the twenty-seven-year-old Lachlan Macquarie, then on his way to India but who in 1809 would succeed Bligh as Governor of New South Wales.

101   "with much . . . rain . . . the man . . . bruised": Bligh, *Voyage*, p. 47.

101   "to find fault": UKNA/ADM/1/5328 pt. 2.

101   "most . . . reprehensible . . . there . . . ship . . . could not . . . man": Bligh, *Log of the Bounty*, August 23, 1788.

102   "no one . . . worked": UKNA/ADM/1/5328 pt. 2.

102   "were sown . . . general": Morrison, "Memorandum," September 11, 1788.

102   "found fault . . . disputes": Morrison, "Journal," p. 20.

102–3   Bligh set . . . Cape Horn: All quotes in these three paragraphs are from Bligh, *Voyage*, pp. 51–58.

103   "light . . . candle": Bligh, *Log of the Bounty*, October 3, 1788.

103   "he had . . . on board . . . this troublesome . . . books": Bligh, *Log of the Bounty*, October 9, 1788.

103   "I sign . . . hereafter": Morrison, "Journal," p. 21.

104   "each taking . . . cabins . . . with . . . reserve": Ibid., p. 20.

104   "some . . . complaints . . . the doctor . . . scurvy": Bligh, *Log of the Bounty*, October 19, 1788.

104   "I think . . . my life": Ibid.

104   "half . . . vitriol": UKNA/ADM/1/5328 pt. 2.

104   "I am . . . it is": Ibid.

105   "*Pahi* . . . ship!": Quoted in Salmond, *Bligh*, p. 132.

105   "would . . . great degree": Bowes Smyth, *Journals*, July 12, 1788.

105   "there . . . people": Ibid., July 24, 1788.

105   "ill-founded suppositions": Bligh, *Log of the Bounty*, October 25, 1788.

105   "not only . . . degree": Ibid., October 24, 1788.

105   "perfectly . . . hours": Ibid., October 25, 1788.

105   "perfectly . . . complaint": Bligh, *Voyage*, p. 60.

105–6   Bligh next . . . commodities: All quotes in these two paragraphs are from Bligh's "Answer to Certain Assertions." Among many other places there is a copy on UKNA/ADM/1/1509.

106   The next day . . . offshore: All quotes in this paragraph are from Bligh, *Voyage*, p. 60.

CHAPTER NINE

As above, for brevity quotes from the personal accounts of Collins, Clark, Tench, and White are only referenced where especially significant, not obviously attributed to them, or out of time sequence.

107   "prevent . . . European power": April 25, 1787, HRNSW, vol. 1, pt. 2, p. 89.

109   "trouble and embarrassment": Hughes, *The Fatal Shore*, p. 88.

109 "upon being given . . . have anything": Bowes Smyth, *Journals*, February 5, 1788.

109 "dressed in general . . . tidy . . . some . . . dressed": Ibid., February 6, 1788.

109 "had not . . . I saw": Ibid.

109–10 "make merry . . . ships": Ibid.

110 "It is . . . the night . . . some . . . almost suffocating": Ibid.

110 "with music . . . flying": Tench, *Narrative*, chapter 10.

110 "Cape York . . . Captain Cook": Collins, *An Account of the English Colony in New South Wales*, vol. 1, ch. 1.

110 "to act . . . own judgement": Clark, "Journal," February 7, 1788.

111 "that there . . . shame . . . freely . . . forget . . . the law . . . course": Worgan, "Journal," February 9, 1788.

111 "Indiscriminate . . . intercourse": White, "Journal of a Voyage to New South Wales," February 7, 1788.

111 "those . . . eat": Worgan, "Journal," February 9, 1788.

112 "200 . . . back": Clark, "Journal," February 9, 1788.

112 "marines . . . dye": Bowes Smyth, *Journals*, February 23, 1788.

112–13 "Could I . . . convicts": Quoted in Parker, *Arthur Phillip*, 151.

113 "heaven . . . together . . . the whole . . . forgiven": Clark, "Journal," February 28, 1788.

113 "the duty . . . executioner . . . reluctantly": White, "Journal of a Voyage," February 30[sic], 1788.

114 "some degree of taste": Hunter, quoted in Parker, *Arthur Phillip*, p. 122.

114 "bound . . . tinfoil": Bowes Smyth, *Journals*, February 9, 1788.

114 "they . . . themselves": Tench, *Narrative*, ch. 10.

114 "naturally indolent . . . authority": Phillip to Lord Sydney, May 15, 1788, HRNSW, vol. 1, pt. 2, p. 123.

114 "decline[d] . . . garrison duty": Phillip to Sydney, July 9, 1788, Ibid., p. 153.

114 "as many . . . storehouses": Phillip to Sydney, May 15, 1788, Ibid., p. 124.

115 "from . . . circumference . . . either . . . dozen": Hunter, quoted in Keneally, *The Commonwealth of Thieves*, p. 114.

115 "for . . . lime": Tench, *Narrative*, ch. 16.

116 "the very . . . females . . . makes . . . necessary": Phillip to Sydney, May 15, 1788, HRNSW, vol. 1, pt. 2, p. 127.

116 "for . . . islands . . . in . . . situation . . . would . . . misery": Ibid.

116 "had the . . . surgeon": White, "Journal," August 25, 1788.

117 "considered as a dainty": Ibid., June 1788.

117 "forcing . . . this . . . I am . . . thought of": Campbell to his patron Lord Ducie, received July 12, 1788, "Letters of James Campbell." State Library of New South Wales, Collection 16. MLMSS 5366.

118 "the scarcity of boats": White, "Journal," June 24, 1788.

118 "swelled . . . debility": Quoted in Salmond, *Bligh*, p. 133.

119 "in the . . . country . . . so . . . rotted . . . now . . . away": Ross to Nepean, November 16, 1788, HRNSW, vol. 1, pt. 2, p. 212.

119 "what little . . . Excellency": Ross to Nepean, July 10, 1788, HRNSW, vol. 1, pt. 2, p. 176.

119 "this . . . them": Parker, *Arthur Phillip*, p. 152.

119 "fatal": Phillip to Sydney, July 9, 1788, HRNSW, vol. 1, pt. 2, p. 147.

119–20 "if fifty . . . convicts . . . Some of . . . receive them . . . the most . . . stop here": Phillip to Nepean, July 9, 1788, Ibid., pp. 153–54.

120 "blankets . . . necessary": White to Phillip, January 7, 1788, HRNSW, vol. 1, pt. 2, p. 142.

120 "troops and convicts . . . sugar . . . saucepans": White to Nepean, July 1788, HRNSW, vol. 1, pt. 2, p. 175.

120 "such a . . . away": Quoted in Judith Cook, *To Brave Every Danger*, p. 121.

121 "a creeping . . . vine . . . sweet tea . . . like . . . root": White, August 16, 1788.

121 "barbed . . . motion . . . dilating . . . depth . . . had penetrated . . . inches": Ibid., May 21, 1788.

121 "torn . . . spears": Collins, *An Account*, vol. 1, ch. 3.

121 "there is . . . philosopher": Worgan, "Journal," May 24, 1788.

121 "the unprovoked . . . experienced": Tench, *Complete Account*, chapter 1.

121 "most . . . butchered": Tench, *Narrative*, ch. 11.

121–22 "transfixed . . . spears . . . sticking . . . birds": White, "Journal," May 30, 1788.

122 "fear . . . wet": Ibid.

122 "they . . . natives": Quoted in Keneally, *Commonwealth*, p. 176.

122 "I have . . . revenge": Bradley, "Journal," acd.library.usyd.edu.

122 "inflict . . . punishment": Tench, *Narrative*, chapter 11.

122 "I think . . . them": Phillip to Marquis of Lansdowne, July 3, 1788, State Library of New South Wales, Collection 19, MLMSS 7241.

122 "the savages . . . officers" Letter from unnamed female convict, Port Jackson, November 14, 1778, HRNSW, vol. 2, p. 747.

CHAPTER TEN

124 "seemed . . . much": Bligh, *Log of the Bounty*, October 26, 1788.

125 "*Toote* . . . Tahiti": Ibid., October 26, 1788.

125 "not . . . stout . . . the . . . saluting": Bligh, *Voyage*, pp. 65–74.

128 "each man . . . day": Morrison, "Journal," p. 22.

129 "very . . . attentive": Quoted in Hough, *Captain Bligh*, p. 120.

129 "the Paradise . . . all": Quoted in Alexander, *Bounty*, p. 107.

129–30 Though Bligh . . ."inclinations": All quotes in these paragraphs are from Bligh, *Log of the Bounty*, November 21, 1788.

130–31 The aspect . . . Bligh grumbled: All quotes in these four paragraphs are from Bligh, *Voyage*, pp. 75–78.

131 "remissness . . . stolen": Bligh, *Log of the Bounty*, December 1, 1788.

131–32 The prickly . . ."orders": All quotes in this paragraph are from Bligh, *Log of the Bounty*, December 5, 1788.

132 If Bligh . . ."plentiful": Morrison, "Journal," p. 22.

133 "drunkenness and indolence . . . exercise . . . nuisance": Bligh, *Log of the Bounty*, December 10, 1788.

134 "might . . . way": Ibid., December 25, 1788.

134 had . . . sight: Morrison, "Journal," p. 24.

134 Although . . . grog: All quotes in this paragraph are from Bligh, *Log of the Bounty*, December 26–27, 1788.

134–35 "eight . . . ammunition": Morrison, "Journal," p. 27.

135 "Had the mate . . . improve": Bligh, *Log of the Bounty*, January 5, 1789.

135 "and informed . . . them": Morrison, "Journal," p. 27.

135–36 The next day . . . sails: Quotes in this paragraph are from Bligh, *Log of the Bounty*, January 17, 1789.

136 "the night . . . windy": Ibid., January 23, 1789.

136 "fatal consequences": The escapees' letter is in UKNA/ADM/1/1509.

137 "for . . . duty": Morrison, "Journal," pp. 27–28.

137 "the cables . . . day": Ibid., p. 26.

137 "with . . . us": Bligh, *Log of the Bounty*, March 4, 1789.

138   "and . . . tent": Morrison, "Journal,"
p. 28.

138   "I had . . . given . . . decent young
officers": Bligh, *Log of the Bounty*, March 7,
1789.

138-39   On March 25 . . ."pudding": All
quotes in these two paragraphs are from
Bligh, *Voyage*, p. 122.

139   "to show . . . store": Morrison, "Journal," p. 29.

140   "truly . . . scene": Ibid.

140   "Everybody . . . waft them": Ibid.

CHAPTER ELEVEN

Comments on what occurred during the
mutiny are from the Bounty court-martial
papers in UKNA/ADM/1/5330, part 2, and
the minutes of the prosecution case recorded
by Stephen Barney, Muspratt's lawyer, later
published with the report by Edward Christian's committee. References to this material are only given where the speaker is
unclear, in which case the reference is
speaker's name/BCM (Bounty court-
martial papers).

141   "which . . . English": Bligh, *Log of the
Bounty*, April 6, 1789.

141   "had . . . legs": Bligh, *Voyage*, p. 125.

141-42   Sailing on . . . to land: All quotes
in this paragraph are Ibid., pp. 127 and 129.

142   "Mr. Bligh . . . words . . . Sir your
abuse . . . with you": Fryer, *Narrative*, April
28, 1789.

142   "a little sickly": Bligh, *Voyage*, p. 130.

142   "dreadful sores . . . breasts . . . bloody
. . . little fingers": Bligh, *Log of the Bounty*,
April 24, 1785.

142   "for want of a little exertion": Ibid.,
April 24, 1789.

142   "considering . . . without them": Ibid.,
April 25, 1785.

143   "for a cowardly . . . 'being used'":
Morrison, "Journal," p. 32.

143   "As to the officers . . . trust them":
Bligh *Log of the Bounty*, April 25, 1789.

143   "the loss . . . great to me": Fryer,
Narrative.

144   "while we . . . nothing rascals": Ibid.

144   "lubberly rascals . . . that he . . . all of
them . . . for . . . attention":   Morrison,
"Journal," p. 34.

144   "distress . . . was worth": Bligh, *A
Book of the "Bounty"*, p. 108.

144   "peel . . . them . . . cut themselves . . .
prevented": Morrison, "Memorandum,"
April 28, 1789.

144   Toward . . ."Endeavour Strait": All
quotes in this paragraph are from Morrison,
"Journal," p. 35.

145   "Stop these . . . a quarter": Ibid.

145   "were heard . . . of them": Ibid.,
pp. 35–36.

145   "was more than their allowance":
Fryer, *Narrative*.

145   Some like . . ."scandalous usage": All
quotes are from Purcell in the report written by the committee set up after the
mutiny by Edward Christian.

145   "to quit . . . very night": Morrison,
"Memorandum," April 27, 1789.

145   "gave away . . . overboard": Edward
Christian report.

145   "he applied . . . pleased": Ibid.

146   "went below . . . at dinner . . . in
a . . . Christian's cot": Ibid.

146   "we . . . speaking terms": Ibid.

146   "a very pleasant watch": Ibid.

146   "upon deck . . . usual": Ibid.

146   "much . . . mind . . . much . . .
order": Morrison, "Journal," p. 39, and
"Memorandum," April 27, 1789.

146   "this made . . . his mind": Morrison,
"Journal," p. 39.

147   "called up . . . in hand": Ibid.

147   "by others . . . come to me": Bligh,
Log of the Bounty, April 28, 1789.

147 "was a dead man": Fryer/BCM.

147–48 "Our eyes . . . of them": Bligh, *Log of the Bounty*, April 28, 1789.

148 When Fryer . . . nightgown down: All quotes in this paragraph are Fryer/BCM.

148 "suffering . . . my hands": Bligh, *Voyage*, p. 134.

148 "seemed to . . . possible description": Quoted in Alexander, *Bounty*, p. 140.

148 "the cause . . . right hand.": Bligh, *Log of the Bounty*, April 28, 1789.

148 "Hold . . . weeks past . . . Captain Bligh . . . himself": Fryer/BCM.

148 "almost . . . worms": Fryer, *Narrative*.

148 "was a friend . . . If you . . . through": Fryer/BCM.

149 "No, Sir . . . about it": Ibid.

149 "Sir . . . too late now": Ibid.

149 Below deck . . . the hatchway: All quotes in this paragraph are Peckover/BCM.

149 "restore . . . time . . . if we stay . . . pirates": Fryer/BCM.

149 "not for . . . with him": Ibid.

150 "full of . . . clothes": Peckover/BCM.

151 "dancing . . . his life": Edward Christian report.

151 "This is . . . Mr. Young . . . Yes . . . belly full": Ibid.

151 "No, by God . . . you through": Fryer/BCM.

151 "would go . . . among the mutineers": Quoted in Mackaness, *Life of Vice-Admiral Bligh*, vol. 1, p. 141.

151 "they . . . doctors": Hayward/BCM.

151 "journal . . . papers . . . my honour . . . suspected": Bligh, *Voyage*, p. 136.

151 "Shoot the bugger": Fryer/BCM.

151 "Consider . . . your knee": Edward Christian's report.

152 "Hold your . . . consider now . . . I have . . . with you": Purcell/BCM.

152 "If you . . . a villain": Morrison, "Journal," p. 37.

152 "Captain . . . going": Fryer/BCM.

152 "took his own . . . 'good one'": Morrison, "Journal," p. 37.

152 "You bugger . . . brains out . . . We . . . mischief": Cole/BCM.

152 "Huzza for Tahiti": Edward Christian's report.

152 "the most . . . company": Bligh, *Voyage*, p. 138.

152 "remember . . . own will": Norman/BCM.

152 "My lads . . . justice": Hayward/BCM.

CHAPTER TWELVE

There are four main sources giving Bligh's account of the launch voyage:

- the notebook in which Bligh recorded his daily observations and comments during the voyage itself;
- Bligh's official Admiralty logbook, which he wrote using the notebook as his base;
- Bligh's first published book on the mutiny, *A Narrative of the Mutiny on board His Majesty's Ship Bounty* (1790), which concentrates on the mutiny and the voyage of the launch;
- Bligh's second published book, *A Voyage to the South Sea* (1792), which covers the whole voyage including the mutiny and the journey of the launch.

Neither the notebook nor logbook was published at the time, although all four of the above have now appeared widely in print and online. All four contain marked similarities in wording, et cetera. For brevity, the particular source of Bligh's words is only given where it seems important to know whether they were published at the time or not, or where the source of the words is unclear. All Fryer's comments come from his narrative, unpublished in the eighteenth century (but later published as *A Narrative of the Mutiny on HMS Bounty*), unless otherwise indicated.

153 "so . . . rocky": Bligh, *Voyage*, p. 142.

155 "he was . . . provisions": Mackaness, *Life of Vice-Admiral Bligh*, vol. 1, p. 188.

156 "the sun . . . gale": Bligh, *Voyage*, p. 151.

159 "a new . . . morning": Fryer, *Narrative*.

159 "showed . . . silent": Bligh, *Log of the Bounty*, May 29, 1789.

160 "idlers . . . insolent . . . degree": Bligh, notebook, May 31, 1789.

160 "taking hold . . . to death": Bligh, *Log of the Bounty*, May 31, 1789.

162–63 Bligh's letter to his wife of August 19, 1789 is widely published, including in Mackaness, ed., *A Book of the "Bounty"*, pp. 304–05.

CHAPTER THIRTEEN

164 "an inflammatory fever . . . imprudently . . . clothing": Bligh, *Voyage*, p. 199.

164–65 After five weeks . . . would do Purcell: the quotes in these three paragraphs come from Bligh's logbook for the *Resource*, contained in *Log of the Bounty*.

166 "It may be . . . conceived": Enclosure with Bligh's letter to Banks, October 13, 1789, from Batavia; reproduced in full in Mackaness, ed., *A Book of the "Bounty"*, pp. 310–21.

Bligh's description of Christian is from HRNSW, vol. 1, pt. 2, p. 704.

167 "unless . . . relations": Quoted in Salmond, *Bligh*, p. 232.

167–68 Just two . . . lost in time: Among the newspapers in which the advertisements appeared were the *Gazetteer and New Daily Advertiser*, May 15, 1790, and the *Diary, or Woodfall's Register* of May 11, 1790.

169–70 The families . . ."fierce and resentful": The quotes in these three paragraphs are from MS 09381, in the Manx National Heritage Library, Douglas, Isle of Man, and reproduced widely, for example in C. Alexander, *The Bounty*, and G. Christian, *Fragile Paradise*.

169 In a letter . . ."without much concern": The quotes in this paragraph come

from Mary Heywood, Letter Book, Mitchell Library, MS 5719.

The papers for both Bligh's court-martial for the loss of the *Bounty* and Purcell's court-martial are contained in UKNA/ADM/1/5328 Pt. 2.

170 "exceeding . . . my evidence . . . as it . . . life": Bligh to Banks, October 24, 1790, Letter 109, in Chambers, ed., *Indian and Pacific Correspondence*, vol. 3, p. 171.

170–71 Edwards's orders . . . Port Jackson: All quotes in these two paragraphs are from Captain Edwards's instructions, October 25, 1790, reproduced in full on the Fateful Voyage website, http://archive.is/www.fatefulvoyage.com.

171–72 Of the loyal . . . off his ship: The two quotes in this paragraph are from Schreiber, *The Fortunate Adversities of William Bligh*, p. 64.

172 "little . . . conversions": Quoted in Salmond, *Bligh*, p. 335.

CHAPTER FOURTEEN

173 "free . . . underwood": Collins, *An Account of the English Colony in New South Wales*, vol.1, ch. 5.

173–74 Phillip . . ."manners of his country": All quotes in these four paragraphs come from Tench, *Complete Account*, ch. 3.

175 "secreting . . . fish": Collins, *Account*, vol. 1, ch. 6.

175 "to receive . . . family": Quoted in Judith Cook, *To Brave Every Danger*, p. 117.

175 With the *Sirius* . . ."terror only": All quotes in this paragraph come from Tench, *Complete Account*, ch. 3.

175 "hardly . . . men": John Easty, *Memorandum*, p. 111.

175 "notwithstanding . . . cart": Collins, *Account*, vol. 1, ch. 6.

176 *galgalla*: Quoted in Keneally, *The Commonwealth of Thieves*, p. 209.

176–77 The *Sirius*'s bounty . . . "New South Wales": the quotes in this paragraph are from Tench, *Complete Account*, ch. 5.

177 "twelve of . . . matrons": Collins, *Account*, vol. 1, ch. 8.

177 "whether . . . prolonged": Tench, *Complete Account*, ch. 5.

177 "by far . . . execute": Quoted in Keneally, *Commonwealth*, p. 244.

177–78 Tench . . . carelessness: All quotes in this paragraph are from Tench, *Complete Account*, ch. 5.

178 "Had he . . . troublesome": Ibid.

179 "Surely . . . forgotten us?": Captain Campbell, quoted in Cook, *To Brave Every Danger*, p. 136.

180 For Phillip . . ."lodged in it": All quotes in this paragraph are from Tench, *Complete Account*, ch. 6.

181 "nimbly . . . paling . . . and . . . adieu": Quoted in Keneally, *Commonwealth*, p. 253.

181 "under . . . kangaroos": Tench, *Complete Account*, ch. 6.

181 "found quite empty": Collins, *Account*, vol. 1, ch. 9.

182 "dangerous . . . illness": Ibid., ch. 10.

182 "in the course . . . Port Jackson": Grenville to Phillip, June 20, 1789, HRNSW, vol. 1, pt. 2, p. 252.

182 "artificers": Ibid.

183 "The contractors . . . being broken": Captain Hill to Wathen, July 26, 1790, HRNSW, vol. 1, pt. 2, p. 366.

183 "the slave trade . . . this fleet": Ibid.

183 "some creeped . . . backs of others": Ibid., Rev. Johnson to Mr. Thornton, p. 387.

184 "and went . . . scarcely bear it": Ibid.

185 "disordered and helpless . . . we have many . . . the settlement": Phillip to Grenville, July 17, 1790, HRNSW, vol. 1, pt. 2, p. 361.

CHAPTER FIFTEEN

186 Pleased . . ."his back": All quotes in this paragraph are from Tench, *Complete Account*, ch. 8.

187 "highly scorbutic": Quoted in Keneally, *The Commonwealth of Thieves*, p. 306.

187 "not mortal": Collins, *Account*, vol. 1, ch. 11.

187 "it might . . . forget": Ibid.

187 "as readily . . . box": Quoted in Keneally, *Commonwealth*, p. 308.

188 "treated . . . disdain": Tench, *Complete Account*, ch. 11.

188 "I am a dead man": Ibid., ch. 12.

189 "unofficerlike behaviour": Quoted in Keneally, *Commonwealth*, pp. 324–25.

189 "frantic . . . behaviour": Tench, *Complete Account*, ch. 13.

190 "who had wives . . . to the settlement": Collins, *Account*, vol. 1, ch. 12.

191 "navigator": Quoted in Currey, *The Transportation, Escape and Pardoning of Mary Bryant*, p. 14.

191 "a mariner": Newgate Prison register, quoted in Currey, *Transportation*, p. 15.

192 "After clearing . . . cove": Hunter, quoted in Judith Cook, *To Brave Every Danger*, p.p. 149–50.

192 "now so fully . . . be past": Phillip to William Grenville, March 25, 1791, HRNSW, vol. 1, pt. 2, p. 483.

192 "I am sorry . . . bodies": Quoted in Keneally, *Commonwealth*, p. 339.

192 "a handsaw . . . rice": Collins, *Account*, vol. 1, ch. 12.

193 "very desperate . . . this country": Easty, *Memorandum*, p. 127.

194 "to embrace . . . of society": Collins's letter to his father, quoted in Hughes, *Fatal Shore*, p. 105.

CHAPTER SIXTEEN

There are two versions of James Martin's "Memorandoms [sic]," made available by the Bentham Project—the "fair copy," shown below as FC, and the "original version," shown below as O—which differ slightly in wording though not in overall content.

195 For two days . . ."well satisfied": All quotes in this paragraph are from James Martin's "Memorandoms" (FC).

195 "superior to Sydney": Judith Cook, *To Brave Every Danger*, p. 161.

195–96 Early on . . ."we could": All quotes in this paragraph are from James Martin's "Memorandoms" (FC).

196 "a little . . . island": Ibid.

196 "with . . . we had": Martin, "Memorandoms" (O).

196 "running . . . hard": Ibid.

196 "much distressed . . . wood": Ibid.

196 "it was . . . water": Ibid.

196 "without . . . damage": Cook, *To Brave Every Danger*, p. 163.

196 "which . . . well": Martin, "Memorandoms" (O).

196 "no . . . kind": Martin, "Memorandoms" (FC).

196 "expecting . . . perish . . . as . . . have it": Ibid.

197 "with great . . . wet . . . the natives . . . numbers . . . They dispersed . . . them": Martin, "Memorandoms" (O).

197 "to keep her up": Ibid.

197 "crying . . . way": Ibid.

197 "a great . . . natives": Ibid.

197 "a heavy . . . wind . . . every moment . . . bottom . . . running . . . high": Ibid.

197 "coming . . . us": Ibid.

197 "I will . . . at night": Ibid.

197 "bore . . . them": Bryant's journal referred to by Tobin, *Captain Bligh's Second Chance*, p. 276.

198 "so very high . . . if . . . perish": Martin, "Memorandoms" (O).

198 "without much damage": Ibid.

198 "which with . . . cook": Martin, "Memorandoms" (FC).

198 "a great . . . turtles . . . had a noble meal": Ibid.

198 "our boat . . . of it . . . great . . . fowls . . . a kind . . . pepper . . . tasted very well": Ibid.

198 "none . . . God for it": Ibid.

198 "we must have starved": Ibid.

198–99 In urgent need of . . . "his shoulders": Martin, "Memorandoms" (FC).

199–200 In desperation . . . tottered ashore: All quotes in these two paragraphs are quoted in ibid.

200 "the captain . . . boat": Quoted in Currey, *The Transportation, Escape and Pardoning of Mary Bryant*, p. 25.

200 "behaved . . . clothed us": Martin, "Memorandoms" (FC).

200 "the favourite . . . places": Hamilton in *Voyage of HMS Pandora*, p. 160.

200 "drew . . . Government . . . supplied . . . need of": Ibid., p. 143.

200 "William Broad": Quoted in Cook, *To Brave Every Danger*, p. 170.

Chapter Seventeen

201–4 On becoming . . ."Mr. Bligh": All quotes in these ten paragraphs are from Morrison, "Journal," pp. 41–47.

204 "set little store . . . 9 men . . . at sea": Ibid., p. 47.

All quotes in the remainder of the chapter come from Morrison, "Journal," pp. 50–58, 69–70, except for "drunkenness . . . life," which come from Heywood/BCM.

Chapter Eighteen

All quotes from Captain Edwards's reports to the Admiralty are from Edward Edwards and George Hamilton, *Voyage of H.M.S. Pandora . . . the Narratives of Captain Edward Edwards, RN, Commander, and George Hamilton, Surgeon,* and are designated Pandora/E.

209 "long since": Hamilton, *A Voyage Round the World in His Majesty's Frigate* Pandora, p. 24.

209 "killed . . . chief": Pandora/E, p. 30.

210   "Knowing . . . villains!": Letter from Peter Heywood to his mother, Elizabeth Heywood, November 20, 1791, quoted in Mackaness, *Life of Vice-Admiral Bligh*, vol. 1, pp. 256–57.

210–12   In the eighteen months . . . his arrival: All quotes in these five paragraphs are from Morrison, "Journal", pp. 74, 79, 81, 96, and 110.

212   Edwards . . . muster: All quotes in this paragraph are from Pandora/E, p. 31.

212–13   Morrison . . . peacefully: All quotes in these three paragraphs are from Morrison, "Journal," pp. 73, 111, 112, and 114.

213   "not to . . . language . . . plenty of coconuts . . . any . . . ship": Ibid., p. 114.

213   "their . . . ships's company": Pandora/E, p. 34.

213   "a kind . . . reception": Morrison, "Journal," p. 114.

213   "round . . . healthy": Pandora/E, p. 34.

213   "The poop . . . disagreeable . . . setting . . . gloves": Morrison, "Journal," pp. 114–15.

214   Morrison . . ."rites": All quotes in this paragraph from Morrison, "Journal," p. 115.

214   "different people . . . journals . . . Tahiti . . . he . . . shipping . . . was . . . islands": Pandora/E, pp. 34 and 38.

214   "decked . . . boat": Hamilton, *Voyage Round the World*, p. 60.

214–15   While . . . disease": All quotes in these two paragraphs are Hamilton, *Voyage Round the World*, p. 37–39 and p. 54.

215   "filled . . . fruit . . . as many . . . hold . . . dismal day . . . heavy mourn": Ibid., p. 59.

215   "melt . . . heart": Morrison, "Journal," p. 115.

215   "plausible": Pandora/E, p. 40.

215–16   En route . . ."Tahiti": All quotes in these two paragraphs are from Hamilton, *Voyage Round the World*, pp. 67–69 and 78–79.

216   "The . . . naked": Morrison, "Journal," p. 117.

216   "the quarter-deck . . . familiarities . . . an old . . . nail": Hamilton, *Voyage Round the World*, p. 87.

216–17   "when . . . us . . . the surgeon . . . alive": Morrison, "Journal," p. 116.

217   "we saw . . . inhabited": Pandora/E, pp. 67–68.

217   "insane labyrinth": Quoted in Hough, *Captain James Cook*, p. 185.

217   "exceeding . . . night": Hamilton, *Voyage Round the World*, p. 104.

217   "expected . . . board": Morrison, "Journal," p. 118.

217   "dreadful . . . water": Hamilton, *Voyage Round the World*, pp. 104–05.

217–18   By dawn . . ."away": All quotes ibid., pp. 107–08.

218   "the . . . irons": Ibid., p. 107.

218   "would . . . together . . . as we . . . ourselves . . . informed . . . done . . . we should . . . lives . . . he ordered . . . purpose . . . with orders . . . motion . . . there was . . . lay down": Morrison, "Journal," p. 118.

218–19   At daybreak . . ."followed": All quotes in these two paragraphs are Morrison, "Journal," pp. 119–20.

219   "89 . . . lost": Pandora/E, pp. 74–75.

219–20   Edwards . . . drink saltwater: All quotes in this paragraph from Hamilton, *Voyage Round the World*, pp. 109–10.

220   "we had . . . day": Morrison, "Journal," p. 120.

220   "a musket-ball weight": Hamilton, *Voyage Round the World*, pp. 115–16.

220   "As I . . . punishment . . . Silence . . . expect . . . in . . . rage": Morrison, "Journal," p. 123.

220   "very savage . . . avoid them . . . a shower . . . us": Hamilton, *Voyage Round the World*, p. 117–18.

221   "we . . . New South Wales": Pandora/E, p. 78.

221 "little squadron": Hamilton, *Voyage Round the World*, p. 113.

221 "the . . . sucked": Morrison, "Journal," p. 123.

221 "hideous growling . . . had . . . rush out . . . our . . . water-logged": Hamilton, *Voyage Round the World*, pp. 121–22.

221 "As . . . continued . . . they . . . temper": Ibid., p. 129.

221 On September 13 . . ."mercy": All quotes in this paragraph ibid., pp. 130, 134, and 136.

221–22 When . . . clothes: All quotes in this paragraph from Morrison, "Journal," p. 124.

222 "We . . . months . . . castle": Martin, "Memorandoms" (O).

222 "not . . . contracted": Morrison, "Journal," p. 124.

222 "one . . . as the rest": Quoted in Currey, *The Transportation, Escape and Pardoning of Mary Bryant*, p. 26.

222 "The . . . taken": Hamilton, *Voyage Round the World*, p. 143.

222 "two . . . more": Martin, "Memorandoms" (O).

223 "to know . . . prisoners": Ibid.

223 "to . . . escape . . . liable to punishment": Pandora/E, p. 82.

223 On October 6 . . . to say: Morrison, "Journal," pp. 124–26.

223 "attended . . . experienced . . . The Dutch . . . rage": Hamilton, *Voyage Round the World*, p. 149.

223 "the death . . . globe": CJB, vol. 1, p. 443.

224 "Golgotha . . . all the . . . pleasure-grounds": Hamilton, *Voyage Round the World*, pp. 156–57.

224 "pestilential vapours . . . thick stinking fog": Morrison, "Journal," p. 127.

224 "a cadaverous . . . prison": Hamilton, *Voyage Round the World*, p. 160.

224 "surrounded . . . dissolution": "Voyage of the Matavy Tender," Midshipman David Thomas Renouard, Fateful Voyage website, http://archive.is/www.fatefulvoyage.com.

224 "we lost . . . taken bad": Martin, "Memorandoms" (O).

224 "heavy gales . . . mountainous sea": "Voyage of the Matavy Tender."

224–25 "It was . . . speculation": Tench, *Complete Account*, ch. 13.

225 "crowded . . . animals": Quoted in Currey, *The Transportation, Escape and Pardoning of Mary Bryant*, p. 33.

225 On April 6 . . ."to the deep": All quotes are from Clark's journal.

Chapter Nineteen

226 "they declared . . . money": *London Chronicle*, June 30–July 3, 1792.

226 "declared . . . assist them": *Evening Mail*, June 29–July 2, 1792.

226 "a paradise . . . voyage": Quoted in Brady, *James Boswell: The Later Years*, p. 465.

227 "remain . . . law": Quoted in Pottle, *Boswell and the Girl from Botany Bay*, p. 23.

227 "I had . . . there . . . most . . . shocked . . . gloomy . . . Erskine": Boswell's London Journal, 1762–63, May 4, 1763.

227–28 The execution . . . better of it: All quotes in this paragraph come from Brady, *James Boswell*, p. 101.

228 "Government . . . escape": Quoted in Pottle, *Boswell*, p. 23.

228 The *Dublin Chronicle* article is dated July 21, 1792, and is reproduced in HRNSW, vol. 2, p. 800.

228 "The only . . . precedent": Boswell's letter is reproduced in photographic form following page 24 of Pottle, *Boswell*.

229 "I asked . . . I desired it": Quoted in Danziger and Brady, eds., *Boswell: The Great Biographer*, p. 271.

229   The account of Boswell's mugging is from the issue of the *London Chronicle* dated June 8–11, 1793.

229   "The resolution . . . sinking": This account is from the Annual Register of Events from 1792.

229–31   Boswell's journal entry for August 18, 1793, is given in eds. Danziger and Brady, *Boswell*, p. 226. His journal entry for August 25, 1793, is at page 229 of the same work and that about accompanying Mary Broad to the boat is from his journal for October 12, 1793, on p. 241.

232   The poem about Mary Broad pining for Boswell is quoted in Judith Cook, *To Brave Every Danger*, pp. 225–26.

232   "by trade . . . in London": Danziger and Brady, *Boswell*, p. 228.

232   "on the River Hawkesbury": HRNSW, vol. 2, p. 355.

233   The burial of a Mary Broad at Lanteglos-by-Fowey on December 23, 1799, is from record 2907912 on the burial database, Cornwall Record Office, which also holds records of the baptisms of Mary (1147129) and her sister Dolly (1147047) among other family details.

CHAPTER TWENTY

The Bounty court-martial papers are in UKNA/ADM/1/5330 part 2. The minutes of the prosecution case were published by Stephen Barney, Muspratt's lawyer, at Edward Christian's request on May 1, 1794. They are reproduced, among many other places, in Mackaness, ed., *A Book of the "Bounty" and Selections from Writings of William Bligh*, pp. 194–246. The quotations from the trial come from both the Admiralty and Barney documents and are not individually sourced unless it is unclear who is speaking.

234   "beloved brother's": Nessie Heywood's deep affection for her brother runs through all her correspondence.

234   "the man . . . his captain": Letter from Pashley to N. Heywood, July 15, 1792. Fateful Voyage website, http://archive.is/www.fatefulvoyage.com.

236   "that the officers . . . his service": Morrison, "Memorandum," April 27, 1789.

237   "Bliss . . . not at all!": Wordsworth, "Prelude, or Growth of a Poet's Mind," Book 11.

237   "we have . . . priests": Quoted in Salmond, *Bligh*, p. 236.

238   "roasted . . . in a wine shop": Quoted in Hibbert, *The French Revolution*, p. 175.

241   "Heywood's . . . defaming [Captain Bligh]": Quoted in Alexander, *Bounty*, p. 319.

242   "If it would not . . . acquaintance": Heywood's letter was published in the *Cumberland Packet* in November 1792 and subsequently in various London newspapers. A copy is included in Bligh's "Answer to Certain Assertions" in UKNA/ADM/1/1509.

243   Edward Christian's committee's report is given in *A Book of the "Bounty" and Selections from Writings of William Bligh*, ed. G. Mackaness, pp. 247–266.

244   "It is very . . . nature": letter 48.01 from Sir Joseph Banks electronic archive, http://www.slnsw.gov.au/Banks.

246   "Few more engaging . . . colour . . . Our countrymen . . . caution": Oliver, *Return to Tahiti*, pp. 192 and 111.

246–47   Bligh was also . . . Port Jackson: Quotes in this paragraph are from Bligh's journal and Mackaness, ed., *Life of Bligh*, vol. 2, p. 24.

247   "violent . . . of fever . . . but he . . . through it": Bligh, *Log of the Proceedings of HM Ship Providence*.

248   "deprived": Quoted in Schreiber, *Fortunate Adversities of Captain Bligh*, p. 71.

248   "since the credit . . . monopolised [by Bligh]": Letter from Flinders to Banks, HRNSW, vol. 6, p. 207.

248 "of the injustice . . . unfavourable eye": Ibid., p. 274.

248–49 Frank Bond's undated letter to his brother is in the archives of the UK National Maritime Museum, Greenwich, London, ref. BND/1 and reproduced in Mackaness, *Fresh Light on Bligh*, pp. 68–69.

249 Frank Bond's son's recollection of his father's condemnation of Bligh is quoted in Kennedy, *Captain Bligh*, p. 194.

249 Tobin's letter to Bond is dated December 15, 1817, just after Bligh's death. The original is in the Mitchell Library archives, Sydney, but is widely reproduced, for example in Mackaness, ed., *Some Correspondence of Captain William Bligh*, pp. 32–33.

250 "Of those . . . voyage": January 16, 1794, UKNA/ADM/1/1509.

250 "astonished . . . a slight": Quoted in Alexander, *Bounty*, p. 318.

250 "Never . . . state": Quoted in Wulf, *The Brother Gardeners*, p. 217.

250 Bligh's response to Edward Christian's report—"Answer to Certain Assertions"—is in UKNA/ADM/1/1509.

250–51 The correspondence between Frank Bond and Bligh about Byrne is given in Mackaness, *Fresh Light on Bligh*, pp. 57–58.

251 "every part . . . stated": Edward Christian's "A Short Reply to Captain Bligh's Answers."

CHAPTER TWENTY-ONE

252 "I impute . . . truth": Reproduced in Mackaness, *Fresh Light on Bligh*, pp. 67–68.

253 "Captain Bligh . . . testimony": Letter of April 14, 1801, reproduced in full in Mackaness, *Life of Bligh*, vol. 2, p. 64.

253 "His manners . . . distant civility": Quoted in Schreiber, *Fortunate Adversities of Captain Bligh*, 122.

253 "uncomfortably situated . . . frequently hurt . . . company": Ibid., p. 126.

253–54 "an habitual . . . ankle": UKNA/ADM/1/5367.

254 "publicly . . . of war": UKNA/ADM/1/5368.

254 "very much swelled": Ibid.

254 Bligh's own . . . "its execution": All quotes in this paragraph are from UKNA/ADM/1/5368.

254 "in part proved . . . reprimanded . . . admonished . . . language": Ibid.

255 "a very . . . heard of . . . the most . . . ship": Quoted in Mackaness, *Life of Bligh*, vol. 2, p. 93.

255 Banks's letter to Bligh of March 15, 1805, is reproduced in full in Mackaness, *Life of Bligh*, vol. 2, p. 96.

255–56 "her undertaking . . . thunder": Bligh to Banks, March 21–29, 1805, Letter 1, Chambers, ed., *Indian and Pacific Correspondence of Sir Joseph Banks*, vol. 7, p. 1.

256 "to procure . . . affluence": Bligh's letter to Banks, September 17, 1805, quoted in Mackaness, *Life of Bligh*, vol. 2, p. 97.

257 "I am very . . . no more": Quoted in Parker, *Arthur Phillip*, p. 266.

259 "There is . . . motive": Quoted in Mackaness, *Life of Bligh*, vol. 2, p. 136.

259 "His employment . . . in motion": UKNA/CO/201/20.

260 "luxuriant pastures . . . tall . . . grass": Quoted in O'Brian, *Joseph Banks*, p. 273.

261 "They were . . . censure": Quoted in Schreiber, *Fortunate Adversities*, p. 148.

262 "I enquired . . . land": Quoted in Mackaness, *Life of Bligh*, vol. 2, p. 143; and Schreiber, *Fortunate Adversities*, p. 179.

263 "the colony . . . encouragement": Quoted in Mackaness, *Life of Bligh*, vol. 2, p. 153.

264 "accustomed . . . jurisprudence": Mitchell Library/MS A85 10/10/1807.

265 "no court . . . Judge Advocate": HRNSW, vol. 6, p. 427.

265 "She hastened . . . opposed": Mackaness, *Life of Bligh*, vol. 2, p. 189.

265 "retired": HRNSW, vol. 6, p. 548.

265–66 "some dirt . . . skirts": Quoted in Mackaness, *Life of Bligh*, vol. 2, p. 193.

266 Bligh's version . . . papers: Ibid.

266 "the soldiers . . . triumphant manner": Ibid., p. 202.

266 "I have been . . . do the like!": HRNSW, vol. 6, p. 594.

266 "his honour . . . gentleman": Quoted in Kennedy, *Captain Bligh*, p. 297.

267 "revengeful . . . government": Quoted in Schreiber, *Fortunate Adversities*, p. 202.

267 "certainly . . . poor": Quoted in Salmond, *Bligh*, p. 463.

267 "I gave . . . to him": Quoted in Kennedy, *Captain Bligh*, p. 300.

267 "not well . . . broke": Quoted in Salmond, *Bligh*, p. 464.

CHAPTER TWENTY-TWO

The account of Folger's arrival at Pitcairn is from Amasa Delano's *A Narrative of Voyages and Travels in the Northern and Southern Hemispheres*, p. 139. Delano was a friend of Folger.

269–70 After Folger . . . massacre: Quotes in these three paragraphs are from *Quarterly Review*, (1810): 23–24.

271–72 Jenny's account comes from the *United Service Journal* 1829, vol. 2, pp. 581–93, and a much shorter version in the *Sydney Gazette*, July 17, 1819.

273–74 "why . . . man . . . humanely . . . only": Beechey, *Narrative of a Voyage to the Pacific and Beering's Strait*, vol. 1, p. 83.

274 "in her zeal . . . upset . . . according to expectation": Ibid., p. 89.

274–75 Three months . . . "than their own": The quotes in this paragraph come from Beechey, *Narrative*, pp. 90–91.

275 "intoxicated . . . [liquor eventually] produced . . . killed": Ibid., p. 92.

275 "Of course . . . an axe": Ibid., p. 98.

276 "an asthmatic . . . laboured": Ibid., p. 94.

276 "even . . . discipline": Quoted in Alexander, *Bounty*, p. 373.

276 "The loss of . . . his life": Beechey, *Narrative*, p. 95.

POSTSCRIPT

277 "a blamer": Quoted in Mackaness, *Fresh Light on Bligh*, p. 68.

283 "the pure . . . Christ": Quoted in Skevington Wood, *Thomas Haweis*, p. 198.

283 "No region . . . favour": Ibid., p. 197.

284 "A plain . . . compensate": Ibid., p. 198.

284 "godly mechanics": Quoted in Garrett, *To Live Among the Stars*, p. 14.

285 "during sermon . . . order": Ibid.

285 "offered . . . alone": Ibid., p. 15.

285 "You . . . or cloth": Ibid., p. 16.

285–86 "The brethren . . . almost dead": Reproduced from a report of March 26, 1798, by Roland Hassell, quoted in Lansdown, ed., *Strangers in the South Seas*, p. 139.

286 "all hopes . . . present": Ibid., p. 140.

286 "Tahiti . . . 1769": Quoted in Moorehead, *Fatal Impact*, p. 89.

286–87 Gradually . . . to her: All quotes in these two paragraphs come from Bellingshausen, *Voyage of Captain Bellingshausen to the Antarctic Seas*, vol. 1, pp. 269, 285, 279, and 275, respectively.

287 "not a fire . . . people . . . The inhabitants . . . howling aloud": Quoted in Moorehead, *Fatal Impact*, p. 84.

287 "mildness . . . civilisation . . . unwittingly . . . word 'Missionary'": Darwin, *Voyage of the Beagle*, pp. 430 and 438.

When I visited Pitcairn in early spring 2016, I traveled on the same small supply vessel—the only regular means of reaching the island—as legal and court teams on their way to try another islander, this time for Internet child pornography offenses.

289 "to convey . . . by direct sea voyage": Quoted in Marks, *Trouble in Paradise*, p. 313.

Graham Ford made comments about the similarity of this order to the transportation orders to New South Wales and its uniqueness thereafter, both to the author in person on Pitcairn in 2016 and to Kathy Marks.

INDEX

Note: The abbreviation WB refers to William Bligh.

A NOTE ON THE AUTHOR

Diana Preston is an acclaimed historian and author of the definitive *Lusitania: An Epic Tragedy*, *Before the Fallout: From Marie Curie to Hiroshima* (winner of the Los Angeles Times Book Prize for Science and Technology), *A Pirate of Exquisite Mind*, and *A Higher Form of Killing*, among other works of narrative history. She and her husband, Michael, live in London.